LEGAL SKILLS

LEGAL SKILLS

EMILY FINCH • STEFAN FAFINSKI

OXFORD
UNIVERSITY PRESS

OXFORD

UNIVERSITY PRESS

Great Clarendon Street, Oxford OX2 6DP

Oxford University Press is a department of the University of Oxford.
It furthers the University's objective of excellence in research, scholarship,
and education by publishing worldwide in

Oxford New York

Auckland Cape Town Dar es Salaam Hong Kong Karachi
Kuala Lumpur Madrid Melbourne Mexico City Nairobi
New Delhi Shanghai Taipei Toronto

With offices in

Argentina Austria Brazil Chile Czech Republic France Greece
Guatemala Hungary Italy Japan Poland Portugal Singapore
South Korea Switzerland Thailand Turkey Ukraine Vietnam

Oxford is a registered trade mark of Oxford University Press
in the UK and in certain other countries

Published in the United States
by Oxford University Press Inc., New York

British Library Cataloguing in Publication Data

Data available

Library of Congress Cataloging in Publication Data

Data available

Typeset by Newgen Imaging Systems (P) Ltd., Chennai, India
Printed in Great Britain
on acid-free paper by
CPI Bath

ISBN 978-0-19-920390-1

10 9 8 7 6 5 4 3 2 1

First, our thanks must go to Professor Rosemary Pattenden who had the initial vision for *Legal Skills*.

We would like to thank Kate Hickey, Nicola Haisley, Sarah Hyland, and Francesca Griffin at OUP for guiding us meticulously throughout this project and their seemingly endless patience throughout the process from contract to bookshelf. Kate must be singled out for her particular good humour in the face of unforeseen challenges, technology failures of all sorts, and our propensity for changing our minds shortly after telling her we had finally decided upon something.

We also wish to extend our very grateful thanks to the many reviewers who were involved throughout all the stages of the writing of the book for their insightful and invaluable feedback, which was both positive and constructive:

Nicola Aries, Kingston University

Vanessa Bettinson, De Montfort University

Jo Boylan-Kemp, Nottingham Trent University

Tim Conner, Bradford University Law School

Lynn Cousins, Leeds Law School, Leeds Metropolitan University

Amy Croft, Kingston University

Cath Crosby, University of Teesside

Dr Haydn Davies, University of Central England

Dennis Dowding, Bournemouth University

Professor Kim Economides, University of Exeter

Nicola Isaacs, University of Plymouth

Dr Martina Gillen, Oxford Brookes University

Beverley Hopkins, University of Central England

Matthew Humphreys, University of Surrey

Robert Jago, University of Surrey

Neil Kibble, University of Wales, Aberystwyth

Lesley Lomax, Sheffield Hallam University

Dr Claire McGourlay, University of Sheffield

Jeanette Porteous, University of Lincoln

Dr Sue Prince, University of Exeter

Stephanie Roberts, University of Westminster

Dr Charlotte Smith, University of Reading

Dr Rhiannon Talbot, Newcastle University

Andy Vi-Ming Kok, Staffordshire University

Roger Welch, University of Portsmouth

Tony Wragg, University of Derby

We have learnt something from all of you and this book is inevitably stronger as a result.

The library-based research for this book was undertaken at the Bodleian Law Library in the University of Oxford and the respective libraries of the University of Leeds and the

University of Wales, Aberystwyth whose resources—both paper and people—were essential to its completion.

Finally, we would like to thank John, Linda, Stuart, Neil, Wendy, Gerald, and Mulan of Island Farm Donkey Sanctuary in Brightwell-cum-Sotwell, Oxfordshire for providing us with a safe and peaceful alternative existence and Anna Kavanagh of Trallwyn Cottages, Mynachlog-ddu, Sir Benfro (Pembrokeshire), Wales, where many draft chapters of this book were written in perfect isolation and a peculiar mix of scorching sunshine and intermittent light drizzle.

EF and SF
Wokingham
October 2006

Grateful acknowledgement is made to the publishers of copyright material which appears in this book.

Crown Copyright is reproduced under Class License Number C2006010631 with the permission of OPSI and the Queen's Printer for Scotland.

Material from Law Reports and, in particular, from *R* v *Morrison*, reproduced by permission of the Incorporated Council of Law Reporting for England and Wales.

Extracts from Halsbury's Statutes, Halsbury Laws of England, and Halsbury Statutory Instruments reproduced by permission of Reed Elsevier (UK) Limited, trading as LexisNexis® Butterworths.

Screenshots reproduced by permission of BAILLI, Thomson Publishing Services, The Stationery Office Ltd, Office of Public Sector Information, Privy Council Office, Merrill Legal Solutions, Her Majesty's Courts Service, Europa, JustCite, Copac, Council of Europe, William S. Hein & Co. Inc., HERO, LexisNexis® Butterworths.

Acknowledgement is given to The English Speaking Union for use of *Eric Pollard* v *Viv Windsor*.

Acknowledgement is given to Microsoft for use of screen capture software.

OUTLINE CONTENTS

DETAILED CONTENTS

Legal Skills is enriched with a range of features to help support a practical approach to learning. This Guided Tour shows you how to fully utilize your textbook and get the most out of your study of legal skills.

LEARNING OUTCOMES

After studying this chapter, you will be able to:

- Use online library catalogues and legal bibliographies to find books on a particular topic
- Understand journal citations
- Recognize the more common journal abbreviations
- Find journals in a library and online
- Distinguish between the various series of Command Papers
- Locate official publications in both paper and electronic form
- Use *Halsbury's Laws of England* to find the law on a specific topic

Learning outcomes

Each chapter begins with a bulleted outline of the main concepts and ideas you will encounter. These serve as a useful signpost to what you can expect to learn by reading the chapter.

Trial and appellate functions are often combined within one court as you will see when ~~ering~~ the functions of each court in more detail.

4.3.2 Superior and inferior courts

Superior courts have unlimited geographic and financial jurisdiction. They generally hear th~~~~ important and/or difficult cases.

Inferior courts have limited geographic and financial jurisdiction. They hear the majority of straightforward cases.

The courts are divided into superior and inferior courts as shown in the following tab~~~~ Remember that the vast majority of cases are dealt with by the inferior courts. Most da~~~~

Definition boxes

Key terms are highlighted in colour when they first appear and are clearly, concisely explained in definition boxes. These terms are collected in a glossary which can be found on the Online Resource Centre that accompanies this book.

? Self-test questions

1. Which piece of legislation amended s. 39 of the Terrorism Act 2000?
2. Which section was added to the Terrorism Act 2000 by s. 117(1)(2) of the Anti-terror~~~~ Security Act 2001?

Answers to the self-test questions can be found on the Online Resource Centre.

Since the *Chronological Table of the Statutes* is usually two to three years out of d~~~~ used with care. It remains of use for historical purposes when trying to trace th~~~~ tory of older (and long-repealed) statutes.

Current Law Legislation Citator
The *Current Law Legislation Citator* is divided into a number of volumes cov~~~~

Self-test questions

Throughout each chapter self-test questions will help you assess your understanding of key skills, concepts, and your readiness to progress to the next topic. You will find answers to all self-test questions on the Online Resource Centre that accompanies the book.

Practical Exercise

The following exercise can be used to help you determine the relevance of the material presentation.

1. Write your title at the top of a blank sheet of paper (or at the start of a new documen~~~~
2. Make a bullet point list of all the points that you could include.
3. Review the list, grouping similar points together and eliminating any repetition or ov~~~~
4. Draw three columns headed: essential, peripheral, and irrelevant and allocate each ~~~~ one of the columns, remembering that the question of relevance is determined by re~~~~ specific details of your presentation title and not to the general topic of the presenta~~~~
5. Use this as guidance when determining the content of your presentation, starting wi~~~~ you have categorized as essential. If you still feel that you have too much informatio~~~~ repeat the exercise, this time using the three columns to divide up the points that yo~~~~ categorized as essential.

Practical exercises

When you feel confident you understand the principles underpinning each skill, it is important that you practise applying them. To help you foster a 'hands on' appreciation of legal skills practical exercises are provided throughout each chapter.

Diagrams and flowcharts

Numerous diagrams and flowcharts are used to provide a colourful representation of concepts and processes.

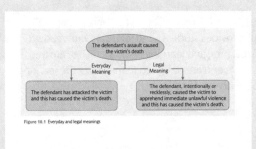

Figure 10.1 Everyday and legal meanings

Screen shots

Screen shots from important electronic databases such as Lexis Nexis and Westlaw will help you to familiarize yourself with these vital online resources.

Chapter summaries

The central points and concepts covered in each chapter are distilled into summaries providing a useful point for you to reinforce your understanding.

 CHAPTER SUMMARY

Language

- Strive for an appropriate level of formality in your written style; the approach u textbooks and articles will provide a useful example
- Avoid casual language such as text speak and the use of the first person
- Be alert for the conventions relating to gender-neutral language and the use of
- Be aware that words that have legal and non-legal meanings, such as assault, c reader

Grammar and punctuation

- Take care to ensure that your work is grammatical as this contributes towards a precision

Further reading

Selected further reading is included at the end of chapters to provide a springboard for further study. This will help you to broaden your learning by guiding you to the key literature in the field.

FURTHER READING

- This chapter aimed to give an overview of legislation as a source of law and bri how it comes into being. For an extremely detailed account, see Zander, M. (20 *Making Process* (6th edn), Cambridge: Cambridge University Press: in particul 'Legislation—the Whitehall stage' (pp. 1–52) and Chapter 2, 'Legislation—the ' (pp. 53–126).
- The House of Commons Information Office factsheet L4 on Private Bills can be http://www.parliament.uk/documents/upload/l04.pdf
- The House of Commons Information Office factsheet L5 on Hybrid Bills can be http://www.parliament.uk/documents/upload/l05.pdf
- The House of Commons Information Office factsheet L3 on the success of Priva can be found online at http://www.parliament.uk/documents/upload/l03.pd

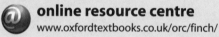

online resource centre
www.oxfordtextbooks.co.uk/orc/finch/

The Online Resource Centre that accompanies this book provides students and lecturers with ready-to-use teaching and learning resources. They are free of charge and are designed to maximize the learning experience.

FOR STUDENTS

The following resources are accessible to all, with no registration or password required.

Web links

EUROPA (europa.eu)
EUROPA is the main website of the European Union. It contains over 1.5 million pages and links to the EC legal portal, EUR-Lex.

EUR-Lex (www.europa.eu.int/eur-lex/en)
EUR-Lex is updated daily and provides a free searchable database of EC legislation.

Annotated web links allow you to easily research those topics that are of particular interest to you.

Glossary

Consolidating statutes

A **consolidating statute** is one which re-enacts particular legal subject matter which was previously contained in several different statutes.

Consolidation does *not* change the law. As Lord Simon stated in *Farrell* v *Alexander*:[1]

A useful one-stop reference point for all the keywords and terms used within the text.

Answers to self-test questions
Self-test questions help you assess your own knowledge and understanding. Answers are provided, along with a commentary to help you understand how and why the correct answer was reached.

Essay writing
Advice on good essay writing practice to help you improve your writing skills in a legal context.

Problem solving
Samples of good and bad answers to problem questions are provided as marking exercises to help improve your ability to spot strengths and weaknesses in your own answers.

Exam strategy
Reference materials and practical exercises for improving your performance in exams. Answers written by students to the same question provide insight into the different approaches that can be taken to the same question; a commentary points out the strengths and weaknesses of each answer.

Mooting
Sample moots, including examples of mooting preparation plans and skeleton arguments provide insight into the process of preparing for and participating in a moot.

Negotiation
Hints and tips for undertaking negotiation and examples of scenarios for you to practise your negotiation skills.

Presentations
A worked example of a presentation plan and examples of good practice in presentations.

FOR LECTURERS

Password protected to ensure only lecturers can access these resources.

Video clips
Video clips of students participating in a range of practical activities bring these skills to life and provide examples of good practice to emulate and bad practice to avoid. Clips featuring different individuals demonstrating their skills and talking about their experiences can be used to help students to overcome nerves, avoid common errors, and develop their own style.

Mooting

Watch mooting in action with clips of students at key moments of the moot demonstrating effective mooting strategies, illustrating core skills such as outlining their submissions, dealing with judicial interventions and handling case law. The clips also give an engaging illustration of common mistakes with commentary on how to avoid them.

Negotiation
Video clips of a negotiation are interspersed with commentary on good and bad technique bringing this activity to life and providing an engaging demonstration of different negotiation styles. Comments from students about their own experiences provide helpful advice for inexperienced negotiators.

Presentations
Clips of student performances demonstrate the desirable and undesirable characteristics of presentations and are interspersed with comments from students on their own fears about delivering a presentation and their views on their own performances.

Lectures
Short lecture clips highlight the variety of ways that information can be recorded as part of an effective note-taking strategy.

Test bank

Chapter 03 - Question 04
All Acts are divided into sections, but sections may be further subdivided. Which of the following lists the correct division of statutes from largest to smallest?
○ Sections, subsections, parts, sub-parts.
○ Sections, subsections, sub-subsections, schedules.
○ Sections, paragraphs, sub-paragraphs, sub-sub-paragraphs.
⦿ Sections, subsections, paragraphs, sub-paragraphs.

1 out of 1
Correct. This is the correct order of the further division of sections.
Page reference: 69

A fully customizable resource containing ready-made assessments with which to test students.

Diagrams
All of the diagrams in the textbook are available to download electronically and can be used in lectures to aid student understanding.

PART I

Sources of law

This part of the book covers the skills that you will need to get to grips with various sources of law. These include UK Acts of Parliament and delegated legislation as well as legislation made by the European Community; case law derived from common law, equity, custom, and decisions of the European Court of Justice and European Court of Human Rights. As well as legislation and case law, this part will also consider the role of books, journals, and official publications as supplementary sources of law.

This part is divided into three sections—section A deals with legislation, section B with case law, and section C with books, journals, and official publications. Each section will explain the role of the various sources, together with information on how to find them, both in a library and online, before giving you the skills needed to use them effectively.

PART I

Sources of law

SECTION A

Legislation

This section of the book covers the skills required to understand legislation as a source of law. This will include UK Acts of Parliament and delegated legislation as well as legislation emanating from Europe. In the first chapter, the different types of legislation will be *explained*. This then leads on to chapter 2, in which you will learn the skills to *find* both the UK and European legislation discussed in the first chapter. Finally, chapter 3 will demonstrate how to *use* legislation, developing the skills you need to read and interpret legislation.

Legislation

1

INTRODUCTION

This chapter will begin by looking at the process by which an Act of Parliament comes into existence before turning to consider delegated legislation—that is, law that is made by other bodies under Parliament's authority. It will then move on to consider European legislation, which has an increasingly significant effect since the United Kingdom joined the European Economic Community in 1973. Although a large part of domestic law remains unaffected, certain high-profile areas are significantly affected; these include employment law, commercial and consumer law, environmental law, and the law relating to the free movement of goods and workers throughout Europe. This chapter will therefore discuss the various Community institutions and their role in the law-making process before looking at the different types of European legislation in detail and explaining the circumstances in which individuals may use them in domestic courts. Finally, the chapter will discuss the impact of the European Convention on Human Rights and the Human Rights Act 1998.

Understanding legislation as a source of law is a fundamentally important legal skill. Every legal topic that you study will generally involve a mixture of legislation, delegated legislation, case law, and equitable principles. Therefore, a thorough understanding of national legislation is key. Furthermore, you must also understand the operation of European legislation as a source of law since it impacts many areas of domestic law. Without understanding the effects of the European sources on our domestic law, you will not be able to see the 'whole picture' of a particular area of legal study—particularly in areas such as employment, commercial, environmental, and discrimination law.

LEARNING OUTCOMES

After studying this chapter, you will be able to:

- Explain the process by which Acts of Parliament come into being

- Describe various types of delegated legislation and their function

- Understand the roles of the various institutions of the European Community

- Describe the process by which European Community legislation comes into being

- Explain the differences between Treaty Articles, Regulations, Directives, Decisions, Recommendations, and Opinions

- Distinguish between direct *applicability* and direct *effect*

- Explain the principles underlying the supremacy of European law

- Discuss the effect of the European Convention on Human Rights and the Human Rights Act 1998

1.1 Domestic legislation

Legislation is a broad term which covers *statutes* (**Acts of Parliament**) and other types of legislation, such as **delegated** (or **subordinate**) legislation and **European Community** legislation.

1.1.1 Statute law

Parliament passes legislation in the form of statutes, or Acts of Parliament. On average, Parliament enacts around sixty or seventy statutes per session and, although this figure remains largely constant, the length of statutes seems to have expanded in recent years, hence increasing the overall volume of legislation.

An Act of Parliament will begin life as a Public Bill, Private Bill or Hybrid Bill.

The procedure for enacting Private and Hybrid Bills is different to that for Public Bills. This chapter will concentrate on Public Bills and the resulting Public General Acts, although a brief overview of Private Bills, Hybrid Bills, and Private Members' Bills is included here for completeness.

1.1.1.1 Public Bills

Public Bills are introduced by the government as part of its programme of legislation. Although many people think that most Public Bills arise from the commitments made by the government as part of its election manifesto, in fact most Public Bills originate from government departments, advisory committees or as a political reaction to unforeseen events of public concern (such as the Dangerous Dogs Act 1991 in response to public and media outcry over a number of attacks by pit-bull terriers in which some unfortunate individuals were severely or disfiguringly injured).

If enacted, most Public Bills result in Public General Acts which, as their name suggests, affect the general public as a whole.

1.1.1.2 Private Bills

Private Bills are introduced for the benefit of particular individuals, groups of people, institutions, or a particular locality. They are promoted by organizations outside the House to obtain powers for themselves in excess of, or in conflict with, the general law. They often fail to become law due to insufficient time in a particular Parliamentary session. For example, before divorce became generally available under the public law, it was granted by Private Act of Parliament. Nowadays, personal Private Bills are extremely rare. There are now only a few Private Bills in each session. Private Bills tend to deal with nationalized industries, local authorities, companies, and educational institutions.

If enacted, Private Bills generally result in Private Acts (for example, The Marquess of Abergavenny's Estate Act 1946), unless (as with Public Bills) they deal with local authorities, in which case the resulting legislation is known as a Local Act (for example, the Liverpool City Council Act 2006).

Take care not to confuse Private Bills with Private Members' Bills which are a type of Public Bill and are covered later in section 1.1.5.

1.1.1.3 Hybrid Bills

Hybrid Bills are a cross between Public Bills and Private Bills. They have been defined by House of Commons Speaker, Hylton-Foster, as:

> A Public Bill which affects a particular private interest in a manner different from the private interests of other persons or bodies in the same category or class.

Bills which propose works of national importance that only affect a local area are generally Hybrid Bills. The Channel Tunnel Bill of 1986–7 provides a good example of a Hybrid Bill, in that the Channel Tunnel was generally viewed as a project which benefited the country as a whole, although it clearly affected the private interests of those in south-east Kent much more than those in Powys.

1.1.1.4 Private Members' Bills

Private Members' Bills are non-government Bills (Public, Private, or Hybrid) that are introduced by private Members of Parliament (MPs of any political party who are neither government ministers nor members of the House of Lords). They may be introduced in a variety of ways. Relatively few Private Members' Bills end up as Acts of Parliament. Although they often deal with relatively narrow issues (such as mock auctions and drainage rates), they may also be used to draw attention to issues of concern that are not within the legislative agenda of government. Significant pieces of legislation that have begun life as Private Members' Bills include the Abortion Act 1967 and the Hunting Act 2005.

Be careful not to confuse Private Members' Bills with Private Bills.

1.1.1.5 Consolidating and codifying statutes

Statutes may also be passed to consolidate or codify the law.

Consolidating statutes

A **consolidating statute** is one which re-enacts particular legal subject matter which was previously contained in several different statutes.

Consolidation does *not* change the law. As Lord Simon stated in *Farrell* v *Alexander*:[1]

> All consolidation Acts are designed to bring together in a more convenient, lucid and economical form a number of enactments related in subject-matter [which were] previously scattered over the statute book.

Examples of consolidation Acts include the Children Act 1989, the Limitation Act 1980, and the Insolvency Act 1986.

Codifying statutes

A **codifying statute** is one which restates legal subject matter previously contained in earlier statutes, the common law, and custom.

---

1. [1977] AC 59.

The meaning of 'common law' and 'custom' is considered in chapter 2.

Unlike consolidation, codification *may* change the law. An example of a codifying Act is the Theft Act 1968.

1.1.1.6 The domestic law-making process

White Papers and Green Papers

Before a Bill is introduced into Parliament, it may be preceded by a White Paper or a Green Paper.

White Papers set out government proposals on topics of current concern. They signify the government's intention to enact new legislation and may set up a consultative process to consider the finer details of the proposal.

Green Papers are issued less frequently. They are introductory higher-level government reports on a particular area put forward as tentative proposals for discussion without any guarantee of legislative action or consideration of the legislative detail.

Drafting the Bill

Proposed government legislation is passed to the Parliamentary draftsmen (officially the 'Parliamentary Counsel to the Treasury') who draft the Bill acting on the instructions of the government department responsible for the proposal. Oddly, it is conventional practice that the ministers responsible for the Bill do not usually see the instructions sent from their departments!

Procedure for Public Bills

Once drafted, the Parliamentary procedure for Bills introduced in the House of Commons can be depicted as shown in Figure 1.1.

Bills introduced in the House of Lords

A Government Bill can be introduced into either the House of Commons or the House of Lords. Most Bills begin life in the House of Commons; particularly Bills which deal primarily with taxation or public expenditure. The House of Commons has priority in such matters by virtue of its financial privileges (see Parliament Acts 1911 and 1949). Conversely, Bills relating to the judicial system, Law Commission Bills, and consolidation Bills conventionally begin their passage in the House of Lords. An example of this can be found in the Local Government Act 1988 which began in the House of Lords and became famous for introducing the controversial section 28 into law which prohibited Local Authorities from promoting in the specified category of schools 'the teaching of the acceptability of homosexuality as a pretended family relationship'.

House of Commons—First Reading

The First Reading in the House of Commons is a formality. The Title of the Bill is read by the Clerk of the House and a date is fixed for the Second Reading. Conventionally, the Second Reading does not normally take place before two weekends have passed.

House of Commons—Second Reading

The Second Reading in the House of Commons involves the main debate on the principles of the Bill. For government Bills, the debate is usually opened by the Minister responsible for the Bill and closed by a junior Minister. A vote is generally taken on the Bill as a whole at the end of the Second Reading. The Bill will then move to a Standing Committee (unless it is moved that the Bill be sent to a Committee of the whole House, a Select Committee, or a Special Standing Committee).

House of Commons—Standing Committee

Following the Second Reading in the House of Commons, most Bills are sent to a Standing Committee. The name 'Standing Committee' was coined from the time when Bills were sent to

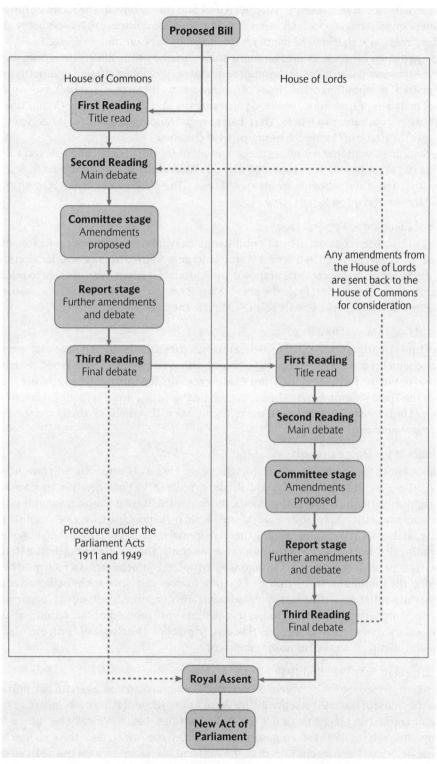

Figure 1.1 The Parliamentary procedure for Bills introduced in the House of Commons

large, permanent committees which considered all Bills they received. The membership of the Standing Committees now varies for each Bill. Standing Committees can have as many as fifty members or as few as sixteen. The members are chosen by the Committee of Selection by virtue of their particular expertise or interest in the subject matter of the Bill and to ensure that the party political composition of the Committee is, so far as possible, representative of the overall party political composition of the House of Commons: in other words that the relative proportions of members of the various political parties are roughly the same in the Committee as in the House of Commons as a whole. The Chair of each Standing Committee is selected by the Speaker of the House of Commons from a panel of chairmen.

The Standing Committee examines the provisions of the Bill in detail and votes on whether each clause, as proposed, 'stands part of the Bill'. Amendments may be moved in Standing Committee. These amendments are also voted upon. The Bill (as amended in Standing Committee) then moves into a Report Stage.

House of Commons—Report Stage

Unless a Bill has been considered by a Committee of the whole House without amendment, the Committee stage is followed by a Report Stage (sometimes referred to as a Consideration Stage). Here, further amendments may be proposed and introduced, often in an attempt to undo the changes made in Committee. Once the Report Stage is complete—which may take two or three days—the Bill finally proceeds to its Third Reading in the Commons.

House of Commons—Third Reading

In the Third Reading of the Bill, its contents are debated for a final time. It is unusual for any further amendments to be made at this stage. Indeed, unless six members table a motion that 'the Question be not put forthwith', the Third Reading does not have to involve any debate at all.

Once the Third Reading is over, the Bill is then tied up with a green ribbon and taken to the House of Lords by the Clerk of the House of Commons with a message kindly requesting the Lords' agreement to its content.

Procedure in the House of Lords

The procedure in the House of Lords mirrors that in the House of Commons. Bills have a formal First Reading, are debated on a Second Reading, proceed to consideration in Committee (although, unlike in the House of Commons, the committee stage is almost invariably taken in the Committee of the whole House), are debated again on Report and then receive a final Third Reading. At the end of the Third Reading there is a formal motion 'that this Bill do now pass'.

Assuming that the Bill survives the motion at the end of the Third Reading in the House of Lords, it is returned to the House of Commons with the Lords' amendments which must be considered in the Commons. If the House of Commons does not agree with the Lords' amendments it can send it back with counter-amendments and its reasons for doing so. Therefore a Bill can go back and forth between the Houses several times until proceedings are terminated or the parliamentary session runs out of time. However, in practice, the House of Lords often accepts the second offering from the House of Commons.

The Parliament Acts 1911 and 1949

These Acts provide a means by which the House of Commons can under certain circumstances bypass the House of Lords to present a Bill for Royal Assent without it having been passed by the House of Lords. The procedure under the Parliament Acts has historically been used infrequently, although the 1997 Labour government has used the Acts to force through legislation on more occasions since its election than the Acts had been used in total before its election. Recent examples include the European Parliamentary Elections Act 1999, the Sexual Offences (Amendment) Act 2000, and the Hunting Act 2005.

Royal Assent

Royal Assent is required before any Bill can become law. The monarch is not required by the constitution to assent to any Act passed by Parliament. However, it is conventionally given by the monarch acting on ministerial advice. It has not been refused since Queen Anne refused to assent to the Scottish Militia Bill of 1707.

Indeed the Royal Assent Act 1967 has marginalized the personal involvement of the monarch to the extent that all that is now required for Royal Assent by Notification is a formal reading of the short title of the Act with a form of words signifying the fact of assent in both Houses of Parliament.

Without express provision to the contrary, an Act of Parliament is deemed to come into force on the day (and for the whole of the day)[2] that it receives Royal Assent. Otherwise it will come into force on a date specified within the Act itself, or via an 'appointed day' provision which allows the Act to be brought into force via a statutory instrument.

Statutory instruments are described in section 1.1.2.1.

Parts of the Act may be brought into force on different dates (e.g. the provisions of the Anti-Social Behaviour Act 2003 relating to high hedges did not come into force until June 2005).

For more information on the coming into force of statutes, see chapter 3.

1.1.1.7 The impact of the Human Rights Act 1998

Section 19 of the Human Rights Act 1998 provides that the Minister in charge of each new Bill in either House of Parliament must, before the Second Reading of the Bill, either:

- make a statement of compatibility—that is, state that the provisions of the Bill are compatible with the European Convention on Human Rights; or
- make a statement acknowledging that it is not possible to make a statement of compatibility, but, despite this, the Government still wishes the House to proceed with the Bill.

The courts have no power to set aside any Act of Parliament that is incompatible with Convention rights; this is a function that is exercised by Parliament (who has a fast-track procedure which it may use in such cases if it wishes to do so). The courts may, however, make a 'statement of incompatibility' under s. 4 of the Human Rights Act 1998 if it is satisfied that the provision is incompatible with a Convention right. Such a statement does not affect the validity, continuing operation, or enforcement of the provision in respect of which it is given; and is not binding on the parties to the proceedings in which it is made.

1.1.2 Delegated legislation

Parliament has delegated legislative power to various other persons and bodies.

....

Delegated legislation is law made by persons or bodies with the delegated authority of Parliament. It is sometimes referred to as 'subordinate legislation'.

....

1.1.2.1 Statutory instruments

An Act of Parliament may grant the power to make statutory instruments, usually to a Minister of the Crown. The scope of this power can vary greatly, from the technical (for example, varying the dates on which different provisions of an Act will come into force or changing the levels of fines or penalties for offences) to much wider powers such as filling out the broad provisions in Acts.

---

2. *Tomlinson v Bullock* (1879) 4 QBD 230.

Often, Acts only contain a broad framework and statutory instruments are used to provide the necessary detail that would be considered too complex to include in the body of an Act. Statutory instruments can also be used to amend, update, or enforce existing primary legislation.

'Statutory instruments' is a general term including Regulations, Rules and Orders. A very common form of statutory instrument is a 'Commencement Order' which brings all, or part, of an Act into force.

For examples of Commencement Orders, see chapter 3.

The procedure for introducing a statutory instrument is usually laid down partly in the enabling (parent) Act and partly in the Statutory Instruments Act 1946. The use of statutory instruments is becoming increasingly widespread as a means of introducing some flexibility into the legislative process as well as helping to contain the ever-increasing length and complexity of statutes. For instance Parliament passed forty-five Acts in 2003; almost 3,500 statutory instruments were made in the same year.

Procedures for creating statutory instruments

The procedure for creating a statutory instrument is laid down in the parent Act. These procedures can be categorized as:

- negative resolution;
- positive resolution;
- no approval by Parliament.

Approximately two-thirds of all statutory instruments are made under the negative resolution procedure. It is named as such since it does not require Parliament to act unless it disapproves of the statutory instrument. It takes one of two forms depending on the state of the statutory instrument at the time that it is presented to ('laid before') Parliament. In the first form, the statutory instrument is laid before Parliament in draft and cannot be made if Parliament votes its disapproval within forty days. In the second form, the statutory instrument is actually made and laid before Parliament. If Parliament votes its disapproval within forty days, then the statutory instrument cannot remain in force.

A further 10 per cent of statutory instruments require positive resolution—in other words they require positive Parliamentary approval. This procedure takes one of three forms. The first of these requires the draft statutory instrument to be laid before Parliament. It can only come into force if approved by resolution of the House or Houses specified in its parent Act. The second form is similar, except that the statutory instrument is made before being laid before Parliament. However, it cannot come into force until approved by resolution as before. The final situation occurs where the statutory instrument has been made, comes into immediate effect, and is then laid before Parliament. It cannot continue beyond the period specified in the parent Act without positive resolution.

The final two-fifths of statutory instruments require no approval by Parliament. This either means that they do not need to be laid before Parliament at all, or that they do, but do not require any subsequent form of approval.

1.1.2.2 By-laws

By-laws are laws which are made by a local authority and only apply within a specific geographical area. By-laws are usually only created when there is no general legislation that deals with particular matters of concern to local people, such as waste collection and public park opening hours. By-laws are made under the Local Government Act 1972. However, by-laws can only come into force once they have been affirmed by the relevant minister. By-laws come into force one month after affirmation unless a specific date is specified within the by-law itself.

1.1.2.3 The Rule Committees

The Rule Committees have delegated power to make procedural rules for the courts. These consist of the Civil Procedure Rule Committee (who are responsible for the Civil Procedure Rules 1998 and their subsequent amendments), the Criminal Procedure Rule Committee and the Family Procedure Rule Committee.

1.1.2.4 The Privy Council

The role of the Privy Council is described further in chapter 2.

The Privy Council may make Orders in Council, such as emergency regulations. These have the force of law. It may also implement resolutions of the United Nations Security Council.

1.1.2.5 Validity of delegated legislation

Unlike Acts of Parliament, delegated legislation may be challenged in the courts via the doctrine of *ultra vires*.

Ultra vires is a Latin term meaning 'outside (their) powers'.

If a body acts beyond the powers that are delegated to it by the parent Act, then the delegated legislation can be declared void by the court. The body is said to have acted *ultra vires* by exceeding its powers. The delegated legislation may also be referred to as being *ultra vires*.[3]

Delegated legislation is also *ultra vires* if it conflicts with an earlier Act of Parliament or, following s. 2(4) of the European Communities Act 1972, European legislation.

Decisions which are made by the public bodies granted power by delegated legislation can also be challenged via judicial review. See section 4.1.4.5.

1.1.2.6 Advantages and disadvantages of delegated legislation

Advantages

The main advantage of delegated legislation is that detailed rules and regulations can be introduced relatively quickly without the need for full debate in Parliament that Acts would require. There is insufficient Parliamentary time available to debate all Bills in full and delegated legislation enables the most effective use of this limited time.

Moreover, Members of Parliament may not have the particular specialist knowledge to debate certain subject areas. It is therefore preferable to delegate authority to individuals or bodies with the requisite degree of specialist, technical, or local knowledge.

Disadvantages

Since delegated legislation is not debated before Parliament in the way that Acts are, the opportunity for public objection is minimized. Nor is delegated legislation publicized before and after implementation in the same way as some new Acts of Parliament. For instance, the Civil Partnership Act 2004 and the Identity Cards Act 2006 both received wide media coverage, whereas a mass of delegated legislation was also introduced over the same period without any significant attention. While it could be argued that media attention derives from the very nature of primary legislation and its general public impact, it is also true that delegated legislation can have a

---

3. For examples of the ways in which the courts have approached the issue of *ultra vires*, see *Commissioners of Customs & Excise* v *Cure & Deeley Ltd* [1962] 1 QB 340 and *R* v *Secretary of State for Social Security, ex parte Joint Council for the Welfare of Immigrants* [1996] 4 All ER 385.

significant public impact (for example, the majority of the Identity Cards Act 2006 will be brought into force by delegated legislation).[4]

Finally, the proliferation of delegated legislation means that in researching any area of law, it is important to be sure that your research is up-to-date.

1.2 European legislation

An increasingly influential range of sources of law emanates from Europe. The majority of this arises by virtue of the UK's membership of the European Communities from 1 January 1973.

With regard to human rights issues, individual citizens of the United Kingdom had the right to petition the European Court of Human Rights from 1966. Building on this, the Human Rights Act 1998 came into force in October 2000, allowing individuals to rely on (most) of the rights guaranteed by the European Convention on Human Rights directly in national courts as well as enabling courts to overrule earlier incompatible decisions. This section will consider European legislation in the form of Treaty Articles, Regulations, and Directives. It will also consider the European Convention on Human Rights as a further European source of law. However, it is important to remember throughout that the European Court of Human Rights is separate from the European Court of Justice.

1.2.1 European law

1.2.1.1 A brief history

The UK became a member of the European Communities on 1 January 1973 when the European Communities Act 1972 came into force. The 'European Communities' at this time were:

- The European Coal and Steel Community, established by the 1951 Treaty of Paris; and
- The European Atomic Energy Community ('Euratom') and the European Economic Community (the 'EEC'), established by the Treaty of Rome 1957.

The 1992 Treaty of the European Union (also known as the Maastricht Treaty or TEU) renamed the EEC as the European Community (EC) and the geographical entity formed by the member states became the European Union (EU) when it came into force on 1 November 1993. As such, the EU has evolved from a trade body into an economic and political partnership.

The Maastricht Treaty is not the only Treaty that you will encounter. The Single European Act 1986 (which is actually a Treaty rather than an Act of Parliament—despite its name) initiated moves toward the harmonization of laws across the member states. The 1997 Treaty of Amsterdam made further changes, not least of which was the renumbering of the pre-existing Treaty provisions.

The impact of the renumbering of Treaty provisions by the Treaty of Amsterdam is covered in chapter 2 when we discuss how to find Treaty Articles.

The Maastricht Treaty established the three 'pillars' of the European Union which can be broadly depicted as shown in Figure 1.2.

The 2001 Treaty of Nice effected further changes relating to the enlargement of the Community which allowed the addition of ten new member states on 1 May 2004, and two

---

4. Identity Cards Act 2006, s. 44(3).

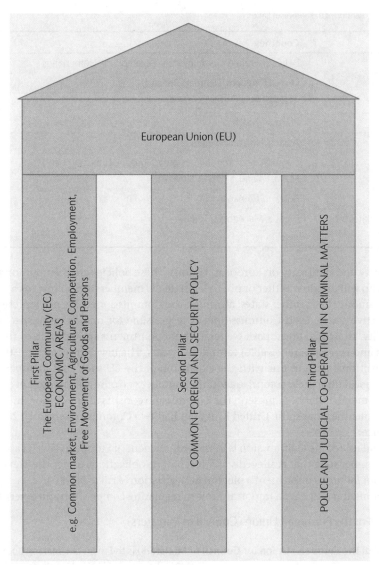

Figure 1.2 The pillars of the European Union

more on 1 January 2007, increasing the membership from fifteen to twenty-seven. The table on page 16 illustrates the expansion of the EU over time (Table 1.1).

1.2.1.2 The institutions of the European Community

It is important to be able to distinguish between the different Community institutions established by the EC Treaty and to understand their functions.

The European Commission

. . . .

The **European Commission** is the main policy-making and law enforcement institution of the EU.

. . . .

The European Commission was established by Articles 211–19 EC. Its first main role lies in the formulation of policies which are consistent with the various Treaties of the European Union

Table 1.1 The expansion of the European Union

Year	Countries	Membership
1957	Belgium, France, Germany, Italy, Luxembourg, Netherlands	6
1973	United Kingdom, Denmark, Ireland	9
1981	Greece	10
1986	Portugal, Spain	12
1995	Austria, Finland, Sweden	15
2004	Cyprus, Czech Republic, Estonia, Hungary, Latvia, Lithuania, Malta, Poland, Slovakia, Slovenia	25
2007	Bulgaria, Romania	27
Current candidates for membership	Croatia, Macedonia, Turkey	

(the EC Treaty and the Treaty on European Union). These policies are then put forward to the Council, who will decide whether or not to legislate. Its members are politicians appointed by agreement among the member states, although the Commissioners are not representatives of their respective states. Each Commissioner is responsible for one or more specific areas of responsibility, known as Directorates-General. The appointments are approved by the European Parliament and run for a (renewable) term of five years. The new European Constitution provides a transitional path in line with the expansion of the EU such that membership of the Commission will ultimately comprise a rotating number of Commissioners equivalent to two-thirds of the member states. At present, the Commission consists of one or more members from each of the member states; the United Kingdom had two Commissioners until 2004 and has had one since.

The second role of the Commission is in the enforcement of European law. It can take action against a member state that is allegedly in breach of its obligations under the Treaties (Article 226 EC) or for failure to implement a piece of EC legislation (Article 228 EC).

The Commission also has an important role in regulating competition and external trade.

The Council of the European Union (Council of Ministers)

The **Council of the European Union** (or **Council of Ministers**) is the main law-making body of the EU.

The Council of the European Union (also known as the 'Council of Ministers', or more usually simply 'The Council') was established by Article 202 EC. It is responsible for decision-making and coordination and passes law, usually legislating jointly with the European Parliament. It also coordinates the broad economic policies of the Member States and defines and implements the EU's common foreign and security policy, based on guidelines set by the European Council. The Council coordinates the actions of Member States and adopts measures in the area of police and judicial cooperation in criminal matters. The Council and the European Parliament constitute the budgetary authority that adopts the Community's budget. Finally, it enters into international agreements, on behalf of the Community and the Union, between the EU and other states or international organizations.

It is the main law-making body of the EU. Its members are politicians who are ministers in their respective national governments. Each minister has the authority to commit its government to a particular policy or decision. Its membership fluctuates according to the subject matter under debate. For instance, if the debate concerns environmental issues, the UK would be represented by the Secretary of State for Environment, Food, and Rural Affairs. The presidency of the Council is held for six months by each Member State on a rotational basis.

Take care not to confuse the Council of the European Union with the European Council or the Council of Europe. The Council of Europe is a separate body and has responsibility for the European Court of Human Rights.

The European Parliament

The **European Parliament** originated as a discussion chamber, but is now part of the legislative process.

The European Parliament was established by Articles 182–201 EC. It has over 600 members (MEPs) distributed among the member states according to the size of their population. Its original function was as a discussion and debating chamber for EC policies. However, its powers have increased since it began in 1957. Originally, it only had the right to be consulted. Proposals originating from the European Commission were considered by Parliament (a Parliamentary Standing Committee would produce a report on the proposals for discussion by the full Parliament), although the Commission were not compelled to amend their proposals if Parliament differed.

Since 1979, MEPs have been directly elected. Before then, they were simply appointed by Parliaments of member states from amongst their own members. A cooperation procedure was then introduced,[5] followed by a co-decision process[6] in which the European Parliament shares decision-making power with the Council. If the Parliament rejects a proposal from the Council it cannot be adopted, although there is provision for a conciliation committee comprising members of Parliament, the Council, and the Commission to be convened in cases of such disagreement. The co-decision process effectively gives the European Parliament the power to veto proposals from the Council.

The European Parliament also controls the EU budget for non-compulsory expenditure (that is, expenditure which does not fall under Treaty Articles or EC legislation). This represents around 40 per cent of the entire EU budget. With respect to compulsory expenditure, Parliament can only propose changes to the Council.

The European Parliament appoints the European Ombudsman. Citizens of member states can appeal to the Ombudsman in respect of cases of maladministration by EU institutions.

Finally, the European Parliament approves the nomination of the President of the Commission and the Commissioners (as a body)[7] and can censure the Commission, forcing its members to resign. However, the power of censure has been described as 'illusory at best and misdirected at worst': the reality is that the Parliament lacks clout.[8]

The Court of Justice of the European Communities

The **Court of Justice of the European Communities** (commonly *European Court of Justice* or *ECJ*) originated as a discussion chamber, but is now part of the judicial process.

---

5. Under Art. 252 EC; Arts 6 and 7, Single European Act 1986.
6. Art. 251 EC; Maastricht Treaty.
7. Art. 214 EC.
8. Weiler, J.H.H. (2002) *The Constitution of Europe*, 78–9 in Zander, M. (2004) *The Law-Making Process*, 6th edn, Cambridge: Cambridge University Press, 430 (n.30).

It is vitally important not to confuse the European Court of Justice (which sits in Luxembourg) with the European Court of Human Rights (which sits in Strasbourg). They are separate courts with separate jurisdictions.

The Court of Justice was established by Articles 220–44 EC. It sits in Luxembourg. It is comprised of one judge from each of the member states. The judges sit in chambers of three or five as well as in plenary session (where all judges sit to hear a case). They are assisted by nine Advocates-General whose role is to make reasoned submissions to the court. The Advocates-General have the same status as the judges themselves. The court delivers a single judgment. Separate concurring or dissenting judgments are not permitted.

The Court of Justice gives 'preliminary rulings'. National courts may make interim references directly to the Court of Justice if they need clarification on how a particular piece of European legislation should be interpreted. The need for such references will arise during the course of a domestic action. In England and Wales this will typically occur in the House of Lords (although it has been done directly from a magistrates' court). In other words, if a court cannot make a ruling because it is unsure how to interpret a piece of European legislation, then it can effectively suspend the proceedings before it to ask the Court of Justice for its opinion. These are made under Article 234 EC, so they are often referred to as 'Article 234 references'. The case will then proceed in the national court with the assistance of the European Court's ruling. It is the role of the national courts to give effect to and enforce the rulings of the Court of Justice.

The Court of Justice also hears actions for failure of a Member State to fulfil its obligations under European law. Proceedings before the Court of Justice are preceded by an investigation conducted by the Commission, which gives the Member State the opportunity to reply to the complaints against it. If that procedure does not result in termination of the failure by the Member State, an action for breach of Community law may be brought before the Court of Justice. That action may be brought by the Commission—as is practically always the case—or by another Member State. If the Court finds that an obligation has not been fulfilled, the Member State concerned must terminate the breach without delay. If, after new proceedings are initiated by the Commission, the Court of Justice finds that the Member State concerned has not complied with its judgment, it may, upon the request of the Commission, impose on the Member State a fixed or a periodic financial penalty.

The Court of Justice may also hear applications seeking the annulment of a Regulation, Directives, or Decision. Such actions may be brought by a Member State, by the European Parliament, the Council of the European Union or the European Commission, or by individuals to whom a measure is addressed or which is of direct and individual concern to them.

The Court of Justice may also review the legality of a failure to act on the part of a Community institution. Where the failure to act is held to be unlawful, it is for the institution concerned to put an end to the failure by appropriate measures.

Finally, appeals on points of law only may be brought before the Court of Justice against judgments given by the Court of First Instance. If the appeal is admissible and well founded, the Court of Justice may set aside the judgment of the Court of First Instance. The Court may decide this itself or may refer the case back to the Court of First Instance, which is bound by the decision given on appeal.

The Court of First Instance

The **Court of First Instance** deals with a limited range of cases.

The Court of First Instance was established by the Single European Act of 1986 to ease some of the burden of cases on the Court of Justice. It also comprises judges appointed by the member states who sit in chambers of three or five judges. It deals primarily with competition cases, anti-dumping cases, and staff cases (that is, disputes between the officials and employees of the Community and the Community itself). There is a route of appeal to the Court of Justice within two months on points of law only.

For the distinction between points of law and points of fact, see chapter 6.

The Court of First Instance has jurisdiction to hear and determine at first instance all direct actions brought by individuals and the Member States, with the exception of those to be assigned to a 'judicial panel' and those reserved for the Court of Justice.

It is vitally important not to confuse the Court of Justice (which sits in Luxembourg) with the European Court of Human Rights (which sits in Strasbourg). They are separate courts with separate jurisdictions.

The European Council

The **European Council** is composed of the Heads of State or Government of the EU member states.

Strictly speaking, the European Council is an EC body, rather than an instituation established by the EC Treaty, although it is included here for completeness. The European Council was introduced in 1974 in an attempt to deal with policy matters at the highest level, comprising the individual Heads of State or Governments of each of the member states. It meets twice a year in so-called 'European Summits'. The Presidency changes every six months.

Take care not to confuse the European Council with the Council of the European Union or the Council of Europe.

1.2.1.3 The European law-making process

The basic steps in the European law-making process are shown in Figure 1.3 on p.20.

For more information regarding the Official Journal, see section 2.2.1.

1.2.1.4 Sources of European law

A number of primary sources of European law have already been mentioned. These are the various Treaties themselves. These Treaties provide the basic principles upon which European law is founded and its objectives. These set out a broad framework and establish fundamental legal concepts, often in very general terms. These Treaty Articles are supplemented by secondary sources of law which provide the detailed law on a given area and establish how the principles and objectives identified in the Treaty Articles are to be achieved. The secondary sources of European law comprise regulations and directives. In addition the Commission may also issue Decisions which are measures directed at member states, companies, or individuals.

Decisions issued by the Commission should not be confused with decisions of the Court of Justice.

The sources of European law can be summarized in a table shown on p.20 (Table 1.2).

The interrelationship between European law and domestic law

The body of European law became part of domestic law by virtue of the European Communities Act 1972. Section 2(1) of the Act provides that:

All such rights, powers, liabilities, obligations and restrictions from time to time created or arising by or under the Treaties, and all such remedies and procedures from time to time provided for by or under the Treaties, as in accordance with the Treaties are without further enactment to be given legal effect or used in the United Kingdom shall be recognised and available in law, and be enforced, allowed and followed accordingly; and the expression 'enforceable Community right' and similar expressions shall be read as referring to one to which this subsection applies.

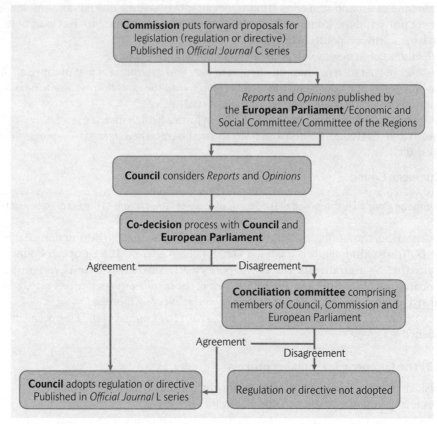

Figure 1.3 The basic steps in the European law-making process

Table 1.2 Primary and secondary sources of European law

Primary sources of European law	Secondary sources of European law
The European Community Treaty	Regulations
The European Coal and Steel Community Treaty	Directives
The Euratom Treaty	Decisions issued by the Commission
Single European Act	
Treaty on European Union (the Maastricht Treaty)	
Treaty of Amsterdam	
Treaty of Nice	

This meant that all directly applicable European law, regardless of whether it has already been made or is to be made in the future, became part of national law.

Before proceeding much further, we must cover some important terminology.

Direct applicability and *direct* effect

It is important that you understand the distinction between provisions of European law which are directly applicable and provisions that are directly effective.

A provision of European law is **directly applicable** if it automatically becomes part of the law of a member state without the need for the member state to enact any further legislation.

A provision of European law is **directly effective** if (and only if) it creates rights upon which individuals may rely in their national courts and which are enforceable by those courts.

Thus, direct *applicability* is concerned with the incorporation of European law into the legal system of a member state, whereas direct *effect* is concerned with its enforceability.

Before considering which of the different types of European law have direct effect (that is, can be relied upon by individuals in national courts and which are enforceable by those courts) it is necessary to understand the distinction between vertical direct effect and horizontal direct effect (Figure 1.4 below).

A provision of European law has **vertical direct effect** if it can be enforced against a member state in its own courts.

A provision of European law has **horizontal direct effect** if it can be enforced against another individual in the courts of a member state.

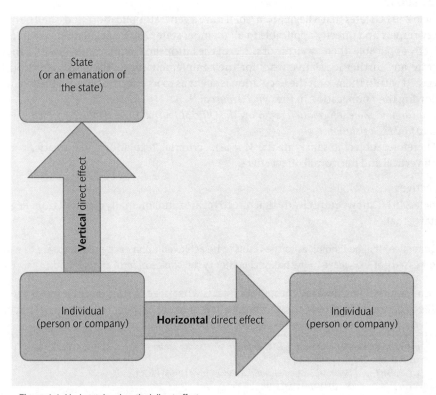

Figure 1.4 Horizontal and vertical direct effect

Therefore, provisions of European law with vertical direct effect can be enforced against the UK itself. Vertically directly effective provisions may also be enforced against emanations of the state, such as local authorities and health authorities[9] and nationalized industries.[10]

You should take care when reading cases which consider the distinction between direct applicability and direct effect since the European Court of Justice does not always distinguish consistently between its use of the two terms.

We have looked at the different sources of European law and the rules of direct applicability and direct effect which determine how those provisions operate within domestic law. To complete the puzzle, we finally have to establish the applicability and effect of each type of provision.

Treaty Articles

Although it is for the Court of Justice to determine, Treaty Articles are normally held to be directly applicable. Therefore, by virtue of s. 2(1) of the European Communities Act 1972, they require no further legislative action by the UK to take effect as law.

A Treaty Article will have vertical direct effect (it will create individual enforceable rights against the state) if its terms are 'clear, precise and unconditional' and its implementation required no further legislation in member states (i.e. it was directly applicable).[11] These are often referred to as the *Van Gend* criteria from the case in which the matter was first considered. In other words, an Article has vertical direct effect if the member states had no discretion in the means of its implementation.

Treaty Articles may also have horizontal direct effect.[12] Therefore, provided that the *Van Gend* criteria are satisfied, Treaty Articles can be enforced directly in UK courts, regardless of any other domestic legislation.

Regulations

Article 249 EC states that a Regulation 'shall have a general application' and 'shall be binding in every respect and directly applicable in all member states'. Since Regulations are immediately directly applicable, then by virtue of s. 2(1) of the European Communities Act 1972 they do not require any further legislative work for their implementation. They take effect on the day specified within them, or if the Regulation is silent as to its effective date, on the twentieth day following their publication in the *Official Journal*.[13]

You can find more information regarding the Official Journal in section 2.2.1 which demonstrates how to find EC legislation.

Therefore, subject to satisfying the *Van Gend* criteria, Regulations, like Treaty Articles, have both vertical and horizontal direct effect.

Directives

Article 249 EC shows quite clearly that directives are fundamentally different from Regulations. It states that:

> A directive shall be binding as to the result to be achieved upon each member state to which it is addressed but shall leave to the national authority the choice of form and method.

In other words, Directives tell the member states what needs to be done, but leaves the member states to decide what provisions of domestic law to enact in order to implement that directive.

---

9. *Marshall v Southampton and South West Hampshire Area Health Authority (No. 2)* [1993] 4 All ER 586.
10. *Foster* v *British Gas plc* [1990] 3 All ER 897.
11. *Van Gend en Loos* v *Nederlandse Administratie der Belastingen* [1963] ECR 1.
12. *Defrenne* v *Sabena (No. 2)* [1976] CMLR 98.
13. Case 39/72 *Commission* v *Italy* [1973] ECR 101; [1973] CMLR 439.

There is always a specified period of time for the member states to implement any given directive.

Directives often provide the fine detail on a given area; here, the EC recognizes that individual member states may need to implement them in slightly different ways, to reflect their own national cultures or customs. Therefore, as long as the objective of the Directive is met, the EC gives each state a measure of discretion as to its precise method of implementation in its domestic law. Many pieces of important and influential UK legislation have arisen from the implementation of EC Directives, such as the Equal Pay Act 1970 and the Sex Discrimination Act 1975.

Since Directives require domestic legislation for their implementation, they are not directly applicable forms of European law. Moreover, if the Directive has been properly implemented, an individual who wishes to bring an action based on that Directive will use the national law rather than relying on the Directive itself; therefore, in general, Directives do not have horizontal direct effect.[14]

However, a Directive will have vertical direct effect if it satisfies the *Van Gend* criteria and the time for implementation specified in the Directive has passed.

Directives may also be said to have indirect effect, since the Court of Justice also requires national law to be interpreted in accordance with Directives.[15]

Finally, a member state who has failed to implement a directive may be liable to compensate individuals who have suffered as a result.[16] In other words, if an individual has lost out because of defective implementation of a Directive, they may be able to sue the state for their losses provided that the state's breach was sufficiently serious (which will be so if the member state 'manifestly and gravely disregard[ed]' its obligations).[17]

Decisions

The final secondary sources of European law are decisions. Article 249 EC provides that a decision 'shall be binding in every respect for the addressees named therein'. The addressees may be individuals, companies, or member states. Thus, they are not directly applicable, but may be capable of having direct effect.

1.2.1.5 'Soft law'—Recommendations and Opinions

Recommendations

Recommendations are not legally binding. However, courts of member states are required to interpret their own law in the light of recommendations.[18]

Opinions

In common with recommendations, opinions also have no legal authority. However, the opinion of the Commission may be a precursor to legal proceedings. If the Commission states an opinion that a member state is in breach of an obligation, then it would be foolhardy for a member state to ignore it.

Despite their evidently persuasive nature, Article 249 EC states that 'Recommendations and opinions shall have no binding force'.

---

14. However, see Case C-1994/94 *CIA Security International SA* v *Signalson SA and Securitel SPRL* [1996] ECR I-2201 and Case C 443/98 *Unilever Italia* v *Central Food* [2000] ECR I-7535 where it appears that, in some instances, Directives may be pleaded against an individual or non-State body.

15. Case 14/83 *Von Colson and Kamann* v *Land Nordheim-Westfalen* [1984] ECR 1891; Case C-106/89 *Marleasing SA* v *La Commercial Internacionale de Alimentacion SA* [1990] ECR I-4135; [1992] 1 CMLR 305.

16. Cases C-6/90 and C-9/90 *Francovich and Bonifaci* v *Italian Republic* [1991] ECR I-5357; [1993] 2 CMLR 66.

17. Cases C-178/94, etc. *Dillenkofer and Others* v *Germany* [1996] ECR I-4845.

18. Case 322/88 *Grimaldi* v *Fonds des Maladies Professionelles* [1989] ECR 4407.

1.2.1.6 The supremacy of European law

From the point of view of the Community, where there is a conflict between European law and the law of member states, European law prevails. This has been clear since *van Gend en Loos* in 1963 where the European Court of Justice clearly stated that 'the Community constitutes a new legal order . . . for whose benefit the states have limited their sovereign rights'.[19]

In *Costa* v *ENEL*[20] the following year, the European Court of Justice made two important observations regarding the relationship between Community law and national law; firstly, that the Member States have definitively transferred sovereign rights to a Community created by them. They cannot reverse this process by means of subsequent unilateral measures which are inconsistent with the concept of the Community. In other words, the autonomy of the member states to act as they wish has been limited by virtue of their membership of the Community.

Moreover, it is a principle of the Treaty that no Member State may call into question the status of Community law as a system uniformly and generally applicable throughout the Community. Therefore, it follows that Community law, which was enacted in accordance with the Treaties, has priority over any conflicting law of the Member States. Therefore, in *Costa* v *ENEL* the European Court of Justice emphatically established the primacy of Community law over national law.

This implies that the enactment of the European Communities Act 1972 prevents Parliament from introducing new statutes which conflict with European law. This impacts upon the constitutional principle of Parlimentary sovereignty which, in essence, requires that Parliament has unlimited legislative competence (that is, it may enact any law that it wishes) and that there is no competing legislative body (that is, no body may challenge the validity of a properly-enacted Act of Parliament). Initially, the courts viewed that national law remained supreme. In *Felixstowe Dock Railway Co* v *British Transport Docks Board*[21] Lord Denning stated that:

> It seems to me that once the Bill is passed by Parliament and becomes a statute that will dispose of all discussion about the Treaty. These courts will have to abide by the Statute without regard to the Treaty.

However, in *Macarthys* v *Smith*[22] the courts considered that national law *was* subservient to Europe, although if Parliament deliberately and consistently breached European law, 'it would be the duty of our courts to follow the statute'.[23]

This situation was not tested in the domestic courts for some years. It was eventually considered in the *Factortame* cases.[24] Here, a conflict arose between certain provisions of the EC Treaty which prevent discrimination on the grounds of nationality and Part II of the Merchant Shipping Act 1988 which provided that fishing boats registered in the UK which were fishing for the quotas allocated to the UK by the EC must be owned and managed by UK citizens.

The House of Lords upheld the opinion of the European Court of Justice that it could grant an interim injunction against the Crown to prevent it enforcing an Act which contravened European law. The act of binding the Crown was previously constitutionally impossible. The House of Lords later held that parts of the Merchant Shipping Act 1988 were incompatible with the relevant provisions of the EC Treaty. This conundrum was cleverly and carefully

---

19. *Van Gend en Loos* v *Nederlandse Administratie der Belastingen* [1963] ECR 1.
20. Case 6/64 *Costa* v *ENEL* [1964] ECR 585.
21. [1976] 2 CMLR 655, [1976] 2 Lloyd's Rep 656, CA.
22. [1979] 3 All ER 325.
23. Per Lord Denning MR.
24. *R* v *Secretary of State for Transport, ex p Factortame Ltd (No. 2)* [1990] 2 AC 85.

reconciled by Lord Bridge who firstly considered s. 2(4) of the European Communities Act 1972 which provided that:

> Any enactment passed or to be passed . . . shall be construed and have effect subject to the foregoing provisions of this section.

In other words, any legislation passed or to be passed in the UK must be interpreted with applicable European law in mind.

Lord Bridge argued that, since s. 2(4) of the European Communities Act 1972 states that any enactment must have regard to Community obligations, this effectively meant that Parliament's intention was that *all* future legislation would be EC-compliant and would contain a fictional 'invisible clause' to this effect, unless the incompatibility was so important, in which case it could be explicitly excluded in the new legislation. Lord Bridge stated that:

> Whatever limitation of its sovereignty Parliament accepted when it enacted the European Communities Act 1972 it was entirely voluntary . . . when decisions of the Court of Justice have exposed areas of United Kingdom law which failed to implement Council Directives, Parliament has always loyally accepted the obligation to make appropriate and prompt amendments. Thus there is nothing in any way novel in according supremacy to rules of Community law.

Therefore the relevant provisions of the Merchant Shipping Act 1988 took effect subject to directly enforceable Community rights. In doing so, the House of Lords affirmed that, for all future cases, where a statute is silent on a matter covered by European law, it is presumed that it is intended to comply with European law.

1.2.2 The European Convention on Human Rights

1.2.2.1 A brief history

The European Convention on Human Rights and Freedoms is a creation of the Council of Europe although it is, at least in part, based upon the 1948 United Nations Declaration of Human Rights. The Council of Europe was formed in 1949, shortly after the end of the Second World War, with its aim of international cooperation and the prevention of the kinds of widespread atrocious violations of human rights which had occurred during the war. The European Convention on Human Rights was signed in Rome in 1950, ratified by the UK a year later and came into force in 1953.

1.2.2.2 Convention Rights

The European Convention on Human Rights establishes a number of fundamental rights and freedoms as follows (Table 1.3).

Table 1.3 Convention rights by Article number

Article	Convention right
1	Obligation to respect human rights
2	Right to life
3	Prohibition of torture
4	Prohibition of slavery and forced labour
5	Right to liberty and security

Table 1.3 (*Cont.*)

Article	
6	Right to a fair trial
7	No punishment without law
8	Right to respect for private and family life
9	Freedom of thought, conscience and religion
10	Freedom of expression
11	Freedom of assembly and association
12	Right to marry and found a family
13	Right to an effective remedy
14	Prohibition of discrimination

1.2.2.3 The European Court of Human Rights

The European Court of Human Rights was established in 1959 as a final avenue of complaint for claimants who had exhausted the remedies available to them in their domestic courts for alleged breaches of Convention rights. At the same time, the European Commission of Human Rights was also established. The Commission's role was to decrease the caseload of the European Court of Human Rights by filtering out some cases and attempting to resolve others by conciliation. The individual's right to petition the European Court of Human Rights became available to UK citizens in 1966.

The European Court of Human Rights and the European Commission of Human Rights were abolished on 31 October 1998 and replaced by a single Court of Human Rights. Questions of admissibility (formerly dealt with by the Commission) are now dealt with by its judges sitting in committee.

It is worth repeating the point that it is vitally important not to confuse the European Court of Human Rights (which sits in Strasbourg) with the European Court of Justice (which sits in Luxembourg). They are separate courts with separate jurisdictions.

CHAPTER SUMMARY

Statute law

- Public Bills are introduced by the Government as part of its programme of legislation

- Private Bills are introduced for the benefit of particular individuals, groups of people, institutions, or a particular locality

- Hybrid Bills are a cross between Public and Private Bills

- Private Members' Bills are non-government Bills that are introduced by private Members of Parliament

- Consolidating statutes re-enact a topic contained in several earlier statutes

- Codifying statutes restate a topic previously contained in statute, common law, and custom

- Government Bills can be introduced in the House of Commons or House of Lords

- The Parliament Acts 1911 and 1949 provide a means by which the House of Commons can (under certain circumstances) bypass the House of Lords to present a Bill for Royal Assent without it having been passed by the House of Lords

- Royal Assent is required before any Bill can become law; it is customarily given

- The Human Rights Act 1998 requires that new Bills must be accompanied by a statement of compatibility (or a declaration that a statement of compatibility is not possible)

- The courts may make a declaration of incompatibility for Acts of Parliament which are incompatible with the European Convention on Human Rights; this does not affect the validity of the Act

- Delegated legislation is made under powers delegated by Parliament

- Delegated legislation includes statutory instruments (Rules, Regulations, and Orders) and by-laws

European bodies

- The European Commission is the main policy-making and law enforcement institution of the EU

- The Council of the European Union is the main law-making body of the EU

- The European Parliament originated as a discussion chamber but is now part of the legislative process

- The European Court of Justice also originated as a discussion chamber, but is now part of the judicial process

- The European Court of Justice and the European Court of Human Rights are different

- The Court of First Instance deals with a limited range of cases

- The European Council is composed of the Heads of State or Government of the EU member states

Interrelationship between European law and domestic law

- A provision of European law is directly applicable if it becomes part of the law of a member state without need for further legislation

- A provision of European law is directly effective if it creates rights upon which individuals may rely in their national courts (and which are enforceable by those courts)

- A provision of European law has vertical direct effect if it can be enforced against a member state in its own courts

- A provision of European law has horizontal direct effect if it can be enforced against another individual in the courts of a member state

- Treaty Articles and Regulations have both vertical and horizontal direct effect if they satisfy the *Van Gend* criteria: that its terms are 'clear, precise and unconditional' and its implementation required no further legislation in member states.

- Directives do not have horizontal direct effect

- Directives may have vertical direct effect if they satisfy the *Van Gend* criteria and the time limit for their implementation has expired

- Where a statute is silent on a matter covered by European law, it is presumed that it is intended to comply with European law

European Convention on Human Rights

- The European Convention on Human Rights establishes a number of fundamental rights and freedoms

- The European Court of Human Rights is a final avenue of complaint for individuals who have exhausted national remedies available for alleged breaches of Convention Rights

- The European Court of Human Rights is not the same as the European Court of Justice

 FURTHER READING

- This chapter aimed to give an overview of legislation as a source of law and briefly to describe how it comes into being. For an extremely detailed account, see Zander, M. (2004) *The Law-Making Process* (6th edn), Cambridge: Cambridge University Press: in particular, Chapter 1, 'Legislation—the Whitehall stage' (pp. 1–52) and Chapter 2, 'Legislation—the Westminster stage' (pp. 53–126).

- The House of Commons Information Office factsheet L4 on Private Bills can be found online at http://www.parliament.uk/documents/upload/l04.pdf

- The House of Commons Information Office factsheet L5 on Hybrid Bills can be found online at http://www.parliament.uk/documents/upload/l05.pdf

- The House of Commons Information Office factsheet L3 on the success of Private Members' Bills can be found online at http://www.parliament.uk/documents/upload/l03.pdf. It provides a list of all Private Members' Bills which have been enacted since the Second World War.

- Discussion of the circumstances in which a Bill may be sent to a Committee of the whole House, a Select Committee, or a Special Standing Committee is beyond the scope of this chapter. See Zander, M. (2004) *The Law-Making Process* (6th edn), Cambridge: Cambridge University Press, pp. 68–73 for details.

- The House of Commons Information Office factsheet L1 on the Parliamentary Stages of a Government Bill can be found online at http://www.parliament.uk/documents/upload/l01.pdf.

- This chapter gives a very brief overview of the European institutions and the sources of law which come from Europe. It does not attempt to cover the substantive European law. European law is a huge subject area in its own right. For further detail, see Weatherill, S. (2005) *Cases and Materials on EC Law* (7th edn), Oxford: Oxford University Press; Fairhurst, J. (2005) *Law of the European Union* (5th edn), Harlow: Pearson; Foster, N. (2006) *EC Legislation* (17th edn), Oxford: Oxford University Press.

Finding legislation

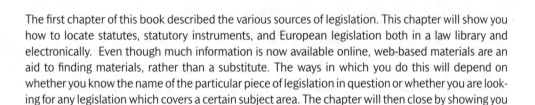

INTRODUCTION

The first chapter of this book described the various sources of legislation. This chapter will show you how to locate statutes, statutory instruments, and European legislation both in a law library and electronically. Even though much information is now available online, web-based materials are an aid to finding materials, rather than a substitute. The ways in which you do this will depend on whether you know the name of the particular piece of legislation in question or whether you are looking for any legislation which covers a certain subject area. The chapter will then close by showing you where to find the European Convention on Human Rights.

The ability to find legislation is an important legal skill. Legislation is a primary source of law affecting virtually every area of legal study. Clearly, you will not be able to read, understand, and use legislation without finding it first.

LEARNING OUTCOMES

After studying this chapter, you will be able to:

- Find Acts of Parliament and statutory instruments in a library and online
- Determine whether there is any statute law on a particular topic
- Work out whether a piece of legislation is in force
- Locate the official texts of European Community Treaty Articles, Regulations, and Directives
- Source the official current text of the European Convention on Human Rights

 Practical exercise

Although this chapter will use a number of extracts from various materials to demonstrate the ways in which they can be used, these are no substitute for your own experience and practice. Go to a law library and try to find as many of these example resources as you can. Bear in mind that not all resources will be available in all law libraries. However, for those that are, you will become familiar with their contents and layout and you will also know their location in the library which could save a lot of searching time in the future.

2.1 Finding domestic legislation

2.1.1 Finding statutes

This section will describe the various ways in which statutes can be located, both in a library and online. By way of example, we will use the Serious Organised Crime and Police Act 2005, an Act which made a large number of changes to the law relating to the policing of crime in general, and serious crime in particular.

2.1.1.1 In a library

Public General Acts and Measures

At the end of each year, the Public General Acts which have been enacted during the year are published together in the official series *Public General Acts and Measures.* This series includes:

- an index to all Acts passed during the year in alphabetical order;
- a chronological index to all Acts passed during the year (by chapter number);
- the full text of all Public General Acts enacted during the year in chapter number (chronological) order;
- the full text of all the General Synod Measures of the Church of England passed in the year;
- a list (but not the full text) of Local and Personal Acts enacted during the year.

Therefore, the Serious Organised Crime and Police Act 2005 can be found in the 2005 volume of *Public General Acts and Measures.* An excerpt is shown below. You will see that this includes s. 115, which deals with the powers of police constables to stop and search for fireworks possessed 'in contravention of a prohibition imposed by fireworks regulations'.[1] We will return to s. 115 later in this chapter.

Fireworks

115   Power to stop and search for prohibited fireworks

  (1) Section 1 of PACE (powers of constables to stop and search) is amended as follows.

  (2) In subsection (2), for "or any article to which subsection (8A) below applies" substitute, "any article to which subsection (8A) below applies or any firework to which subsection (8B) below applies".

  (3) In subsection (3), for "or any article to which subsection (8A) below applies" substitute, "any article to which subsection (8A) below applies or any firework to which subsection (8B) below applies".

  (4) In subsection (6), for "or an article to which subsection (8A) below applies" substitute, "an article to which subsection (8A) below applies or a firework to which subsection (8B) below applies".

  (5) After subsection (8A) insert–

     "(8B) This subsection applies to any firework which a person possesses in contravention of a prohibition imposed by fireworks regulations.

     (8C) In this section–

        (a) "firework" shall be construed in accordance with the definition of "fireworks" in section 1(1) of the Fireworks Act 2003; and

        (b) "fireworks regulation" has the same meaning as in that Act".

Extract 2.1 Serious Organised Crime and Police Act 2005, s. 115

---

1.   Serious Organised Crime and Police Act 2005, s. 115(5).

Law Reports—Statutes

The Incorporated Council of Law Reporting publishes the *Law Reports—Statutes* series.

This comprises a set of annual volumes, combined with several parts for the current year, each of which contains the full text of one or more Acts. These parts are then republished as a single bound volume at the end of the year. However, *Law Reports—Statutes* is of limited use, since there is usually a delay of a few months between publication of the Queen's Printer copy (*Public General Acts and Measures*) and the *Law Reports—Statutes*. Furthermore *Law Reports—Statutes* does not provide any value-added information such as commentary on the statute, so for all practical purposes, it is hardly worth waiting for.

Chronological Table of the Statutes

The *Chronological Table of the Statutes* provides historical as well as current information. As its name suggests it lists all statutes enacted since 1235 (the Statute of Merton). It then shows, for each, whether it has been repealed or amended. Take a look at the extracts provided. These show the opening page, and a more recent example (the Terrorism Act 2000).

Chronological Table of the Acts of the Parliaments of England, Great Britain and the United Kingdom

Square brackets enclosing bold type indicate that that particular Act has no statutory short title (see preface)

Acts of the Parliaments of England

1235 (20 Hen 3)

Stat Merton

c 1	*Damages on writ dower*—*rep* SLR and Civil Procedure, 1881 c 59, s 3 SLR 1950
c 2	*Widow's bequest of corn on her land*—*rep* SLR 1948
c 3	*Redisseisin*—rep SLR 1863; SL(I)R 1872
c 4	*Commons*—rep SLR 1953
c 5	*Usury*—rep SLR 1863; SL(I)R 1872
cc 6, 7(a)	*Wardship*—rep SLR 1863; SL(I)R 1872
c 8	*Limitation of writs*—rep SLR 1863; SL(I)R 1872
c 9	*Special Bastardy*—rep SLR 1948
c 10	*Attorneys in county courts*—rep Civil Procedure Acts Repeal. 1879 c 59
c 11	*Trespassers in parks*—rep SLR 1863; SL(I)R 1872

Extract 2.2 *Chronological Table of the Statutes*—opening

c 11 **Terrorism**

see—SIs 2001/425, art 2; 2001/427, art 2

s 1 appl—(prosp) Highways, 1980c 66, s 329 (as amended by 2004 c 36, s 32(1), sch 1 pt 3 para 15(2)); (19.1.2005) Road Traffic Regulation, 1984 c 27, ss 22C(6), 67(1A) (as added by 2004 c 36, s 32(1), sch 2 pt 3 para 16(1)–(3)); (19.1.2005) Roads (Scotland), 1984 c 66, s 40 (as amended by 2004 c 36, s 32(1), sch 2 pt 3 para 17(2)); (19.1.2005) ibid, s 39BA (as added by 2004 c 36, s 32(1), sch 2 pt 3 para 17(1)): Anti-terrorism, Crime and Security, 2001 c 24, s 21(5)

s 9 am—Regulation of Investigatory Powers, 2000 c 23, s 82(1), sch 4 para 17(1)

ss 15–23 appl—SI 2001/192, reg 3

s 19 am—Anti-terrorism, Crime and Security, 2001 c 24, s 3, sch 2 pt 3 para 5(1)(3)(4) excl—SI 2001/192, reg 4

> s 20 am—Anti-terrorism, Crime and Security, 2001 c 24, s 3, sch 2 pt 3 para 5(1)(5)
> ss 21A, 21B added—Anti-terrorism, Crime and Security, 2001 c 24, s 3, sch 2 pt 3 para 5(1)(2)
> ss 24–31 rep—Anti-terrorism, Crime and Security, 2001 c 24, ss 1(4), 125, sch 8 pt 1
> s 34 am—Anti-terrorism, Crime and Security, 2001 c 24, s 104, sch 7 paras 29, 30; Railways and
>   Transport Safety, 2003 c 20, s 73, sch 5 para 4(1)(a)2(k), SI 2004/1573, art 12(6)(a)(b)
> s 36 am—(prosp) (EWI Crime Justice, 2003 c 44, s 280(2)(3) sch 26 para 35(1)(2)
> s 38A added—Anti-terrorism, Crime and Security, 2001 c 24, s 3 Sch 2 pt 1 para 1(2)
> s 38 B added—Anti-terrorism, Crime and Security, 2001 c 24, s 117(1)(2)
> s 39 am—Anti-terrorism, Crime and Security, 2001 c 24, s 117(1)(3)
>   appl—SI 2001/192, reg 3

Extract 2.3 *Chronological Table of the Statutes*—Terrorism Act 2000

The statutes are listed in year and chapter order.

Statutes shown in *italic* are not in force. The repealing legislation is shown for each. For example, the Attorneys in county courts Act of 1255 was repealed by the Civil Procedure Act of 1879, six hundred and twenty-four years later!

Statutes shown in **bold** are (at least partly) in force. Where part of such an Act has been repealed, again, the repealing legislation is shown. An example of this can be found in the Terrorism Act 2000 although you can see that ss 24–31 were repealed by the Anti-terrorism, Crime and Security Act 2001 (ss 1(4) and 125).

? Self-test questions

1. Which piece of legislation amended s. 39 of the Terrorism Act 2000?
2. Which section was added to the Terrorism Act 2000 by s. 117(1)(2) of the Anti-terrorism, Crime and Security Act 2001?

Answers to the self-test questions can be found on the Online Resource Centre.

Since the *Chronological Table of the Statutes* is usually two to three years out of date, it should be used with care. It remains of use for historical purposes when trying to trace the legislative history of older (and long-repealed) statutes.

Current Law Legislation Citator

The *Current Law Legislation Citator* is divided into a number of volumes covering different periods as follows (Table 2.1).

Table 2.1 The volumes comprising the *Current Law Legislation Citator*

1947–71	*Current Law Statute Citator*—covers Acts (of whatever age) which were either amended or cited in court between 1947 and 1971
1972–88	*Current Law Legislation Citator*
1989–95	*Current Law Legislation Citator* also includes a *Statutory Instrument Citator* for 1993–5
1996–9	*Current Law Legislation Citator* also includes a *Statutory Instrument* citator
2000–1	*Current Law Legislation Citator* also includes a *Statutory Instrument* citator
2002–	Volumes published annually. The most recent changes can be found in the *Current Law Monthly Digest*

The *Current Law Legislation Citators* since 1972 provide an alphabetical list of statutes at the start of each volume. This can be useful if you know the name of the Act but are unsure of its year or chapter number.

Here is an extract from the alphabetical table of statutes from the *Current Law Legislation Citator 2005*. You will see the Serious Organised Crime and Police Act 2005 listed as (c. 15).

ALPHABETICAL TABLE OF STATUTES

Sea Fisheries (Shellfish) Act 1967 (c. 83)

Security Service Act 1989 (c. 5)

Self-Governing Schools etc (Scotland) Act 1989 (c. 39)

Serious Organised Crime and Police Act 2005 (c. 15)

Settled Estates Act 1877 (c.18)

Settled Land Act 1925 (c.18)

Severn Bridges Act 1992 (c.3)

Statute Law (Repeals) Act 1989 (c. 43)

Statute Law (Repeals) Act 1993 (c. 50)

Statute Law (Repeals) Act 1998 (c. 43)

Statutory Instruments Act 1946 (c.35)

Statutory Orders (Special Procedure) Act 1945 (c.18)

Statutory Orders (Special Procedure) Act 1965 (c.43)

Extract 2.4 Alphabetical table of statutes

The *Current Law Statute Citator* is included within the *Legislation Citator*. It covers public and local Acts which have been:

- enacted during the period covered by the *Citator*;
- affected by later statute or statutory instrument during the period;
- considered by the judiciary in a case during the period;
- repealed and amended during the period;
- the parent Act under which statutory instruments have been made during the period.

The entries in the *Statute Citator* are organized by calendar year and then by chapter number.

Since we know from the index that the Serious Organised Crime and Police Act 2005 was chapter number 15 in 2005, we can find its full entry in the *Statute Citator* by moving forward to the section covering 2005 and then looking for chapter number 15. Its full entry is as follows:

STATUTE CITATOR 2005

9. **Mental Capacity Act 2005**
   Royal Assent, April 07, 2005
   Sch.6 para.28. amended: 2005 c.4 Sch.11
   para.1
   Sch.7, amended: 2005 c.4 Sch.11 para.1

10. **Public Services Ombudsman (Wales) Act 2005**
   Commencement Orders: SI 2005/2800
   Art.3, Art.4, Art.5, Sch.1 Part1, 2
   Royal Assent, April 07, 2005
   Part 2, applied: SI 2005/2800 Art.6
   s.40, enabling: SI 2005/2008
   s.43, enabling: SI 2005/2800
   s.44, enabling: SI 2005/2800
   Sch.2 para.7, repealed (in part): SI 2005/
   3238 Sch.1 para.93

   Sch.3, amended: SI 2005/3225 Sch.2
   para.7, SI 2005/3226 Sch.2 para.15,
   SI 2005/3238 Sch.1 para. 94

11. **Commissioners for Revenue and Customs Act 2005**
   Commencement Orders: SI 2005/1126 Art.2
   Royal Assent, April 07, 2005
   s.27, enabling: SI 2005/1133
   s.28, enabling: SI 2005/3311
   s.29, applied: SI 2005/1133 Reg.9
   s.29, enabling: SI 2005/3311
   s.37, varied: 2005 c.15 s.38
   s.38, varied: 2005 c.15 s.38
   s.53, enabling: SI 2005/1126
   Sch.3 para.6, applied: 2005 c.15 s.39

15. **Serious Organised Crime and Police Act 2005**	s.133, varied: SI 2005/1521 Art.3, Art.4
	s.134, applied: SI 2005/1537 Art.2
Commencement Orders: SI 2005/1521 Art.2,	s.135, applied: SI 2005/1537 Art.2
Art.3, Art.4, Art.5: SI 2005/2026 Art.2: SI	s.136, applied: SI 2005/1537 Art 2
2005/3136 Art.2, Art.3: SI 2005/3495	s.137, applied: SI 2005/1537 Art.2
Art.2: SSI 2005/358 Art.2	s.138, enabling: SI 2005/1537
Royal Assent, April 07, 2005	s.142, amended: SI 2005/3496 Art.2
s.9, disapplied: SI 2005/3495 Art.2	s.153, enabling: SI 2005/2833
s.101, disapplied: SI 2005/1521 Art.2	s.162, applied: SI 2005/1522 Art. 2
s.128, applied: SI 2005/3447 Art.2	s.162, enabling: SI 2005/1522
s.128, enabling: SI 2005/3447	s.172, applied: SI 2005/3496
s.129, applied: SI 2005/3447 Art.2	s.172, enabling: SI 2005/2833
s.129, enabling: SI 2005/3447	s.173, applied: SI 2005/2240, SI 2005/2241,
s.132, applied: SI 2005/1537 Art.2	SI 2005/3496
s.132, varied: SI 2005/1521 Art.4	s.173, enabling: SI 2005/2240, SI 2005/2241,
s.133, applied: SI 2005/1537 Art.2	SI 2005/3389, SI 2005/3496

Extract 2.5 *Statute Citator*

This shows that the Act received Royal Assent on 7 April 2005.

It is perhaps interesting to note that the other Acts listed in this extract—the Mental Capacity Act 2005, the Public Services Ombudsman (Wales) Act 2005, and the Commissioners for Revenue and Customs Act 2005—all received Royal Assent on the same day. This should give you some idea of the volume and diversity of legislation enacted by Parliament as well as demonstrating the marginalization of the role played by the monarch in granting Royal Assent.

The entry in the *Statute Citator* also shows the various Commencement Orders that were made under the Act. For example, the first Commencement Order was SI 2005/1521 (Arts 2, 3, 4, and 5)—the title of the instrument is not shown in the entry, but the reference is sufficient for you to be able to find it.

You will also see a list of the various legislative effects and their sources. The terms used are listed in the following table (Table 2.2).

Table 2.2 Legislative effects in the *Statute Citator*

Term	Meaning
Added	New provisions are inserted into this Act by subsequent legislation
Amended	This provision of the Act is modified by subsequent legislation
Applied	This provision of the Act was brought to bear or exercised by subsequent legislation
Consolidated	This provision of the Act consolidates provisions of earlier legislation. For more information on consolidation statutes, see chapter 1.
Disapplied	An exception was made to the application of earlier legislation
Enabling	This provision gives power for a statutory instrument to be made under it
Referred to	This provision was referred to from within other legislation, without any specific effect or application
Repealed	This provision was taken out of force by subsequent legislation
Restored	This provision was reinstated by subsequent legislation (after previously having been repealed)
Substituted	This provision was replaced in its entirety by subsequent legislation
Varied	The text of this provision remains unchanged, although its application to particular circumstances was modified

Self-test questions

3. Which piece of delegated legislation brought the Commissioners for Revenue and Customs Act 2005 into force?

4. Look at the full entry for the Commissioners for Revenue and Customs Act 2005. Which provision of which Act varied ss 37 and 38?

Answers to the self-test questions can be found on the Online Resource Centre.

Current Law Statutes Annotated

Current Law Statutes Annotated provides the full text of all Public General Acts shortly after the official Act is published by the Queen's Printer (as will ultimately be bound into *Public General Acts and Measures*). They are supplied as individual booklets and filed in a loose-leaf service binder in chapter number order. First of all, they are supplied on off-white (blue-grey) paper which indicates that the booklet contains only the actual text of the Act itself. At this stage it is indistinguishable from the Queen's Printer copy. Within a few months, the Act is published with annotations, this time on white paper.

The annotations generally provide a detailed account of the legislative history of the Act including references to the key debates in *Hansard*, provision by provision. Although these annotations carry no legal authority, they are extremely useful.

Look at the extract from *Current Law Statutes Annotated* provided here. It deals with s. 115 of the Serious Organised Crime and Police Act 2005. You will recall from looking at the reprint of the Act in *Public General Acts and Measures* that it deals with the powers of police constables to stop and search for fireworks possessed 'in contravention of a prohibition imposed by fireworks regulations'.

Fireworks

115. Power to stop and search for prohibited fireworks

(1) Section 1 PACE (power of constables to stop and search) is amended as follows.

(2) In subsection (2), for "or any article to which subsection (8A) below applies" substitute, "any article to which subsection (8A) below applies or any firework to which subsection (8B) below applies"

.

.

.

(5) Alter subsection (8A) insert–

"(8B) This subsection applies to any firework which a person possesses in contravention of a prohibition imposed by fireworks regulations.

(8C) In this section–

(a) "firework" shall be construed in accordance with the definition of fireworks in section 1(I) of the Fireworks Act 2003; and

(b) "fireworks regulations" has the same meaning as in that Act.

GENERAL NOTE

Note that by Art.3(f) of the Serious Organised Crime and Police Act 2005 (Commencement No.1 Transitional and Transitory Provisions) Order 2005 (SI 2005/1521 (C.66)). s.115 came into force on July 1, 2005, but subject to Arts 4 and 5. These make transitional arrangements

Paragraph 252 of the Government's Explanatory Notes decribed the effect of the section as follows
"252. The Fireworks Regulations 2004 (SI 2004/1836), which were made under the Fireworks Act 2003, make it an offence, subject to certain exceptions, for persons under the age of 18 to possess adult fireworks in public places, and for any person to possess category 4 fireworks (professional display fireworks). This section amends section 4 of PACE to provide the police with the power to stop and search in respect of these two offences. Where any prohibited fireworks are found as a result of a search, the constable conducting the search will be able to seize the fireworks in question. The use of the power will be governed by the procedures and safeguards set out in PACE Code A (Exercise by police officers of statutory powers of stop and search)"
In Parliament there was no opposition to this provison, but there was wider concern about the use of stop and search powers
" . . . the extension of stop and search powers to include a power to stop and search for prohibited fireworks is not in itself an unreasonble provision. Like all extensions of such powers, however, it raises important questions about the potential misuse of stop and search. In particular its racially biased use, which has caused so much damage to relations between minority ethnic groups and the police" (*Hansard*, Lord Dholakia, col.1184 (March 14, 2005))

Extract 2.6 *Current Law Statutes Annotated*

You will see that this extract not only reproduces that wording of the provision as before, but it also includes a detailed commentary on its meaning and effect. For instance, we now know that this provision extends the police powers of stop and search to persons under 18 in respect of adult fireworks in public places and any person in respect of professional display fireworks. We also know that there was some concern expressed by Lord Dholakia during the Parliamentary debate regarding the danger posed to relations between minority ethnic groups and the police by the extension to stop and search powers, although this comment seemed to be a general sweeping statement rather than founded on anything specifically to do with fireworks themselves.

 Practical exercise

Lord Dholakia's comment was reported in *Hansard* column 1184 on 14 March 2005. Find it. The skills you will need are covered in section 8.6.

Halsbury's Statutes of England

Halsbury's Statutes of England aims to provide current versions of all Public General Acts in force in England and Wales (despite its name). As you would probably imagine, it is a mammoth undertaking which comprises a number of different volumes, all of which work together to keep the publication overall as up-to-date as possible (Table 2.3).

The information listed in the main volumes is brought up to date annually via the *Cumulative Supplement* with more recent (i.e. this year's) developments being available via the *Noter-Up Service*. Therefore, whenever using *Halsbury's Statutes* to find legislation, you should always consult the main volumes, *Cumulative Supplement* and *Noter-Up Service* in that order (Figure 2.1).

Table 2.3 The volumes comprising *Halsbury's Statutes*

Component	Content
Main volumes	*Halsbury's Statutes* comprises fifty main volumes, arranged alphabetically by subject from Admiralty to Wills.
Current Statutes Service	Six loose-leaf volumes which contain more recent legislation post-dating that in the main volumes.
Cumulative Supplement	An annually-published single volume that summarizes the effects of new legislation on the main volumes and the *Current Statutes Service.*
Noter-Up Service	A loose-leaf volume that contains very recent changes to the main volumes, the *Current Statutes Service*, and the *Cumulative Supplement.*
Consolidated Index	An annually-published single-volume index to the main volumes and the *Current Statutes Service.*
Is It In Force?	An annually-published single volume which records the commencement dates of all Public General Acts enacted since 1961. It also includes a list of statutes which are *not* yet in force.
Destination Tables: A Guide to the Consolidation of Legislation since 1957	The *Destination Tables* provide a means of tracing the provisions of consolidation statutes back to the earlier legislation. For more information on consolidation statutes, see section 1.1.1.5

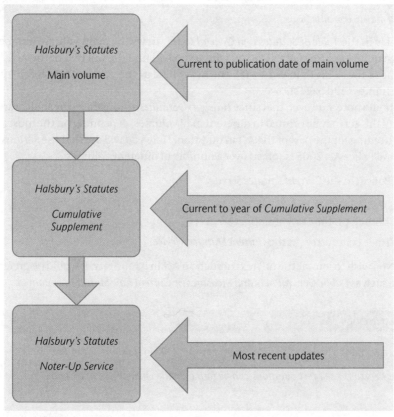

Figure 2.1 *Halsbury's Statutes*

Using *Halsbury's Statutes* when you know the name of the Act

If you know the name of the Act you are looking for, it is quite straightforward to find information upon it in *Halsbury's Statutes*.

First of all, look up the name of the Act in the *Alphabetical List of Statutes* found in the *Consolidated Index* volume. Here is an extract from that table:

Septennial	*Alphabetical List of Statutes*
Septennial Act 1715 . . . . 32, 860	
Sequestration Act 1849 . . . . 14, 174	
Sequestration Act 1871 . . . . 14, 236	
Serious Organised Crime and Police Act 2005—	
ss 1–59, 120, 122, 123, 139, 141, 150, 151, 153, 155–170, 172–174, 176–179,	
Schs 1–4, 8, 9, 11–14, 17 . . . . 33(S), Police 125	
ss 60–76, 78–94, 96, 97, 102, 109–114, 116–118, 121, 124, 126, 128–138, 145–149,	
172, 174, 175, 177–179, Schs 5–7, 16, 17 . . . . 12(2), 1887	
ss 144, 172, 177–179, Sch 10 . . . . 6(S), Children 149	
ss 171, 172, 177–179, Sch 15 . . . . 47(S), Trade & Industry 1	
Servants' Characters Act 1792 . . . . 12(1), 66	
Settled Land Act 1882 . . . . 22, 417	

Extract 2.7 *Alphabetical List of Statutes*

Each entry in the *Table of Statutes and General Index* shows the main volume number (in bold) and page number of *Halsbury's Statutes* where you will find the full text of the Act. However, if the name of the Act is followed by (S), the Act will be in the *Current Statutes Service* under the volume number and page shown.

You should note, however, that since *Halsbury's Statutes* are organized by subject area, the provisions of the Act may be printed in different mail volumes, depending on the most appropriate subject heading for the part of the Act in question. Here you will see that the Serious Organised Crime and Police Act 2005 is spread over a number of different volumes:

- 33(S) Police (in the *Current Statutes Service*)
- 12(2)
- 6(S) Children (in the *Current Statutes Service*)
- 47(S) Trade & Industry (in the *Current Statutes Service*)

Should you wish to look at the full text of such an Act in its entirety, it would be preferable to use a source such as *Public General Acts and Measures* or *Current Law Statutes Annotated*.

 Self-test questions

5. Where would you find the Servants' Characters Act 1792 in *Halsbury's Statutes*?

 Answers to the self-test questions can be found on the Online Resource Centre.

If you want to find a very recent Act, look in the table of contents in the first volume of the *Current Statutes Service*.

The entry in the main volume of the *Current Statutes Service* will provide the text of the Act, as shown in the extract here:

PART 1

THE SERIOUS ORGANISED CRIME AGENCY

CHAPTER 1

SOCA: ESTABLISHMENT AND ACTIVITIES

Establishment of SOCA

1   Establishment of Serious Organised Crime Agency

(1) There shall be a body corporate to be known as the Serious Organised Crime Agency ("SOCA").

(2) Schedule 1 makes provision about the constitution, members and staff of SOCA and other matters relating to it.

(3) Each of the following bodies shall cease to exist on such date as the Secretary of State appoints by order—

(a) the National Criminal Intelligence Service and its Service Authority, and

(b) the National Crime Squad and its Service Authority.

NOTES

Commencement

See 178(8) post and the note "Order under this section" thereto.

General Note   This part is (59 and Schs 1–4) establishes the Serious Organised Crime Agency (SOCA) following proposals set out in the government white paper. *One Step Ahead A 21st Century Strategy to Defeat Organised Crime* (March 2004) (Cm 6167) "The point of establishing SOCA is to bring together the National Crime Squad, the National Criminal Intelligence Service, drugs investigation by Customs and Excise and . . . the immigration crime side of the immigration department of the Home Office. We are not creating a police organisation or a merger; SOCA is a new organisation bringing together talent and skills from different sectors to assist us in combatting serious and organised crime" Parliamentary Under-secretary of State for the Home Department, Caroline Flint, HC Official Report SC D (Serious Organised Crime and Police Bill) col 9.

Sub-s (1): Serious Organised Crime Agency   For the functions of the Agency (SOCA) and the general considerations in the exercise thereof, see ss 2–4 post; for SOCA's general powers, see s 5 post, as to SOCA's annual plans and reports, see ss 6, 7 respectively post.

For provisions relating to the supervision and direction of SOCA by the Secretary of State and the Scottish Ministers, including provision as to inspections of SOCA by Her Majesty's Inspectors of Constabulary, see ss 8–16 post. As to grants made to SOCA in each financial year by the Secretary of State, see ss 17, 18 post; as to charges made by SOCA, see s 19 post and as SOCA's accounts, see s 20 post.

Extract 2.8 *Halsbury's Statutes*—main entry

You will see that each section of the Act is followed by notes with useful information such as definitions and any cases which have considered the interpretation of that section. It will also list any amendments and statutory instruments which have been made under the authority of that part of the Act.

Finally, to ensure that you have the most up-to-date information available, check the *Cumulative Supplement* and the *Noter-Up Service* for any updates.

Is it in force?

The quickest way to determine whether a particular statutory provision is in force is to use *Is It In Force?* which is part of the *Halsbury's Statutes* suite. However, it only covers statutes enacted since 1961. For older statutes, you should use the *Chronological Table of the Statutes*.

The Chronological Table of the Statutes *is described in section 2.1.1.1.*
Take a look at the extract below from *Is It In Force?*

Serious Organised Crime and Police Act 2005 (c 15)

RA: 7 Apr 2005
Commencement provisions: s 178; Serious Organised Crime and Police Act 2005 (Commencement No 1. Transitional and Transitory Provisions) Order 2005, SI 2005/1521; Serious Organised Crime and Police Act 2005 (Commencement No 1) (Scotland) Order 2005 SSI 2005/328; Serious Organised Crime and Police Act 2005 (Commencement No 2) Order 2005, SI 2005/2026, Serious Organised Crime and Police Act 2005 (Commencement No 3) Order 2005, SI 2005/3136; Serious Oganised Crime and Police Act 2005 (Commencement No 4 and Transitory Provisions) Order 2005 SI 2005/3495.

Section		
1	(1)	*Not in force*
	(2)	See Sch 1 below
	(3)	1 Jan 2006 (SI 2005/3495)
2–7		*Not in force*
		.
		.
		.
101		1 Jul 2005 (SI 2005/1521)
102		*Not in force*
103, 104		1 Jul 2005 (SI 2005/1521)
105–108		1 Jul 2005 (SI 2005/1521)
109		See Sch 6 below
110, 111		1 Jan 2006 (SI 2005/3495)
112		1 Jul 2005 (SI 2005/1521)
113		1 Jul 2006 (SI 2005/3495)
114	(1)–(8)	1 Jan 2006 (SI 2005/3495)
	(9)	*Not in force*
115		1 Jul 2005 (SI 2005/1521)
116	(1)	1 Aug 2005 (SI 2005/2026)

Extract 2.9 *Is It In Force?*

As you will see, this provides the date of Royal Assent ('RA') and the various Commencement Orders that have brought parts of the Serious Organised Crime and Police Act 2005 into force. It then goes on to list, provision by provision, whether or not that provision is in force (and if so, the date and any Commencement Order that brought it into force).

Following on from our fireworks example, *Is It In Force?* shows that s. 115 was brought into force on 1 July 2005 by SI 2005/1521 which section 2.1.2.1 later in this chapter will show you is the Serious Organised Crime and Police Act 2005 (Commencement No.1 Transitional and Transitory Provisions) Order 2005.

 Self-test questions

6. Is s. 110 of the Act in force? If so, which piece of delegated legislation brought it into force?

 Answers to the self-test questions can be found on the Online Resource Centre.

Is It In Force? also contains a table of statutes that are not yet in force. This is an alternative way of checking whether or not a particular statutory provision is in force:

Serious Organised Crime and Police Act 2005 (c 15)

RA 7 Apr 2005
Section

1	(1)		Not in force
	(2)		See Sch 1 below
2–7			Not in force
9	(2)	(a)	In force 1 Jan 2006; does not apply during the period up to 31 Mar 2006
11–16			Not in force
19–26			Not in force
28–38			Not in force

Extract 2.10 *Statutes Not Yet In Force*

Is It In Force? is updated via the *Noter-Up Service*. You should always check the *Noter-Up* for any recent changes.

Alternative means of checking whether legislation is in force can be found in the *Current Law Legislation Citator* which notes amendments and repeals and which is updated by the relevant section in the *Current Law Monthly Digest* and the *Legislation Not Yet in Force* table in the current year binder of *Current Law Statutes Annotated* which cites all Acts or sections that have received Royal Assent but which have not yet been brought into force. It is also updated by the relevant section in the *Current Law Monthly Digest*.

Using *Halsbury's Statutes* to find statutes on a particular topic

If you want to find if there are any statutes relating to a particular topic, you should start with the *Table of Statutes and General Index* which contains an extensive *Consolidated Index* arranged by topic.

Returning to our example concerning police powers of stop and search in relation to finding prohibited articles, take a look at this extract from the *Consolidated Index* under 'police':

Police
  special constables—
    appoinment, **33**, 1304
      declaration on, **33**, 1199
      nominations for, **33**, 1199
    defence establishments, service at, **33**, 1180
    disciplinary proceedings, conduct of, **33**, 1655–6
    pension regulations, **33**, 521–2, 1329
    regulations, **33**, 1328–9
    remuneration, **33**, 1329
  special services, provision of, **33**, 1303
  station—
    arrested person to be taken to, **12(1)**, [842]
    designated—
      custody officer. *See* custody officer *above*
      detention, for, **12(1)**, [851]

detainee, search of, **12(1)**, [875]
fingerprinting at, **12(1)**, [883]
suspect, photographing, **12(1)**, [891]
voluntary attendance at, **12(1)**, [841]
station, riotous or indecent behaviour in, **38**, [15]
stop and search powers—
exercise of, **12(1)**, [814]
firearms, for, **12(1)**, [541]
garden or yard, in, **12(1)**, [814]
information, giving, **12(1)**, [815]
length of detention, **12(1)**, [815]
no search made, where, **12(1)**, [815]
persons, of, **12(1)**, [817]
prohibited article, finding, **12(1)**, [814]
records, making, **12(1)**, [816], [818]
reports of, **12(1)**, [818]
road checks, **12(1)**, [817]–[818]
seizure of articles, **12(1)**, [814]
unattended vehicle, **12(1)**, [815]
vehicles, of, **12(1)**, [814]–[816]
violence, in anticipation of, **12(1)**, [1219]
street collections, regulation of, **33**, 1178

Extract 2.11 *Consolidated Index*

You will see that 'stop and search powers' is listed as a sub-category of 'police' and is then further divided into more detailed topics. One of these is 'prohibited articles, finding', with the full entry as:

police—
stop and search powers—
prohibited article, finding, **12(1)**, [814]

This means that the subject can be found in volume **12(1)** of *Halsbury's Statutes* at section 814. The volume number is denoted in **bold** and section is denoted by square brackets. If the reference after the bold volume number is not in brackets, it denotes a page reference. For example:

police—
street collections, regulation of, **33**, 1178

This means that statutes relating to police regulation of street collections can be found in volume **33** of *Halsbury's Statutes* at page 1178.

Self-test questions

7. Where would you find statute law relating to special constables?

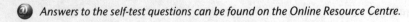 *Answers to the self-test questions can be found on the Online Resource Centre.*

If you then go to volume 12(1) in the main volumes and look for section 814, you will find:

PART I
POWERS TO STOP AND SEARCH

1   Power of constable to stop and search persons, vehicles etc [814]

(1) A constable may exercise any power conferred by this section—

(a) in any place to which at the time when he proposes to exercise the power the public or any section of the public has access, on payment or otherwise, as of right or by virture of express or implied permission: or

(b) in any other place to which people have ready access at the time when he proposes to exercise the power but which is not a dwelling.

.

.

.

(8) The offences to which subsection (7)(b)(i) above applies are—

(a) burglary;

(b) theft;

(c) offences under section 12 of the Theft Act 1968 (taking motor vehicle or other conveyance without authority); . . .

(d) offences under section 15 of that Act (obtaining property by deception) [and

(e) offences under section 1 of the Criminal Damage Act 1971 (destroying or damaging property)

[(8A) This subsection applies to any article in relation to which a person has committed, or is committing or is going to commit an offence under section 139 of the Criminal Justice Act 1988]

[(8B) This subsection applies to any firework which a person possesses in contravention of a prohibition imposed by fireworks regulations.

(8C) In this section—

(a) "firework" shall be construed in accordance with the definition of "fireworks" in section 1(1) of the Fireworks Act 2003; and

(b) "fireworks regulations" has the same meaning as in that Act.]

NOTES

Amendments

Sub-s (2): words in Square brackets (as inserted by the Criminal Justice Act 1988, s 140 (1)(a)(b)) substituted by the Serious Organised Crime and Police Act 2005, s 115(1), (2)

Sub-s (3) words in square brackets (as inserted by the Criminal Justice Act 1988, s 140(1)(a)(b)) substituted by the Serious Organised Crime and Police Act 2005, s 115(1), (3).

Sub-s (6): words in Square brackets (as inserted by the Criminal Justice Act 1988, s 140(1)(b)) substituted by the Serious Organised Crime and Police Act 2005, s 115(1), (4).

Sub-s (8)(c): word omitted repealed by the Criminal Justice Act 2003, s 332, Sch 37, Pt 1.

Sub-s (8)(e) (and word "and" preceding it): inserted by the Criminal Justice Act 2003, s 1(2)

Sub-s (8A) inserted by the Criminal Justice Act 1988, s 140(1)(e)

Sub-s (8B), (8C) inserted by the Serious Organised Crime and Police Act 2005, s 115(1), (5)

Extract 2.12 *Halsbury's Statutes*

You will see that this refers to s. 1 of the Police and Criminal Evidence Act 1984 (commonly referred to as 'PACE'). Note, in particular, sub-sections 8B and 8C. These are shown in square brackets which indicate that they were added to PACE by some subsequent legislation. Detail of this can be found in the notes section which follows section 1 of PACE under 'Amendments' which tells us:

Sub-ss (8B)(8C) inserted by the Serious Organised Crime and Police Act 2005, s 115(1), (5).

The notes also give a variety of other information concerning s. 1 of PACE and its interpretation.

After looking at the entry in the main volume, you should also consult the *Cumulative Supplement* and *Noter-Up* to see if there have been any further changes.

Older statutes

Most legal research will involve the study of (comparatively) recent statutes. However, older statutes can be found in *Statutes of the Realm* which covers the period from 1235 to 1713. It includes statutes that are no longer in force. In addition *Statutes at Large* covers statutes from the Magna Carta (1215) to the late 1700s.

2.1.1.2 Online

You will see throughout this part of the book that a vast amount of legal information is available online. Some online resources are free to acccess, although many of the commercially-produced databases (typically, the ones with the better search facilities!) require a subscription. Most institutions will subscribe to most of the main databases that are covered in this book. These typically require you to log in to gain access and most are accessible via the Athens access management system, which will allow you use a single login to access the whole range of databases to which your institution subscribes. Each institution will have its own registration procedures, so if you do not have an Athens login and password, a good first point of enquiry will be your institution's library.

You may find other perfectly-reputable sources of statute law online—such as websites from local authorities and law firms. However, these sometimes provide a summary or paraphrase of the law—often to make it more accessible to the non-lawyer—rather than using the precise wording of the statute. You should therefore make sure that your sources use the official wording. All the resources listed in this section do so.

 Links to the sites mentioned in this section can also be found on the Online Resource Centre.

 Practical exercise

Find as many of the legal databases from this section as you can. Make a list of those to which you are allowed access. Have a look at each of them. Perform a few practice searches.

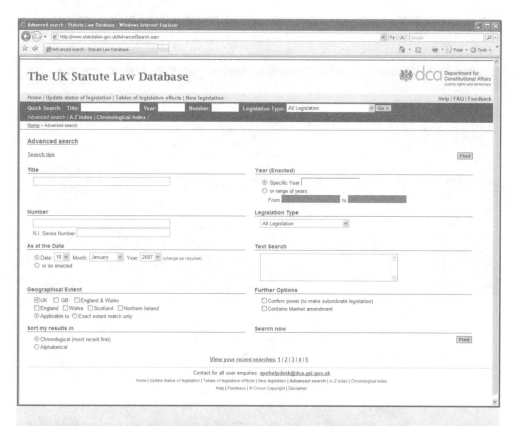

The UK Statute Law Database (http://www.statutelaw.gov.uk)

The UK Statute Law Database (SLD) is the official revised edition of the primary legislation of the United Kingdom made available online. It is a free service and was released to the public by the Department for Constitutional Affairs in December 2006. Most types of primary legislation on the database are held in 'revised' form. This means that amendments made to them by subsequent legislation are incorporated into the text. Most types of secondary legislation on SLD are not revised and are held only in the form in which they were originally made. New legislation is loaded onto SLD as soon as possible after it is received from the publisher.

All legislation held on SLD in revised form has been updated at least to the end of 2001. The remaining updates will be applied progressively throughout 2007. While this work continues, it is important to determine the point in time to which any given item of legislation has been revised and also how to obtain details of any effects that have not yet been applied. Instructions for this can be found on the site.

The SLD allows both quick (title and year) and advanced searches.

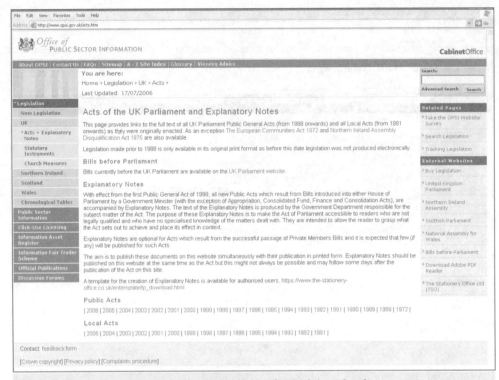

Office of Public Sector Information (http://www.opsi.gov.uk/acts.htm)

The OPSI site provides links to the full text of all UK Parliament Public General Acts (from 1988 onwards) and all Local Acts (from 1991 onwards) as they were originally enacted. The European Communities Act 1972 and Northern Ireland Assembly Disqualification Act 1975 are also available. Legislation made prior to 1988 is not included here since it was not produced electronically.

With effect from the first printed Statutory Instrument of 1987, the full text of all published Statutory Instruments is available. With effect from June 2004 the Explanatory Memorandum, setting out a brief statement of the purpose of an instrument and providing information about its policy objective and policy implications, which are produced to accompany any Statutory Instrument or Draft Statutory Instrument laid before Parliament, have also been published on this website.

OPSI's aim is to publish all UK Statutory Instruments on the Internet simultaneously with or, at least within 24 hours of their publication in printed form.

Bailii (http://www.bailii.org/uk/legis/num_act/)

BAILII is the abbreviated name of the 'British and Irish Legal Information Institute'. It is a free service which provides a fully searchable collection of statutes and statutory instruments as enacted or passed. The data is derived from OPSI.

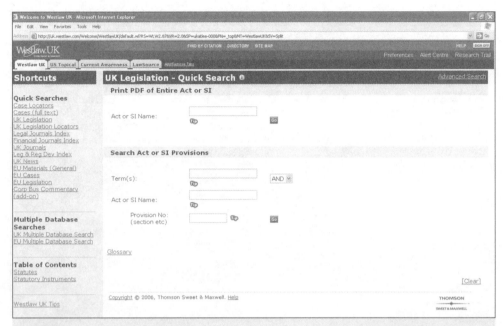

Westlaw

Westlaw provides a range of search facilities which can be used to find both Acts of Parliament and statutory instruments.

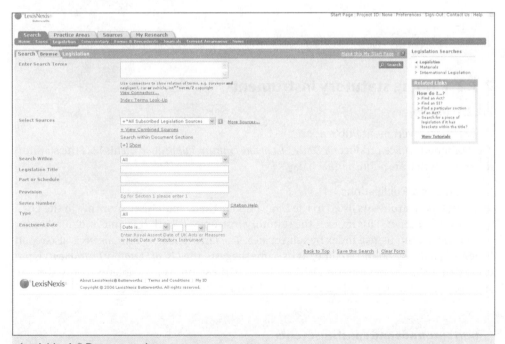

LexisNexis® Butterworths

LexisNexis® Butterworths (LexisNexis) provides searchable legislation and statutory instrument databases as well as cross-references to *Halsbury*.

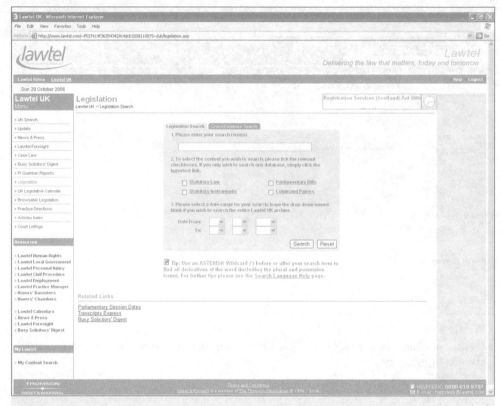

Lawtel

Lawtel provides a good legislation search facility. It also has a full range of browsable legislation.

2.1.2 Finding statutory instruments

2.1.2.1 In a library

Daily List of Government Publications

The Stationery Office produces a *Daily List of Government Publications*. This lists the statutory instruments that are published each day.

List of Statutory Publications

The statutory instruments listed in the *Daily Lists* are then republished monthly in the *List of Statutory Publications*. This indexes the statutory instruments both by name and number and also provides a cumulative index by subject area. The *List of Statutory Instruments* is also republished annually as a bound volume. As its name suggests, the *List of Statutory Instruments* is precisely that—a list. It does not contain the full text of the statutory instruments themselves. The statutory instruments are indexed by subject heading and also by number.

Sports grounds and sporting events

The London Olympic Games and Paralympic Games Act 2006 (Commencement No.1) Order 2006 No. 2006/1118 (C.38). Enabling power: London Olympic Games and Paralympic Games Act 2006, s. 40 (2) to (4) (9). Bringing into operation certain provisions of the 2006 Act on 30.05.2006.

Issued: 25.04.2006. Made: 19.04.2006. Effect: None. Territorial extent & classification: E/W/S/NI. General. - 4p.: 30 cm. - 0 11 074507 8 *£3.00*

Sports grounds and sporting events, England and Wales

The Football Spectators (2006 World Cup Control Period) Order 2006 No. 2006/988. Enabling power: Football Spectators Act 1989. ss. 14(6), 22A (2). - issued: 05.04.2006. Made: 29.03.2006. Laid: 03.04.2006. Coming into force: 24.04.2006. Effect: None. Territorial extent & classification: E/W. General. - 2p.: 30 cm. - 0 11 074435 7 *£3.00*

Extract 2.13 *List of Statutory Instruments*

Halsbury's Statutory Instruments

Halsbury's Statutory Instruments provides current information on all statutory instruments of general application to the whole of England and Wales which are in force. Like *Halsbury's Statutes*, it is made up of a number of components (Table 2.4).

Table 2.4 The volumes comprising *Halsbury's Statutory Instruments*

Component	Content
Main volumes	*Halsbury's Statutory Instruments* comprises twenty-two main volumes, arranged alphabetically by subject.
Main Service Binder (Service Binder 1)	Notes of changes to the instruments contained within the main volumes
Additional Texts Service Binder (Service Binder 2)	The full text of selected new statutory instruments which post-date the main volumes
Consolidated Index and Alphabetical List of Statutory Instruments	An annually-published single volume providing a consolidated index by subject and an alpabetical list of statutory instruments by title

Its use is similar to that of *Halsbury's Statutes*.

If you know the name and number of the statutory instrument for which you are looking, then it is easiest to find it in the *Alphabetical List*.

Alphabetical List of Instruments

Note that the first column indicates the serial number (SR & O from 1894, SI from 1948) or date of the instrument; the years reference may be taken from the title of the instrument except where indicated in brackets following the title description.

Serial No	Description	Title
797	Abolition of the Central Council for Education and Training in Social Work Order 2002	Employment
3680	Abolition of the Intervention Board for Agricultural Produce (Consequential Provisions) (Wales) Regulations 2001 (W 301)	Agriculture
3744	Abolition of the NHS Tribunal (Consequential Provisions) Regulations 2001.	NHS
1920	Abolition of the NHS Tribunal (Consequential Provisions) 2002	NHS
887	Abortion (Amendment) (England) Regulations 2002.	Medicine
2879	Abortion (Amendment) (Wales) Regulations 2002 (W 275)	Medicine

Extract 2.11 *Alphabetical List of Instruments*

Alternatively, the statutory instruments for a particular subject matter area can be found from the *Consolidated Index* by topic:

	Consolidated Index
fishing	**flood defence**
fishing boats—*contd*	
financial assistance schemes **8**, [668]; [687]	codes of practice on environmental procedures—
foreign, stowage of gear **8**, [655]	Environment Agency **22**, [783]
generally **17**, 267, 268	internal drainage boards and local
grants by ministers towards— expenses **8**, [668]	authorities **22**, [784] Environment Agency, functions of **22**,
harmonised safety regime, Directive **17**, 418–420	[581] local committee, functions of **22**, [581]
health and safety provisions 17, 374, 375	regional committee, membership, etc **22**, [581]

Extract 2.15 *Consolidated Index*

This gives a reference to the main volume and section or page number in exactly the same way as *Halsbury's Statutes*.

As with *Halsbury's Statutes*, you should also always check for current updates in the *Service Binder*.

Current Law Legislation Citator

The *Current Law Legislation Citator* also includes an alphabetical table of statutory instruments and a *Statutory Instrument Citator*. Here is an extract from the alphabetical table:

Alphabetical Table of Statutory Instruments

Food (Figs, Hazelnuts and Pistachios from Turkey) (Emergency Control) Regulations (Northern Ireland) 2002 (140)

Food (Forces Exemptions) (Revocations) Regulations (Northern Ireland) 1992 (464)

Food (Forces Exemptions) (Revocations) Regulations 1992 (S.I. 2596)

Food (Hot Chilli and Hot Chilli Products) (Emergency Control) (England) Regulations 2003 (S.I. 1940)

Food (Hot Chilli and Hot Chilli Products) (Emergency Control) (Scotland) Amendment Regulations 2003 (S.S.I. 493)

Food (IIot Chilli and Hot Chilli Products) (Emergency Control) (Scotland) Regulations 2003 (S.S.I. 382)

Food (Hot Chilli and Hot Chilli Products) (Emergency Control) (Wales) Regulations 2003 (S.I 2455)

Extract 2.16 *Alphabetical Table of Statutory Instruments*

This extract should give you an idea as to the more specific nature of many statutory instruments as opposed to general Acts of Parliament—for instance, the little-known Food (Hot Chili and Hot Chili Products) (Emergency Control) (Wales) Regulations 2003 (SI 2455)!

Like the *Current Law Statute Citator*, the *Statutory Instrument Citator* lists:

- statutory instruments amended, repealed, or modified by statute passed or statutory instrument issued during the period;

- statutory instruments judicially considered during the period;
- statutory instruments consolidated during the period;
- statutory instruments made under the powers or any powers of any statutory instrument issued during the period.

Just as with the *Statute Citator*, each statutory instrument is shown with a list of its effects.

The terms used in the Statutory Instrument Citator are the same as those used in the Statute Citator. These are listed in Table 2.2 above.

You will recall from looking at the extract from the Serious Organised Crime and Police Act 2005 that it was brought into force by SI 2005/1521. You can find its full entry in the *Statutory Instrument Citator* by turning to the section covering 2005 and looking for number 1521.

STATUTORY INSTRUMENT CITATOR 2005

No

2005 cont.

1521. **Serious Organised Crime and Police Act 2005 (Commencement No.1, Transitional and Transitory Provisions) Order 2005**

Art. 3 see *R. (on the application of Haw) v Secretary of State for the Home Department* [2005] EWHC 2061. Times, August 4, 2005 (QBD (Admin)), Smith, L.J.

Art. 4, see *R. (on the application of Haw) v Secretary of State for the Home Department* [2005] EWHC 2061, Times, August 4, 2005 (QBD (Admin)), Smith, L.J.

1528. **Waste Mangement Licensing (England and Wales) (Amendment and Related Provisions) (No.2) Regulations 2005**

No

2005 cont.

1656. **Offshore Installations (Safety Zones) Order 2005**

Sch.1. amended: SI 2005/2669 Sch.2 para.1

1711. **Restriction on the Preparation of Adoption Reports Regulation 2005**

Reg.3, referred to: SI 2005/2795 r.155

1714. **Climate Change Levy (Combined Heat and Power Stations) Regulations 2005**

Reg.2, referred to: SI 2005/3320 Reg.10

1721. **Street Works (Sharing of Costs of Works) (Wales) Regulations 2005**

applied: SI 2005/1810 Reg.4

Reg.2, referred to: SI 2005/1810 Reg.4

1725. **Pesticides (Maximum Residue Levels in Crops, Food and Feeding Stuffs) (England and Wales) (Amendment) (No.2) Regulations 2005**

Extract 2.17 *Statutory Instrument Citator*

You now know that the full title of SI 2005/1521 is the 'Serious Organised Crime and Police Act 2005 (Commencement No.1 Transitional and Transitory Provisions) Order 2005'. The entry in the *Statutory Instrument Citator* also tells us that two Articles of the Order have been judicially considered.

    Practical exercise

Once you know how to find and understand cases (chapters 5 and 6), use your skills to find *R (on the applications of Haw) v Secretary of State for the Home Department* [2005] EWHC 2061, *Times*, August 4, 2005 (QBD (Admin)), Smith LJ and examine its effect on Arts 3 and 4 of this Commencement Order. This will test your skills in finding and understanding cases in depth.

2.1.2.2 Online

Daily List

The Stationery Office website provides an overview of the **Daily List** on its online bookshop at www.tsoshop.co.uk. From the main menu, select 'Daily List' for an overview. You can select 'Full Daily List' from here if you want to see all the government publications for the day.

Other databases

The databases listed in section 2.1.1.2 above all provide access to statutory instruments.

2.2 Finding European legislation

2.2.1 The *Official Journal of the European Communities*

The *Official Journal of the European Communities* (generally referred to as the *Official Journal* or just the *OJ*) is the only official source of the officially adopted texts of the EC.

The *Official Journal* is published almost daily (usually around six times a week). It is vast—running to over 30,000 pages annually![26] It comprises several parts, as follows (Table 2.5).

Table 2.5 Parts of the Official Journal

Part	Contents
L series (Legislation)	The L series provides the text of all enacted legislation. It is divided into two sections:
	• Acts whose publication is mandatory (most regulations and directives addressed to all member states)
	• all other legislation
	Note that this distinction carries through to the *Official Journal: Index*. In other words, the L series contains all legislative acts, but the *Index* divides them into two as above.

26.   The figure of 30,000 pages only refers to the *L series* and the *C series*. Adding the material that is only available electronically clearly expands the mass of information in the *Official Journal* even more.

Table 2.5 *(Cont.)*

Part	Contents
C series (Communications)	The *C series* is divided into three parts: • Part I contains information from the Commission, Court of Justice, Court of First Instance, European Parliament, and the Economic and Social Committee • Part II contains the text of *proposed* EC legislation • Part III contains notices of invitation to tender for contracts and staff vacancies
S series (Supplemental)	The *S series* publishes details of public contracts which are open to competitive tender
Annex	Contains full text transcripts of debates in the European Parliament
Special Edition	Contains official English translations of all EC legislation in force as at 1 January 1973 when the United Kingdom joined the European Communities.

Note that the *S series*[27] and the *Annex*[28] are only available electronically. The *S series* can be found as Tenders Electronic Daily (TED) at ted.eur-op.eu.int

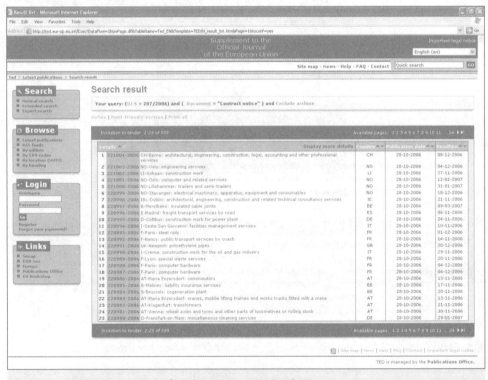

Debates of the Parliament can be found at www.europarl.eu.int

---

27. Since 1997.
28. Since 2000.

2.2.1.2 Citing the *Official Journal*

There are two forms of citation which can be used to refer to the *Official Journal.* These are best illustrated by way of example (Figures 2.2, 2.3).

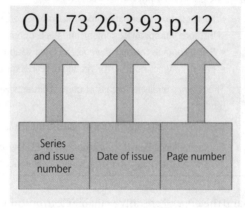

Figure 2.2 Citing the *OJ*

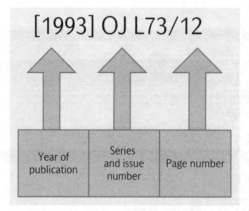

Figure 2.3 Citing the *OJ*—an alternative

Since there is no standard form of citation for the *Official Journal*, you must be familiar with both forms.

Self-test questions

8. Give an alternative citation for OJ C204 20.1.06 p.14

9. What does [2001] OJ C98/17 mean?

Answers to the self-test questions can be found on the Online Resource Centre.

2.2.2 Citing European legislation

The full citation of European legislation must include the following components:

• The Community institution that is responsible for the act. This is usually the Commission, but may be the Council

- The type of the act (Regulation, Directive, Decision, etc.)
- A unique number by which to identify the act
- The year of the enactment
- The institutional treaty under which the act was made (EEC, EC, ECSC or Euratom)
- The date on which the act was passed

It is important to note that references to Regulations are written with the number first followed by the year, for example:

Regulation (EC) 852/2004 on the hygiene of foodstuffs.

However, references to Directives and Decisions are written with the year first followed by the number, for example:

Directive 95/45/EC as regards Sunset Yellow FCF (E 110) and Titanium Dioxide (E 171)

2.2.3 Finding Treaty Articles

As you will recall from chapter 1, the underlying source of European law is found in the various treaties:

- The European Community Treaty
- The European Coal and Steel Community Treaty
- The Euratom Treaty
- Single European Act
- Treaty on European Union (the Maastricht Treaty)
- Treaty of Amsterdam
- Treaty of Nice

The EC Treaty itself has been amended by the Single European Act and the Treaties of Maastricht, Amsterdam, and Nice.

2.2.3.1 The Treaty of Amsterdam: renumbering treaty provisions

One of the potentially more confusing changes introduced by the Treaty of Amsterdam[29] was the renumbering of the provisions of the EC Treaty and the Treaty on European Union (Maastricht). For example, Article 119 EC of the EC Treaty became Article 141 EC. When looking for EC Treaty Articles you therefore need to be sure whether the Article number refers to the Treaty before or after the renumbering by the Treaty of Amsterdam. Some materials refer to the old and new numbers together in the form Article 141 EC (ex 119), although as more time has passed since the renumbering, the dual-form is encountered less frequently.

2.2.3.2 In a library

The authoritative text for all European legislation is the *Official Journal*.[30] However, for ease of access, the official publisher of the European Union (the Office for Official Publications of the

---

29. Art. 12.
30. For instance, the text of the Treaty of Nice was found in the *Official Journal C series* on 10 March 2001.

European Communities or OOPEC) publishes *European Union—Selected Instruments taken from the Treaties.*

An unofficial, but nonetheless very useful, compilation of the unannotated texts of the main treaties can be found in Foster, N. *Blackstone's EC Legislation*, published and updated regularly by Oxford University Press.

2.2.3.3 Online

The text of the Treaties can be found online on the EUR-Lex website at www.europa.eu.int/eur-lex/en

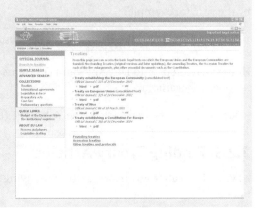

2.2.4 Finding European secondary legislation

2.2.4.1 In a library

The *Official Journal Index*

Despite its helpful sounding name, the *Official Journal Index* does not greatly assist in navigating the vast expanse of material that is the *Official Journal*. For instance, it only indexes the *L series* (of enacted legislation) and the case lists and summaries (from the Court of Justice and Court of First Instance) from the *C series*.

It is published monthly, with a cumulative index only being published annually. This means that you may have to search through a number of monthly copies of the *Index*.

Given its cumbersome and incomplete nature, the better way of searching for European materials is via one or more of the electronic sources available.

2.2.4.2 Online

EUROPA (www.europa.eu)

EUROPA is the main website of the European Union. It contains over 1.5 million pages and links to the EC legal portal, EUR-Lex.

EUR-Lex (www.europa.eu.int/eur-lex/en)

EUR-Lex is updated daily and provides a free searchable database of European legislation.

CELEX

CELEX is the official multilingual legal database of the European Union. It is available as a subscription service via EUROPA, or commercially via a number of commercial publishers such as Justis CELEX and Eurolaw. The commercial variants offer a wider range of search facilities than CELEX itself.

Other databases

LexisNexis, Lawtel, and Westlaw also provide search facilities for European legislation.

2.3 European Convention on Human Rights

The official text of the European Convention on Human Rights and the various protocols which amend it can be found online at conventions.coe.int. (http://conventions.coe.int/ Treaty/en/Treaties/Html/005.htm)

Individual copies of the Convention on Human Rights are also published by the Council of Europe.

CHAPTER SUMMARY

Domestic statutes

- *Public General Acts and Measures* contains the full text of all statutes

- *Law Reports—Statutes* also contains full text, but its publication is often delayed

- The *Chronological Table of the Statutes* is useful for tracing very old statutes, but is of less use for modern statutes as it is often two or three years out of date

- The *Current Law Legislation Citator* lists all statutes and provides information as to where and how that legislation has been used

- *Current Law Statutes Annotated* provides the full text of all Public General Acts annotated with a detailed account of the history of the Act (including Parliamentary debate) and other useful notes and cross-references

- *Halsbury's Statutes of England* aims to provide current volumes of all Public General Acts, arranged by subject matter. Although comprehensive it is sometimes cumbersome to use. It does contain a very useful *Is It In Force?* volume

- The Office of Public Sector Information (OPSI) provides free links to the full text of all Public General Acts from 1988 and Local Acts from 1991

- BAILII provides a searchable list of statutes, but the content is sourced from OPSI

- Westlaw, Lexis-Nexis, and Lawtel all provide commercially-available legislation search engines

Domestic statutory instruments

- The *Daily List* and *List of Statutory Publications* list all SIs by subject heading and number. They do not contain the full text of the SIs themselves

- *Halsbury's Statutory Instruments* provides full text to all SIs of general application to the whole of England and Wales arranged by subject area

- The *Current Law Legislation Citator* also includes an alphabetical table of SIs and a *Statutory Instrument Citator*

- The *Daily List* can be found online on the TSO website

- Westlaw, Lexis-Nexis, and Lawtel all provide commercially-available legislation search engines

European law

- The *Official Journal of the European Communities* is the only official source of the officially adopted texts of the EC

- The *OJ* is unfortunately vast and difficult to navigate

- The *S series* and *Annex* to the *OJ* are only available electronically

- Compilations of European legislation are widely available in student statute texts

- European legislation can be found online for free via EUROPA and EUR-Lex

- CELEX is the official multilingual legal database of the European Union but is difficult to use

- Westlaw, Lexis-Nexis, and Lawtel all provide commercially-available European legislation search engines which are much easier to use

- The European Convention on Human Rights and various protocols which amend it can be found on the Council of Europe official website

FURTHER READING

This chapter demonstrates the basic skills that you will need to find legislation in a law library.

- Clinch, P. (2001) *Using a Law Library* (2nd edn) London: Blackstone Press, pp. 28–98.

- Thomas, P.A. and Knowles, J. (2001) *Dane and Thomas: How to Use a Law Library* (2nd edn) London: Sweet & Maxwell, pp. 57–83.

- Borchardt, K. (2000) *The ABC of Community Law* (4th edn) European Commission.
  For a table of the old and new numbering European legislation schemes as well as a useful general introduction to European law.

Using legislation

3

The place of legislation within the range of sources of law was covered in chapter 1 while various means of finding legislation were considered in chapter 2. Having learnt where legislation fits into the structure of the legal system and how it can be found, this chapter will discuss how to use legislation. It will firstly look at the 'anatomy' of an Act of Parliament and describe each of its composite parts. It will then move on to consider the various means by which the courts can interpret the wording of statutory provisions, including a discussion of the impact of the European Communities Act 1972 and the Human Rights Act 1998.

Using legislation is an important legal skill. Legislation is a primary source of law and represents the will of Parliament as the legislature. Therefore it is essential that you are able to negotiate your way around a piece of legislation and understand how it all fits together. You will also need to be able to interpret potentially ambiguous legislative provisions to determine whether they will support your argument or whether an interpretation could be found that might go against your argument. Most importantly, using and understanding legislation is vital to the study of every area of law.

LEARNING OUTCOMES

After studying this chapter, you will be able to:

- Navigate an Act of Parliament and a statutory instrument and distinguish its component parts

- Interpret the possible meanings of a legislative provision in the case of ambiguity

- Describe the impact that the European Communities Act 1972 and the Human Rights Act 1998 have had on the interpretation of legislation

3.1 Anatomy of an Act of Parliament

In order to make any sense at all of a statute, you will need first to understand the way in which it is structured. We will use the London Olympic Games and Paralympic Games Act 2006 as an example. Look at the extracts from the statute provided. You will see that a number of areas of the statute have been highlighted. These will be covered in turn (Figures 3.1, 3.2).

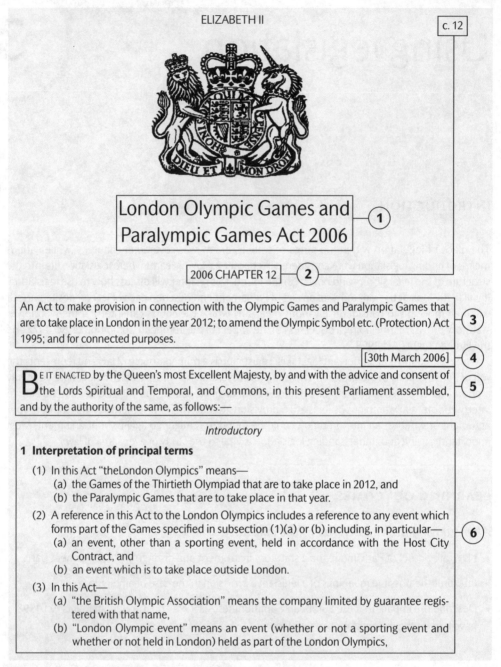

ELIZABETH II

c. 12

London Olympic Games and Paralympic Games Act 2006 —①

2006 CHAPTER 12 —②

An Act to make provision in connection with the Olympic Games and Paralympic Games that are to take place in London in the year 2012; to amend the Olympic Symbol etc. (Protection) Act 1995; and for connected purposes. —③

[30th March 2006] —④

BE IT ENACTED by the Queen's most Excellent Majesty, by and with the advice and consent of the Lords Spiritual and Temporal, and Commons, in this present Parliament assembled, and by the authority of the same, as follows:— —⑤

Introductory

1 Interpretation of principal terms

(1) In this Act "theLondon Olympics" means—
    (a) the Games of the Thirtieth Olympiad that are to take place in 2012, and
    (b) the Paralympic Games that are to take place in that year.

(2) A reference in this Act to the London Olympics includes a reference to any event which forms part of the Games specified in subsection (1)(a) or (b) including, in particular—
    (a) an event, other than a sporting event, held in accordance with the Host City Contract, and
    (b) an event which is to take place outside London. —⑥

(3) In this Act—
    (a) "the British Olympic Association" means the company limited by guarantee registered with that name,
    (b) "London Olympic event" means an event (whether or not a sporting event and whether or not held in London) held as part of the London Olympics,

Figure 3.1 London Olympic Games and Paralympic Games Act 2006

3.1.1 Short title (1)

The short title of this Act is the 'London Olympic Games and Paralympic Games Act 2006'. The short title is the normal way in which to refer to a statute—the Theft Act 1968, the Computer Misuse Act 1990 and the Human Rights Act 1998 are all examples of short titles. In this example the Act states its own short title itself in s. 42 at the very end (Figure 3.3).

39. Offences: arrest ————————————————————————— (7)

(1) At the end of Schedule 1A to the Police and Criminal Evidence Act 1984 (arrestable offences) add—

    "*London Olympic Games and Paralympic Games Act 2005*

    270 An offence under section 21(1), 27(1) or 31(1) of the London Olympic Games and Paralympic Games Act 2006 (unauthorised advertising trading and ticket)."

(2) A constable in Scotland may arrest without a person who the constable reasonably believes is committing or has committed an offence under section 21(1), 27(1) or 31(1).

(3) Subsection (2) is without prejudice to any power of arrest which is otherwise exercisable by a constable in Scotland.

40 Commencement and duration ————————————————— (8)

(1) The following provisions of this Act shall come into force on Royal Assert—
    (a) section 1,
    (b) section 3 to 5 and Schedule 1,
    (c) section 32 and paragraphs 1 to 11 of Schedule 3,
    (d) section 33 and Schedule 4,
    (e) sections 34 and 35(1) and (2),
    (f) section 36(3)(a) and (d),
    (g) section 37, and
    (h) section 38.

(2) The other preceding provisions of this Act (including paragraphs 12 to 14 of Schedule 3) shall come into force in accordance with provision made by order of the Secretary of State.

Figure 3.2 London Olympic Games and Paralympic Games Act 2006, ss 39 and 40

42 Short title
    This Act may be cited as the London Olympic Games and Paralympic Games ——— (1)
    Act 2006.

Figure 3.3 London Olympic Games and Paralympic Games Act 2006, s. 42

Sometimes, the short title might be quite long—as is the case with this statute. If the Act is referred to constantly then the short title may be abbreviated further. For instance, the London Olympic Games and Paralympic Games Act 2006 might be referred to as the 'Olympics Act 2006'; however, the short title remains the London Olympic Games and Paralympic Games Act 2006.

More extreme examples of short-title abbreviation can be found with the Police and Criminal Evidence Act 1984 and the Trusts of Land and Appointment of Trustees Act 1996 which for reasons of manageability are almost universally referred to as PACE and TOLATA respectively.

3.1.2 Citation (2)

The official citation for this statute is '2006 Chapter 12'. Each Act passed in any calendar year is given its own number, known as the chapter number. The official citations—comprising year and chapter number—are therefore unique. In this case, the London Olympic Games and Paralympic Games Act 2006 was the twelfth statute passed in 2006. The word 'chapter' can be abbreviated to 'c.'—an example of this can be seen in the top right-hand corner of the page. The citation is not usually used in referencing, although some international journals (particularly American journals) do require full citations to be used, often in connection with the short title; for example, the London Olympic Games and Paralympic Games Act 2006 (c.12).

This system has been used for Acts passed since 1 January 1963 when the Acts of Parliament Numbering and Citation Act 1962 came into force. Prior to that a more complex system involving regnal years was used. *See Further reading.*

3.1.3 Long title (3)

The long title of this statute is 'An Act to make provision in connection with the Olympic Games and Paralympic Games that are to take place in London in the year 2012; to amend the Olympic Symbol etc. (Protection) Act 1995; and for connected purposes'. Generally speaking, the long title of an Act gives an indication as to its purpose and content.

3.1.4 Date of Royal Assent (4)

This Act received the Royal Assent on 30 March 2006. This is the date upon which the preceding Bill became law. The provisions of the Act come into force on the date of Royal Assent unless the Act itself states otherwise. For example, the Act, or various parts of it, may come into force by order of a government minister. This will be provided for within the Act itself and will involve the passing of a commencement order (which is a statutory instrument).

In section 3.2 below, you will see how the Sustainable and Secure Buildings Act 2004 (Commencement No. 1) Order 2006 brings part of the Sustainable and Secure Buildings Act 2004 into force.

The date of the Act in its short title can sometimes be misleading. For example, the European Communities Act 1972 actually came into force on 1 January 1973. An Act or provision of an Act comes into force at the beginning of the day where provision is made for it to come into force on that day, or if not, at the beginning of the day on which the Act receives the Royal Assent[1] (see section 3.7 on 'Commencement').

3.1.5 Enacting formula (5)

The enacting formula introduces the main provisions of the statute. It declares that the law derives its authority from having been properly passed by the legislature. The enacting formula is generally the same, namely:

> BE IT ENACTED by the Queen's most Excellent Majesty, by and with the advice and consent of the Lords Spiritual and Temporal, and Commons, in this present Parliament assembled, and by the authority of the same, as follows:

However, if the Parliament Acts 1911 and 1949 have been used to force legislation through Parliament against the wishes of the House of Lords, the enacting formula used is different:

> BE IT ENACTED by the Queen's most Excellent Majesty, by and with the advice and consent of the Commons in this present Parliament assembled, in accordance with the provisions of the Parliament Acts 1911 and 1949, and by the authority of the same, as follows:

---

1.   Interpretation Act 1978, s. 4.

This formula removes references to the 'advice and consent of the Lords Spiritual and Temporal'. Examples of this may be found in the Hunting Act 2004 which prohibited hare coursing and most hunting of wild mammals, particularly foxes, with dogs and the Sexual Offences (Amendment) Act 2000 which lowered the age of consent for male homosexual activities from 18 to 13.

3.1.6 Main body (6)

The main body of the Act is divided into sections, subsections, paragraphs, and subparagraphs. When referencing particular parts of an Act, it is important to be precise. You should identify exactly where the wording of the law can be found.

In this Act, s. 1 deals with the interpretation of principal terms. Subsection 1(1) provides a definition of 'the London Olympics' as comprising two events. The first of these is in para. 1(1)(a), namely 'the games of the thirtieth Olympiad that are to take place in 2012'. The second is in para. 1(1)(b), namely 'the Paralympic Games that are to take place in that year'. Some paragraphs are further divided into subparagraphs. An example can be found in subpara. 40(9)(b)(i), highlighted in the extract from the Act (Figure 3.4).

(9) In respect of section 36(3)—
   (a) paragraph (a) shall have effect in relation to compulsory purchase orders made on or after 1st October 2005,
   (b) an order bringing paragraph (b) into force on a date ("the commencement date")—
      (i) may provide for paragraph (b) to have effect in relation to purchases (whether compulsory or voluntary) completed before, on or after the commencement date, but
      (ii) must include provision modifying section 295 of the Housing Act 1985 in its application by virtue of section 36(3)(b) so that extinguishment of rights and easements takes effect, in the case of a purchase completed before the commencement date, on the commencement date,

Figure 3.4 London Olympic Games and Paralympic Games Act 2006, subparagraph 40(9)(b)(i)

'Section' is commonly abbreviated to 's.'—the examples highlighted above could be therefore be referred to as s.1, s.1(1), s.1(1)(a), s.1(1)(b) and s.40(9)(b)(i). However, many consider it to be poor written style to begin a sentence with the abbreviated form. Therefore, it is better style to start a sentence with 'Section 3 of the Human Rights Act 1998 . . . ' than with 'S. 3 of the Human Rights Act 1998 . . . '

See chapter 10 for more discussion on written style.

3.1.6.1 Headings (7)

Each section in this particular Act has a heading. For example the heading to s. 39 is 'Offences: arrest'. The headings give some indication of the content of the particular section, but are not especially helpful in resolving matters of interpretation.

Some statutes have marginal notes instead of headings. Look at the extract from the Misrepresentation Act 1967 in Figure 3.5. You will see an example of a marginal note highlighted alongside s. 1 of the Act. This shows that s. 1 is concerned with the 'Removal of certain bars to recission for innocent misrepresentation'. This is similar to the information provided by headings.

However, there is one key difference between marginal notes and headings. The headings are part of the Act (they are debated during the passage of the legislation) and marginal notes are

Misrepresentation Act 1967

1967 CHAPTER 7

An Act to amend the law relating to innocent misrepresentation and to amend sections 11 and 35 of the Sale of Goods Act 1893.   [22nd March 1967]

B E IT ENACTED by the Queen's most Excellent Majesty, by and with the advice and consent of the Lords Spiritual and Temporal, and Commons, in this present Parliament assembled, and by the authority of the same, as follows:—

1. Where a person has entered into a contract after a misrepresentation has been made to him, and—

(*a*) the misrepresentation has become a term of the contract;

or

(*b*) the contract has been performed;

or both, then, if otherwise he would be entitled to rescind the contract without alleging fraud, he shall be so entitled, subject to the provisions of this Act, notwithstanding the matters mentioned in paragraphs (*a*) and (*b*) of this section.

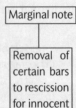

Marginal note

Removal of certain bars to rescission for innocent misrepresentation

Figure 3.5 Misrepresentation Act 2006, marginal note

not. This means that marginal notes have no direct legal effect. Despite this distinction, both marginal notes and headings are of limited use beyond being a useful means of navigating around the Act.

? Self-test questions

1. When did the Misrepresentation Act 1967 receive Royal Assent?

2. What is its long title?

3. What is its citation?

4. What does '1967 Chapter 7' signify?

@ *Answers to the self-test questions can be found on the Online Resource Centre.*

3.1.7 Commencement (8)

As we have found, the provisions of the Act come into force on the date of Royal Assent unless the Act itself states otherwise. The commencement provisions are normally found towards the end of the Act. In this example, the commencement provisions are found in s. 40. You will see that s. 40(1) details the parts of the Act which came into force on Royal Assent—that is, 30 March 2006.

Section 40(2) provides that the other preceding provisions of the Act come into force 'in accordance by provision made by order of the Secretary of State'. Therefore, the Secretary of State has the power to decide when certain parts of the Act become law. He will bring those parts of the Act into effect by passing a statutory instrument known as a commencement order—a piece of delegated legislation.

This means that certain statutory provisions might *never* come into force at all. For example, the Family Law Act 1996 was intended to revolutionize the divorce process. It received Royal Assent on 4 July 1996 but at the time it was not expected to be brought into effect until 2000. Amongst other things, it was to dispense with the principle of 'fault-based divorce' whereby unreasonable behaviour and adultery were relied upon to obtain the so-called 'quickie divorce'. This is where the parties do not have to wait two years and rely on either unreasonable behaviour or adultery. The Act was also to promote mediation in an attempt to reduce acrimony between the parties. The new law proposed Information Meetings as a prerequisite to divorce. A Statement of Marital Breakdown could then be prepared three months after the Information Meeting. Filing of this Statement at the Court would then start proceedings. After that there would be a period for reflection and consideration commencing fourteen days after the Statement was received by the Court and ending nine months after that (with limited exceptions). After the period of reflection either party could then apply for a Divorce or Separation Order, normally being granted if less than a year had elapsed after the Period of Reflection had ended and financial matters had been settled. Unfortunately, the results from a pilot study established that such meetings were ineffective. This led to the Government abandoning the reforms altogether and consequently Part 2 of the Act will never be brought into force.

Alternatively, an Act might specify that it comes into force on a fixed date, or a date relative to its receiving Royal Assent.

Acts do not take effect retrospectively unless expressly provided for within the Act. Examples of retrospective legislation are rare, but one example can be found in s. 1 of the War Crimes Act 1991; an Act which confers jurisdiction on UK courts in respect of certain grave violations of the laws and customs of war committed in German-held territory during the Second World War.

 Self-test questions

5. When did the Misrepresentation Act 1967 come into force?

 Answers to the self-test questions can be found on the Online Resource Centre.

3.1.8 Schedules (9)

Some statutes have one or more schedules at the end (Figure 3.6). These may contain a number of different things, such as:

- Definitions of terms used in the Act (e.g. Schedule 1, Interpretation Act 1978)
- Detailed provisions which are referred to in the main Act (e.g. Schedule 1, Football (Disorder) Act 2000)
- Details of minor and consequential amendments to other legislation (e.g. Schedule 2, Football (Disorder) Act 2000)
- Repeals of pre-existing legislation (e.g. Schedule 3, Football (Disorder) Act 2000)

SCHEDULES

SCHEDULE 1   Section 3
THE OLYMPIC DELIVERY AUTHORITY
PART 1
CONSTITUTION

Membership

1 (1) The Secretary of State shall, having consulted the Mayor of London—

　　(a) appoint the members of the Olympic Delivery Authority, and

　　(b) appoint one of the members as Chairman.

 (2) The Secretary of State aim to ensure that the Authority has neither less than 7 nor more than 11 members at any time.

 (3) In appointing members of the Authority the Secretary of State shall have regard to the desirability of their having experience relevant to—

　　(a) the nature of the Authority's functions, and

　　(b) the places in relation to which they are likely to be exercised.

Figure 3.6 Schedule 1—The Olympic Delivery Authority

In this example, Schedule 1 refers to the 'Olympic Delivery Authority' which is set up in the main Act. The schedule provides more details as to the constitution and working of the authority. It is split out into a schedule to enable easier navigation around the main body of the Act.

Schedules are divided into paragraphs and subparagraphs. In this example, schedule 1, paragraph 1, subparagraph 2 provides that 'the Secretary of State shall aim to ensure that the Authority has neither less than seven nor more than eleven members at any time'. 'Schedule' is often abbreviated to 'sch.' and paragraph to 'para.'. It is incorrect to refer to the divisions of a schedule as sections.

3.1.9 Preambles

Older statutes contain preambles, which describe the purpose of the Act in more detail than the long title. For example, the preamble to the Statute of Charitable Uses 1601 sets out a list of charitable purposes or activities.

The Statute of Charitable Uses (1601), 43 Elizabeth I c. 4

An Acte to redresse the Misemployment of Landes Goodes and Stockes of Money heretofore given to Charitable Uses

Whereas Landes Tenementes Rentes Annuities Profittes Hereditamentes, Goodes Chattels Money and Stockes of Money, have bene heretofore given limitted appointed and assigned, as well by the Queenes most excellent Majestie and her moste noble Progenitors, as by sondrie other well disposed persons, some for Releife of aged impotent and poore people, some for Maintenance of sicke and maymed Souldiers and Marriners, Schooles of Learninge, Free Schooles and Schollers in Universities, some for Repaire of Bridges Portes Havens Causwaies Churches Seabankes and Highwaies, some for Educacion and prefermente of Orphans, some for or towardes Reliefe Stocke or Maintenance of Howses of Correccion, some for Mariages of poore Maides, some for Supportacion Ayde and Helpe of younge tradesmen Handicraftesmen and persons decayed, and others for reliefe or redemption of Prisoners or Captives, and for aide or ease of any poore Inhabitantes concerninge payment of Fifteenes, setting out of Souldiers and other Taxes; Whiche Landes Tenementes Rents Annuities Profitts Hereditaments Goodes Chattells Money and Stockes of Money nevertheles have not byn imployed according to the charitable intente of the givers and founders thereof, by reason of Fraudes breaches of Truste and Negligence in those that shoulde pay delyver and imploy the same . . .

However, since the list was in the preamble, rather than in the main body of the Act, it did not form part of the statute. However, the list in the preamble to the 1601 statute has nevertheless formed the foundation of the modern definition of charitable purposes. Almost 300 years later in *Commissioners for Special Purposes of Income Tax* v *Pemsel*,[2] Lord MacNaughten identified the four heads of charity which still apply today:

- Relief of poverty
- Advancement of education
- The advancement of religion
- Other purposes considered beneficial to the community

For a purpose to fall into the fourth category, the courts will usually refer to the preamble of the 1601 Statute of Charitable Uses, and decide by analogy to the purposes listed there.

Preambles in older statutes are also useful if you need to evaluate whether an old piece of legislation has actually achieved what it set out to achieve. The purposes set out in the preamble can then be compared to the effect of the Act's application by the courts.

3.1.10 Explanatory notes

Most recent Acts will carry accompanying Explanatory Notes. These are useful information but are not legally binding. The Office of Public Sector Information (www.opsi.gov.uk) describes Explanatory Notes as follows:

With effect from the first Public General Act of 1999, all new Public Acts which result from Bills introduced into either House of Parliament by a Government Minister (with the exception of Appropriation, Consolidated Fund, Finance and Consolidation Acts), are to be accompanied by Explanatory Notes. The text of the Explanatory Notes will be produced by the Government Department responsible for the subject matter of the Act. The purpose of these Explanatory Notes is to make the Act of Parliament accessible to readers who are not legally qualified and who have no specialised knowledge of the matters dealt with. They are intended to allow the reader to grasp what the Act sets out to achieve and place its effect in context.

The Explanatory Notes can give an indication of the purpose of a particular statute which might be useful background when trying to establish the meaning behind any seemingly ambiguous provision.

See section 3.3 for a discussion of statutory interpretation.

3.2 Anatomy of a statutory instrument

Chapter 1 describes statutory instruments as sources of law.

Statutory instruments are also built up from a number of standard components. Look at the Sustainable and Secure Buildings Act 2004 (Commencement No. 1) Order 2003. As before, a number of the parts of the statutory instrument have been highlighted (Figure 3.7).

2. [1891] AC 531.

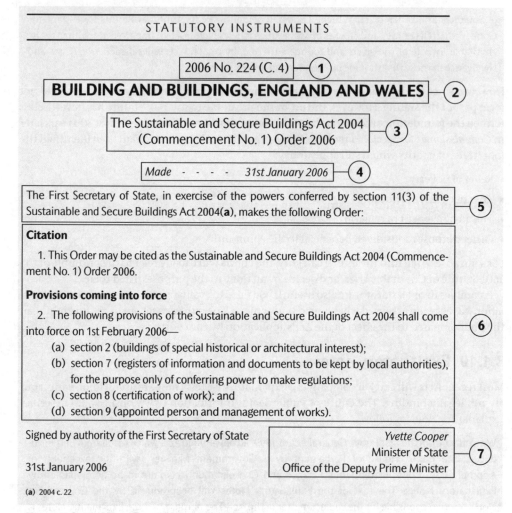

STATUTORY INSTRUMENTS

2006 No. 224 (C. 4) — 1

BUILDING AND BUILDINGS, ENGLAND AND WALES — 2

The Sustainable and Secure Buildings Act 2004 (Commencement No. 1) Order 2006 — 3

Made - - - - 31st January 2006 — 4

The First Secretary of State, in exercise of the powers conferred by section 11(3) of the Sustainable and Secure Buildings Act 2004(**a**), makes the following Order: — 5

Citation

1. This Order may be cited as the Sustainable and Secure Buildings Act 2004 (Commencement No. 1) Order 2006.

Provisions coming into force

2. The following provisions of the Sustainable and Secure Buildings Act 2004 shall come into force on 1st February 2006— — 6
    (a) section 2 (buildings of special historical or architectural interest);
    (b) section 7 (registers of information and documents to be kept by local authorities), for the purpose only of conferring power to make regulations;
    (c) section 8 (certification of work); and
    (d) section 9 (appointed person and management of works).

Signed by authority of the First Secretary of State

Yvette Cooper
Minister of State
Office of the Deputy Prime Minister — 7

31st January 2006

(**a**) 2004 c. 22

Figure 3.7 Sustainable and Secure Buildings Act 2004 (Commencement No. 1) Order 2006

3.2.1 Citation (1)

The citation for this example is '2006 No. 224 (C.4)' This means that it is the 224th statutory instrument of 2006. The chapter number (4) refers to that of the parent Act.

3.2.2 Subject matter (2)

The subject matter of the statutory instrument in this case is building and buildings in England and Wales.

3.2.3 Title (3)

The title of the statutory instrument Sustainable and Secure Buildings Act 2004 (Commencement No. 1) Order 2006. This refers to its parent Act, namely the Sustainable and Secure Buildings Act

2004 and to its purpose as a commencement order. The 'No. 1' refers to it being the first commencement order made under the parent Act.

3.2.4 Date made (4)

The date shown in the statutory instrument (31st January 2006) is that on which it was made (or in the case of instruments that are required to be laid before Parliament, the date on which it was laid before Parliament). If the statutory instrument comes into force after the date of the order, then it will give the commencement date.

3.2.5 Authority (5)

This section of the statutory instrument shows the authority by which it is made. In this case, the order was made under the power delegated to the First Secretary of State by s. 11(3) of the Sustainable and Secure Buildings Act 2004.

3.2.6 Main body (6)

The main body of the statutory instrument contains paragraphs or articles if it is an order (as here), regulations if it is a regulation, or rules if it is a set of rules. Regulations are often abbreviated to 'reg.' and rules to 'r.'.

3.2.7 Minister (7)

The name of the Minister signing the order. In this case, Yvette Cooper.

3.2.8 Explanatory note (8)

EXPLANATORY NOTE
(This note is not part of the Order)

This Order brings the following provision of the Sustainable and Secure Buildings Act 2004 into force on 1st February 2006:

(a) sections 2 (buildings of special historical or architectural interest), 8 (certification of work) and 9 (appointed person and management of works); and

(b) for the purposes of making regulations only, section 7 (registers of information and documents to be kept by local authorities).

All those provisions amend the Building Act 1984 (c. 55).

Figure 3.8 Explanatory Note

As with statutes, the explanatory note is not part of the order. It generally either:

- explains the purpose of the statutory instrument;
- details amendments or revocations of previous statutory instruments; or
- notes implementation of European legislation.

3.3 Statutory interpretation

Once you have found a statutory provision, you will need to interpret it in order to find its meaning. Language is an imperfect tool and consequently problems can arise when attempting to discern the meaning of and purpose behind the form of words used in the statute.

The words of an Act of Parliament are authoritative. It is the constitutional role of the judiciary to apply the law. In this sense, it is often said that the role of the courts in statutory interpretation is to discover Parliament's intention from the words of the statute. However, it may be that the particular set of circumstances before the court were never actually foreseen or considered by Parliament (or indeed considered and left out), and therefore Parliament's intention could *never* be ascertained. In this case, it can be argued that the courts are trying to guess what Parliament *would have* meant had it directed its mind to the circumstances in question.[3]

Whatever the reasons for interpretation, the situation is straightforward. If the wording of the legislation is ambiguous or unclear, then its meaning will need to be interpreted. While the ordinary meaning of a word in the English language is a matter of fact, its legal meaning is, self-evidently, a matter of law. Ambiguity or lack of clarity may arise because the Act has been poorly drafted or does not cover all eventualities or circumstances, particularly where the subject matter is highly technical or complex.

Bennion identified a number of factors that may prove problematic:[4]

1. The draftsman may refrain from using certain words that he or she regards as necessarily implied. The problem here is that the users may not realize that this is the case.

2. The draftsman may use a broad term ('a word or phrase of wide meaning') and leave it to the reader to judge what situations fall within it.

3. Ambiguous words may be used.

4. There may be unforeseeable developments.

5. There are many ways in which the wording may be inadequate. There may be a printing error, a drafting error, or another error.

A word, phrase, or sentence is ambiguous if it can be understood in two or more possible ways. There are two types of ambiguity.

. . . .

Lexical ambiguity occurs where the meaning of a single word is ambiguous.

. . . .

There are many examples of lexical ambiguity; indeed most words have more than one meaning. For instance, 'set' has some forty-eight meanings as a noun alone, ranging from 'the action of setting or condition of being set' or 'a place where stationary fishing nets are fixed' to 'the series of movements or figures that make up a square dance or country dance'. Even the word 'ambiguity' has more than one meaning—an uncertainty, capable of being understood in two or more ways, or a word susceptible of more than one meaning.

Words can change their everyday and legal meaning over time. For example, the word 'gay', originally recorded in the early fourteenth century as meaning 'full of or disposed to joy and mirth', came to mean 'homosexual' from the 1930s. In *Fitzpatrick* v *Sterling Housing Association*[5]

---

3. Per Lord Edmund-Davies in *Farrell* v *Alexander* [1977] AC 59, 95B.

4. Bennion, F.A.R (1990) *Bennion on Statute Law* (3rd edn), Harlow: Longman.

5. [2001] 1 AC 27.

the House of Lords held that for the purposes of the Rent Act 1977 the definition of 'family' included the homosexual partner of a deceased tenant. The court recognized that a same-sex relationship can embody essential familial characteristics signifying that evolving social conditions enlarged the number of people who qualified as belonging to the same family under the legislation.

. . . .

Structural ambiguity refers to a sentence or clause with multiple possible meanings.

. . . .

For example, in 'Gerald enjoys painting his models nude' it is not clear whether Gerald or the models are without clothes. Equally, if we read that 'visiting relatives can be so boring', we are not sure who is doing the visiting. The ambiguity here arises since 'visiting' could be used as both a verb or an adjective in this context.

A combination of lexical and structural ambiguity can lead to a statutory provision with more than one meaning. This can prove to be a great source of legal argument. For that reason, an understanding of the approaches that can be used to interpret a statutory provision is of vital importance as a fundamental building block of legal skills. As Lord Steyn commented: 'The preponderance of enacted law over common law is increasing year by year . . . and the subject of interpretation has moved to the centre of the legal stage'.[6] In other words, the sheer volume of legislation and the pace with which it is introduced provides more opportunities for creative arguments before the courts. Knowledge of how to interpret a statutory provision in your favour—or know how it might be used against you—is therefore of paramount importance.

3.3.1 How to interpret a statutory provision

Judges use a variety of different approaches when faced with an issue of statutory interpretation. These are commonly referred to as the 'rules' of interpretation, although they are not strict rules. They are sometimes referred to as the 'rules of construction'. This is derived from the verb 'to construe', meaning 'to interpret'.

Judges are not bound to follow one, or indeed any, of them and do not have to state which 'rule' they have used. It is perhaps better, then, to think of them as *approaches* to interpretation, rather than as hard-and-fast rules. As A.T.H. Smith says:

> I take the view that the student might . . . benefit from considering the difficulties inherent in the apparently straightforward tasks of interpretation and that the three 'rules' afford a framework for discussion, not a 'cure-all' for decision-making.[7]

The 'rules' in question are:

- The literal rule
- The golden rule, and
- The mischief rule

In addition to these rules, the purposive approach considers the wider purpose of the legislation and the teleological approach is particularly important in the interpretation of European law. There are also various rules of language, presumptions and extrinsic aids that can be used to help.

---

6. Lord Steyn, '*Pepper* v *Hart*: a Re-examination' (2001) 21 OJLS 59.
7. Smith, ATH (2002) *Glanville Williams: Learning the Law* (12th edn), London: Sweet & Maxwell, 122, n.1.

3.3.1.1 The literal rule

The **literal rule** provides that words must be given their plain, ordinary, and literal meaning.

The rationale behind the use of the literal rule is that if the words of the statute are clear they must be applied as they represent the intention of Parliament as expressed in the words used. This is so even if the outcome is harsh or undesirable. This was made clear in the *Sussex Peerage Case* (1844) 1 Cl & Fin 85:

> The only rule for construction of Acts of Parliament is that they should be construed according to the intent of the Parliament which passed the Act. If the words . . . are themselves precise and unambiguous, then no more can be necessary than to expound those words in that natural and ordinary sense.

An example of the use of the literal rule can be found in *Cutter* v *Eagle Star Insurance Co Ltd*.[8] The claimant was sitting in his friend's car in a car park and was injured when a can of lighter fuel exploded. The driver was insured as required by the Road Traffic Act 1988, for injury caused while on a 'road'. Here the House of Lords ruled that a car park is not a 'road' for the purposes of the Road Traffic Act 1988, since the purpose of a road is a means for cars to move along it to a destination and the purpose of a car park is for cars to stand still. Parking a car on a road does not make it a car park. Driving a car across a car park does not make it a road as it is incidental to its main function.

Moreover, in *Whiteley* v *Chappell*[9] the defendant had impersonated a dead person and voted in an election in his name. The relevant statute provided that it was an offence to impersonate 'any person entitled to vote' at an election. Since the person impersonated was dead he was not entitled to vote, and thus Whiteley could not be convicted. Of course, this application of the literal rule went *against* Parliament's intention, which was to ensure that only those entitled to vote were able to do so, and then only to do so once at each election.

Although use of the literal rule gives utmost primacy to the precise words used by Parliament, emphasizing the literal meaning of statutory provisions can lead to 'unthinking' decisions where the meaning in the wider context is ignored or lost. It assumes perfection in parliamentary draftsmen and ignores the natural limitations of language.

3.3.1.2 The golden rule

The **golden rule** provides that words must be given their plain, ordinary, and literal meaning as far as possible but only to the extent that they do not produce absurdity (the 'narrow golden rule' approach) or an affront to public policy (the 'wide golden rule' approach).

The rationale behind the golden rule is that it mitigates some of the potential harshness arising from use of the literal rule. An early reference to it can be found in *Grey* v *Pearson*:[10]

> The grammatical and ordinary sense of the words is to be adhered to unless that would lead to some absurdity or inconsistency with the rest of the instrument, in which case the grammatical and ordinary sense of the words may be modified so as to avoid that absurdity or inconsistency, but not farther.

---

8. [1998] 4 All ER 417, HL.
9. (1868) LR 4 QB 147.
10. (1857) 6 HL Cas 61.

Absurdity

R v *Allen*[11] concerned the application of s. 57 of the Offences against the Person Act 1861. This provided that 'whosoever being married shall marry any other person during the lifetime of his spouse' shall commit bigamy. If 'marry' had been interpreted literally the offence could never have been committed, since no one married could ever marry another. The court interpreted the words 'shall marry' as if they said 'shall go through the ceremony of marriage'.

Affront to public policy

A more unpleasant example was provided by *Re Sigsworth*.[12] Under the Administration of Estates Act 1925 the estate of a person dying intestate (i.e. without leaving a will) was to be divided among the 'issue'. Mrs Sigsworth was murdered by her son who stood to inherit her estate. Even though there was only one possible interpretation of the word 'issue' the court held that the son could not inherit the estate as it would be contrary to the public policy principle that a murderer should not benefit from his crime. Here the golden rule was applied in preference to the literal rule.

3.3.1.3 The mischief rule

The **mischief rule** (or the rule in *Heydon's Case*)[13] involves an examination of the former law in an attempt to deduce Parliament's intention ('mischief' here means 'wrong' or 'harm').

The mischief rule asks four questions, the answers to which provide some sort of structured evaluation of Parliament's intention in passing the Act in question:

1. What was the common law before the making of the Act?
2. What was the mischief and defect for which the common law did not provide?
3. What was the remedy proposed by Parliament to rectify the situation?
4. What was the true reason for that remedy?

The rule was restated by Lord Diplock in *Jones* v *Wrotham Park Settled Estates*[14] where he identified three necessary conditions:

- It must be possible to determine precisely the mischief that the Act was drafted to remedy
- It must be apparent that Parliament had failed to deal with the mischief
- It must be possible to state the additional words that would have been inserted had the omission been drawn to Parliament's attention

Corkery v *Carpenter*[15] concerned the interpretation of s. 12 of the Licensing Act 1872. This provided that a person drunk in charge of a 'carriage' on the highway could be arrested without a warrant. The defendant was found drunk in charge of a bicycle. Although it was argued that a bicycle is not a carriage in the normal meaning of the word (the term generally refers to a vehicle of some kind), the Divisional Court held that a bicycle was a carriage for the purposes of the Act. The mischief here was the prevention of drunken persons from being on the highway in charge of some form of transportation and was addressed by the Act for the purposes of public order and safety.

---

11. (1872) LR 1 CCR 367.
12. [1935] Ch 89.
13. (1584) 3 Co Rep 7a.
14. (1980) AC 74.
15. [1951] 1 KB 102.

More recently, *Royal College of Nursing* v *DHSS*[16] considered the wording of the Abortion Act 1963. This allows abortions by 'a registered medical practitioner'. The first part of the procedure was carried out by a doctor. The second part was performed by nurses but without a doctor being present. The House of Lords narrowly held by a 3–2 majority that this procedure *was* lawful because the mischief Parliament was trying to remedy was back street abortions performed by unqualified people. However, it is both important and interesting to note the strength of the dissenting judgments.

In *Manchester City Council* v *McCann*,[17] the defendant had threatened a witness who had given evidence against his wife on his return home from court. Section 118(1)(a) of the County Courts Act 1984 provides that county courts may deal with anyone who 'wilfully insults the judge . . . or any juror or witness, or any officer of the court'. The Court of Appeal held that a threat was an insult for the purposes of the Act. The mischief here was protection of various participants in the civil process. Even though a threat is not necessarily an insult using the normal meanings of the words, the ability for the court to deal with insults but not threats was contrary to Parliament's intention.

3.3.1.4 The purposive approach

....

The **purposive approach** involves seeking an interpretation of the law which gives effect to its general purpose. It is based upon the mischief rule.

....

The purposive approach is based upon the mischief rule and allows the courts to look beyond the wording of the legislation to find an interpretation which furthers its general purpose. In that sense it is similar to the mischief rule, which attempts to deduce Parliament's intention (or purpose) in enacting a particular provision. It is now regarded as the predominant approach to statutory interpretation in the UK.

The shift towards the use of the purposive approach was recognized by the House of Lords in *R (Quintavalle)* v *Secretary of State for Health*.[18] Here, the House of Lords endorsed the decision of the Court of Appeal who adopted a purposive approach to the interpretation of s. 1(1) of the Human Fertilisation and Embryology Act 1990. Lord Steyn explained that:

> . . . the adoption of a purposive approach to construction of statutes generally, and the 1990 Act in particular, is amply justified on wider grounds. In *Cabell* v *Markham* (1945) 148 F 2d 737 Justice Learned Hand explained the merits of purposive interpretation, at p. 739:
>
>> Of course it is true that the words used, even in their literal sense, are the primary, and ordinarily the most reliable, source of interpreting the meaning of any writing: be it a statute, a contract, or anything else. But it is one of the surest indexes of a mature developed jurisprudence not to make a fortress out of the dictionary; but to remember that statutes always have some purpose or object to accomplish, whose sympathetic and imaginative discovery is the surest guide to their meaning.
>
> The pendulum has swung towards purposive methods of construction. This change was not initiated by the teleological approach of European Community jurisprudence, and the influence of European legal culture generally, but it has been accelerated by European ideas . . . In any event, nowadays the shift towards purposive interpretation is not in doubt. The qualification is that the degree of liberality permitted is influenced by the context, e.g. social welfare legislation and tax statutes may have to be approached somewhat differently.

16.   [1981] 1 All ER 545.
17.   [1999] 2 WLR 590, CA.
18.   [2003] 2 AC 687.

3.3.1.5 The teleological approach

The **teleological approach** requires that the spirit of the legislation, rather than merely its purpose, is considered. It is therefore much broader than the purposive approach.

The teleological approach is particularly important when considering European law, since European law is often drafted in terms of wide general principles and not in the detailed manner found in domestic legislation. It is the predominant approach used in civil law jurisdictions which tend to favour simplified drafting and a high degree of abstraction. It is also used by the European Court of Justice and the UK courts in interpreting European law.

You may wish to refer back to chapter 1 which considered the various types of European legislation.
Section 2(4) of the European Communities Act 1972 provides that:

> . . . any enactment passed or to be passed . . . shall be construed and have effect subject to the foregoing provisions of this section.

The primary foregoing provision is s. 2(1) of the Act which effectively incorporates all directly applicable European law into the legal system.

> . . . all rights, powers, liabilities, obligations and restrictions from time to time created or arising by or under the Treaties, and all such remedies and procedures from time to time provided for by or under the Treaties, as in accordance with the Treaties are without further enactment to be given legal effect or used in the United Kingdom shall be recognised and available in law, and be enforced, allowed and followed accordingly.

In other words, when interpreting legislation which implements European law, the courts should give preference to an interpretation which gives effect to the general spirit of the legislation. This necessarily means that questions of wide economic or social policy are often considered by the courts.

In some circumstances this approach involves the courts reading certain words into legislation. This is a clear departure from using the literal words as chosen by Parliament. In *Pickstone* v *Freemans plc*,[19] the House of Lords held that it was proper to give a broad construction to the Equal Pay Act 1970, as amended by the Sex Discrimination Act 1975, so as to arrive at a result consistent with the UK's obligations under Community law.

A further example is provided by *Litster* v *Forth Dry Dock and Engineering Co. Ltd.*[20] Here, employees were dismissed one hour before a business was transferred to a new owner. The employees claimed they were unfairly dismissed. The Transfer of Undertakings (Protection of Employment) Regulations 1981[21] (commonly referred to as 'TUPE') implements a European Directive to protect employees who are employed during the transfer of a business. However, taking a literal approach, the employees here were not actually employed at the moment of transfer, having been dismissed an hour previously and therefore their situation seemed to fall outside the protection offered by TUPE. However, the House of Lords read in additional words such that the regulations covered an individual who was employed 'or would have been so employed if he had not been unfairly dismissed as a reason connected with the transfer before the transfer'. In doing so, the spirit of the Directive, to protect the employees on the transfer of a business, was upheld.

---

19. [1998] 2 All ER 803, HL.
20. [1989] 1 ALL ER 1134, HL.
21. SI 1981 No. 1794.

3.3.1.6 Rules of language

In addition to the rules of construction, there are also rules of language which the courts may use. They are known by the following Latin terms:

- *Ejusdem generis*
- *Noscitur a sociis*
- *Expressio unius est exclusio alterius*

Ejusdem generis

Ejusdem generis means 'of the same type'.

In other words, if a word with general meaning follow a list of specific words, then the general word only applies to things of the same type as the specific words.

In *Powell* v *Kempton Park Racecourse*,[22] the defendant was operating an outdoor betting ring. It was an offence to use a 'house, office, room or other place for betting'. The court held that since the specific places listed are all indoors, an outdoor betting ring was not covered within the statute and the defendant was found not guilty.

Wood v *Commissioner of Police of the Metropolis*[23] considered whether a piece of (accidentally broken) glass was covered by 'any gun, pistol, hangar, cutlass, bludgeon or other offensive weapon'. It was held that the list contains items made or adapted for the purposes of causing harm. Therefore a piece of accidentally broken glass was not included, although presumably it would have been if it had been smashed in order for it to be used as a weapon.

Noscitur a sociis

Noscitur a sociis means that a word is 'known by the company it keeps'.

Words in a statute derive meaning from the words surrounding them. There is a presumption that words in a list have related meanings and are to be interpreted in relation to each other.

In *Pengelley* v *Bell Punch Co. Ltd*[24] it was held that the word 'floors' in a statute requiring 'floors, steps, stairs, passages and gangways' to be kept clear did not include part of a factory floor used for storage, since the words listed related to passageways and not static storage.

Muir v *Keay*[25] concerned a café owner. All houses kept open at night for 'public refreshment, resort and entertainment' had to be licensed. The defendant argued that his café did not need a licence because he did not provide entertainment. The court held that 'entertainment' did not mean musical entertainment but the reception and accommodation of people. Therefore the owner was required to have a licence by law.

Expressio unius est exclusio alterius

Expressio unius est exclusio alterius means that to 'express one thing is to exclude others'.

In other words, a list of a number of specific things may be interpreted as impliedly excluding others of the same type. For example, in *R* v *Inhabitants of Sedgley*[26] it was held that the poor rate

---

22. [1899] AC 143.
23. [1986] 2 All ER 570.
24. [1964] 1 WLR 691.
25. (1875) LR 10 QB 594.
26. (1831) 2 B & Ald 65.

levied on owners of 'lands, houses, tithes and coal mines' could not be levied on owners of limestone mines, as these were impliedly excluded by the specific mention of coal mines.

3.3.1.7 Presumptions

A legal **presumption** is an inference established by the law as universally applicable to certain circumstances.

In addition to the rules of construction and rules of language, there are also a number of presumptions which are made when interpreting legislation. These are generally expected to be taken 'as read' without the need for Parliament specifically to address them in the wording of a statute, since they deal with traditional ideas of natural justice and fairness or matters so uncontroversial that they would almost certainly represent the intention of Parliament. A number of these presumptions are as follows:

Against alteration of the common law
Although Parliament can change the existing common law, such an intention cannot be implied (e.g. *Beswick* v *Beswick*).[27]

Against retrospective operation of statute
It is presumed that statutes do not operate retrospectively (this is particularly important in Acts which criminalize, since it could lead to criminal liability arising for acts which were lawful at the time they were committed). This presumption can, however, be rebutted by express words by Parliament (e.g. War Crimes Act 1991; War Damage Act 1965 overruling the House of Lords decision in *Burmah Oil Co Ltd* v *Lord Advocate*).[28]

Against deprivation of liberty
Parliament is presumed not to intend to deprive a person of his liberty; if it does, clear words must be used and will be construed so as to interfere with the subject's liberty as little as possible (e.g. *R(H)* v *London North and East Region Mental Health Review Tribunal*).[29]

Against deprivation of property and against interference with private rights
Parliament is presumed not to wish to interfere with a person's private rights or deprive him of his property without compensation (e.g. *Glassbrook Bros* v *Leyson*;[30] *Bowles* v *Bank of England*).[31]

Against binding the Crown
Parliament is presumed not to bind the Crown except expressly or by necessary implication of the statute (e.g. Equal Pay Act 1970; Sex Discrimination Act 1975).

Against ousting the jurisdiction of the courts
Even where clear ouster clauses have been used, the courts will try to construe them in a way which permits judicial review (e.g. *Anisminic Ltd* v *Foreign Compensation Commission*).[32]

---

27. [1968] AC 58.
28. [1965] AC 75.
29. [2001] 3 WLR 512.
30. [1933] 2 KB 91.
31. [1913] 1 Ch 57.
32. [1969] 2 AC 147.

Against criminal liability without *mens rea* (a guilty mind)

There is a presumption that, for statutory criminal offences, Parliament intended no liability without proof of *mens rea* (e.g. *R* v *K*).[33] This can be rebutted by express words or by implication in offences of strict liability (such as exceeding the speed limit).

3.3.1.8 Intrinsic aids to interpretation

. . . .

Intrinsic aids to interpretation are found within the statute itself.

. . . .

Any statute must be read as a whole. That is to say that before looking outside the statute to seek its meaning, every word within the statute should be considered in the search for meaning. There are a number of areas within the statute which could potentially be used as an intrinsic aid to construction.

Look back at section 3.1 which describes the anatomy of an Act of Parliament.

Short title

This is usually descriptive only and therefore of limited value.

Long title

The long title may be considered but only where there is ambiguity within the body of the Act (e.g. *R(Quintaville)* v *Secretary of State for Health*).[34]

Preamble

Preambles tend not to be found in recent statutes. Where preambles do exist, they may be considered for guidance purposes in cases of ambiguity.

Marginal notes

These are not debated in Parliament and are not normally used in determining the precise scope of a provision (*DPP* v *Schildkamp*);[35] they can however give some general indication of the provision's purpose (*DPP* v *Johnson*).[36]

Punctuation

Old statutes did not use punctuation at all. Punctuation may be used as an aid to interpretation where there is ambiguity (*DPP* v *Schildkamp*).[37]

In *R* v *Casement*,[38] Roger Casement was charged under the Treason Act of 1351[39] after conspiring with the Germans during the First World War while outside of the country. His counsel contended that, because the Act was unpunctuated, the phrase 'if the man be adherent to the king's enemies in his realm giving to them aid and comfort in the realm or elsewhere' referred only to the King's enemies 'in his realm' since 'or elsewhere' technically applied only to 'aid and comfort'. In other words, his counsel contended that plotting abroad fell outside the ambit of the Act. Upon examination of the original legal document written in 1351 on parchment, the Court of Appeal found extra large spaces between a couple of words. They inferred that these spaces must have been for commas that had since faded away. This, according to Darling J, proved that 'giving aid

---

33. [2001] 3 WLR 471.
34. [2003] 2 WLR 692, HL.
35. [1971] AC 1, HL.
36. [1995] 4 All ER 53, DC.
37. [1971] AC 1, HL.
38. [1916–1917] All ER Rep 214, CA.
39. 25 Edw 3, st 5, c 2.

and comfort' were words of apposition. Therefore, being on the side of the king's enemies meant being on their side whether within the realm or otherwise. Casement was duly hanged.

Examples

Statutes may provide examples to illustrate how the Act might work or how terminology within it might be used. These are part of the statute and carry great persuasive authority (examples include s. 44(6) Criminal Justice Act 2003; Consumer Credit Act 1974; Law of Property Act 1925).

Schedules

Some statutes may contain a Schedule which includes an interpretation and definition section of terms used in the Act (e.g. Schedule 1, Interpretation Act 1978). These definitions are part of the statute and are strongly persuasive.

3.3.1.9 Extrinsic aids to interpretation

Extrinsic aids to interpretation are found outside the statute.

The Interpretation Act 1978 defines words that are commonly used within legislation. For example:

- In any Act, unless the contrary intention appears, words importing the masculine gender include the feminine and vice versa (section 6)

- 'Land' includes buildings and other structures, land covered with water, and any estate, interest, easement, servitude or right in or over land (Schedule 1)

- 'Writing' includes typing, printing, lithography, photography and other modes of representing or reproducing words in a visible form, and expressions referring to writing are construed accordingly. (Schedule 1)

Where a word has no specific legal meaning, dictionaries may also be used. Courts may also consider the interpretation of the same words used in earlier or related statutes.

Historically, since the court was only allowed to interpret the words used, reference to preparatory works (*travaux préparatoires*) was not permitted. Article 9 of the Bill of Rights 1689 provides:

> That the freedom of speech and debates or proceedings in Parliament ought not to be impeached or questioned in any court or place out of Parliament.

Therefore, members of the Houses of Parliament had the right to say whatever they wished and to discuss whatever they wished. Until 1993, the protection given by Article 9 was held to prevent the courts from using statements made in Parliament concerning the purpose of Bills as a guide to the interpretation of ambiguous statutory provisions. This meant that courts could not refer to records of Parliamentary debate on the statute in *Hansard*.

However, this rule was relaxed in 1993 following the ruling of the House of Lords in *Pepper* v *Hart*.[40] Here the House of Lords held that the rule against the use of *Hansard* as an extrinsic aid to interpretation would be relaxed to permit reference to Parliamentary materials where:

(a) the legislation is ambiguous or obscure, or its literal meaning leads to an absurdity;

(b) the material relied on consists of statements by a minister or other promoter of the Bill together with such other Parliamentary material as is necessary to understand such statements and their effect; and

(c) the statements relied upon are clear.

---

40. [1993] 1 All ER 42, HL.

The House of Lords held such use of statements did not infringe Article 9 because it did not amount to questioning a proceeding in Parliament. Indeed, they considered that far from questioning the independence of Parliament and its debates, the use of *Hansard* would allow the courts to give effect to what was said and done there.

Note that the use of *Hansard* is only permitted under the circumstances outlined in *Pepper* v *Hart*. It is a common mistake to state that reference to *Hansard* may always be made.

Although *Pepper* v *Hart* concerned the use of *Hansard*, its principles extend to the reports of recommendations made by the Law Commission and government departmental committees. For example, in *R.* v *Allen*,[41] the House of Lords considered the report of the Criminal Law Revision Committee when considering the meaning of s. 3 of the Theft Act 1978. The Act was silent on the point in question—specifically, whether intent never to pay had to be proved as an element of the offence of making off without payment—but the committee report made it clear that such intention *did* have to be proved.

3.3.2 Interpretation and the European Communities Act 1972

Section 2(4) of the European Communities Act 1972 provides that:

> Any enactment passed or to be passed . . . shall be construed and have effect subject to the foregoing provisions of this section.

In other words, any legislation passed or to be passed in the United Kingdom must be interpreted with applicable European law in mind. There is therefore a strong presumption of compliance with European law.

In *Garland* v *British Rail Engineering*,[42] Lord Diplock suggested that where words of domestic law were incompatible with the Community law in question, they should be construed so as to comply with it. This creative approach—not applying the plain meaning of words in a statute, if that meaning will conflict with Community law—was also taken by the House of Lords in *Pickstone* v *Freemans plc*.[43] The Court of Appeal had declared that the Equal Pay (Amendment) Regulations 1983 were inconsistent with Article 141 (ex 119) of the EC Treaty. However, the House of Lords rules that the Regulations should in fact, be interpreted in a manner compatible with the provisions of the Treaty.

The supremacy of European law is considered in general in chapter 1.

3.3.3 Interpretation and the Human Rights Act 1998

The Human Rights Act 1998 has had an effect on the traditional role of the courts in the interpretation of statutes.

Section 3 of the Act provides that:

> (1) So far as it is possible to do so, primary legislation and subordinate legislation must be read and given effect in a way which is compatible with the Convention rights.
> (2) This section—
>   (a) applies to primary legislation and subordinate legislation whenever enacted;
>   (b) does not affect the validity, continuing operation or enforcement of any incompatible primary legislation; and

---

41. [1985] AC 1029.
42. [1983] 2 AC 751.
43. [1989] AC 66.

(c) does not affect the validity, continuing operation or enforcement of any incompatible subordinate legislation if (disregarding any possibility of revocation) primary legislation prevents removal of the incompatibility.

Section 3(1) imposes a duty upon the courts to try and discern a meaning *so far as it is possible to do so* with Convention rights. This is a weaker presumption of compliance than that concerning European law; s. 2(4) of the European Communities Act 1972 uses the imperative 'shall' rather than 'so far as it is possible'. If the courts are unable to find a compatible interpretation, then they may make a 'declaration of incompatibility' under s. 4. The effect of such a declaration is that the law must then be changed to remove the incompatibility. Section 10(2) provides a fast-track route by which this may be done:

If a Minister of the Crown considers that there are compelling reasons . . . he may by order make such amendments to the legislation as he considers necessary to remove the incompatibility.

The section 3 power has been considered in a number of cases since the provision came into force on 2 October 2000.

R v *A*[44] concerned the interpretation of s. 41 of the Youth Justice and Criminal Evidence Act 1999 which placed the court under a restriction that seriously limited the evidence that could be raised in cross-examination of a sexual relationship between an alleged rape victim and the accused. Section 41(1) provided that:

If, at a trial, a person is charged with a sexual offence, then, except with the leave of the court—
  (a) no evidence may be adduced, and
  (b) no question may be asked in cross-examination, by or on behalf of any accused at the trial, about any sexual behaviour of the complainant.

This remained so even in a case where the defendant claimed that the complainant had consented. *A* argued that s. 41 of the Act was incompatible with Article 6 of the Convention to the extent that it prevented him from putting forward a full and complete defence. The House of Lords held that s. 3 required them to consider Article 6 and its concomitant right to a fair trial. This allowed them to read s. 41 as permitting the admission of evidence or questioning relating to a relevant issue in the case where it was considered necessary by the trial judge to make the trial fair.

In reaching its decision, the House of Lords was well aware that its interpretation of s. 41 went against its actual meaning, but it nonetheless (by a majority) felt it within its power to do so. As Lord Steyn stated:

In my view s 3 of the 1998 Act requires the court to subordinate the niceties of the language of s 41(3)(c) of the 1999 Act, and in particular the touchstone of coincidence, to broader considerations of relevance judged by logical and commonsense criteria of time and circumstances. After all, it is realistic to proceed on the basis that the legislature would not, if alerted to the problem, have wished to deny the right to an accused to put forward a full and complete defence by advancing truly probative material. It is therefore possible under s 3 of the 1998 Act to read s 41 of the 1999 Act, and in particular s 41(3)(c), as subject to the implied provision that evidence or questioning which is required to ensure a fair trial under Art 6 of the convention should not be treated as inadmissible.[45]

---

44. [2001] 1 WLR 789.
45. Ibid. [45].

Lord Hope (dissenting) felt that the courts were going too far towards legislating:

> The rule of construction which s 3 lays down is quite unlike any previous rule of statutory interpretation. There is no need to identify an ambiguity or absurdity. Compatibility with convention rights is the sole guiding principle. That is the paramount object which the rule seeks to achieve. But the rule is only a rule of interpretation. It does not entitle the judges to act as legislators.[46]

However, Parliament *did* seek to limit the rights of the defence to question alleged victims of rape. *R* v *A* could therefore be considered to be an act of quasi-legislation by the House of Lords.

In *Re S* (Care Order: Implementation of Care Plan)[47] Lord Nicholls explained the operation of s. 3 as follows:

> The Human Rights Act reserves the amendment of primary legislation to Parliament. By this means the Act seeks to preserve parliamentary sovereignty. The Act maintains the constitutional boundary. Interpretation of statutes is a matter for the courts; the enactment of statutes, are matters for Parliament.

In *Ghaidan* v *Godin- Mendoza*[48] the House of Lords significantly clarified the force to be given when construing legislation under s. 3. Lord Nicholls stressed that the intention of Parliament in enacting s. 3 was, to the extent bounded only by what is 'possible', to allow the court to modify the meaning and hence the effect of primary and secondary legislation,[49] pointing out that s. 3 is the principal remedial measure and that declarations of incompatibility were a measure of last resort.[50]

He also rejected the literal approach to interpretation, emphasizing a broad approach, concentrating amongst other things, in a purposive way on the importance of the fundamental right involved.[51] The practical effect of *Mendoza* is to establish a strong, but rebuttable, presumption in favour of an interpretation consistent with Convention rights.[52]

CHAPTER SUMMARY

Anatomy of an Act of Parliament

- The short title is the normal way in which to refer to a statute

- The chapter number of an Act (since 1963) is the sequence number of the Act in the particular calendar year

- The long title of an Act gives an indication of its purpose and content

- Royal Assent is needed before an Act can come into force

- The enacting formula declares that the law derives its authority from being properly passed by the legislature

---

46. [2001] 1 WLR 108.
47. [2002] 2 AC 291.
48. [2004] UKHL 30.
49. Ibid. [33].
50. Ibid. [39].
51. Ibid. [42].
52. Ibid. [50].

- The main body of an Act is divided into sections, subsections, paragraphs, and subparagraphs

- Any commencement provisions are normally found towards the end of an Act

- Schedules may contain further information such as definitions, further detail, minor and consequential amendments to other legislation or repeals of pre-existing legislation

- Older statutes may contain preambles which describe the purpose of the Act in more detail than the long title; these are not part of the Act itself

- Most recent Acts will carry accompanying Explanatory Notes which contain useful information but are not legally binding.

Anatomy of a statutory instrument

- Statutory instruments show the authority by which they are made

- Orders are divided into paragraphs or articles

Statutory interpretation

- Lexical ambiguity occurs where the meaning of a single word is ambiguous

- Structural ambiguity refers to a sentence or clause with multiple possible meanings

- The literal rule provides that words must be given their plain, ordinary, and literal meaning

- The golden rule provides that words must be given their plain, ordinary, and literal meaning as far as possible but only to the extent that they do not produce absurdity (narrow approach) or an affront to public policy (wide approach)

- The mischief rule (or the rule in *Heydon's Case*) involves an examination of the former law in an attempt to deduce Parliament's intention

- The purposive approach involves seeking an interpretation of the law which gives effect to its general purpose. It is based upon the mischief rule

- The teleological approach requires that the spirit of the legislation, rather than merely its purpose, is considered. It is therefore much broader than the purposive approach

- *Ejusdem generis* is a rule of language meaning 'of the same type'

- *Noscitur a sociis* is a rule of language meaning that a word is 'known by the company it keeps'

- *Expressio unius est exclusion alterius* is a rule of language meaning that to 'express one thing is to exclude others'

- A legal presumption is an inference established by the law as universally applicable to certain circumstances

- Intrinsic aids to interpretation are found within the statute itself

- Extrinsic aids to interpretation are found outside the statute

- *Pepper* v *Hart* allows courts to refer to clear statements made by a Minister or other promoter of a Bill in *Hansard* where the legislation is ambiguous or obscure or its literal meaning leads to absurdity

- Section 2(4) of the European Communities Act 1972 requires that legislation must be interpreted with applicable European law in mind. There is a strong presumption of compliance with European law

- Section 3(1) of the Human Rights Act 1998 requires that legislation must be interpreted *so far as it is possible to do so* in a way that is compatible with Convention rights. There is a rebuttable presumption of compliance with the European Convention on Human Rights

 FURTHER READING

- Clinch (2001) *Using a Law Library* (2nd edn), London: Blackstone Press, pp. 47–9. For a detailed explanation of the complexities of the regnal year citation system.

PART I
Sources of law

SECTION B
Cases

The first section in this part of the book covers the skills required to understand legislation as a source of law. This section will take a similar approach to building the skills required to deal with case law as a further source of law. Chapter 4 will *explain* the role of the common law, equity, and custom as case-based sources of law, as well as explaining the different courts that are involved in deciding cases. This then leads on to chapter 5, in which you will learn the skills to *find* cases from the UK, the European Courts and the European Court of Human Rights. Finally, chapter 6 will give you the skills to *use* cases, describing how legal principles can be extracted from the case and the extent to which those principles are binding on other courts in the future.

Case law

4

INTRODUCTION

This chapter will begin our investigation into case law as a source of law. Case law can be broken down into common law, equity, and custom. This chapter will begin with a discussion of common law and equity, including a very brief history to help you understand how these sources came into being. We will then take a brief look at custom as a further source of law. Since the common law comprises a great many cases decided by judges in different courts, this chapter will also include an overview of the court system to help you understand how the various courts in the system link together in a hierarchy before closing with a discussion of the European Court of Human Rights and the impact of the Human Rights Act 1998 on case law.

Understanding the sources of case law is as fundamental a legal skill as understanding the role of legislation. Since all legal topics will generally include some case law, equitable principles or both, you would not otherwise be able to understand how the particular area of law you are studying came into existence or has evolved over time. The law is a constantly changing creature which takes its shape from a whole range of sources. You must therefore undertand these sources if you wish properly to understand the law and its development.

LEARNING OUTCOMES

After studying this chapter, you will be able to:

- Distinguish between the common law and equity as sources of law

- Chart the historical development of the common law and equity

- Appreciate the role of custom as a further source of law

- State the hierarchy of the courts and the types of case heard in the various courts

- Discuss the effect of the European Convention on Human Rights and the Human Rights Act 1998 on case law

4.1 Common law and equity

Having considered the role of legislation as a source of law in Part 1A, the next sources of law to consider are the common law and equity. However, before looking at them in detail, it will be useful to provide a very brief legal history. This will help you to understand the development of the common law and equity as two key sources of law and their interrelationship today. It will also greatly assist us later in dealing with some terminology.

4.1.1 A brief legal history

A timeline to give you an overview of the history that we are about to cover is provided in Figure 4.1.

4.1.1.1 The emergence of the common law

Before the Norman Conquest in 1066 there was no single system of law common to the whole country. There was a range of local customs which were unwritten and varied throughout the country, although the general effect of the local laws was similar in practice.

The use of custom as a source of law today is covered later in section 4.2.

Disputes according to these laws were judged by the local sheriffs sitting in the courts of the Shires and Hundreds (subdivisions of the Shires) and feudal courts held by landowners. In an attempt to create some level of uniformity and consistency in the law, the King sent itinerant commissioners into the country to perform various tasks on his behalf, such as checking on local administration and tax collection and hearing cases. The judicial functions of the itinerant commissioners increased, evolving a system of itinerant justices who held Assizes (or sittings) of the Royal courts in each county, three or four times a year, to hear serious criminal cases. Less serious cases were still dealt with by the local sheriff.

This system was extended to hear civil cases in 1285. Over time the judges began to establish a system of law common to the whole country—the common law—by the universal application of the best local customs (from outside the county if necessary) and rules derived from the judges' own decisions in cases. Therefore the common law emerged from a combination of local custom and case law.

The Royal Courts at Westminster comprised three main common law courts. By 1400 they were staffed by professional judges. The three courts were:

- The Court of Common Pleas dealing with disputes between the King's subjects
- The Court of Exchequer dealing primarily with matters concerning taxes but also later dealing with some common law matters
- The Court of King's Bench dealing with cases of particular concern to the King

The common law developed as a system because the judges tended to follow the decisions of earlier judges in similar cases. Over time, and in certain circumstances, judicial precedents became binding rather than merely being useful persuasive guidance.

The operation of the doctrine of judicial precedent is covered in detail in section 6.2.

4.1.1.2 Problems with the common law

An action could only be started in the Royal courts by a writ purchased from the office of the Chancellor. Since the existence of a common law right depended on there being a procedure for enforcing that right, an action could only be brought if an appropriate writ already existed which covered the facts of the case. As a result, the number of writs grew to many hundreds.

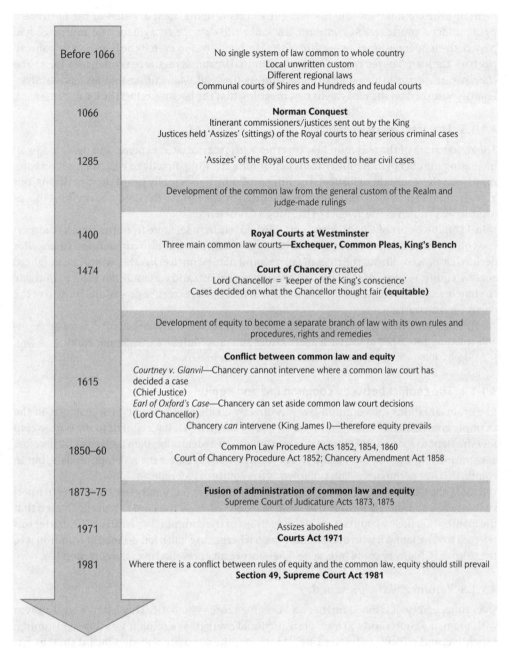

Figure 4.1 Timeline of legal developments

Moreover, the procedure for bringing an action before the courts was very formal and inflexible, leading to delay and expense. The only remedy generally available to a successful claimant was monetary damages—which was not always adequate. For instance, the courts could not compel individuals to do (or stop doing) something; not even to return personal property.[1]

---

1. Although actions for recovery of land, known as 'real actions', did enable the successful claimant to recover their land at common law.

Finally, the common law did not recognize certain rights, such as trusts or the borrower's rights under a mortgage. At common law, once the date for repayment of a mortgage had passed, the lender regained ownership of the land. This was so even if the borrower was able to pay back the loan. The repayment had to be counted by sunset on the repayment day for it to be effective and prevent the lender from reclaiming the land. Many unscrupulous lenders mysteriously vanished on the repayment day, meaning that the borrowers lost the land.

4.1.1.3 The emergence of equity

The rigid nature of the common law, together with its associated expense and delay led to an increasing number of unhappy citizens petitioning the King directly to exercise his Royal prerogative as the 'fountain of justice'. The King (in Council) originally heard these petitions, but as their number increased, this duty was delegated by the King to the Lord Chancellor, who, as a result, was known as the 'Keeper of the King's Conscience'.

In 1474, the Court of Chancery was established, entirely separate from the King's common law courts. Proceedings in the Court of Chancery did not require a writ, and the Chancellor decided cases according to the rules of fairness and natural justice. In other words, he sought to achieve equity. He was able to develop new equitable rights and equitable remedies to mitigate the harshness of the common law and was not bound by the excessive procedural burden of the common law courts.

Although the Chancery was more concerned with equity in individual cases, general equitable maxims developed along with a set of rules and procedures for their application.

Equitable maxims, rights, and remedies are covered later in section 4.1.3.

4.1.1.4 The conflict between common law and equity

In certain situations the common law was directly challenged by equity. For instance, in the example given earlier regarding mortgages, equity deemed that it was unfair to the borrower to lose the right to redeem the mortgage even though the redemption date had passed. Therefore at common law, the borrower could not repay the mortgage after the redemption date, but in equity, this was permissible. This is known as the equity of redemption.

In 1615 the Chief Justice held that the Court of Chancery (i.e. equity) had no power to intervene where a common law court had decided a case[2] whereas the Lord Chancellor stated that the Court of Chancery could set aside the decision of the common law courts.[3] The matter was referred to King James I, who decreed that, even where a case had been decided at common law, the Court of Chancery could intervene. Therefore equity prevailed over the common law.

4.1.1.5 Reform and the present day

Over time, equity developed further and became more systematic. This led to a legal system with too many courts and too much jurisdictional overlap. As a result it was time-consuming, expensive, and difficult to resolve cases. Moreover, the disparate remedies meant that, in certain cases, a claimant would have to bring two actions arising from the same dispute: one in the common law courts for monetary damages and the other in the Court of Chancery for an equitable remedy.

---

2. *Courtney v Glanvil* (1615) Croke Jac 343, 79 ER 294.
3. *Earl of Oxford's Case* (1615) 1 Rep Ch 1.

Bleak House by Charles Dickens[4] illustrates the problems that could be caused by long drawn-out suits in the Courts of Chancery. Dickens had observed the inner workings of the courts as a reporter in his youth and observed that the 'one great principle of the English law is to make business for itself'.

The overhaul of this unsatisfactory system began in the 1850s with the Common Law Procedure Acts 1852, 1854, and 1860, the Court of Chancery Procedure Act 1852, and the Chancery Amendment Act 1858. This enabled equitable remedies and defences to be available in the common law courts and allowed the Court of Chancery to make monetary awards of damages.

The Supreme Court of Judicature Acts 1873 and 1875 fused the administration of law and equity into a single court structure regulated by a single set of procedures. However, in cases of conflict (which are rare since equity evolved to supplement the common law), equitable principles still prevail.[5] In 1981, the Supreme Court of Judicature was renamed the Supreme Court of England and Wales.

An overview of the court structure and the jurisdictions and personnel of the courts is given in section 4.3.

4.1.2 The common law

With the brief history of the law in mind, you will have seen that, originally, the common law was the law that was common to the whole of England. Although this is true, it is not nowadays the usual meaning of the phrase.

'The common law' is usually taken to mean either the law that is not the result of legislation; in other words the law which derives from cases decided by judges and the value of the judicial precedents that these decisions set. Case law is a major source of domestic law, since a great deal of law has not been enacted as legislation, and is therefore found in the results of decided cases.

The operation of the doctrine of judicial precedent is explained in section 6.3.

4.1.3 Equity

Equity is a source of law. You may hear, or read, of the contrast between 'law' and 'equity'. However, in this case 'law' is an abbreviation for 'the common law'. Therefore equity *is* law in that it is part of the law of England and Wales. However, it is *not* part of the common law. Although the *administration* of common law and equity has been fused into the Supreme Court of England and Wales the distinction between common law principles and equitable principles is still important. For instance, common law remedies are granted as of *right* whereas equitable remedies remain within the *discretion* of the court and are subject to equitable principles.

The brief history provided earlier referred to equitable maxims, rights, and remedies. These will be explained here in more detail.

4.1.3.1 Equitable maxims

Equitable maxims are sometimes referred to as 'equitable doctrines'.

There are a number of equitable maxims that have developed over the years. The following table (Table 4.1) sets out some of the more commonly encountered.

---

4. Published in monthly parts between March 1852 and September 1853.
5. Supreme Court Act 1981, s. 49.

Table 4.1 Some equitable maxims

Maxim	Meaning
He who comes to equity must come with clean hands	Equity will not be available to a party that has behaved unreasonably in relation to the disputed matter
Equity looks on that as done which ought to be done *Equity looks to intent rather than to form*	Equity will enforce the intentions of the parties rather than enforcing the position reached by inflexible adherence to the common law. For example, if one party wished to transfer property to another as a gift but died before the formalities relating to the transfer were complete, the gift would fail at common law but equity would intervene to perfect the imperfect gift.
Delay defeats equity	Equity will not be available to someone who seeks it after an unreasonable delay
Equity is a shield not a sword	A party cannot bring a claim in equity (sword) but may rely on equity to protect their own position (shield)
Equity will not suffer a wrong to be without a remedy	Equity will allow a party that has been wronged the capacity to ask for a remedy.
Equity follows the law	Equity will not allow a remedy that is contrary to law
Where there is equal equity, the law will prevail	Equity will not provide a remedy where the parties are equal, or where neither has been wronged
Equity will not assist a volunteer	Equity will not assist someone who has given no consideration for a promise

4.1.3.2 Equitable rights

Equity also evolved to recognize new rights that were not within the scope of the common law. These include the equity of redemption discussed earlier, which protects the rights of borrowers under a mortgage. A further example is that of the equitable rights of beneficiaries under a trust. Although the law of trusts (or, at the time, 'uses') developed in the 1200s as a means of protecting the land of crusaders and land held for the benefit of religious orders, it is still relevant today in matters of, for example, co-ownership of property, wills, charity, pension funds, and taxation.

4.1.3.3 Equitable remedies

As mentioned in the brief history, the Court of Chancery developed a range of new equitable remedies. These still exist, but remember that they are only available at the discretion of the court. The most common equitable remedies sought are injunction, specific performance, and recission.

Injunction

An **injunction** is a court order which compels a person or body to perform some action or to cease some action.

There are different types of injunction. Examples include:

- Mandatory injunctions compelling someone to perform an act
- Prohibitory injunctions restraining someone from committing some act
- Interim injunctions granted before trial to preserve the status quo until the case is decided

Specific performance

An order of **specific performance** compels a person or body to perform their obligations under a contract or trust.

Specific performance is not generally available where damages (i.e. the common law remedy as of right) would provide an adequate remedy. It is therefore usually only relevant to special situations (such as a contract for the sale of land).

Recission

An order of **recission** sets aside a contract.

As well as being subject to the usual equitable principles, recission is only generally available where it is possible to restore the parties to the contract to the positions that they were in before entering into the contract.

4.2 Custom

In order to enforce a local custom as an exception to the common law, it is necessary to show that the custom meets seven main tests. These were introduced by judges as a means of giving them the power to disregard any local custom which they considered unsuitable for recognition as a legal right. As you will see, the tests are very difficult to establish:

- The custom must have existed from time immemorial. This was arbitrarily defined as meaning the year 1189 (or the start of the reign of Richard I). If it can be proved that the custom did not exist in 1189, then it will fail.
- It must have existed without interruption since 1189.
- It must have been enjoyed without force, stealth, or permission
- It must have been observed because people felt that it was obligatory
- It must be capable of being precisely defined
- It must be reasonable. It must also have been reasonable throughout its entire period of use.
- It must be consistent with other local customs.

In other words, in order to claim the benefit of a local custom, you simply have to prove that people have felt obliged to observe it since 1189 and have done so continuously since then without opposition; that it has been reasonable at all times since 1189, that it is precise, and that it is not at variance with other local practices! In practice, if the custom has been observed 'in living memory', this raises a presumption that it has been observed since 'time immemorial' unless evidence can be provided to rebut this presumption.

Custom is typically used in connection with land disputes, such as rights of way or access. However, as you might imagine, the difficulties involved in passing these tests means that claims to local custom are nowadays extremely rare and success is rarer still. For instance in *Beckett Ltd* v *Lyons*[6] the claimant company sued in trespass to land after the defendant had been removing sea coal from a shore over which the company held the right to do so. The defendants attempted to rely on lawful custom, claiming that the inhabitants of County Durham had a customary right

---

6.   [1967] 1 All ER 833.

to take the sea coal. They introduced witnesses who had lived locally since 1886 who confirmed their story. However, the Court of Appeal held that the practice could also be considered to have been mere tolerance on the part of the landowner in earlier times, when the collection of the coal was not a business enterprise. Moreover, the evidence put forward by the witnesses related to the removal of the coal by means of buckets and wheelbarrows, as opposed to the more recent removal by the defendants in lorries!

Despite the inherent difficulties in proving local custom, examples of relatively recent successful claims include *Egerton* v *Harding*[7] involving a customary duty to erect a fence to prevent cattle straying from the common; *New Windsor Corporation* v *Mellor*,[8] in which the customary right of the mayor, bailiff, burgess, and others to indulge in lawful sports (including shooting) on land in a local borough was upheld; and the 1992 decision in the High Court[9] allowing anglers to dig for worms as bait on the foreshore for their own use as an ancillary customary right to that to fish in tidal waters, which has existed since the Magna Carta (1215).

4.3 The courts, their personnel, and their jurisdictions

Without a set of institutions to enforce legal rules, there would be no legal system. A set of rules cannot usefully exist in isolation. There needs to be a system of courts to hear cases at first instance, as well as higher courts which offer the mechanism for individuals to bring appeals arising from the outcome of cases in lower courts.

As you will see when looking at the doctrine of judicial precedent in section 6.2, there are rules which determine whether or not a particular court will be bound by a decision of a higher court—generally meaning that it will have to follow the particular legal reasoning of that higher court.

Therefore, a thorough understanding of the institutions of the modern court system is vital to your study of law. This section will provide an overview of the various courts, the types of case which they hear and the personnel who hear and decide those cases.

The domestic courts can be depicted as shown in Figure 4.2.

4.3.1 Classification of the courts

Courts may be classified in a number of different ways:

- Criminal and civil courts
- Trial and appellate courts
- Superior and inferior courts

4.3.1.1 Criminal and civil courts

Criminal courts determine the guilt or innocence of defendants according to the parameters of the criminal law and dispense punishment to convicted offenders.

---

7. [1974] 3 All ER 689.
8. [1974] 2 All ER 510 (Ch D).
9. *The Guardian*, 12 December 1992.

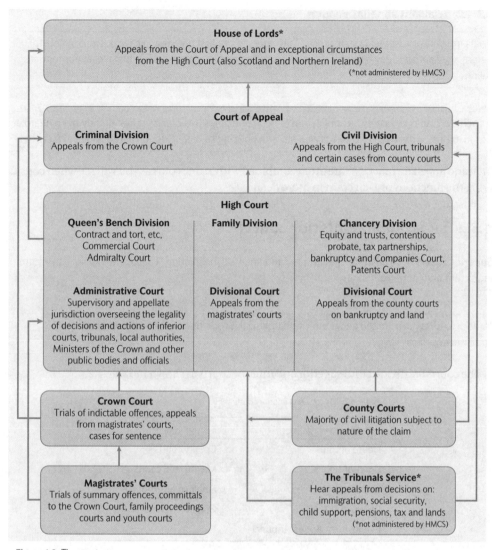

Figure 4.2 The courts

Civil courts primarily deal with the resolution of disputes between individuals and award appropriate remedies to successful claimants. These remedies are normally in the form of monetary damages.

You should note that a particular set of facts can give rise to proceedings in both the criminal and civil courts. For instance, if you were knocked down and injured by a reckless driver while walking down the street, this could lead to a case in the criminal courts (for a possible breach of the Road Traffic Acts) and in the civil courts (to seek compensation for your injuries).

The Crown Court deals almost exclusively with criminal matters. The county court has only civil jurisdiction. However, all the other courts have both criminal and civil jurisdictions.

4.3.1.2 Trial and appellate courts

Trial courts hear cases 'at first instance'. This refers to the first time that a case is heard in court, before any appeals. They consider the matters of fact and law in the case and make an appropriate ruling.

Appellate courts consider the application of legal principles to a case that has already been heard at first instance. Some appellate courts also have jurisdiction to reconsider disputed issues of fact.

Trial and appellate functions are often combined within one court as you will see when considering the functions of each court in more detail.

4.3.2 Superior and inferior courts

Superior courts have unlimited geographic and financial jurisdiction. They generally hear the more important and/or difficult cases.

Inferior courts have limited geographic and financial jurisdiction. They hear the majority of straightforward cases.

The courts are divided into superior and inferior courts as shown in Table 4.2.

Table 4.2 Superior and inferior courts

Superior courts	Inferior courts
House of Lords	County courts
Court of Appeal	Magistrates' courts
High Court	Employment Tribunal
Crown Court	Coroners' courts
Employment Appeal Tribunal	

Remember that the vast majority of cases are dealt with by the inferior courts. Most day-to-day court proceedings take place in the inferior courts and only a tiny proportion of these end up in the superior courts. With the exception of the magistrates' court and the Employment Tribunal the courts shown in the table are also courts of record. This means that records of their proceedings are kept at the Public Record Office and are available for inspection by members of the general public.

4.3.3 House of Lords

The House of Lords (strictly speaking, the 'Appellate Committee of the House of Lords') has jurisdiction in both civil and criminal matters.

As its position in the hierarchy of the courts might suggest, its function is almost entirely appellate, although it does have an extremely limited jurisdiction at first instance concerning matters such as disputed succession to peerages and breaches of Parliamentary privilege.

The House of Lords does not hear evidence from witnesses but instead considers legal argument and documentary evidence. Its decisions are given as opinions (although these are commonly referred to—inaccurately—as judgments, even by lawyers). Therefore the Lords opine, rather than judge!

The House of Lords hears appeals in criminal cases from the Court of Appeal (Criminal Division) and exceptionally from the High Court (typically the Queen's Bench Divisional Court). It hears appeals in civil cases from the Court of Appeal (Civil Division) and (again, rarely) the High Court (via the so-called 'leapfrog' procedure).

It comprises three to seven (but usually five) Lords of Appeal in Ordinary who are commonly referred to as the 'Law Lords'.

4.3.3.1 Supreme Court of the United Kingdom

The Constitutional Reform Act 2005[10] establishes a Supreme Court of the United Kingdom consisting of twelve judges with a President and a Deputy President. The judges other than the President and Deputy President are to be styled 'Justices of the Supreme Court'. The Lords of Appeal in Ordinary become justices of the Supreme Court; the senior Lord of Appeal in Ordinary becomes the President of the Court, and the second senior Lord of Appeal in Ordinary becomes the Deputy President of the Court.[11]

According to the Department for Consitutional Affairs:

> The introduction of a Supreme Court for the United Kingdom will provide greater clarity in our constitutional arrangements by further separating the judiciary from the legislature and the executive. It will assume the jurisdiction of the current Appellate Committee of the House of Lords and the devolution jurisdiction of the Judicial Committee of the Privy Council.

The Supreme Court will:

(a) hear appeals on arguable points of law of general public importance;

(b) act as the final court of appeal in England, Wales, and Northern Ireland;

(c) hear appeals from civil cases in England, Wales, Northern Ireland, and Scotland;

(d) hear appeals from criminal cases in England, Wales, and Northern Ireland;

(e) assume the devolution jurisdiction of the Judicial Committee of the Privy Council, while the Commonwealth jurisdiction of the Council will remain unchanged (see section 4.3.10).

The UK Supreme Court is scheduled to open in October 2009 and will be located in Middlesex Guildhall, on the corner of Parliament Square, opposite the Houses of Parliament and alongside Westminster Abbey and the Treasury Building.

4.3.4 Court of Appeal

The Court of Appeal is one court which is divided into two divisions—the Civil Division and the Criminal Division. The Court of Appeal does not hear witnesses but instead considers legal argument and documentary evidence. The majority decision will prevail, so, in practice, an odd number of judges—usually three—sit. In certain cases of major public importance, sometimes

---

10. Section 23.
11. Constitutional Reform Act 2005, s. 24.

five or even seven Lord Justices of Appeal will sit. Note that, although unlikely in practice, the court is properly constituted even if only one judge sits.

4.3.4.1 Court of Appeal (Criminal Division)

The Court of Appeal (Criminal Division), as its name suggests, has a predominantly appellate jurisdiction. It also has jurisdiction to hear certain other matters to which it may be referred. It mainly deals with appeals from Crown Court against conviction, sentence or both; references made by the Attorney-General following an acquittal on indictment under s. 36 of the Criminal Justice Act 1972 on a point of law (although the defendant will remain acquitted whatever happens); references made by the Attorney-General under s. 36 of the Criminal Justice Act 1988 against an unduly lenient sentence; cases referred by the Criminal Cases Review Commission under s. 9 of the Criminal Appeal Act 1995 where there has been a possible miscarriage of justice; and applications for leave (permission) to appeal to the House of Lords.

It is comprised of Lord and Lady Justices of Appeal. Its head is the Lord Chief Justice.

4.3.4.2 Court of Appeal (Civil Division)

The Court of Appeal (Civil Division) deals with appeals from the High Court, county courts, and certain tribunals (for example, the Employment Appeal Tribunal).

It is also comprised of Lord and Lady Justices of Appeal. Its head is the Master of the Rolls.

4.3.5 High Court

The High Court is one court. However, it is divided into three 'divisions' for administrative purposes. These are the Queen's Bench Division, Chancery Division, and Family Division.

It is staffed by High Court judges (also known as puisne judges—pronounced 'puny' and meaning 'junior'). The head of the Queen's Bench Division is the Lord Chief Justice. The nominal head of the Chancery Division is the Lord Chancellor (who never actually sits in the Chancery Division); in effect it is headed by the Vice-Chancellor. The Family Division is headed by the President of the Family Division.

None of the Divisions has any practically significant criminal jurisdiction at first instance.

4.3.5.1 Queen's Bench Division

The Queen's Bench Division hears criminal appeals from magistrates' courts by way of case stated and from the Crown Court sitting without a jury (for example, a Crown Court hearing an appeal from the magistrates' court). Its civil jurisdiction includes contractual disputes and actions in tort (with no upper limit on value) at first instance and appeals from the county court. It also has three notable specialist subdivisions: the Administrative Court (which deals with applications for judicial review), the Admiralty Court (dealing with shipping and aircraft), and the Commercial Court (covering banking, insurance, and finance).

4.3.5.2 Judicial review

Judicial review is a procedure by which, on the application of an individual, the courts may determine whether a public body (or a private body exercising a public function) has acted lawfully. It is available to applicants with 'sufficient interest' in the matter to which the application relates.[12]

---

12. Supreme Court Act 1981, s. 31.

The most common classification of grounds of challenge in judicial review is that of Lord Diplock who defined three broad (and arbitrary) headings: illegality, irrationality, and procedural impropriety.[13] Illegality was defined as failure to recognize and give effect to the law which regulates a decision-making power: to determine whether a public body has acted *ultra vires*. Irrationality was described as a decision that was so outrageous in its defiance of logic or accepted moral standards that no reasonable decision maker could have arrived at it. Procedural impropriety covers both any statutory procedural requirements and the common-law rules of natural justice, namely bias and failure to give a fair hearing.

It is also unlawful for a public body to act in a way which is incompatible with the European Convention on Human Rights.[14] The victim of the breach of Convention rights relating to the actions of a public body (or a private body exercising a public function) may also challenge by judicial review. In reaching its decision, the court will consider:

- What Article was breached? How was it breached?
- Was the interference with the right prescribed by law?
- Was the interference necessary in a democratic society or in pursuit of a legitimate aim?
- Was the interference proportional?

4.3.5.3 Chancery Division

The Chancery Division has first instance jurisdiction over disputes over wills; the administration of estates and contentious probate; land actions; mortgage actions; trusts; company law; partnership and intellectual property (such as trade marks and copyright). Its specialist subdivisions are the Patents Court and the Court of Protection (which deals with matters concerning the care of disabled persons). It also hears various appeals from county courts, concerning matters such as bankruptcy.

4.3.5.4 Family Division

The Family Division has the inherent jurisdiction to deal with cases of defended divorce, adoption, and wardship.[15] It also considers certain wills and probate cases along with matters relating to family homes and domestic violence, declarations in medical treatment cases, and final dissolution matters in Civil Partnerships. It hears appeals from the magistrates' court and Crown Court in family cases.

4.3.6 Crown Court

The Crown Court deals with trials on indictment (by jury); cases where the magistrates have declined jurisdiction before trial; offences triable either-way where the defendant has elected for trial by jury in the Crown Court; and referrals for sentence from the magistrates' court where the magistrates consider that their sentencing powers are inadequate for the case in question (by virtue of the statutory limit on sentences in magistrates' courts).

The Crown Court hears appeals from defendants against conviction or sentence or both in the magistrates' court.

---

13. *Council for Civil Service Unions* v *Minister for Civil Service* [1985] 1 AC 374.
14. Human Rights Act 1998, s. 6.
15. Any person may, by issuing proceedings, make the High Court guardian of any child within its jurisdiction a 'ward of court'. No important decision concerning the child's life can then be taken without the court's permission.

Its first instance civil jurisdiction is limited so much as to be practically insignificant (for example, it hears certain disputes as to whether particular highways are in disrepair!)

It is staffed by High Court judges, circuit judges, deputy circuit judges (part-time), recorders (part-time), assistant recorders (part-time), and a jury (for trials).

4.3.7 County court

The county court deals with all but the most complicated civil law matters, such as:

- Claims for repayment of debt
- Claims for compensation in personal injury cases
- Cases involving breach of contract concerning goods or property
- Family issues including divorce or adoption
- Administration of wills
- Bankruptcy proceedings
- Housing disputes, including mortgage and council rent arrears and re-possessions.

There are 218 county courts throughout England and Wales.

The jurisdiction of the county court to hear certain types of case may be limited geographically and/or financially. Generally, the county court will hear contractual disputes (up to £5,000 in value); actions in tort (e.g. negligence and nuisance) where compensation sought for personal injuries is not more than £1,000; probate (administration of wills); divorce, and bankruptcy.

Its staff comprises circuit judges, deputy circuit judges, district judges (formerly known as registrars), and deputy district judges (part-time).

4.3.8 Magistrates' court

All criminal proceedings begin in the magistrates' courts and well over 90 per cent end there. The main types of hearing are the trial of summary offences; applications for bail; issue of summonses and warrants for arrest or search; Youth Courts (formerly known as Juvenile Courts) for defendants between the ages of 10 and 18; plea before venue hearings; committal proceedings for Crown Court trial or sentence.

Magistrates' courts also have an extensive civil jurisdiction, much of which concerns local government matters. The main categories of civil hearing include highways, public health and licensing; recovery of civil debts such as national insurance contributions and income tax; Family Proceedings Court, covering certain family or matrimonial matters (but not divorce), and care proceedings in respect of children in the Youth Court.

Magistrates' court proceedings are either heard by Justices of the Peace (lay magistrates), usually sitting as a bench of three, or a single district judge (magistrates' courts) working on a full-time salaried basis (these were formerly known as stipendiary magistrates).

4.3.9 Coroners' court

The Coroners' court is responsible for investigating violent, unnatural, or sudden deaths where the cause of death is unknown. This can include bodies brought into their jurisdiction for burial or cremation from abroad.

The Coroners' court is an inquisitorial court unlike the other adversarial courts in the court system. The Coroner is not bound by any rules of evidence relating to hearsay, nor governed by

THE COURTS, THEIR PERSONNEL, AND THEIR JURISDICTIONS

any requirement for a case to be determined beyond any particular standard of proof. The Coroners' court has a statutory duty to discover:

(a) the identity of the deceased;

(b) how, when, and where the deceased came by his or her death.[16]

If the coroner has reason to suspect murder, manslaughter, or infanticide, then a jury must be summonsed.

It is important to realize that the Coroner's function is relatively limited: the court does not determine any civil or criminal liability for the death.[17]

The usual verdicts available to a Coroner are:

- Accidental death
- Death by misadventure
- Unlawful killing
- Open verdict
- Suicide

4.3.10 The Judicial Committee of the Privy Council

The Privy Council is not, strictly speaking, a court at all. Its function is to advise the Crown. Therefore it cannot really be said to be 'deciding' cases. However, in practice, the 'advice' given to the Queen in the 'opinion' of the Judicial Committee of the Privy Council is almost always followed. This is generally because of the seniority of its members.

When we consider the doctrine of judicial precedent in section 6.2, you will see that decisions of the Privy Council are not binding on any domestic court, but are highly persuasive. Again, this is a result of the high judicial standing of its members.

The Judicial Committee of the Privy Council hears appeals from certain Commonwealth countries; appeals relating to disciplinary proceedings brought by various professions; ecclesiastical appeals; questions relating to the competence and function of the Scottish Parliament and the National Assembly of Wales.

It comprises at least three, and usually five, of the following:

- Lord Chancellor
- Lords of Appeal in Ordinary (the 'Law Lords')
- Lord President of the (Privy) Council and any former Lord Presidents
- Members of the Privy Council with experience of senior judicial posts
- Members of the Privy Council who are also Commonwealth judges

4.3.11 Tribunals

Tribunals were originally established to provide a quicker, cheaper, and therefore more accessible route to justice that is available through the courts system. The original intention was that individuals could represent themselves without needing to go to the expense of legal representation

---

16. Coroners' Act 1988, s. 11(5)(b).
17. Rule 42 of the Coroners Rules 1984.

by solicitors or barristers. Since tribunals are also staffed by experts in the particular field, they are familiar with the types of issue that arise and can therefore usually reach a judgment more quickly than the normal court system.

However, tribunals are tending towards increasing formality. Since tribunal chairs have legal qualifications more people are using the services of legal professionals so that they can present their case more effectively, although public funding is not always available for this type of professional representation.

The most commonly-encountered tribunal is probably the Employment Tribunal which investigates allegations of wrongful or unfair dismissal from ex-employees against their former employers (although employment tribunal awards for breaches of contract are subject to an upper limit, currently £25,000); claims of sex and racial discrimination in the workplace; considers claims for redundancy payments, and alleged breaches of maternity rights.

Additional tribunals include:

- Employment Appeal Tribunals, which hear appeals from the Employment Tribunal on points of law

- Immigration Appeal Tribunals, which hear appeals from individuals who have been refused entry into the UK or who have had an application to extend their leave to remain turned down

- Rent Tribunals, which resolve disputes between tenants and landlords over payment or amount of rent

- Mental Health Tribunals, which consider issues involving the secure detention of psychiatric patients

4.4 The European Court of Human Rights

4.4.1 A brief history

The European Convention on Human Rights and Freedoms is a creation of the Council of Europe although it is, at least in part, based upon the 1948 United Nations Declaration of Human Rights. The Council of Europe was formed in 1949, shortly after the end of the Second World War, with its aim of international cooperation and the prevention of the kinds of widespread atrocious violations of human rights which had occurred during the war. The European Convention on Human Rights was signed in Rome in 1950, ratified by the UK a year later and came into force in 1953.

The European Court of Human Rights was established in 1959 as a final avenue of complaint for claimants who had exhausted the remedies available to them in their domestic courts for alleged breaches of Convention rights. At the same time, the European Commission of Human Rights was also established. The Commission's role was to decrease the caseload of the European Court of Human Rights by filtering out some cases and attempting to resolve others by conciliation. The individual's right to petition the European Court of Human Rights became available to UK citizens in 1966.

The European Court of Human Rights and the European Commission of Human Rights were abolished on 31 October 1998 and replaced by a single Court of Human Rights. Questions of admissibility (formerly dealt with by the Commission) are now dealt with by its judges sitting in committee. It is based in Strasbourg.

Remember that the Court of Justice and the European Court of Human Rights are different, as are the Council of the European Union and the Council of Europe.

4.4.2 The Human Rights Act 1998 and case law

The Convention is an international treaty that binds the states which sign it to certain standards of behaviour towards individuals. However, the treaty was not enacted as part of the law of England and Wales until the Human Rights Act 1998 which received Royal Assent on 9 November 1998 and came into force on 2 October 2000. This means that individuals may rely on (most) Convention rights in domestic proceedings.

Section 2 of the Human Rights Act 1998 requires courts to take into account any previous decision of the European Court of Human Rights. This effectively allows the overruling of any previous English case authority that was in conflict with a previous decision of the European Court of Human Rights. This will enable the courts to build a new body of case law where human rights issues are raised.

The impact of the Human Rights Act 1998 on the doctrine of judicial precedent is dealt with in section 6.3. Section 5.4 describes how to find decisions of the European Court of Human Rights.

CHAPTER SUMMARY

Common law and equity

- The common law evolved following the Norman Conquest in 1066

- It emerged from a combination of local custom and case law

- The common law became very bureaucratic in operation, costly and time-consuming

- The common law did not recognize certain rights

- Equitable rights and remedies became available from the Court of Chancery

- Where there was conflict between law and equity, equity prevailed

- The administration of common law and equity was fused by the Supreme Court of Judicature Acts 1873 and 1875

- Equity has its own system of equitable maxims (doctrines), rights and remedies including injunctions, specific performance and recission

Custom

- Local customs can be enforced as exceptions to the common law

- In order to enforce a custom, it is necessary to show that it meets a very stringent set of conditions

- Custom is consequently very difficult to prove

- Custom is typically used in connection with disputes over land

The courts and their jurisdictions

- Criminal courts determine guilt or innocence of defendants and dispense punishment to convicted offenders

- Civil courts primarily deal with the resolution of disputes between individuals

- Trial courts hear cases at first instance—before any appeals

- Appellate courts consider the application of legal principles to cases that have already been heard at first instance

- Superior courts have unlimited geographic and financial jurisdiction and hear the most important and/or difficult cases

- Inferior courts have limited geographic and financial jurisdiction and hear the majority of straightforward cases

- The House of Lords has an almost entirely appellate function

- The Constitutional Reform Act 2005 establishes a Supreme Court of the United Kingdom, scheduled to open in October 2009

- The Court of Appeal is divided into the Civil and Criminal Divisions

- The High Court is divided into three divisions for administrative purposes—the Queens' Bench, Family, and Chancery Divisions.

- The Crown court primarily deals with trial by jury in criminal cases

- The county courts deal with all but the most complicated civil law matters

- All criminal proceedings begin in the magistrates' court

- The Coroners' court is responsible for investigating violent, unnatural, or sudden deaths where the cause of death is unknown

- The Privy Council hears appeals from certain Commonwealth countries, appeals in professional disciplinary cases, ecclesiastical appeals, and matters relating to the Scottish Parliament and the National Assembly of Wales

- The Privy Council's role is to advise the Crown—although its advice is highly persuasive. This is due to the high judicial rank of its members.

- Tribunals are specialist bodies established with the aim of providing quicker, cheaper, and more accessible routes to justice—examples include Employment Tribunals, Immigration Appeal Tribunals, Rent Tribunals, and Mental Health Tribunals.

The European Court of Human Rights

- Not to be confused with the European Court of Justice

- The European Court of Human Rights is based in Strasbourg

- The European Convention on Human Rights was signed in Rome in 1950, ratified by the UK in 1951 and came into force in 1953

- The individual's right to petition the European Court of Human Rights became available to UK citizens in 1966

- The Human Rights Act 1998 came into force on 2 October 2000. This means that individuals may rely on (most) Convention rights in domestic proceedings

- Section 2 of the Human Rights Act 1998 requires courts to take into account any previous decision of the European Court of Human Rights

- This will enable the courts to build a new body of case law where human rights issues are raised

 FURTHER READING

- Ingman, T. (2004) *The English Legal Process* (10th edn), Oxford: Oxford University Press. For a very detailed view of the court system, civil and criminal procedure and the appeals process.

- Greer, F.A. 'Custom in the Common Law' (1893) 9 *Law Quarterly Review* 157.

- Braybrooke, E.K. (1951) 'Custom as a Source of English Law' (1951) 50 *Michigan Law Review* 70. For more detail on custom as a domestic source of law.

Finding cases

5

INTRODUCTION

The previous chapter explained the role of case law as a source of law. This chapter will give you the skills to find cases. It will start by explaining the meanings of case citations before moving on to discuss how to locate domestic cases both in a law library and electronically via a number of the online databases which are currently available. It will then explain how to find decisions of the European Courts—namely the European Court of Justice, the Court of First Instance, and the European Court of Human Rights.

The ability to locate case law is as important as finding legislation. Without being able to find the primary sources of law you will struggle in every area of your legal study. You will need to be able to find the cases that you encounter during your studies in order to read and understand them. This is important both in terms of analysing the operation of particular areas of the law as well as more practically in constructing legal arguments based on the outcomes of previous cases.

LEARNING OUTCOMES

After studying this chapter, you will be able to:

- Understand the meaning of case citations

- Explain the use of the neutral citation system

- Distinguish between reported and unreported cases

- Find domestic and European cases in a law library and online

5.1 Law reporting

Unless you are actually present in court at the time that the judgment in a particular case is made, you will have to rely on a report of the case to find out what happened. Clearly, then, accurate law reporting is extremely important. Before learning how to find cases in the various law reports, it will be helpful to provide a very brief history of law reporting. This will come in useful later.

5.1.1 A brief history

5.1.1.1 The Year Books (1272–1535)

The Year Books are the medieval equivalent of the modern law reports. They are annual collections of case reports from 1272 to 1535 and are mostly handwritten in law French. They are of limited use today other than to students of legal history. Some modern reprints (with translations) can be found in the *Rolls* series and the Selden Society series.

5.1.1.2 The Nominate Reports (1535–1865)

The Nominate Reports comprise collections of cases published commercially under the name of the individual reporter (hence 'nominate' reports). The standard of reliability varied considerably, although the reports of Coke, Burrow, and Plowden are generally the most well-respected of the many series. Between 1571 and 1865 there were over 500 different series of reports published; of these, 176 volumes have been reproduced in the *English Reports* and some of the more important cases between 1558 and 1935 were also reprinted in the *All England Law Reports Reprint* series.

5.1.1.3 Modern Reports (from 1865)

The Law Reports

In 1865 the Council of Law Reporting was established to report:

- All cases which introduce, or appear to introduce, a new principle or a new rule
- All cases which materially modify an existing principle or rule
- All cases which settle, or materially tend to settle, a question upon which the law is doubtful
- All cases which for any reason are peculiarly instructive

In other words, the reports publish those cases which are considered to be the most important. This means that a large number of cases (particularly those heard at first instance) go unreported. In fact, only around 2,500 of the 200,000 or so cases heard each year are reported.

In 1870 it became the Incorporated Council of Law Reporting (ICLR) with the object of 'the preparation and publication, in a convenient form, at a moderate price, and under gratuitous professional control, of reports of judicial decisions of the superior and appellate courts in England'. Since 1970 the Council has operated as a Registered Charity and consists of members nominated by each of the four Inns of Court and by the General Council of the Bar. The two law officers and the President of The Law Society are *ex officio* members. An executive committee sits once or twice a year and the full council meets only once a year.

There are three series of the ICLR reports:

- 1865–1875
- 1875–1890
- 1891 to date

These are bound according to the court as follows:

- Queen's Bench Division
- Chancery Division
- Family Division
- Appeal Cases

You should note that the Appeal Cases series does not actually report all appeal cases. It only covers appeals heard in the House of Lords and by the Privy Council.

The *Law Reports* are published monthly. They summarize the arguments of counsel, and are checked by the bench prior to publication. For this reason, they carry the greatest authority. This was made clear by Lord Woolf CJ in the *Practice Direction (Judgments: Form Citation) (Supreme Court).*[1]

Citation of judgments in court

3.1 For avoidance of doubt, it should be emphasised that both the High Court and the Court of Appeal require that where a case has been reported in the official Law Reports published by the Incorporated Council of Law Reporting for England and Wales it must be cited from that source. Other series may only be used when a case is not reported in the Law Reports.

The requirement to cite cases from the official Law Reports in court wherever possible is of great importance in mooting. See chapter 15.

The Weekly Law Reports

Since 1953, the ICLR has also published the *Weekly Law Reports* which aim to report cases more quickly than the *Law Reports*. This is achieved by dispensing with the need for the bench to revise judgments prior to publication and by not summarizing the arguments of counsel. As their name suggests, they are published weekly in a paper cover and republished as bound volumes at the end of the year (in practice, subscribers send their paper copies back to the ICLR for binding).

There are three volumes of the *Weekly Law Reports* (Table 5.1).

Table 5.1 The volumes of the *Weekly Law Reports*

Volume	Contents
1	Cases of lower importance which are not likely to be re-published in the *Law Reports*.
2 and 3	Cases of higher importance which are intended to be re-published (with counsel's argument and any revision by the bench) in the *Law Reports*.

The All-England Law Reports

The *All England Law Reports* are published by Lexis-Nexis Butterworths Tolley. Reports are usually revised by the bench before publication, but arguments of counsel are not reported. It is a general series of law reports which is updated weekly and provides full text reports on cases heard by the House of Lords, the Privy Council, the Court of Appeal (Criminal and Civil Divisions), and all the divisions of the High Court.

Specialist report series

There are many series of specialist reports which give in-depth coverage of cases in particular areas of law. It is often the case that leading judgments in particular fields will be reported in the specialist reports but not in the general series such as the *Law Reports* or the *All England Law Reports*.

Some examples of specialist report series are:

- *Industrial Relations Law Reports*
- *Family Law Reports*

1.   [2001] 1 WLR 194.

- *Criminal Appeal Reports*
- *Road Traffic Reports*

5.1.2 Making sense of case citations

Case citations are an abbreviated form of reference to a particular report of a case. This section deals with the main citations for cases heard in England and Wales. For an explanation of citations used for European cases, see 'Finding European case law' in section 5.3 below.

5.1.2.1 Law report citations

The citation for *R v Morrison* is [2003] 1 WLR 1859.

R v Morrison *is used as an example in chapter 6 and is used to illustrate how to read and navigate around a law report. This chapter is just concerned with finding the case.*

The citation indicates where this particular reported case can be found (Figure 5.1).

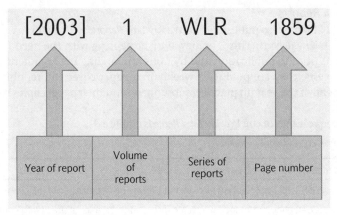

Figure 5.1 Law report citation

Year of report

The year shown here is the year in which the case was reported. Although cases are usually reported in the same year as the judgment, there can be situations where the reports are published later. This can occur if the case was heard late in one year, but reported early in the next year. An example of this can be found in *Wilkey and another v British Broadcasting Corporation and another* [2002] EWCA Civ 1561; [2003] 1 WLR 1. This case was heard on 21 and 22 October 2002 but reported in the first issue of the *Weekly Law Reports* of 2003. Another possible cause of delay between judgment and report can occur if the importance of the case was not appreciated at the time of the judgment. For example, the judgment in *Mesher v Mesher* [1980] 1 All ER 126 which deals with the division of marital property on divorce, was reported in 1980 but delivered on 13 February 1973, some seven years previously.

To complicate matters further, there is a convention surrounding the use of round or square brackets around the year of the report. Prior to 1890, the year was not part of the citation; in other words, it was not necessary to know the year of the report in order to find the case report. However, the date is now inserted for ease of reference, but is put in *round* brackets to indicate that it is for information only. An example of this can be found in the *Sussex Peerage Case* (1844) 1 Cl & Fin 85 which sets out the golden rule of statutory interpretation.

Since 1890 the year of the case *is* part of the citation and so it would be impossible to find the case without knowing its year. In this instance the year is put in *square* brackets.

Citation of the *Law Reports*

Between 1875 and 1890 the system of citation used by the *Law Reports* changed. For example:

Table 5.2 Citation of the *Law Reports*

	1865–1875	1875–1890	1891 to date
Appeal Cases	(1871) LR 1 HL 123	(1881) 2 App Cas 123	[1991] AC 123

From 1865–75 all citations included 'LR' for 'Law Reports'.

The abbreviation for Appeal Cases was 'HL' for 'House of Lords' from 1865–75. From 1875–90 it was 'App Cas' and after 1890 it was further shortened to 'AC'.

The two series from 1865–75 and 1875–90 used a volume number to denote the volume of the series. Volumes often covered more than one year. From 1890 onwards the volume number is the volume of that particular year.

Volume and series of reports

There are many different series of law reports, each of which has its own abbreviation. Some of the more commonly encountered are:

Table 5.3 Some common law report series

AC	Appeal Cases
All ER	All England Law Reports
All ER (EC)	All England Law Reports European Cases 1995
All ER Rep	All England Law Reports Reprints
BCLC	Butterworths Company Law Reports 1983–
C.L.R.	Commonwealth Law Reports 1903–98
ChD	Chancery
CMLR	Common Market Law Reports 1962–
Com.Cas.	Commercial Cases 1895–1941
Cox. CC	Cox's Criminal Law Cases 1843–1934
Cr App R	Criminal Appeal Reports 1909
Cr App R (S)	Criminal Appeal Reports Sentencing 1979–96
Crim LR	Criminal Law Review
ECHR	European Commission of Human Rights Decisions and Reports 1976–98
ECR	European Court Reports 1954 (Court of Justice of the European Community)
ECR I-	European Court of First Instance
EHRR	European Human Rights Reports 1993–
Fam	Family
FLR	Family Law Reports 1980–
IRLR	Industrial Relations Law Reports 1972–

Table 5.3 *(Cont.)*

KB	King's Bench
Lloyd's Rep	Lloyds List Law Report 1919–67, now Lloyds Law Reports 1968–
LTR	Landlord and Tenant Reports 2000–
QB	Queen's Bench
RTR	Road Traffic Reports 1970–87
WLR	Weekly Law Reports 1953–

If there is more than one volume of the reports for a particular year, then the volume number is inserted before the abbreviation for the law report series. For instance *Murphy* v *Brentwood District Council* [1990] 2 All ER 908 was reported in the second volume of the All England Reports for 1990 at page 908. If there is only one volume then the volume number is left out—for example, *Young* v *Bristol Aeroplane Co.* [1944] KB 718.

The ability to translate the citation of a case into words is an important skill in mooting. This is dealt with in chapter 15.

5.1.2.2 Neutral citations

The neutral citation system was introduced to the Court of Appeal and the Administrative Court by the *Practice Direction (Judgments: Form and Citation)* [2001] 1 WLR 194; [2001] 1 All ER 193, issued on 11 January 2001 and extended to all divisions of the High Court on 14 January 2002.

According to the *Practice Direction*, the main reason for these changes was to facilitate the publication of judgments on the World Wide Web and their subsequent use by the increasing numbers of those who have access to the Web and to assist those who use and wish to search judgments stored on electronic databases.

A unique number is given by the official shorthand writers to each approved judgment issued out of the House of Lords, Court of Appeal and High Court. The judgments are numbered in the following way (Figure 5.2).

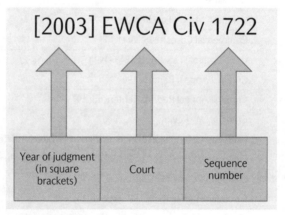

Figure 5.2 Neutral citation

First, the year of the judgment is given in square brackets. This is followed by an abbreviation for the court, preceded by UK (for 'United Kingdom' in relation to the jurisdiction of the House of

Lords and the Privy Council) or EW (for 'England and Wales' in relation to the jurisdiction of the other courts). Therefore, the abbreviations used for each of the courts which use the neutral citation system are set out in the table below:

Table 5.4 Abbreviations used in the neutral citation system

Court	Abbreviation
House of Lords	UKHL {sequence number}
Privy Council	UKPC {sequence number}
Court of Appeal (Criminal Division)	EWCA Crim {sequence number}
Court of Appeal (Criminal Division)	EWCA Civ {sequence number}
High Court (Administrative Court)	EWHC {sequence number} (Admin)
Chancery Division	EWHC {sequence number} (Ch)
Patents Court	EWHC {sequence number} (Pat)
Queen's Bench Division	EWHC {sequence number} (QB)
Commercial Court	EWHC {sequence number} (Comm)
Admiralty Court	EWHC {sequence number} (Admlty)
Technology and Construction Court	EWHC {sequence number} (TCC)
Family Division	EWHC {sequence number} (Fam)

Therefore this particular case (*R v Morrison* [2003] EWCA Civ 1722) was the 1722nd reported judgment of the Court of Appeal (Criminal Division) in England and Wales in 2003.

The neutral citation *precedes* the citation for any Law Report in which the case has been published. If the report has not been published then the neutral citation stands alone.

5.1.3 Reported and unreported cases

We have seen that only a relatively small proportion of cases end up being reported. It follows that there are a vast number of 'unreported' cases each year. There are an increasing number of these unreported cases available online. Since 1996, various unreported judgments have been freely available as courts have published verbatim transcripts online.

 Links to the sites mentioned in this section can also be found on the Online Resource Centre.

 Practical exercise

Visit the free databases listed in this section. Have a look around each to get used to their layout and content. If you are using your own computer, bookmark the sites for quick access later.

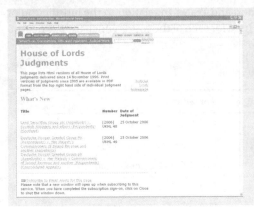

http://www.publications.parliament.uk/pa/ld/ldjudgmt.htm
This contains html versions of all House of Lords judgments delivered since 14 November 1996 with print-friendly versions in PDF format.

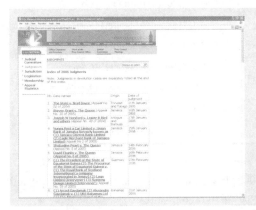

http://www.privycouncil.org.uk
Contains full-text versions of Privy Council decisions from 1999 and a selection of pre-1999 decisions. These are generally available in RTF or PDF format.

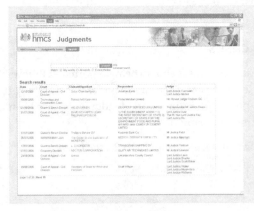

http://www.hmcourts-service.gov.uk/judgments.htm
This site lists judgments dating back to 1996 although it only includes judgments selected by the judge concerned.

5.1.4 Case summaries

In addition to the full reports, there are a number of sources of case summaries and commentaries. For instance, the *Criminal Law Review* and the *Journal of Criminal Law* contain brief summaries of pertinent criminal cases. There are similar journals and digests for other areas of the law. The summaries tend to comprise a brief summary of the facts and the judgment accompanied by a pithy commentary.

However, you should remember that these summaries only provide indications of the law and pointers to the actual cases themselves. You should therefore use case summaries with caution—if you wish to rely on the opinion in a case summary, it would be prudent to seek out the full transcript of the case to try and understand for yourself the reasoning used by the author of the summary.

5.2 Finding case law

5.2.1 In a library

As you will see, there are a range of different paper resources that you can use to find case law in a library. This section will give you an overview of the main resources available with some worked examples of their use. However, this is no substitute for practice.

 Practical exercise

Go to a law library and have a look at as many of these resources as you can. In doing so, you will become familiar with their contents and layout as well as their location in the library.

5.2.1.1 If you know the citation

If you know the citation for the case you want to find, then you simply need to find if the library carries the particular series of reports to which the citation refers. If so, look along the shelf for the year and volume you have identified from the citation. The report you require should be at the page listed in the citation.

Sometimes, however, this will not be so. Citations can sometimes be misprinted, or you may have misinterpreted the abbreviation for the report series. Double-check your citation. If the report still proves elusive, or the library does not carry the particular series of reports you want, then you will have to find an alternative citation. The rest of this section describes a range of ways in which you may do so.

Current Law Case Citator

The *Current Law Case Citator* is published in a number of volumes covering date ranges within which cases have been published or referred to in court as follows:

- 1947–1976
- 1977–1988
- 1989–2002

Updates to the *Citator* are provided annually from 2002. In the current year, monthly updates are printed in the *Current Law Monthly Digest*.

If you do not know the date of the case, you should search through each of the volumes in order, starting with the oldest. You should then move through to the most recent month. By being methodical, you will make sure that you do not miss anything of importance.

The *Citator*'s list cases in alphabetical order by the name of the first party. Criminal cases (such as *R* v *G*[2] for example) are listed under 'R'. Remember here that the *R* is short for 'Regina' or 'Rex' (depending on who was head of state at the time of the case), meaning 'the Queen' or 'the King'.

Look at the extract from the *Current Law Case Citator* 2003. This shows a list of cases. You should be able to find our example of *R* v *G* at the bottom of the page together with a list of places in which this particular case has been reported.

CASE CITATOR 2003	*R* v G
R v Friskies Petcare (UK) Ltd [2000] 2 Cr App. R. (S) 401 CA (Crim Div)	*Digested* 01/3296
	Considered 03/1923 03/3715

R *v* G see Attorney General's Reference (No.1 of 2001), Re
R *v* G see Attorney General's Reference (No.9 of 2003), Re
R *v* G, R *v* R [2003] UKHL 50; [2003] 3 W.L.R. 1060; [2003] 4 All E. R. 765,
    (2003) 167 J.P. 621; (2003) 167 J.P.N. 955; (2003) 100(43) L.S.G. 31;
    Times, October 17, 2003, HL; reversing [2002] EWCA Crim 1992;
    [2003] 3 All E.R. 206; [2003] 1 Cr. App. R. 23; [2002] Cnm. L.R. 926,
    Times, August 1, 2002; *Independent*. October 21, 2002 (C.S),
    CA (Crim Div) . . . . *Digested*, 03/775
    Applied, 03/1692

Extract 5.1 *Current Law Case Citator*

Self-test questions

1. What is the neutral citation for the House of Lords judgment in *R* v *G?*

2. How would you interpret the neutral citation? In which court was the case decided?

3. In which other journals was it reported?

4. Which of the reports (if any) should be cited in court?

Answers to the self-test questions can be found on the Online Resource Centre.

After the list of citations you will see 'Digested 03/775'. This indicates that the case was digested (i.e. summarized) in the *Current Law Yearbook* 2003 as case number 775.

The *Citator* also provides information regarding the judicial history of the case. In this example you will see a references to another (digested) case where R *v* G was applied—03/1692. In other cases you will see that certain decisions have been Applied, Considered, Distinguished, and Followed.

775.   Criminal damage—mens rea—meaning of recklessness in Criminal Damage Act 1971 s.1
        [Criminal Damage Act 1971 s.1.]
        A person acts recklessly within the meaning of the Criminal Damage Act 1971 s.1 in respect of a result when he is aware of a risk that it will occur, and it is, in the circumstances known to him, unreasonable to take that risk. G and R appealed against a decision ([2002] EWCA Crim 1992, [2003] 3 All E.R. 206) upholding their convictions for arson under the Criminal Damage Act 1971 s.1 (1) and s.1 (3). In August 2000 the appellants, who were then aged 11 and 12 respectively, went camping without their parents' permission. During the night they set fire to newspapers in the yard at the back of a shop and threw the lit newspapers under a wheelie bin. They left the yard without putting out the fire. The burning newspapers set fire to the bin and subsequently spread to the shop. Approximately £1 million worth of damage was caused to the shop

---

2.   [2003] 3 WLR 1060.

and adjoining buildings. The appellants' case at trial was that they expected the newspapers to burn themselves out on the concrete floor of the yard and it was accepted that neither of them appreciated the risk of the fire spreading in the way that it did. The trial judge had directed the jury in accordance with the objective test given in *R. V. Caldwell (James)* [1982] A.C. 341, [1981] C.L.Y. 385. The Court of the Appeal certified a point of law of general public importance, namely whether a defendant could properly be convicted under s.1 of the 1971 Act on the basis that he was reckless as to whether property was damaged when he gave no thought to the risk and by reason of his age and/or personal characteristics the risk would not have been obvious to him, even if he had thought about it.

Extract 5.2 *Current Law Yearbook*

This shows the digested report of *R* v *G*. Notice that the *Current Law Yearbook* gives a summary of the case (facts and judgment) only. It is not an official law report. When using the *Current Law Yearbook* you must take care not to confuse the case number with the page number. You will see that case number 775 was summarized on page 346. If you tried looking for page 775 you would quickly find that it is beyond the end of the *Yearbook*.

Law Reports Index

Since 1951, the *Law Reports* have published the *Law Reports Consolidated Index*. These indices are also known as the *Red Index* or the *Red Book* from the distinctive colour of their binding. They are labelled as *Law Reports Index* on the spine of the volume. They are published in hard cover and cover up to a ten-year period. Therefore, there are hardback volumes covering:

- 1951–1960
- 1961–1970
- 1971–1980
- 1981–1990
- 1991–2000

In addition to these, a red paperback volume is also published each year, covering the period from 2001 to the end of the last year.

The *Red Books* are supplemented by *Pink Books*. These are published throughout the present year, usually quarterly (every three months) and list cases covered during the year.

The *Law Reports Index* includes cases from the *Law Reports* (i.e. Queen's Bench Division, Chancery Division, Family Division, and Appeal Cases) as well as cases from other report series as follows:

- *Weekly Law Reports*
- *All England Law Reports*
- *Criminal Appeal Reports*
- *Industrial Cases Reports*
- *Lloyd's Law Reports*
- *Local Government Reports*
- *Road Traffic Reports*
- *Tax Cases*

Look at the extracts from the *Law Reports Index* 2001–05 provided. The list of cases reported also shows a range of possible citations for *R* v *G*.

R v Francom [2001] 1 Cr App R 237, CA
R v G [2002] EWCA Crim 1992; [2003] 3 All ER 206; [2003] 1 Cr App R 343, CA; [2003] UKHL 50; [2004] 1 AC 1034; [2003] 3 WLR 1060; [2003] 4 All ER 765; [2004] 1 Cr App R 237, HL(E)

R v G [2004] EWCA Crim 1240; [2004] 2 Cr App R 638, CA

R v G [2004] EWCA Crim 1368; [2004] 1 WLR 2932; [2004] 2 Cr App R 630, CA

R v G (Autrefois Acquit)[2001] EWCA Crim 1215; [2001]1 WLR 1727; [2001] 2 Cr App R 615, CA

R v G (Interlocutory Appeal: Jurisdiction) [2001] EWCA Crim 442; [2002] 1 WLR 200; [2002]1 Cr App R 147, CA

R v Gibbs. *See* R v Sullivan

Extract 5.3 *Law Reports Index* (Cases Reported)

If, however, you know the subject matter of the case, then the *Law Reports Index* provides an index by subject. You will find *R v G* under the category of 'Arson—*Mens rea*'.

Appeal

Appellate court's discretion

Appeal by prosecution against ruling of no case to answer—Defendant on bail pending trial on related matter—Defendant absconding from jurisdiction before prosecution appeal—Appeal allowed in defendant's absence—Whether defendant procluded from appealing—Appellate court's approach on application to adduce fresh evidence—British Virgin Islands

Benedetto v The Queen, PC [2003] 1 WLR 1545

Arson

Mens rea

Recklessness as to whether or not property would be destroyed or damaged—Whether defendants' acts created obvious risk of damage to property— Whether defendant's age and personal characteristics relevant in assessing obviousness of risk—Criminal Damage Act 1971, s1

R v G, CA [2003] 3 All ER 206; [2003] 1 Cr App R 343

HL(E) [2004] 1 AC 1034; WLR 1060

Extract 5.4 *Law Reports Index* (Subject Matter)

Finally, the *Law Reports Index* also contains a list of cases that have been judicially considered. For instance, *R v G* overruled *R v Caldwell*.[3] Therefore if you look up *R v Caldwell* you will find that it was applied in *R v G* in the Court of Appeal, but departed from in *R v G* in the House of Lords.

R v C (1992) 14 Cr App R (S) 562, CA. Considered, *R v A* [2001] 2 Cr App R 275, CA

R v Caldwell [1982] AC 341; [1981] 2 WLR 509; [1981] 1 All ER 961; 73 Cr App R 13, HL(E). Applied, *R v G* [2003] 3 All ER 206; [2003] 1 Cr App R 343, CA. Departed from, *R v G* [2004] 1 AC 1034; [2003] 3 WLR 1060, HL(E)

R v Camplin [1978] AC 705, 718F; [1978] 2 WLR 679; [1978] 2 All ER 168, HL(E). Applied, *Attorney General for Jersey v Holley* [2005] 2 AC 580; [2005] 3 WLR 29, PC. Considered, *R v Smith (Morgan)* [2001] 1 AC 146; [2000] 3 WLR 654, HL(E). Dictum of Lord Diplock considered, *R v Weller* [2004] 1 Cr App R 1, CA

Extract 5.5 *Law Reports Index* (Cases Judicially Considered)

Practical exercise

Compare the information provided on *R v G* in the *Law Reports Index* 2001–05 with that in the *Current Law Case Citator 2003*. Do you have an opinion as to which resource is easier to use?

The Digest

The Digest was first published in forty-nine volumes between 1919 and 1932. It now comprises over seventy volumes. According to its publisher, its purpose is:

---

3.   [1982] AC 341.

to provide, in digested form, the whole case law of England and Wales, together with a considerable body of cases from the courts of Scotland, Ireland, Canada, Australia, New Zealand and other countries of the Commonwealth. Cases dealing with the law of the European Communities are also included.

The Digest contains summaries of over half a million cases and covers over a thousand different series of law reports. It is currently in its third edition, known as the 'Green Band' edition, due to the green stripe on the spine of each volume. It comprises a number of separate parts:

- Main volumes and *Continuation Volumes*
- *Quarterly Survey*
- *Cumulative Supplement*
- *Consolidated Table of Cases*
- *Consolidated Index*

Main volumes and *Continuation Volumes*

The main volumes and *Continuation Volumes* of *The Digest* contain the digested cases themselves. Each of the volumes deals with a specific subject.

Cumulative Supplement

The *Cumulative Supplement* is published as an annual update to *The Digest*.

Quarterly Survey

The *Quarterly Survey* summarizes cases digested since the last *Cumulative Supplement*. It is *not* cumulative.

Consolidated Table of Cases

The *Consolidated Table of Cases* provides an alphabetical list of digested cases.

Consolidated Index

The *Index* provides an alphabetical list of subjects covered by *The Digest* providing for each the main volume number, an abbreviated subject heading, and the relevant digested case reference numbers.

Using *The Digest* to find a specific case

We will use a particular case to show the ways in which the various parts of *The Digest* interrelate. The 1936 case of *Grant v Australian Knitting Mills Ltd*[4] concerned the purchaser of a pair of woollen long-johns. These long-johns unfortunately contained an excess of sulphite chemicals which should have been removed during the manufacturing process. The presence of these excess sulphites caused the purchaser to contract dermatitis and he sued the manufacturer in negligence. Look at this extract from the *Consolidated Table of Cases*.

Grant v Austen (1816) **1(4) Agcy: 3(2) Bank**
Grant v Australian Knitting Mills Ltd (1933) **16 courts**
Grant v Australian Knitting Mills Ltd (1936) **35(3) Negl; 39(2) S Goods**
Grant v Bagge (1802) **21(2) Exon**
Grant v Baillie (1869) (SCOT) **48(2) Trusts**

Extract 5.6 *Consolidated Table of Cases*

---

4.   [1936] AC 85.

The *Consolidated Table of Cases* shows the entry for this case as follows:

Grant v Australian Knitting Mills Ltd (1936) **35(3) Negl; 39(2) S Goods**

This indicates that it is relevant to two subject areas: namely negligence, which is dealt with in volume 35(3) and sale of goods, which is covered in volume 39(2) (Figure 5.3).

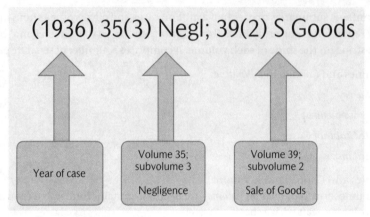

Figure 5.3 A reference in *The Digest*

The subvolume numbers indicate that volumes 35 and 39 are split into more than one physical volume on the shelf.

The next step on finding the digested case is to look at the table of cases at the front of the volumes identified in the *Consolidated Table of Cases*; in this example volume 35(3) and volume 39(2). You will find the case listed again in each of these tables. In volume 35(3) you will find:

xxxi	Vols 35(3) & 35(4) Tables of Cases	
	CASE	CASE
Goldman v Hargrave (1967) 1678	Grant v Australian Knitting Mills Ltd (1936) ...1852	
Goldman v Regina (City) (1967) (CAN) 1444	Grant v Caledoman Ry Co (1870) (CAN) 3191	
Gonzy v Lees (1941) (CAN) 2327	Grant v Drysdale (1883) (SCOT) 4316	

Extract 5.7 Vol 35(3) & 35(4) Table of Cases

and at the front of volume 39(2) the table of cases will show:

Granatta BV v Leievoeders NV (1986) 5107	Guardian Motors Ltd v Canadian Acceptance
Granger v Dacre (1844) 2814	Corpn Ltd (1969) (CAN) 5656
Grant v Australian Knitting Mills Ltd (1936) ..1626	Gueraid v Frith (1957) (CAN) 576
Grant v Cadwell (1851) (CAN) 1767	Gulab Rai-Sagar Mal v Nirbhe Ram-Nagar Mal
Grant v Fletcher (1826) 1012	(1923) (IND) 2358

Extract 5.8 Vol 39(2) & 39(3) Table of Cases

The final step in finding the digested case is to look at the case number provided in the index to each volume. Therefore, *Grant* v *Australian Knitting Mills Ltd* is digested as case number 1852 in volume 35(3) of *The Digest* and also as case 1626 in volume 39(2). These digested cases are listed in order in each of the respective volumes:

1852   Duty to warn purchaser of dangerous character — Liability to third party — Article dangerous owing to unknown defect
Appellant, who contracted dermatitis of external origin as the result of wearing a woollen garment which, when purchased from the retailers, was in a defective condition owing to the presence of

excess sulphites which, it was found, had been negligently left in it in the process of manufacture, claimed damages against both retailers and manufacturers.

.

.

Grant v Australian Knitting Mills Ltd [1936] AC 85; [1935] All ER Rep 209; 105 LJPC 6; 154 LT 18; 52 TLR 38; 79 Sol Jo 815, PC

ANNOTATIONS **Distd** Evans v Triplex Safety Glass Co [1936] 1 All ER 283; Howard v Furness Houlder Argentine Lines Ltd and Brown Ltd [1936] 2 All ER 781; Kubach v Hollands [1937] 3 All ER 907 Consd Dransfield v British Insulated Cables Ltd [1937] 4 All ER 382; Herschtal v Stewart & Ardern Ltd [1940] 1 KB 155; Barnett v Packer & Co [1940] 3 All ER 575; Godley v Perry [1960] 1 All ER 36; Bartlett v Sidney Marcus Ltd [1965] 2 All ER 753; Beale v Taylor [1967] 3 All ER 253; BS Brown & Son Ltd v Craiks Ltd [1970] 1 All ER 823 **Apld** H Parsons (Livestock) Ltd v Uttley Ingham & Co Ltd [1978] 1 All ER 525; (dicta Lord Wright) B v Islington Health Authority [1991] 1 All ER 825

Extract 5.9 Digested case 1852 in Vol 35(3)

1626 Application of rule — Manufactured article — Woollen underwear
Appellant who contracted dermatitis of an external origin as the result of wearing a woollen garment

.

Held

The retailers were liable in contract for breach of implied warranty or condition under exceptions (i) and (ii) of s 14 of the South Australia Sale of Goods Act 1895, which is identical with the English Sale of Goods Act 1893 (c 71) s 14.

Grant v Australian Knitting Mills Ltd [1936] AC 85; [1935] All ER Rep 209; 105 LJPC 6;154 LT 18; 52 TLR 38; 79 Sol Jo 815, PC

ANNOTATIONS **Consd** Bartlett v Sidney Marcus Ltd [1965] 2 All ER 753; Beale v Taylor [1967] 3 All ER 253 **Apld** (dicta Lord Wright) B v Islington Health Authority [1991] 1 All ER 825

Extract 5.10 Digested case 1626 in Vol 39(2)

You will also notice that the reports in *The Digest* are annotated to show cases which have been distinguished (Distd), considered (Consd) and applied (Apld). Other annotations which may appear in *The Digest* are shown in Table 5.5.

Table 5.5 Annotations used in *The Digest*

Annotation	Meaning
Apld	Applied
Apprvd	Approved
Consd	Considered
Disapproved	Disapproved
Distd	Distinguished
Dbtd	Doubted
Expld	Explained
Extd	Extended
Folld	Followed
NF	Not followed
Overd	Overruled

Using *The Digest* to find cases on a specific topic

You can also use *The Digest* to find cases in a specific subject area. For a general review of a wide area, start by consulting the table of contents at the front of the volume which covers the area you wish to review. Alternatively, use the *Consolidated Index* for access to all subjects covered by *The Digest*.

Look at this extract from the *Consolidated Index*.

MANUFACTURER 47(3) *Trade* 357, 423, 424
duty to warn purchaser of danger
    article dangerous in itself **35(3)** *Negl* 1848, 1849, 1873–1898
    article dangerous owing to unknown defect **35(3)** *Negl* 1850–1856, 1886–1898
    corn solvent **35(3)** *Negl* 1864
    generally **35(3)** *Negl* 1870, 1871
    goods not tested by retailer **35(3)** *Negl* 1858–1860
    hair dye **35(3)** *Negl* 1861–1863
    liability of purchaser's employee **35(3)** *Negl* 1866
    onus of proof **35(3)** *Negl* 1857
    toys not complying with safety regulations **35(3)** *Negl* 1869

Extract 5.11 *Consolidated Index*

This shows that cases concerning a manufacturer's duty to warn purchasers of danger where the article is dangerous owing to an unknown defect are:

35(3) *Negl* 1850–1856, 1886–1898

These cases can be found in volume 35(3) as before and will include *Grant* v *Australian Knitting Mills Ltd* (case 1852).

Using *The Digest*: a summary

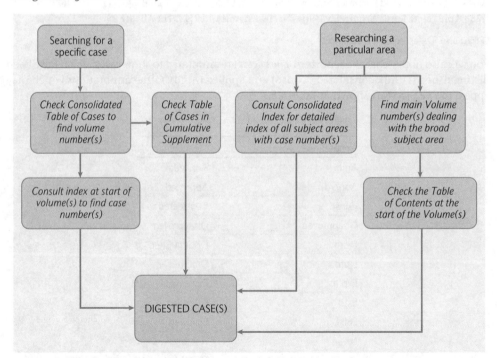

Figure 5.4 Using *The Digest*. Adapted from *The Digest: A User's Guide* (1994) London: Butterworths, p. 12.

Figure 5.4 will show you the steps you need to use *The Digest*. You may wish to use it in conjunction with the previous sections.

5.2.2 Online

 Links to the sites mentioned in this section can also be found on the Online Resource Centre.

 Practical exercise

Find as many of the legal databases from this section as you can. Make a list of those to which you are allowed access. Have a look at each of them. Perform a few practice searches.

5.2.2.1 Which database?

Although there are a number of different legal databases available online, not all databases contain all reports. Table 5.6 table provides a summary of some of the more common report series and the database (or databases in which they are covered).

Table 5.6 Law reports and electronic databases

Series	Citation	Database and dates
The Law Reports	AC, QB, Ch, Fam	Westlaw (1865–)
		Lexis (1865–)
		Justis
Weekly Law Reports	WLR	Westlaw
		Justis
All England Law Reports	All ER	Lexis
English Reports	ER	Justis
All England Law Reports European Cases	All ER (EC)	Lexis (1995–)
Butterworths Company Law Cases	BCLC	Lexis (1983–)
Butterworths Medico-Legal Reports	BMLR	Lexis (1986–)
Common Market Law Reports	CMLR	Westlaw (1962–)
Criminal Appeal Reports	Cr App R	Westlaw (1990–)
European Commercial Cases	ECC	Westlaw (1978–)
European Human Rights Reports	EHRR	Justis, Westlaw (1979/80–)
Family Court Reporter	FCR	Lexis (1998–)
Human Rights Law Reports	HRLR	Westlaw (2000–)
Industrial Cases Reports	ICR	Justis, Westlaw (1972–)
Industrial Relations Law Reports	IRLR	Lexis (1972–)
Landlord & Tenant Reports	L&TR	Westlaw (1998–)
Personal Injury & Quantum Reports	PIQR	Westlaw (1992–)
Tax Cases	TC	Lexis

5.2.2.2 How do the databases work?

A detailed description of the operation of each of the various databases is beyond the scope of this book. Most institutions provide a guide to using each of the main databases and you should check with your law librarian for details. LexisNexis and Westlaw often have student representatives at institutions. They are another useful source of information.

In general terms, the databases allow you to search by a name, citation or keywords, or any combination of the above. The best strategy with all database searches is to try and keep it as simple as possible. For instance if you are searching for a case called *DPP* v *Majewski* it would be simple to put in the appellant's name. It is an uncommon name so you would therefore not expect there to be too many cases involving a party called Majewski.

However, if the case was *R* v *Smith* and you did not know the year, you would need to try to find some appropriate subject-matter keywords to narrow your search results; otherwise you would very likely end up with an unmanageable number of potential cases. The pictures that follow in this chapter show the options available on the main search screen of a range of different online resources.

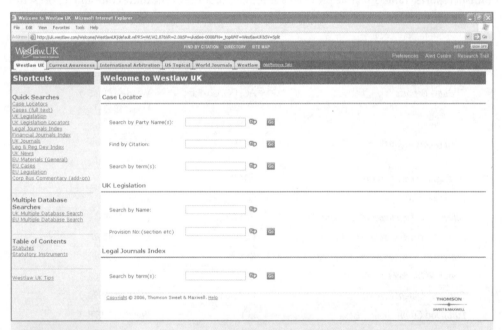

5.2.2.3 Westlaw

Westlaw allows searching for cases by party name, citation, or keyword. Even if the case is not available on full text in Westlaw, links will be given to the location of the report or transcript (if available). Westlaw also contains transcripts of recent cases. However, Westlaw does not contain all series of reports (see the table above) and for this reason it is often best used together with another broad database such as LexisNexis. Westlaw also incorporates the *Current Law Case Citator*, but presents it as its 'Case Locator' service.

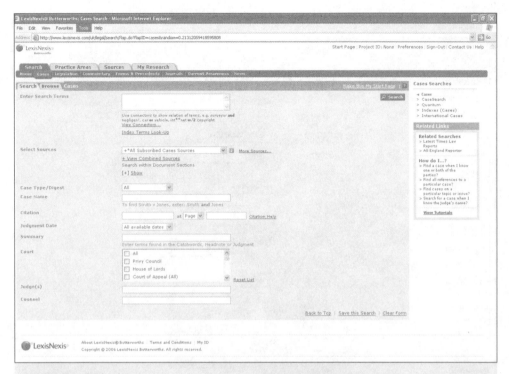

5.2.2.4 LexisNexis

Like Westlaw, LexisNexis is also a subscription service which contains a very broad selection of reports. As well as the standard search criteria it also allows searches by the judge (or judges) or searches for cases which refer to a particular statutory provision. This can be useful if you need to research how a particular piece of legislation has been applied by the courts.

5.2.2.5 Lawtel

Lawtel is updated daily. It includes the following:

- A daily update
- Summaries of cases 1980–, with some links to full text from 1993–
- Personal injury quantum reports
- Practice directions 1980–

It contains summaries and transcripts only. The summaries provide links to full reports. Lawtel covers an immense range of cases and often carries judgments which are not included in the other databases.

(Cont.)

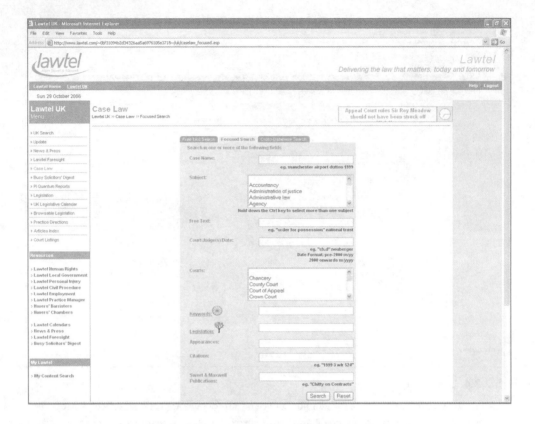

5.2.2.6 Justis

Justis contains the *Law Reports, English Reports, Industrial Cases Reports*, and *Family Law Reports*. It also contains the *Weekly Law Reports*. It is a full text online legal library of UK, Irish, and EU case law dating back to 1163 and legislation from 1235. Justis 2.0 introduced a range of new features including exact replica PDF files of reported cases.

5.2.2.7 Casetrack

Casetrack is a subscription service provided by Merrill Legal Solutions. It contains judgments as follows:

- Court of Appeal (Criminal and Civil Divisions) from April 1996 to present
- Administrative Court from April 1996 to present
- All divisions of the High Court from July 1998 to present
- Employment Appeal Tribunal from July 1998 to present
- VAT Tribunal from January 2002 to present
- Selected judgments from the European Court of Human Rights and the European Court of Justice

Merrill Legal Solutions is the official source of Court of Appeal and Administrative Court transcripts. This means that handed-down approved judgments are often available within hours (and in one instance, 26 minutes).

(Cont.)

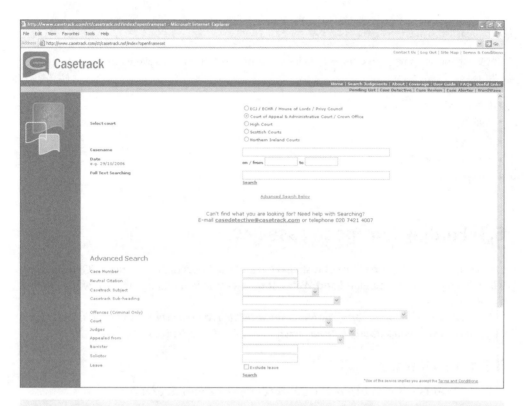

5.2.2.8 BAILII

BAILII is a free service which contains judgments from a wide range of sources. It has an extremely comprehensive coverage of case law. BAILII's coverage extends beyond England and Wales to Scotland, Northern Ireland, and the European Union.

It can be found at **www.bailii.org**. It allows searching by keyword and first named party.

5.2.2.9 JustCite

JustCite includes:

- Primary case law series, such as The *Weekly Law Reports* (ICLR), *All England Law Reports* (Butterworths), *Irish Reports* (ICLRI) and *Session Cases* (SCLR)

- Specialist case law series, including *Criminal Appeal Reports* (Sweet & Maxwell), *Industrial Cases Reports* (ICLR) and *Lloyd's Law Reports* (Informa)

- Transcripts from the Courts of Appeal, Administrative Court, and the High Court (Smith Bernal Reporting)

Practical exercise

Try to find the following cases using each of the databases from their names alone:

- *Dudley* v *Stephens*
- *Eves* v *Eves*
- *Nettleship* v *Weston*
- *Pennington* v *Waine*
- *R* v *Gold; R* v *Schifreen*
- *R* v *Mirza*

5.3 Finding European case law

Decisions of the European Court of Justice (ECJ) and the Court of First Instance (CFI) also have a bearing on the law of England and Wales. It follows that you will need to know how to find European case law.

For a reminder of the operation of the European Institutions and Courts, see section 4.3. The effect of European cases on the doctrine of judicial precedent is covered in section 6.4.

5.3.1 In a library

5.3.1.1 *Reports of Cases before the Court* (*European Court Reports*)

The official reports of cases are found in the *Reports of Cases before the Court*. These are more commonly referred to as the *European Court Reports*, abbreviated to ECR. The reports are structured differently from those of England and Wales. Their component parts are as follows.

Table 5.7 Components of the *European Court Reports*

Reports before 1994	Reports since 1994
Report for the hearing	
Advocate-General's opinion	Advocate-General's opinion
Judgment of the court	Judgment of the court

The report for the hearing was included in reports before 1994. This is a summary of the facts and legal arguments prepared for the court by a 'reporting judge'. The Advocate-General's opinion is precisely that—an opinion. Therefore, it is not binding (although in practice is it usually followed). It contains a detailed analysis of the facts and legal arguments. The judgment of the court is a single judgment, even though there are always at least three judges hearing the case. Unlike the courts of England and Wales, separate concurring or dissenting judgments are not permitted.

Since 1990 the *Reports* have been split into two parts. Part I covers reports of cases from the ECJ and Part II contains cases from the CFI.

The main problem with the *European Court Reports* is the delay in publication. The courts can hear cases in any of the eleven official languages of the European Union, although they work in French. Judgments have to be translated into each of the official languages. This can take up to two years since the translations must be accurate and precise in each of the languages. Therefore, because of this delay, it is very difficult to use the *Reports* for relatively recent cases.

5.3.1.2 Citation of European cases

European cases are cited differently from those in England and Wales. We will use the following two cases by way of example.

Case C-295/95 *Farrell* v *Long* [1997] ECR I-1683

Case T-119/89 *Tellesonié re* v *Commission* [1990] ECR II-7

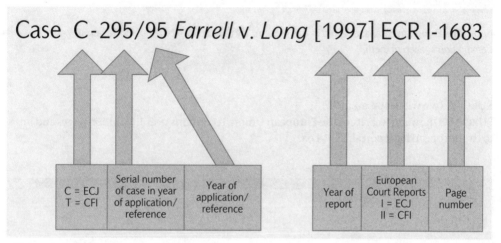

Figure 5.5 Citing European cases

We therefore know that *Farrell* v *Long* was the 295th case (serial number) reported to the ECJ (serial number is prefixed by C and the report appears in Part I of the ECR) in 1995 (the year of application or reference is '95'). It was reported in Part I of the ECR for 1997 at page 1683.

However *Tellesonié re* v *Commission* was heard in the Court of First Instance. The case reference is prefixed by T (from the French *Tribunal*) and it is reported in Part II of the ECR for 1990 at page 7. It was the 119th case heard by the CFI in 1989.

You will notice from both these examples that there is a lapse of time between the hearings (1995 and 1989 respectively) and the official reports (1997 and 1990 respectively). This illustrates the delay in publication.

5.3.1.3 *Common Market Law Reports*

The *Common Market Law Reports* are published commercially by Sweet & Maxwell, first appearing in 1962. They are issued weekly. These reports appear more quickly than those in the *European Court Reports* but you must bear in mind that they are not official reports. It reports significant cases only; not all cases.

5.3.1.4 *All England Law Reports (European Cases)*

The *All England Law Reports (European Cases)* have been published commercially by Butterworths since 1995. They are published ten times a year and includes the full text of a selection of cases.

5.3.1.5 *Proceedings of the Court of Justice*

The *Proceedings of the Court of Justice and the Court of First Instance of the European Communities* is a weekly bulletin which provides brief details of the cases being heard during that week. It is not authoritative, but it is of great use as a source of information on recent judgments, given the lengthy delays in publications of the official reports. Unfortunately, an index is not published until after end of the year which makes its use during the year somewhat more difficult. It does, however, remain useful as a current awareness tool.

Practical exercise

Access the European databases listed in this section. Try to find *Farrell* v *Long and Tellesonié re* v *Commission* in each of them.

EUROPA (www.europa.eu.int)

EUROPA is the main website of the European Union. It contains over 1.5 million pages and links to the European legal portal, EUR-Lex.

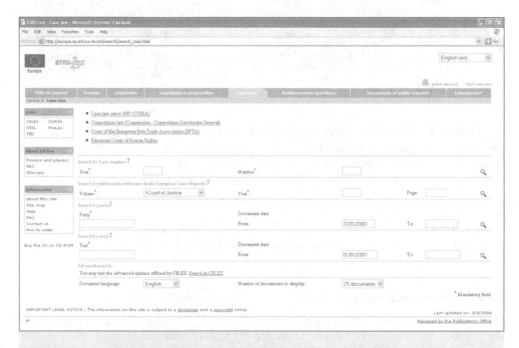

EUR-Lex (www.europa.eu.int/eur-lex/en)

EUR-Lex includes coverage of the judgments of the ECJ and the CFI. It also includes opinions of the Advocates-General as published in the *European Court Reports*. It is updated daily.

CELEX

CELEX is the official multilingual legal database of the European Union. It contains the full text of the *European Court Reports*. It is available as a subscription service via EUROPA, or commercially via a number of commercial publishers such as Justis CELEX and Eurolaw. The commercial variants offer a broader range of search facilities.

Other databases

LexisNexis, Lawtel, and Westlaw also provide search facilities for European cases (see section 5.2 for details).

5.4 Finding decisions of the European Court of Human Rights

The final cases that you will need to find are those decided in the European Court of Human Rights.

The operation of the European Court of Human Rights was dealt with in section 4.4.

5.4.1 In a library

5.4.1.1 Official reports

The first series of official reports were published in *Publications of the European Court of Human Rights, Series A: Judgments and Decisions*. Series B contained pleadings, oral arguments, and other supporting documentation. These reports cover the period up until the end of 1995.

From 1996 onwards, the official reports are published in *Reports of Judgments and Decisions*. There is usually a delay of about a year from the date of the judgment before a case report is published.

5.4.1.2 Citation of cases from the European Court of Human Rights

European Court of Human Rights cases are cited differently from those in England and Wales and differently from those in the European Court of Justice and Court of First Instance.

For cases reported in *Publications of the European Court of Human Rights, Series A: Judgments and Decisions* the correct form of citation is, for example:

Golder v United Kingdom (1975) Series A, no. 18

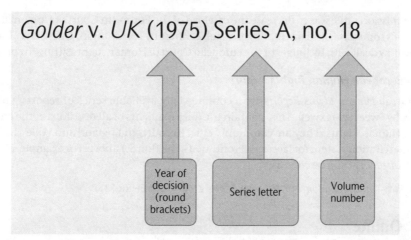

Figure 5.6 Citing ECtHR cases

For cases reported from 1996 in *Judgments and Decisions*, the citations take the following form:

Robins v United Kingdom RJD 1997-V 18, 01

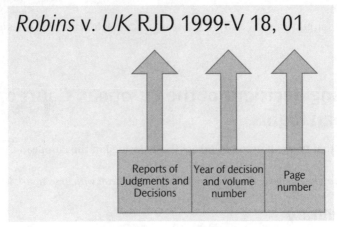

Figure 5.7 Citing cases reported in *Judgments and Decisions*

5.4.1.3 European Commission of Human Rights

The European Commission of Human Rights, which was abolished on 31 October 1998, published its decisions in the following reports:

Table 5.8 Reports of the European Commission of Human Rights

1955–73	*Collection of Decisions of the European Commission of Human Rights* (vols 1–46)
1974–98	*Decisions and Reports* (vol. 46 onwards)

These reports are cited following the usual citation system for law reports outlined in section 5.1 above. For example:

X v UK (1967) 25 CD 76
S v UK (1986) 47 DR 274

The Commission's role was to decrease the caseload of the European Court of Human Rights by filtering out some cases and attempting to resolve others by conciliation. Questions of admissibility are now dealt with by judges of the European Court of Human Rights sitting in committee.

5.4.1.4 *European Human Rights Reports*

The *European Human Rights Reports* are a commercially available series of reports, published monthly by Sweet & Maxwell. They contain the full judgments of all decisions of the European Court of Human Rights. They are commonly cited in courts in England and Wales and follow the normal citation system for law reports outlined in section 5.1 above. For example, *Handyside v United Kingdom* would be cited as:

Handyside v United Kingdom (1976) Series A, No. 24; (1976) 1 EHRR 737

5.4.2 Online

5.4.2.1 HUDOC (http://cmiskp.echr.coe.int/tkp197/search.asp?skin=hudoc-en)

HUDOC is the official database of the European Court of Human Rights and contains all judgments. It is available without charge.

(Cont.)

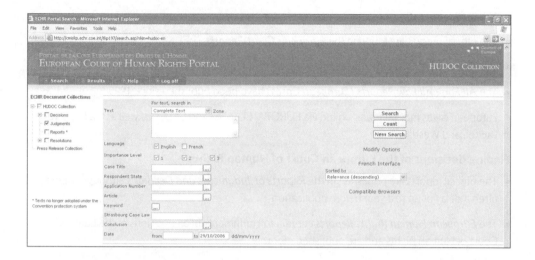

5.4.2.2 Cases pending

A list of ECtHR cases pending can be found online at:

http://www.echr.coe.int/ECHR/EN/Header/Pending+Cases/Pending+cases/Calendar+of+scheduled+hearings/

5.4.2.3 Other databases

Lawtel, Westlaw, Justis, and Casetrack also provide search facilities for cases decided in the ECtHR.

 CHAPTER SUMMARY

Finding case law

- The *Current Law Case Citator* covers cases from 1947

- The *Law Reports Index* covers cases from 1951

- The *Digest* aims to provide the whole case law of England and Wales

- Common case databases include Westlaw, LexisNexis, Lawtel, Justis, Casetrack, BAILII, and JustCite

Finding European case law

- The official reports are found in the *European Court Reports*

- The *Common Market Law Reports* cover significant European Cases from 1962

- The *All England Law Reports (European Cases)* have been published since 1995

- European cases may be found online via EUROPA, EUR-Lex and CELEX as well as via LexisNexis, Lawtel, and Westlaw

Finding decisions of the European Court of Human Rights

- The official reports are published in the *Reports of Judgments and Decisions* although there is often a delay of up to a year before publication

- The *European Human Rights Reports* contain full judgments of all decisions of the European Court of Human Rights and are published monthly

- ECtHR cases may also be found online via HUDOC as well as via Lawtel, Westlaw, Justis, and Casetrack

FURTHER READING

- Clinch P. (2001) *Using a Law Library* (2nd edn) London: Blackstone Press, pp. 99–106.

- Smith, A.T.H. (2002) *Glanville Williams: Learning the Law* (12th edn), London: Sweet & Maxwell, pp. 35–41.
  These give a more detailed account of the history of law reporting.

- http://www.lawreports.co.uk/AboutICLR/history.htm.
  Further detail on the history of the ICLR.

- Smith A.T.H. (2002) *Glanville Williams: Learning the Law* (12th edn), London: Sweet & Maxwell, p. 40.
  For a full description of the evolution of the *Law Reports* from 1865 to 1891

- *The Cardiff Index to Legal Abbreviations* http://www.legalabbrevs.cardiff.ac.uk/.
  An excellent online resource for deciphering unfamiliar citations.

- There are a number of printed guides to legal abbreviations, including Raistrick, D. (1993) *Index to Legal Citations and Abbreviations*, Bowker-Saur; *Current Law; Sweet and Maxwell's Guide to Law Reports and Statutes; Legal Journals Index* and *The Digest*.

- For a detailed description of using *The Digest*, see *The Digest: A User's Guide* (1994) London: Butterworths.

Using cases

6

INTRODUCTION

The two previous chapters described why case law is an important source of law and gave you the skills necessary to find it. This chapter will build on these skills by discussing how to use cases. It will firstly look at the 'anatomy' of a law report, before considering the means by which the key legal principles can be extracted from the case. Once the legal principles are known we will then consider the extent to which those principles are binding on other courts via the doctrine of judicial precedent. Finally, the chapter will consider the impact of both the Human Rights Act 1998 and European law on the operation of precedent.

The ability to use cases is a vital legal skill. You will come across a multitude of cases throughout your legal career, so you must be able to work with them effectively. Knowledge of the operation of precedent is also vital, since you will need to know whether the case which you hope to rely upon will have any legal force in the court where your case is being heard. Equally, when you chart the development of particular areas of law you must understand how the decisions given in cases change the law over time depending on the court in which they are heard. Therefore understanding cases is key to each and every area of law.

LEARNING OUTCOMES

After studying this chapter, you will be able to:

- Navigate a law report and identify its component parts

- Understand the meaning of case citations

- Explain the use of the neutral citation system

- Outline the operation of the doctrine of judicial precedent and explain whether a particular court will be bound by a particular decision

- Determine the *ratio decidendi* of a case and distinguish it from the *obiter dicta*

- Demonstrate how courts can avoid being bound by 'difficult' precedents

- Assess the impact of European law and the Human Rights Act 1998 on the system of precedent

6.1 Reading cases

6.1.1 Anatomy of a case

Before you can start making effective use of cases, you will need to understand the layout of a reported case and the information that the reports provide. You will then be able to move on to

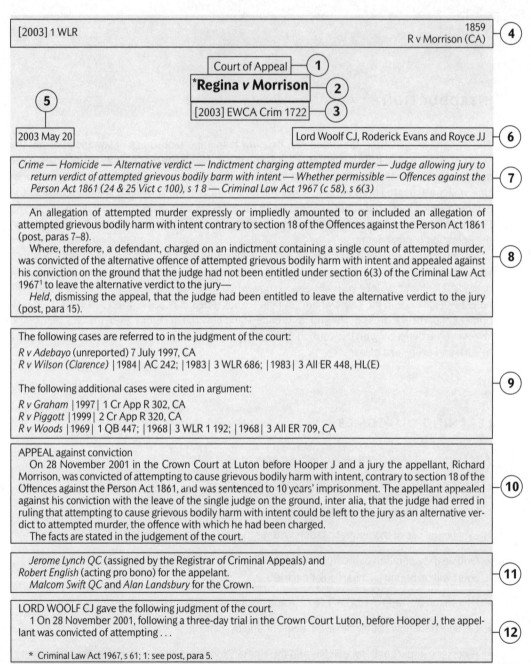

Figure 6.1 *R* v *Morrison*: first page

analysing the information that you have been able to glean from the case before you. We will use a real example: *R v Morrison*.[1] Part of this case is provided as Figure 6.1. Each of the high-lighted areas of the report will be covered in turn.

6.1.2 Case name (2)

The name of this case is *Regina* v *Morrison*. This is a criminal case and, as such, one of the parties involved is the Crown, indicated by *Regina*. If the monarch at the time of the case was a King then the masculine form *Rex* would be used instead of *Regina*. *Regina* (or *Rex*) is often abbreviated to *R.*, so the parties to this case could equally well be referred to as *R v Morrison*. If you were saying the name of the case (in a moot or presentation for example) you would call it 'the Crown against Morrison'. A common mistake is to say the 'v' as 'versus'. This is incorrect. The person against whom a criminal case is brought is referred to as the 'defendant'.

In civil cases, the names of the two parties are used. The first party is the claimant (the person bringing the claim) and the second party is the respondent (the person against whom the claim is brought). For example, in the famous case of *Donoghue* v *Stevenson*,[2] the parties were Mrs Donoghue (claimant) and Stevenson (respondent). The correct way to say the name of this case is 'Donoghue *and* Stevenson'. Once again, the 'v' is not said as 'versus'.

You may also encounter the word 'plaintiff'. This is identical in meaning to 'claimant' in civil proceedings. Under the Civil Procedure Rules, the term 'claimant' should be used.

On appeal, the names of the parties change. The person bringing an appeal is the 'appellant' and the person against whom the appeal is brought is known as the 'respondent'.

There are other commonly encountered forms of case name as shown by the examples in Table 6.1 below:

Table 6.1 Case citations

R v Secretary of State for Foreign and Commonwealth Affairs, ex parte World Development Movement Ltd[3]	Judicial review cases prior to 2001 are cited as the Crown against a particular public body *ex parte* (on behalf of) an applicant. *Ex parte* is sometimes abbreviated to *ex p.*
R (Quintavalle) v Secretary of State for Health[4]	Judicial review cases after 2001 are cited with the applicant's name in brackets after the 'R'. Such cases are spoken as 'the Crown *on the application of* Quintaville against the Secretary of State for Health'
R v R[5]	Family cases are usually kept anonymous. There is some scope for confusion here if one of the parties names begins with 'R'. It would not then be immediately apparent whether the case in question was a criminal matter or a civil matter. However, the facts of the particular case should make this clear very quickly.
Re W; Re: A; Re: B (Change of name)[6]	Cases in the family courts often have some explanatory subject-matter text associated with them in order to aid identification and differentiation.

1. [2003] EWCA Crim 1732; 1 WLR 1859.
2. [1932] All ER Rep 1.
3. [1995] 1 WLR 386.
4. [2003] 2 AC 687.
5. [1992] 1 AC 599.
6. [1999] 2 FLR 930.

Table 6.1 (*Cont.*)

In re: Jones[7] *(or Re Jones)*	'In the matter of' Jones. This citation is often used in cases involving wills or probate.
Liesbosch Dredger[8]	Shipping cases are conventionally referred to by the name of the vessel involved.

6.1.3 Court (1)

The court in which the case was heard; in this case, the Court of Appeal. It is important to know which court heard the case because of the doctrine of judicial precedent.

6.1.4 Neutral citation (3)

The neutral citation of this case is '[2003] EWCA Crim 1722'.
    For information on the operation of the neutral citation system, see section 5.1.2.2.

6.1.5 Case citation—law report (4)

The citation for this particular reported case is '[2003] 1 WLR 1859'.
    For a detailed description of case citations, see chapter 5.

6.1.6 Date of the hearing and judgment (5)

This case was heard and the judgment was given on 20 May 2003. Remember that the year of the judgment might be different from the year of the report.

In a *reserved judgment*, the judges take time after the hearing to consider the issues and provide a written judgment at a later date. The date of the written judgment will be given before the judgment after the words *cur adv vult*. This is short for *curia advisari vult* (literally 'the court wishes to be advised').

In the House of Lords, judgments are always reserved and are usually preceded by the words 'Their Lordships took time for consideration'. Strictly speaking, House of Lords judgments are known as 'opinions'.

6.1.7 Judges (6)

In this case the Court of Appeal comprised Lord Chief Justice Woolf, Mr Justice Roderick Evans, and Mr Justice Royce. It is sometimes useful to know the seniority or reputation of the judges involved in making a particular decision since this may affect the extent to which the judgment may be persuasive (if it is not automatically binding).

6.1.8 Subject matter (7)

This section contains a series of catchwords which are provided by the editors of the law report. It provides a very brief list of the subject matter and key legal points of the case as well as any references to particular statutory provisions which the case considers (in this case, s. 18 of the Offences against the Person Act 1861 and s. 6(3) of the Criminal Law Act 1967). These points are also repeated in the summaries at the start of each volume of the reports.

---

7.   [1931] 1 Ch 375.
8.   [1933] AC 449.

6.1.9 Headnote (8)

The headnote contains a summary of the case. However, the headnote carries no legal authority. It is prepared by the reporter and not by the judges. Although it usually carries an accurate summary of the case, it sometimes does not. For instance in *Young* v *Bristol Aeroplane Co.*[9]—a case which we will return to later in this chapter when we consider the doctrine of judicial precedent—the headnote states that:

> (b) [The Court of Appeal] must refuse to follow a decision of its own which, though not expressly overruled, is inconsistent with a decision of the House of Lords

 whereas the actual text of the judgment says that:

> The third is where this court comes to the conclusion that a previous decision, although not expressly overruled, cannot stand with a *subsequent* (emphasis added) decision of the House of Lords.

Therefore the headnote of the case should always be used with some caution and you should read the whole report.

The headnote may also usefully summarize the effect of the case on the existing case law, using the terms in Table 6.2.

Table 6.2 Headnote terminology

Affirmed	The court in the present case agreed with the decision of a lower court on the same case
Applied	The court in this case considered itself to be bound by the precedent set by an earlier (and different) case and has therefore used the same legal reasoning in the present case
Approved	The court in the present case agreed with the decision of a lower court in a different case
Considered	The court discussed a different case. This is often a case that has been decided by a court at the same level in the hierarchy
Distinguished	The court in the present case does not wish to (or cannot) overrule a previous decision and also does not wish to apply it. It has found sufficient differences between the cases to avoid being bound by the earlier case
Overruled	The court in the present case has overturned a decision in a different case, usually made in a lower court (although occasionally in a court of equal status)
Reversed	The court in the present case on appeal overturned the decision of a lower court in the same case
Semble	(literally 'it appears') The court gives an opinion on a point that is not directly at issue in this case. (This is *obiter dictum*)

The effect of the existing case law is explained in detail in section 6.2 on the doctrine of judicial precedent.

6.1.10 List of cases (9)

The report provides a list of cases in two sections. The first section contains two cases (*Adebayo* and *Wilson* (*Clarence*)) which were referred to by the judges in their judgment. The second section contains a list of cases (*Graham*, *Piggott*, and *Woods*) which counsel also raised in argument

9   [1944] KB 718.

but which were not referred to by the judges. These cases are of less importance than those referred to directly by the judges.

6.1.11 Details of the action (10)

This section of the report provides a brief history of the case proceeding to date. In this case, the Court of Appeal (Criminal Division) is considering an appeal against a ten-year conviction for causing grievous bodily harm with intent. Any relevant statute law is usually stated in this section (as well as in the catchwords).

6.1.12 Counsel (11)

The names of counsel who appeared for each party in the case are listed. These may be barristers or solicitor advocates. Senior barristers are known as 'Queen's Counsel' and designated by the letters QC. The names of the barristers are particularly useful to solicitors. If a similar case comes up again, then solicitors may choose to instruct barristers who have success or experience in similar cases.

This section also informs us that Robert English was acting '*pro bono*'—that is, without charge.

6.1.13 The judgment (12)

The judgment is the most important part of the report. Where there is more than one judge hearing a particular case, each judge may deliver his own judgment. Typically one judge—usually, but not always, the most senior—delivers the first judgment. The other judges may then give their own judgments. These may be as brief as 'I agree' or given at length and dissenting (i.e. disagreeing with) from one or more of the other judgments.

Judgments often (but not always) are broken down as follows:

- Summary of the material facts of the case
- Statement of the applicable law
- Legal reasoning
- Decision

Some reports also contain a summary of the arguments presented by counsel for each side. An example of such a report can be found in *R (Holding & Barnes plc)* v *Secretary of State for the Environment, Transport and the Regions*.[10]

Practical exercise

Look up the *Holding & Barnes plc* case referred to here and find the summary of counsels' arguments.

The judgment in *R* v *Morrison* is divided up into numbered paragraphs. The report also contains marginal letters for ease of reference. Pinpoint referencing provides a useful way of referencing particular quotations from a judgement in a piece of legal writing or to support an argument put forward in a moot. The reader (or judge) may then direct their attention easily to the precise wording to which you wish to draw reference.

Under the neutral citation system, precise (or pinpoint) references to paragraphs of the judgment are given by appending 'at [X]' to the neutral citation, where X is the paragraph number of the judgment (Figure 6.2).

---

10.   [2003] 2 AC 295.

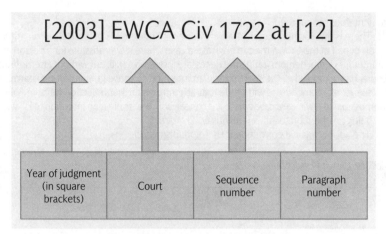

Figure 6.2 The neutral citation for *R* v *Morrison* with paragraph reference

The citation [2003] EWCA Civ 1722 at [12] therefore refers to the twelfth paragraph.

In older cases where numbered paragraphs are not used then the page number is used to pin-point the reference. In this instance, the paragraph in question is on page 1863 and its citation would be [2003] 1 WLR 1859, 1863. It is conventional always to cite the first page of the report.

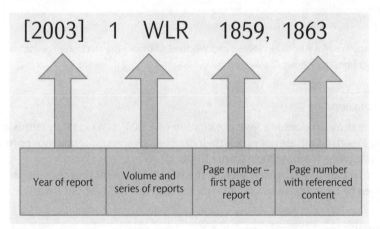

Figure 6.3 *The Weekly Law Reports* citation for *R* v *Morrison* with page reference

For greater accuracy you can also append the marginal letter from the relevant part of the page.

Choose the marginal letter that is closest to the text. For example, the first passage on the page could be cited as [2003] 1 WLR 1859, 1863A.

You should note, however, that if you use one of the electronic databases to retrieve a copy of a case, the paragraph numbers or marginal letters may not be reproduced.

6.1.14 Solicitors and reporter (13)

The end of the report shown in Figure 6.4 gives details of the solicitors who represented each party and instructed counsel on their behalf. Finally, the name or initials of the reporter are provided.

C   argument does not succeed.

   14 There is one further matter to which we should refer. In his helprun skeleton argument, Mr Swift on behalf of the Crown tried to envisage a case where it was possible for a person to attempt to murder his victim, demonstrating the necessary intention to kill, but without attempting to cause grievous harm and without demonstrating an intention to cause grievous bodily harm. Although

D   in his skeleton argument Mr Swift made that attempt, on further reflection he acknowledges that it is impossible to envisage a case where it is conceivable that there is an intention to kill without also there being an intention to inflict grievous bodily harm.

   15 The appeal against conviction is therefore dismissed.

E

Appeal dismissed.

Solicitors: *Crown Prosecution Service, Luton.*

JBS

F

Figure 6.4 *R* v *Morrison*: final page

6.1.15 Electronic reports

As well as paper law reports, many case reports are also available electronically via databases such as LexisNexis and Westlaw. These databases have been chosen to illustrate some of the differences between the electronic and paper presentations of the cases.

Practical exercise

Retrieve *R* v *Morrison* from both LexisNexis and Westlaw. Compare the electronic versions with the printed extract from the *Weekly Law Reports*.

6.1.15.1 Citations

The LexisNexis report does not give the citation of [2003] 1 WLR 1859. This is because the *Weekly Law Reports* (WLR) are not part of their database. However, alternative reports are cited as [2003] 2 Cr App Rep 563 and [2003] Crim LR 801.

   On the other hand, Westlaw *does* include the *Weekly Law Report* version as well as the two references given by LexisNexis and a range of others (such as (2003) 147 SJLB 626).

Self-test questions

1. What does [2003] 2 Cr App Rep 563 mean?
2. What does [2003] Crim LR 801 mean? Why is 2003 in square brackets?
3. What does (2003) 147 SJLB 626 mean? Why is 2003 in round brackets?

6.1.15.2 Content

You will see that the catchwords on the LexisNexis report are different and that there is no headnote at all. There is also no list of the cases considered or used in argument, or any summary of the history of the case. The Westlaw report is identical in content to that in the paper version of the *Weekly Law Reports*.

   Both reports contain paragraph numbers. The Westlaw report also shows the corresponding page numbers from the bound version of the *Weekly Law Reports*. You will see *1859 at the very start of the report. This denotes the start of p. 1859 in the bound version.

Follow paragraph 1 in the bound version and the Westlaw report. You will see that there is a page break after the words 'On 28 November 2001, following a three-day trial in the Crown Court at Luton, before Hooper J, the appellant was convicted of attempting' in the bound version. In the Westlaw transcript the words 'convicted of attempting' are followed by *1860. This denotes the start of p. 1860.

Therefore, if you need to refer to the page number of a particular part of an electronic transcript, you must work backwards until you reach a page number mark. The material you want to reference is on that page.

However, the electronic versions do allow direct links to academic and professional commentary on the case, so despite some key differences from the paper reports, they can in may respects be considered to be a richer resource than the paper report in isolation.

6.2 Judicial precedent

Having worked out how to navigate a law report, we must move on to consider how legal rules arise from these cases and how they might then be applied in later cases. In this section 'judicial precedent' refers to the process by which judges follow previously decided cases.

Before considering the doctrine of judicial precedent in more detail, it is important to recap on the way in which the courts are arranged in a hierarchy and to demonstrate the importance of the status of the courts in relation to the operation of judicial precedent.

6.2.1 Precedent and the hierarchy of the courts

The courts of the English legal system are arranged in a hierarchy which can be depicted as shown in Figure 6.5 overleaf.

Since the courts at the top of the hierarchy are more 'important' than lower courts, their decisions carry a greater legal 'value' than the decisions of lower courts. It is the doctrine of judicial precedent, or *stare decisis,* that explains the way in which these decisions relate to each other.

Stare decisis is a Latin phrase which means 'let the decision stand'.

The doctrine of precedent is based on the principle that *like cases should be treated alike*. This means that once a decision has been reached in a particular case, it stands as good law and should be relied upon in other cases as an accurate statement of law. This is the essence of the doctrine of precedent.

For example, a case which is decided in the Court of Appeal could be relevant in three different directions: vertically up or down the hierarchy (House of Lords and High Court respectively) and horizontally (other Court of Appeal cases). It is the doctrine of precedent that tells us the types of case in which of the courts such a Court of Appeal decision would be relevant and how it would influence the outcome of the case being heard (Figure 6.6).

This preserves legal certainty and consistency in the application of the law. This is important to our ideas of justice and fairness. We would think it questionable if judicial decisions were contradictory or if there was no logical explanation to the pattern of their application.

This principle is encapsulated by Frankena:

> The paradigm case of injustice is that in which there are two similar individuals in similar circumstances and one of them is treated better or worse than the other. In this case, the cry of injustice rightly goes up against the responsible agent or group; and unless that agent or group can

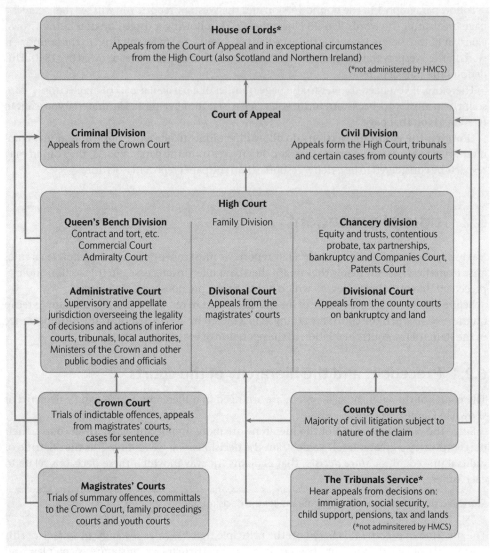

Figure 6.5 The hierarchy of the courts (reproduced from HMCS)

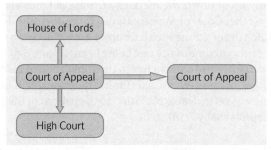

Figure 6.6 Possible directions in which a Court of Appeal case could be relevant

establish that there is some relevant dissimilarity after all between the individuals concerned and their circumstances, he or they will be guilty as charged (Frankena, W.K. (1973) *Ethics*, Prentice-Hall at p. 49).

Therefore, the doctrine of precedent is concerned with the way that decisions in earlier cases are applied in subsequent cases. It is based upon a series of presumptions:

- Cases with the same or similar material facts (that is, facts which are legally relevant) should be decided in the same way

- Decisions made in the higher level courts carry greater weight than those lower in the hierarchy thus a court is normally bound by courts which are higher or equal to them

- Judgments often contain a great deal of legal discussion that is not directly relevant to the issue at the heart of the case so a distinction should be made between the importance of those things that address the principle of law on which the decision is based (known as the *ratio decidendi*, 'the reason for the decision') and those which are peripheral to the outcome of the case (known as *obiter dicta*, 'things said in passing') and the weight given to these concepts in subsequent cases.

Ratio decidendi is a Latin phrase which means 'the reason for the decision' (plural *rationes decidendi*, although often simply stated as *ratios*). This is the (potentially) binding part of a judicial decision.

Obiter dictum is a Latin phrase meaning 'thing said in passing' (plural *obiter dicta*).

The first step in determining whether a precedent is binding or persuasive is to isolate the legally relevant facts and use them to distinguish between the *ratio* of the judgment and the *obiter dicta* as outlined above. Just because a statement is the *ratio* of an earlier case does not mean it is automatically binding in subsequent cases just as the facts that a statement is *obiter* does not mean that it has no precedent value—it all depends on the relationship between the court in which the original decision was made and the case in which the precedent is to be applied.

The general rule is that each court is bound by the decisions of those that are higher and of equivalent level in the hierarchy of the courts. For example, the Court of Appeal is normally bound by decisions of the House of Lords (higher) and other Court of Appeal decisions (equivalent) (Figures 6.7 and 6.8).

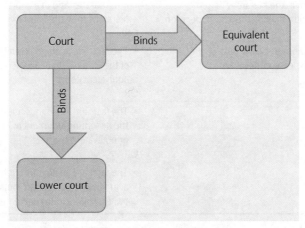

Figure 6.7 Courts binding equivalent and lower courts

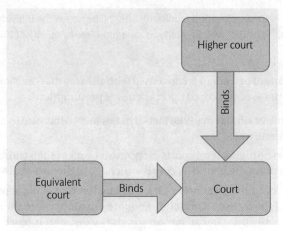

Figure 6.8 Courts being bound by equivalent and higher courts

6.2.2 Binding and persuasive precedents

A binding precedent is a decided case that *must* be applied in a later case—even if it is considered to have been wrongly decided. It exists when the material facts of a case are similar with those of an earlier decision in a higher or equivalent court in which the applicable statement of law was part of the *ratio* of the earlier decision.

A persuasive precedent is one which *may* be followed by a court (provided no binding precedent exists) but there is no compulsion on the courts to do so.

Table 6.3 Binding and persuasive precedents

Binding precedent	Persuasive precedent
• The facts in the decided case and the case before the courts must be sufficiently analogous to justify the imposition of the same legal principle/rule. AND	• The facts in the decided case and the case under consideration may have similar, but not directly analogous, facts. OR
• The decided case must have been heard in a court which is more senior in the hierarchy or at the same level as the court making the instant decision. AND	• The facts are analogous but the relevant legal rule is part of the ratio of a court that is lower in the hierarchy than the court making the decision. OR
• The part of the previous decision must be the *ratio decidendi* of the case rather than *obiter dicta*.	• The facts are analogous but the legal rule was part of the *obiter dicta* of a case heard in a higher or equivalent court. OR
	• The facts are analogous but the legal rule is part of the dissenting judgment of a case heard in a higher or equivalent court. OR
	• The facts are analogous but the legal rule is part of a judgment of a court outside of England and Wales. This includes decisions of the Privy Council.

6.2.3 Finding the *ratio decidendi* and *obiter dicta*

The judgment in a case generally contains a statement of the facts and the relevant law and an explanation by the judge of the way in which the law applies to the particular situation before him and his conclusion as to the outcome of the case. The *ratio* of the case is the legal rule and associated reasoning that is essential to the resolution of the case. It is the conclusion that is reached by the application of the relevant legal rule to the material facts.

This was summed up by Buxton LJ in *R(Kadhim)* v *Brent London Borough Council Housing Benefit Review Board:*[11]

> Cases as such do not bind: their *rationes decidendi* do. While there has been much academic discussion of the proper way of determining the *ratio* of a case, we find the clearest and most persuasive guidance . . . to be . . . the *ratio decidendi* of a case is any rule of law, expressly or impliedly treated by the judge as a necessary step in reaching his conclusion, having regard to the line of reasoning adopted by him.

Therefore, in order to identify the *ratio* of a case, you must first isolate the material, or legally relevant, facts. Most judgments contain a wide general statement of the facts to establish the context in which the events occurred that gave rise to the case before the court. Many of these facts are not legally relevant—the outcome in the case would be the same even if these facts were different as they were not material to the legal question at the heart of the case.

In addition to isolating the material facts and determining what aspects of the reasoning is relevant to making a decision on the outcome of the case in order to identify the *ratio* of a judgment, the following are useful ways to identify *obiter*:

- The discussion, explanation or reasoning of the judge is wider than that which is necessary to reach a decision on the facts of the case
- The judge hypothesises about the decision that he would have reached if the facts had been different
- The judge explains what his decision would have been in this case if he had not been compelled to reach a different decision due to binding precedent
- It is something said by a dissenting judge.

Identifying the *ratio* is often difficult as it can be difficult to separate it from the *obiter*. This can be illustrated by way of example.

In *Donoghue* v *Stevenson*,[12] the claimant's friend purchased a bottle of ginger beer which was served in an opaque bottle. After drinking some of the ginger beer, the claimant discovered that the bottle contained the decomposing remains of a snail. The claimant was distressed as a result and suffered a period of gastric illness. There was no basis for a contractual claim as the claimant did not purchase the ginger beer and the friend could not claim as it was the claimant that suffered harm. The House of Lords held that the claimant could recover damages from the manufacturer due to their negligence, Lord Atkin stating that:

> . . . a manufacturer of products, which he sells in such a form as to show that he intends them to reach the ultimate consumer in the form in which they left him with no reasonable possibility of

---

11.   [2001] 2 WLR 1674.
12.   [1932] AC 562.

> intermediate examination and with the knowledge that the absence of reasonable care in the pre-
> paration or putting up of the products will result in an injury to the consumer's life or property, owes
> a duty to the consumer to take that reasonable care.[13]

This case became the cornerstone of the duty of care in negligence and therefore guides the availability and operation of this tort. Each of the following could have been the *ratio* of this case:

- The manufacturer owes a duty to take reasonable care that the consumer is not injured as a result of a snail in a bottle of ginger beer.

- The manufacturer owes a duty to take reasonable care that the consumer is not injured by a foreign body in a container.

- The manufacturer owes a duty to take reasonable care that the consumer is not injured by defective products.

- A person owes a duty to take reasonable care that he does not commit any act which he could reasonably foresee as injuring another person.

The first option is too specific to the facts and would create an unrealistically narrow ratio that would be unlikely ever to be raised in later cases. The fact that it is a snail and a bottle of ginger beer is not material—the decision would have been no different if it had been a decomposed stag beetle and a pork pie, for example. The second option is wider but it could still be questioned whether a *ratio* that limits the value of a case to foreign bodies in containers is desirable; would it really be sufficiently distinct if the snail had been in a sandwich? The third option seems reasonable; it is sufficiently general to create a legal principle that can be used in a range of situations thus not creating an undue restriction on its use in future cases. The fourth option may seem too wide; it moves beyond the particular relationship (manufacturers and consumers) and the particular negligent behaviour (failing to check the quality of products). However, it was this wide *ratio* that was followed in later cases and which is the basis for the law of negligence as it exists today. This *ratio* is so wide that it has been suggested that it was actually the third option that was the *ratio* and that the wider principle was merely *obiter* but which obtained the status of binding precedent by its use in later cases. The *ratio* from *Donoghue* v *Stevenson* has been applied to products including lifts, chemicals, and motor cars, and manufacturers' liability extended to repairers and assemblers. Therefore it is perhaps more accurate to say that the *ratio decidendi* of a case is ultimately determined by its application by a court in a later case.

6.2.4 The operation of judicial precedent in the courts

6.2.4.1 The European Court of Justice

The European Court of Justice is not bound by its previous decisions, as it does formally have the concept of *stare decisis*. This allows it to take future changes in European policy into account. However, it is strongly persuaded by its own previous decisions and rarely departs from them in practice in the interests of legal certainty. All UK courts are bound by the European Court of Justice on matters of interpretation of EC Treaties themselves and on the interpretation and validity of Regulations and Directives.[14]

6.2.4.2 The House of Lords

Until 1966 the House of Lords was bound by itself. This was established in the mid-nineteenth century and became known as the *London Tramways* rule after the House of Lords affirmed the

---

13. *per* Lord Atkin [1932] AC 562, 599.
14. European Communities Act 1972, s. 3(1).

position in the 1898 case of *London Tramways Co. Ltd* v *London County Council*.[15] Since the House of Lords was the highest appeal court in the hierarchy of the courts, it was considered to be in the public interest for its decisions to be final. The rule was intended to provide absolute certainty in the law and to cut down on cases from being brought to court.

The rigidity of this rule was increasingly criticized throughout the twentieth century, and the *London Tramways* rule was eventually abolished by the 1966 *Practice Statement (Judicial Precedent)*[16] made on behalf of the House of Lords by Lord Gardiner LC who stated:

> Their Lordships regard the use of precedent as an indispensable foundation upon which to decide what is the law and its application to individual cases. It provides at least some degree of certainty on which individuals can rely in the conduct of their affairs, as well as a basis for orderly development of legal rules.
>
> Their Lordships nevertheless recognise that too rigid adherence to precedent may lead to injustice in a particular case and unduly restrict the proper development of the law. They propose, therefore, to modify their present practice and *while treating former decisions of this House as normally binding, to depart from a previous decision where it appears right to do so.*
>
> In this connection they will bear in mind the danger of disturbing retrospectively the basis upon which contracts, settlements of property and fiscal arrangements have been entered into and also the especial need for certainty in the criminal law.
>
> This announcement is not intended to affect the use of precedent elsewhere than in this House.

The impact of the *Practice Statement* gives the law sufficiently flexibility to deal with novel situations and to ensure justice in each particular case. The operation of precedent means that the law can develop in line with the changes in society and that judicial decisions are in line with the morals and expectations of the community.

When will the House of Lords depart from its own previous decisions?

The *Practice Statement* 'does not mean that whenever . . . a previous decision was wrong, we should reverse it' (*Miliangos* v *George Frank Textiles*).[17] This may seem to contradict the *Practice Statement*; in fact it shows that the House of Lords is extremely reluctant to use it, as it is acutely aware of the need for certainty and the dangers attached to departing from its previous decisions (as stated in the *Practice Statement*). Thus, it will require more than just a previous decision to be wrong; it will only be used where a previous decision caused injustices, caused uncertainty or hindered the development of the law. Even if the *Practice Statement* might apply, the Lords still consider whether legislation might provide a better solution than departing from its previous decisions.

In *R* v *Secretary of State for the Home Department ex parte Khawaja*,[18] it was held that, before departing from its own decisions, the House of Lords should be sure that continued adherence to precedent involves the risk of injustice and would obstruct the proper development of the law and departure from the precedent is the safe and appropriate way of remedying the injustice and remedying the law.

Further evidence in support of the reluctance of the House of Lords to exercise its powers to bring about change to well-established law can be seen in the approach taken in *C* v *Director of Public Prosecutions*.[19] Here the House of Lords refused to abolish the presumption of *doli incapax* (the presumption that children under the age of 14 were incapable of criminal wrongdoing) despite finding it to be anomalous and absurd, preferring to call upon Parliament to remedy the situation. Lord Lowry stated the guidelines for judicial law-making as follows:

---

15. [1898] AC 375.
16. [1966] 1 WLR 1234.
17. [1976] AC 433 *per* Lord Cross.
18. [1983] 2 WLR 321.
19. [1994] 4 All ER 43.

(a) judges should exercise caution before imposing a remedy where the solution to the problem is doubtful;

(b) they should be cautious about making changes if Parliament had rejected opportunities of dealing with a known problem or had legislated whilst leaving the problem untouched;

(c) they are more suited to dealing with purely legal problems than disputed matters of social policy;

(d) fundamental legal doctrines should not be lightly set aside; and,

(e) judges should not change the law unless they can achieve finality and certainty.

Therefore, despite the freedom conferred by the *Practice Statement* to set aside their own decisions and exercise greater freedom in the development of the law, it is clear that the House of Lords is reluctant to exercise these powers.

However, there are examples of cases in which the House of Lords has departed from its previous decisions. The first example of this was in *Conway* v *Rimmer*,[20] where the House of Lords unanimously overruled its previous decision in *Duncan* v *Cammel, Laird & Co.*[21] This case involved public interest immunity: the principle by which courts can grant an order allowing one litigant to refrain from disclosing evidence to the other litigants where disclosure would be damaging to the public interest. *Duncan* was decided in wartime: here the House of Lords held that the Crown could claim privilege not to disclose documents in civil cases on the strength of an affidavit sworn by a government minister. In *Conway* the House of Lords held that the ministerial affidavit was *not* binding upon the court.

R v *Shivpuri*[22] saw the first use of the *Practice Statement* in criminal law. Here the House of Lords overruled the decision in *Anderton* v *Ryan*[23] which it had made only one year previously. These cases involved the construction of s. 1(2) of the Criminal Attempts Act 1981 which provides that 'a person may be convicted of attempting to commit an offence . . . even if the facts are such that the commission of the offence is impossible'. In *Anderton* v *Ryan* the appellant was acquitted of attempting dishonestly to handle stolen goods. She believed that the video recorder in question had been stolen, but there was no evidence that it had been. Despite the clear wording of s. 1(2), the House of Lords effectively held that they meant something different. In *Shivpuri*, the appellant's conviction for attempting to deal with and harbour prohibited drugs was upheld after he had been caught with a suitcase which he thought contained drugs, but in fact contained an innocuous substance. Their Lordships reapplied the wording of s. 1(2), effectively admitting their error in *Anderton* v *Ryan*.

As Lord Bridge stated in *Shivpuri:* 'the Practice Statement is an effective abandonment of our pretension to infallibility'.

6.2.4.3 The Court of Appeal

Civil Division

In *Young* v *Bristol Aeroplane Co. Ltd*[24] the Court of Appeal considered whether it is bound by its own decisions. It was held that it is normally bound, subject to three exceptions:

1. **Where its own previous decisions conflict**

    This may arise if the court in the later case was unaware of the decision of the earlier case; for instance, if the earlier case was very recent or unreported, or the second case might have distinguished the first, or one of the cases had been decided *per incuriam* (see below). In such situations, the Court of Appeal can choose which of its previous decisions to follow and which

---

20.   [1968] AC 910.
21.   [1942] AC 624.
22.   [1986] 2 All ER 334.
23.   [1985] AC 560.
24.   [1944] KB 718.

to reject. Whilst this has obvious implications for the future precedent value of the decision which is not followed, its status is not technically affected by the fact that it has not been followed; it could still be adopted in subsequent cases. For example, in *National Westminster Bank plc* v *Powney*[25] the Court of Appeal had to choose between two of its own previous judgments in *W.T. Lamb & Sons* v *Rider*[26] and *Lougher* v *Donovan*[27] which were irreconcilable.

2. **Where its previous decision had been implicitly overruled by the House of Lords**
   This occurs when a previous Court of Appeal decision is inconsistent with a later House of Lords decision. For example in *Family Housing Association* v *Jones*[28] the Court of Appeal refused to follow its own recent decisions which were inconsistent with the House of Lords decision in *AG Securities Ltd* v *Vaughan*[29] and *Street* v *Mountford*,[30] even though the decisions of the Court of Appeal had not been expressly overruled by the House of Lords.

   This situation of inconsistency also occurs where an appeal case has bypassed the Court of Appeal and gone straight to the House of Lords via the so-called 'leapfrog' procedure.[31] The conditions which must be satisfied before such a direct appeal can be taken are that:

   (a) the trial judge has granted a certificate of satisfaction, and

   (b) the House of Lords has given leave to appeal.

   A trial judge can only grant a certificate if all the parties consent and the case involves a point of law of general public importance which is either concerned wholly or mainly with the construction of a statute or of a statutory instrument, or is one where the trial judge is bound by a previous decision of the Court of Appeal or the House of Lords. The granting of a certificate by the trial judge is discretionary. No appeal is possible against the granting or refusal of a certificate.

   Appeals direct from the High Court to the House of Lords are very rare. An example can however be found in *Kleinwort Benson Ltd* v *Lincoln City Council*.[32]

3. **Where its previous decision was made *per incuriam***

   Per incuriam is a Latin phrase meaning 'through carelessness'.

   A decision made *per incuriam* is one made 'through carelessness' or without due regard to the relevant law. It should not be confused with *per curiam* which is a part of a judgment upon which all the judges are agreed.

   Examples of cases in which *per incuriam* decisions have been considered include *Morelle* v *Wakeling*[33] which provided a definition of *per incuriam* as 'decisions given in ignorance or forgetfulness of some inconsistent statutory provision or of some authority binding on the court concerned . . . ' In other words, where the decision was reached without due regard for the correct law. In *Duke* v *Reliance Systems Ltd*,[34] it was held that 'if the court has failed to consider the relevant law, the decision will be *per incuriam* if the court *must* inevitably have reached a different decision had it considered the correct law; it will not suffice that the court

25. [1990] 2 All ER 416.
26. [1948] 2 KB 331.
27. [1948] 2 All ER 11.
28. [1990] 1 All ER 385.
29. [1988] 3 All ER 1058.
30. [1985] AC 809.
31. Administration of Justice Act 1969, ss. 12–15.
32. [1999] AC 358.
33. [1955] 2 QB 379.
34. [1988] QB 108.

might have reached a different decision had it considered the correct law'. In *Williams* v *Fawcett* [35] the Court of Appeal declared several of its previous decisions *per incuriam* which had held that a person could not be committed to prison for breach of a non-molestation order unless the notice had been signed by the 'proper officer' of the court. Since this was not a requirement of the statute or of the procedural rules the decisions lacked a rational legal basis.

More recently, in *Cave* v *Robinson Jarvis & Rolf* [36] the Court of Appeal stated that the decision in question had to be 'manifestly wrong' before it could be declared *per incuriam*.

Criminal Division

All the exceptions from *Young* v *Bristol* Aeroplane that apply in the Civil Division also apply to the Criminal Division. However, the Court of Appeal has a wider discretion in criminal cases where the liberty of the individual is at stake. In *R* v *Gould*, [37] Lord Diplock stated:

> if upon due consideration we were to be of the opinion that the law had been either misapplied or misunderstood in an earlier decision . . . we should be entitled to depart from the view as to the law expressed in the earlier decision notwithstanding that the case could not be brought within any of the exceptions laid down in *Young* v *Bristol Aeroplane Co. Ltd*.

There has been no ruling on whether the Civil and Criminal Divisions are bound by each other. However, their predecessors (the Court of Appeal and the Court of Criminal Appeal) were not. It is also accepted that, when dealing with criminal appeals, a 'full' Court of Appeal (five judges) can depart from decisions made by three judges. The rule in *Young* v *Bristol Aeroplane* gives the Court of Appeal some capacity to depart from its own decisions but only in narrowly defined circumstances. The House of Lords has a broad discretion to depart from its own decisions where it appears right to do so but, in practice, this discretion is exercised sparingly.

6.2.4.4 The Divisional Courts and the High Court

The Divisional Courts (i.e. the Divisional Court of the appropriate division of the High Court for the particular matter) are bound by their own decisions subject to the same exceptions as the Civil Division of the Court of Appeal, and, arguably, the Criminal Division (following the decision in *R* v *Greater Manchester Coroner, ex parte Tal*). [38] Decisions of the Divisional Courts are binding on the High Court.

High Court decisions are not binding on the Divisional Courts (since the Divisional Courts operate at a higher level than the High Court by virtue of the nature of their jurisdiction, which is mostly appellate).

Decisions of individual High Court judges are binding on lower courts but not on other High Court judges.

The structure of the High Court is complicated. You may wish to review the explanation of its organization which is provided in section 4.3.

6.2.4.5 The Crown, county, and magistrates' courts

The Crown Court is not bound by its previous decisions but, in order to promote certainty in the criminal law, is strongly persuaded by them. County and magistrates' courts are not bound by their own decisions and bind no other courts.

In summary, the question 'who is bound by whom?' can be shown in a diagram as shown opposite (Figure 6.9).

---

35.   [1985] 1 All ER 787.
36.   [2001] EWCA Civ 245; [2002] 1 WLR 581.
37.   [1968] 2 QB 65.
38.   [1984] 3 All ER 240.

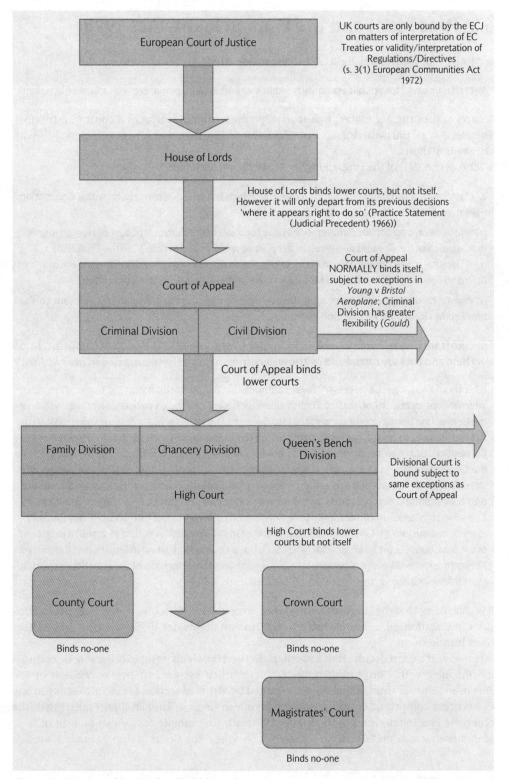

Figure 6.9 A summary of the operation of judicial precedent

6.3 Precedent and the Human Rights Act 1998

Section 6(1) of the Human Rights Act 1998 provides that:

> 6.–(1) It is unlawful for a public authority to act in a way which is incompatible with a Convention right.

Section 6(3) of the Act makes it clear that 'public authority' includes a court or a tribunal. Therefore it is unlawful for courts to deliver a judgment which is incompatible with Convention rights.

Moreover, s. 2(1) of the Human Rights Act 1998 provides that:

> 2.–(1) A court or tribunal determining a question which has arisen in connection with a Convention right must take into account any
>
> (a) judgment, decision, declaration or advisory opinion of the European Court of Human Rights,
> (b) opinion of the Commission given in a report adopted under Article 31 of the Convention,
> (c) decision of the Commission in connection with Article 26 or 27(2) of the Convention, or
> (d) decision of the Committee of Ministers taken under Article 46 of the Convention,
>
> whenever made or given, so far as, in the opinion of the court or tribunal, it is relevant to the proceedings in which that question has arisen.

The courts are only required to take such decisions 'into account'. They are not compelled to follow them and they are not bound by those decisions. As Lord Hoffman stated in *In Re McKerr*:[39]

> 63 It should no longer be necessary to cite authority for the proposition that the Convention, as an international treaty, is not part of English domestic law . . . Although people sometimes speak of the Convention having been incorporated into domestic law, that is a misleading metaphor. What the Act has done is to create domestic rights expressed in the same terms as those contained in the Convention. But they are domestic rights, not international rights. Their source is the statute, not the Convention. They are available against specific public authorities, not the United Kingdom as a state. And their meaning and application is a matter for domestic courts, not the court in Strasbourg.
> 64 This last point is demonstrated by the provision in section 2(1) that a court determining a question which has arisen in connection with a Convention right must 'take into account' any judgment of the Strasbourg court. Under the Convention, the United Kingdom is bound to accept a judgment of the Strasbourg court as binding: article 46(1). But a court adjudicating in litigation in the United Kingdom about a domestic 'Convention right' is not bound by a decision of the Strasbourg court. It must take it into account.

It is clear then, that the House of Lords does not consider itself bound by the judgments, decisions, declarations, or opinions listed in the Human Rights Act 1998—it merely has to 'take them into account'.

However, if a court decides that a previous decision by which it would otherwise be bound is incompatible with Convention rights (as determined by, for instance, a decision of the European Court of Human Rights) it is required by virtue of section 6(1) to give effect to any Convention-compatible decision from the European Court of Human Rights rather than the otherwise binding decision of the higher UK court. An example of this can be seen in *In Re Medicaments and Related Classes of Goods (No. 2)*[40] where the Court of Appeal made a 'modest

---

39. [2004] 1 WLR 807, 825.
40. [2001] 1 WLR 700.

adjustment' to the House of Lords' decision in *R* v *Gough*[41] to make it compatible with the view of the European Court of Human Rights: although this 'modest adjustment' involved substituting an objective test to determine whether or not a tribunal was biased for the earlier subjective test. This fundamentally changed the decision of the House of Lords in *Gough*.

6.4 Precedent and European law

Section 3(1) of the European Communities Act 1972 (as amended by s. 2 of the European Communities (Amendment) Act 1986) provides that:

> 3.–(1) For the purposes of all legal proceedings any question as to the meaning or effect of any of the Treaties, or as to the validity, meaning or effect of any Community instrument, shall be treated as a question of law and, if not referred to the European Court, be for determination as such in accordance with the principles laid down by and any relevant decision of the European Court or any court attached thereto.
>
> (2) Judicial notice shall be taken of the Treaties, of the Official Journal of the European Communities and of any decision of, or expression or opinion by, the European Court or any court attached thereto, on any such question as aforesaid.

Under Article 234 of the EC Treaty, courts may (or in the case of the House of Lords, must) refer any question regarding the interpretation of EC legislation to the European Court of Justice for a ruling. The ruling of the European Court of Justice is then binding in that particular case. This means that domestic courts must follow decisions on European law made by the European Court of Justice in particular cases.

However, such decisions are not binding on the UK courts in the future. Since the European Court of Justice is not bound by its previous decisions, the House of Lords can refer the same point of law to the European Court of Justice again in a later case if it considers that the European Court's earlier decision (by which the House of Lords would have been bound in the particular case) was wrong, or merely if the House of Lords considered it to be unsatisfactory.

6.5 Avoiding difficult precedents

The 1966 *Practice Statement* and the rule in *Young* v *Bristol Aeroplane* give the House of Lords and Court of Appeal respectively the ability to avoid previous decisions of courts at the same level. In the case of the Court of Appeal, the circumstances in which the previous decisions of the Court of Appeal can be avoided are narrowly defined whereas the House of Lords exercises its power with caution because of the wider implications of departing from its own decisions in terms of the legal principle that results.

Other than by the operation of these particular rules, there are several methods that a court (at any level) can use to avoid an otherwise binding precedent. The approach taken depends upon whether the court in which is confronted with the precedent wishes merely to avoid the precedent but to allow it to continue to exist as legal authority or whether the court wishes to deprive the precedent of any future legal effect.

Overruling occurs when a court higher in the hierarchy overturns the decision of a lower court in a different case. This not only means that the higher court is not bound to follow the

---

41.   [1993] AC 646.

earlier decision but that it is negated of any legal force; indeed, it is regarded as never having been the law.

This is to be distinguished from reversing a decision whereby a court higher in the hierarchy overturns the decision of a lower court in the same case. For example, the House of Lords in *R* v *Woollin*[42] refused to follow the approach taken by the Court of Appeal in the same case, upholding the defendant's appeal against his conviction for murder and reversing the decision of the Court of Appeal definition of oblique intention.

In both of these situations, the earlier decision is negated by the later decision of the higher court. An alternative way in which an existing precedent that would otherwise be binding can be avoided is if the court decides that the case before them is materially different, either on the facts or on the point of law. By distinguishing in this way, the court is saying that they will not be applying the earlier case because it is not sufficiently similar to the case before them; the cases can be distinguished (on the facts or the law).

An alternative to this approach is to interpret the *ratio* of the earlier case widely rather than narrowly so that there is greater scope to apply the authority but reach a decision which is consistent with what the judges want to achieve in the case. In many ways, it is true to say that the *ratio* of a case remains unclear until it is identified and applied by a later court. Accordingly, the operation of the doctrine of precedent is contingent not on the judgment at the time it is given but the way in which a case is used by later courts; a case does not necessarily have precedent value until it acquires precedent value by usage. Therefore, the decision as to whether a case has a wide or narrow *ratio* is one for the later courts.

CHAPTER SUMMARY

Reading cases

- Criminal cases *R* v *X* are said as 'the Crown against X'

- Civil cases *A* v *B* are said as 'A and B'

- The party against whom a criminal case is brought is called the defendant

- The party bringing a civil claim is called the claimant

- The party against whom a civil claim is brought is called the respondent

- The party bringing an appeal is called the appellant

- The party against whom an appeal is brought is called the respondent

- The headnote of a case report is not part of the judgment

- The headnote may summarize the effect of the judgment on the existing case law

- Electronic reports may not contain all the information in a printed report, but often provide links to useful academic and professional commentary on the case

Judicial precedent

- *Stare decisis* is a Latin phrase meaning 'let the decision stand'

- *Ratio decidendi* is a Latin phrase which means the 'reason for the decision'. This is the (potentially) binding part of a judicial decision

---

42.   [1999] AC 82.

- *Obiter dicta* is a Latin phrase meaning 'things said in passing'

- Binding precedents must be applied in a later case

- Persuasive precedents may be followed in later cases, but there is no compulsion on the courts to do so

- The European Court of Justice is not bound by its previous decisions

- All UK courts are bound by the European Court of Justice on matters of interpretation of EC Treaties and the interpretation and validity of Regulations and Directives

- The House of Lords may depart from its previous decisions where it appears right to do so (*Practice Statement 1966*) although it is often reluctant to do so

- The Court of Appeal (Civil Division) is normally bound by its previous decisions unless they conflict; its previous decision has been implicitly overruled by the House of Lords, or; its previous decision was made *per incuriam* (*Young* v *Bristol Aeroplane*)

- *Per incuriam* is a Latin phrase meaning 'through carelessness'

- The Court of Appeal (Criminal Division) is also subject to the *Young* v *Bristol Aeroplane* exceptions, but does have greater discretion where the liberty of the individual is at stake (*Gould*)

- The Divisional Courts are bound by their own decisions subject to the *Young* v *Bristol Aeroplane* exceptions

- The High Court is bound by decisions of the Divisional Court

- Decisions of individual High Court judges are binding on lower courts, but not on individual High Court judges

- The Crown Court is strongly persuaded by its previous decisions

- County and magistrates' courts do not bind themselves and bind no other courts

- The House of Lords must take decisions of the European Court of Human Rights into account but is not bound by them (s. 2, Human Rights Act 1998)

- However, courts must act in a way compatible with Convention rights (s. 6, Human Rights Act 1998)

- Domestic courts must follow decisions of the European Court of Justice in matters of Europen law in particular cases

- Difficult precedents may be avoided by distinguishing, reversing, or overruling

- Cases may be distinguished from one another if the material facts of the two cases are different

- Reversing occurs when a court higher in the hierarchy overturns the decision of a lower court in the same case

- Overruling occurs when a court higher in the hierarchy overturns the decision of a lower court in a different case

FURTHER READING

- Ingman, T. (2004) *The English Legal Process* (10th edn), Oxford: Oxford University Press, pp. 313–68.
  For greater depth on the operation of the doctrine of judicial precedent.

- Montrose, J.L. 'The *Ratio Decidendi* of a Case' (1957) 20(6) *Modern Law Review* 587.
  Contains an interesting article concerning *ratio decidendi*.

PART I
Sources of law

Books, journals, and official publications

The final section in this part of the book covers the skills you will need to find sources of law other than legislation and case law. Chapter 7 will describe how books, journals, and official publications can be used as supplementary sources of law whilst chapter 8 will give you the skills you need to find these additional resources.

Books, journals, and official publications

7

INTRODUCTION

The first two sections in this part of the book have explored the primary domestic and European sources of law. As you will have seen, these sources derive either from legislation (an Act of Parliament, statutory instrument, Treaty Article, Regulation, or Directive) or from cases decided before the courts (common law, equity, custom, or decision of the European Court of Justice). However, in addition to these sources, there is a wide range of secondary sources of law. This chapter will complete your appreciation of the spectrum of legal sources by describing the role of books, journals, and official publications among the secondary sources which you might encounter during your legal studies.

Without a good grasp of secondary sources of law you will miss out on an entire range of legal knowledge and comment. Secondary sources are a vital resource for a fully-rounded legal knowledge and will give you the means to start critically analysing the law as well as just reading and describing it. During your legal studies you will be required to demonstrate understanding, analysis, and synthesis skills as well as merely demonstrating simple knowledge of a particular area of law: an appreciation of the range of sources which will help you to develop these skills is therefore essential.

LEARNING OUTCOMES

After studying this chapter, you will be able to:

- Distinguish between textbooks, monographs, and practitioners' books

- Understand the role of legal encyclopedias and digests

- Appreciate the distinction between standard dictionaries, legal dictionaries, and specialist dictionaries

- Choose and use revision guides appropriately

- Understand the use of journals as important sources of information

- Describe the origins and sources of various official publications

- Express an awareness of newspapers, other reports, the Internet and 'soft law' as other potential sources of law

7.1 Books

7.1.1 Student textbooks

Student textbooks collect together, analyse, and criticize the law in particular areas. They traditionally deal with an individual area of legal study. There is a wide range of textbooks within each of the core subject areas:

- Constitutional and administrative law
- Contract law
- Criminal law
- European law
- English legal systems
- Equity and trusts
- Land law
- Tort law

as well as most of the popular optional subject areas such as family law, medical law, employment law, intellectual property law, and company law.

There are usually several textbooks available for each topic. You should be given guidance as to the preferred textbook for your particular course. However, textbooks are written in different styles and have widely varying degrees of difficulty. If you find that you are not getting on with your set text, you should ask your course leader whether there is a different text that might suit you better. For instance, if you find the set text hard to follow, then you might need a more basic book to give you a lower-level grounding in the material before building upon that with the set text. Equally, if you are fortunate enough to think that your textbook is too simple, then a higher-level text will allow you to deepen your understanding and build upon your skills of analysis and critical evaluation.

Textbooks do not generally carry any great legal authority although some established texts are occasionally cited in court. These include *Smith & Hogan*: *Criminal Law*, *Winfield and Jolowicz on Tort*, *Megarry & Wade*: *The Law of Real Property*, and *Treitel*: *The Law of Contract*.

Student textbooks undergo frequent revision to ensure that they stay current and relevant. You should always make sure that you are using the most recent edition of your particular textbook. For that reason, buying second-hand textbooks in student shops or online should be done with care, as you would not want to be working from a book which did not cover or explain more recent developments. If you do, you run the risk of inaccuracy in your research for essays and problem answers.

7.1.2 Cases and materials books

Cases and materials books contain a collection of key cases, statutes, reports, articles, and book extracts arranged by topic area within a subject. These are sometimes stand-alone publications, although an increasing number of textbooks have accompanying books of cases and materials.

These are an extremely useful way of gathering together all the supplementary materials you need to support your studies. However, they should be used with caution since they contain only extracts from the materials and those materials that the editor has considered appropriate. They are not a substitute for finding and reading the original and complete statutes, cases, and articles. Therefore, while very valuable as a starting point for research, a reliance upon cases and materials books can lead to lazy or unthinking research and, at worst, a blinkered view of the subject area.

7.1.3 Monographs

Monographs are a detailed written study of a single specialized topic. They are usually more expensive than student textbooks and cover particular narrow subject areas in much greater depth (often greater than that required for a first degree in law). For example, while you might think that your set criminal law textbook goes into more than enough detail, there are a large number of books which take particular topics and analyse them in very fine detail, such as:

- **Stone:** *Offences Against the Person*
- **Kugler:** *Direct and Oblique Intention in the Criminal Law*
- **Innes:** *Investigating Murder*
- **Smith:** *The Law of Theft.*

When you consider that many of these books are similar in size to an introductory-level student textbook designed to cover the whole of the criminal law, you should begin to appreciate the distinction between textbooks and monographs.

7.1.4 Practitioners' books

As distinct from textbooks which are usually written by law lecturers for student use, practitioners' books are usually written by practising lawyers for practising lawyers (although some practitioners write student texts and academics sometimes write for the practitioner market). These are primarily reference works and often span several volumes. As a result new editions appear much less frequently than for student textbooks and updates may be issued in the form of cumulative supplements. Some practitioner works are entirely loose-leaf, such as:

- *Chitty on Contracts*
- *Palmer's Company Law*
- *Woodfall: Landlord and Tenant*
- *Emmet & Farrand on Title*
- *Kemp & Kemp Personal Injury Law, Practice and Procedure*

They are also generally very expensive—the titles listed above range in price from around £200 to £850.

7.1.5 Legal encyclopedias and digests

There are various legal encyclopedias and digests which are extremely useful research tools.

To see examples of how to use the various encyclopedias and digests to find the law, see chapters 2, 5, and 8.

7.1.5.1 *Halsbury's Laws of England*

Halsbury's Laws of England is a comprehensive legal encyclopedia which aims to provide a complete statement of the law of England and Wales, derived from all sources and arranged by topic. As you can imagine, this is a massive work. It comprises sixty volumes in several parts.

7.1.5.2 *Halsbury's Statutes of England*

Halsbury's Statutes of England aims to provide current versions of all Public General Acts in force in England and Wales. As with *Halsbury's Laws of England* these are arranged by subject area.

7.1.5.3 *Halsbury's Statutory Instruments*

Halsbury's Statutory Instruments provides current information on all statutory instruments of general application to the whole of the England and Wales which are in force. Once again, these are arranged by topic.

7.1.5.4 *The Digest*

The Digest provides, in digested form, the whole case law of England and Wales, together with a considerable body of cases from the courts of Scotland, Ireland, Canada, Australia, New Zealand, and other countries of the Commonwealth. Cases dealing with the law of the European Communities are also included. The case digests are printed with annotations listing the subsequent cases in which judicial opinions have been expressed in the English courts. *The Digest* contains summaries of hundreds of thousands of cases drawn from over a thousand different series of law reports.

7.1.5.5 *Current Law*

Current Law is published in several parts:

- *Current Law Yearbook*
- *Current Law Statutes Annotated*
- *Current Law Case Citator* 1947–1976, 1977–1988 and 1989–2002
- *Current Law Statute Citator* 1947–1971
- *Current Law Legislation Citator* 1972–1988; 1989–2002

Its component parts provide access to both legislation and case law along with commentary.

7.1.6 Dictionaries

7.1.6.1 Conventional and legal dictionaries

The *Shorter Oxford English Dictionary* is the conventional dictionary which is most frequently cited in court, followed by the *Oxford English Dictionary*.[1]

The *OED* is also available online at www.oed.com. You will need a valid Athens account to gain access.

As well as conventional dictionaries, there are a range of legal dictionaries available. If your course does not recommend a particular dictionary, it is a good idea to browse a few in the bookshop. Legal dictionaries are very useful as a quick means of checking whether a word has a specific legal meaning as well as an everyday meaning. They can also be used when you encounter an unfamiliar term—which is likely, particularly if it is in Latin or Law French. Examples of legal dictionaries include:

- Penner, J.E.: *Mozley and Whiteley's Law Dictionary*
- Martin, E.A. and Law, J.: *A Dictionary of Law*

---

1.   Clinch, P. (1989) *Systems of Reporting Judicial Decision Making*, PhD thesis, University of Sheffield 481 cited in Clinch, P. (2001) *Using a Law Library* (2nd edn) London: Blackstone Press.

- Garner, B.A.: *Black's Law Pocket Dictionary*
- Bone, S. and Woodley, M.: *Osborn's Concise Law Dictionary*

Finally, there are also a range of specialist dictionaries which cover definitions that are restricted to certain topics including Employment Law, Company Law, and Commercial Law. These are likely to be too detailed for the purposes of your course of study; therefore, one of the general legal dictionaries will probably be the more appropriate resource.

7.1.6.2 Judicial dictionaries

Judicial dictionaries contain details of the ways in which judges have interpreted particular words or phrases as well as definitions contained in statute. They are very expensive, so are best used as a library resource.

Stroud's Judicial Dictionary of Words and Phrases includes definitions from English, Scottish and Commonwealth sources. Judicial interpretations of words and phrases used in statutes which have been repealed or amended have been retained. It comprised six volumes and is updated annually.

Words and Phrases Legally Defined is similar to *Stroud's Judicial Dictionary* and is also updated via annual cumulative supplements.

Finally, *Halsbury's Laws of England* may also be used to find definitions of words and phrases via the index to the main volumes.

7.1.7 Revision guides

Many students rely upon revision guides as a safety net. Revision guides do exactly what their name suggests—they are guides to revision. They are not a substitute for attendance at lectures and seminars. Moreover, they do not provide an excuse not to read and follow your own course materials and text books and should not cut down on the amount of reading and thinking that you have to do.

If you compare the size of most revision guides to that of your recommended textbook, it follows that a revision guide could never be expected to cover the subject in the depth required to succeed in coursework or examinations. However, they can serve a useful purpose in providing a concise overview of the key areas for revision—reminding you of the headline points to enable you to focus your revision and identify the key points you need to know.

Many series of revision guides, such as *Nutshells* from Sweet & Maxwell tend only to provide a condensed statement of law whereas others, including the *Law Express* series from Pearson Education also provide practical guidance on how to use the law in answering essay and problem questions.

7.2 Journals

. . . .

Journals are also referred to as periodicals.

. . . .

Journals are an important resource which can be used to keep up to date with latest developments in the law. They are also a key source of academic criticism and commentary upon the law which should be used in addition to textbooks, particularly when researching for a piece of written work, a seminar, or a moot. Books are always out of date to a greater or lesser extent. Even with a new book there is usually a delay of some months between the submission of the final manuscript by the author(s) and the book finally appearing on the shelves. New editions rarely come out more frequently than once every two years.

Journals contain a mixture of articles, news, notes, reviews, and digests. They are usually published as individual issues, which combine to make up volumes.

7.2.1 General journals

General journals tend to contain lengthy articles based on extensive academic research. Most include notes of recent cases, news of legal developments, and book reviews. The general journals most frequently encountered are the *Law Quarterly Review*, *Legal Studies*, the *Cambridge Law Journal*, the *Oxford Journal of Legal Studies* and the *Modern Law Review*. They are published relatively infrequently; typically with four or six issues per year.

7.2.2 Specialist journals

Specialist journals are similar to the general journals in that they primarily provide academic commentary and news on the law. However, they focus on particular aspects of the law. Examples of these include the *Journal of Criminal Law* and the *Criminal Law Review*, *Family Law*, *Civil Justice Quarterly*, and the *Journal of Business Law*.

There are also shorter specialist bulletins and newsletters which are focused towards the needs of practitioners, such as *Simon's Tax Intelligence*, *Property Law Bulletin* and *Business Law Brief*. These are of less immediate importance to your studies, although you should at least be aware of their existence.

7.2.3 Practitioner journals

Practitioner journals are usually published weekly or bi-weekly. These tend to contain shorter articles on wide range of topics of interest to lawyers in practice as well as case notes, digests, and practice notes. The articles are not usually covered in as great a depth as in the general or specialist journals and are often written by other practitioners rather than by academic lawyers. They still provide useful information and should not be overlooked, although they do carry less academic weight than the general and specialist academic journals. The journals in this category which you are most likely to come across include the *New Law Journal, Solicitors' Journal*, the *Law Society Gazette, Counsel*, and *Justice of the Peace*.

7.2.4 Foreign journals

English-language journals, in particular those from other common law jurisdictions such as the United States, Canada, Australia, and New Zealand can be useful when undertaking comparisons with the UK. Most libraries will carry a selection of foreign journals, such as the *Harvard Law Review*, the *Australian Law Journal*, and the *Canadian Bar Review*.

7.3 Official publications

7.3.1 Command papers

Command papers derive their name from the fact that they are presented to Parliament 'by Command of Her Majesty'. In fact, they are generally presented by a Government Minister. Command Papers are papers of interest to Parliament where presentation to Parliament is not required by statute. The subjects may include:

- Major policy proposals (White Papers)
- Consultation documents (Green Papers)
- Diplomatic documents such as treaties
- Government responses to Select Committee reports
- Reports of major committees of inquiry
- Certain departmental reports or reviews.

7.3.2 Bills

As you will recall from section 1.1.1, Bills are draft Acts of Parliament, put forward for debate. They are particularly useful when used in conjunction with the reports of Parliamentary debate, as you will be able to follow the various amendments made between versions of the Bill and the final Act of Parliament alongside the debate in Parliament that drove those amendments.

7.3.3 Parliamentary papers

The papers of the House of Commons originate inside the House and are 'Ordered by the House of Commons to be printed . . . ' They comprise the reports and evidence of Select Committees or the proceedings of Standing Committees considering legislation. Other House of Commons papers include:

- Reports of investigations of the National Audit Office
- Financial papers
- Annual reports of official bodies
- Accounts of official bodies
- Various administrative reports.

The House of Lords publishes substantially fewer papers than the Commons. Until the 1986/87 session both Bills and papers were numbered in one single sequence. From 1987/88 House of Lords papers and Bills were split into two separately numbered sequences.

7.3.4 Parliamentary debates (*Hansard* or the Official Report)

Parliament once prohibited all reporting and publishing of its proceedings, believing that it should deliberate in private. Indeed, it regarded any attempt to publicise its proceedings as a serious punishable offence. However, by the late 1700s, dissent both from the public and within Parliament coupled with the attacks of the press, persuaded the Parliament to relax its stance. In 1803 the House of Commons passed a resolution giving the press the right to enter the public gallery and William Cobbett, publisher of *Cobbett's Weekly Political Register* added reprints of reports of speeches taken from other newspapers in a new supplement. In 1812 publication was taken over by Cobbett's assistant, Thomas Hansard, who in 1829, changed the title of the reports to *Hansard's Parliamentary Debates*.

By 1878 dissatisfaction with the accuracy of the report was being expressed, and Hansard received a special subsidy conditional upon his employing special parliamentary reporters. In 1888 a Parliamentary Select Committee recommended that rather than let Hansard publish the debates an authorized version ought to be published. This version was published without using the name *Hansard*.

Hansard was officially adopted by Parliament in 1907 as a 'full report, in the first person, of all speakers alike', with a full report being defined as:

one which, though not strictly verbatim, is substantially the verbatim report, with repetitions and redundancies omitted and with obvious mistakes corrected, but which on the other hand leaves out nothing that adds to the meaning of the speech or illustrates the argument.

In 1943 it was decided to reintroduce the name *Hansard* because of its popular usage.

Therefore *Hansard* (the *Official Report*) is the edited verbatim report of proceedings in both the House of Commons and the House of Lords. Commons *Hansard* covers proceedings in the Commons Chamber, Westminster Hall, and Standing Committees. Lords *Hansard* covers proceedings in the Lords Chamber and its Grand Committees. Both contain Written Ministerial Statements and Written Answers.

7.4 Other secondary sources

7.4.1 The Internet

Although there is a vast amount of material available online, you need to exercise care to ensure that material you do find on the Internet is reliable, valuable, and credible. This can be a difficult task, although the following pointers should be borne in mind:

- Does the material give an author's name? If so, is the author a reputable academic or practitioner? Can you find any biographical information which will enable you to determine the academic value of the material?
- Is the information in a reputable online publication?
- Does the article carry a bibliography? Is it adequately referenced (either using footnotes, endnotes, or Harvard referencing)?
- Is the material on an official website or a personal website? The latter should be used with caution since anyone can set up a personal site.
- Has the material been evaluated independently before publication?

7.4.2 Newspapers

In addition to law reports, newspapers often contain comment and analysis on recent legal developments and interesting background material on topical issues. *The Times* in particular carries a law supplement on Tuesdays.

7.4.3 Think-tanks

Think-tanks are typically research institutes or other organizations who provide specialist advice and ideas on national problems, such as the Centre for Policy Studies, the Commonwealth Policy Studies Institute, or the Institute for Public Policy Research. While their reports are not official, they can sometimes be influential in driving legislative policy.

7.4.4 'Soft law'

. . . .

Soft law is sometimes referred to as *quasi-legislation*—or 'law-which-is-not-law'.

. . . .

There are a number of sources of 'soft law'. Soft law is typically administrative in nature and is probably best explained by way of examples (Table 7.1).

Table 7.1 Some examples of 'Soft Law'

Category	Examples
Prescriptive rules	• Codes of Practice issued under the Police and Criminal Evidence Act 1984 • Highway Code • ACAS (Advisory Conciliation and Arbitration Service) codes relating to employment disputes
Procedural rules	• Practice Directions • Prison Rules • Gaming Board rules for application for gaming licences • Codes of Practice issued under the Police and Criminal Evidence Act 1984
Instructions	• Home Office Circulars to magistrates' courts • Home Office Circulars to Chief Constables • Prison Department Circulars, Orders, and Regulations
Guides to interpretation	• Official statements explaining how terms or rules will be interpreted
Recommendations	• Specimen directions to juries formulated by the Judicial Studies Board • Guidance notes issued by the Health and Safety Executive
Rules of practice	• Tax concessions made by the Commissioners for the Inland Revenue outside those permitted by statute
Voluntary codes	• Broadcasting Complaints Authority • Press Complaints Commission • City Code on takeovers and mergers

The legal effect of these various sources is not certain until they have been tested in court. Sometimes they are given legal effect, others not, and in some instances, inconsistently. The House of Lords[2] has expressed concern regarding the uncertain legal consequences of non-compliance and the Cabinet Office has recently provided some 'Guidance on Codes of Practice and Legislation' in its *Guide to Legislative Procedure*.[3]

. . . .

2. *Hansard* vol. 469 c. 1075–1105 (15 January 1986).
3. September 2003. Available at www.cabinet-office.gov.uk.

CHAPTER SUMMARY

Books

- Student textbooks collect together, analyse, and criticize the law in particular areas

- They do not generally carry any great authority

- Cases and materials books provide a useful starting point for research, but are not a substitute for finding and reading original materials

- Monographs are a detailed written study of a single specialized topic. They cover particular narrow subject areas in much greater depth than student textbooks

- Practitioners' books are primarily reference works for practising lawyers

- Legal encyclopedias and digests such as *Halsbury's Laws of England*, *Halsbury's Statutes* and *The Digest* are extremely useful and comprehensive research tools

- Legal dictionaries exist alongside conventional dictionaries; some specialize on a particular topic

- Judicial dictionaries are large reference works which provide detailed commentary on judicial interpretation of words and phrases

- Revision guides can serve a useful purpose, but are not a substitute for attendance at lectures or seminars or a short cut for reading and thinking

Journals

- Journals are an important resource which can be used to keep up to date with latest developments in the law

- General journals contain articles based on extensive academic research

- Specialist journals also contain academic articles but with a focus on a particular area of the law

- Practitioner journals carry less academic weight but are published more frequently. They tend to contain shorter articles

- Foreign journals from other common law jurisdictions can be a useful resource when undertaking comparative research

Official publications

- Command Papers contain matters of interest to Parliament

- Bills are draft Acts of Parliament put forward for debate

- Papers of the House of Commons primarily comprise reports and evidence of select committees or the proceedings of standing committees

- The House of Lords publishes substantially fewer papers than the Commons

- *Hansard* (the *Official Report*) is the edited verbatim report of proceedings in both the House of Commons and the House of Lords

Other secondary sources

- Online material can be useful but should be used with caution

- Newspapers often contain comment and analysis on recent legal developments

- Think-tank reports can be influential in driving legislative policy

- 'Soft law' comprises rules, guidelines, codes, and recommendations which may be given legal effect when tested in court

 FURTHER READING

- Baldwin, R. and Houghton, J. 'Circular Arguments: The Status and Legitimacy of Administrative Rules' [1986] *Public Law* 239.

- Megarry, R.E. 'Administrative Quasi-legislation' (1944) 60 *Law Quarterly Review* 125.
  For more information on soft law

Finding books, journals, and official publications

8

INTRODUCTION

Chapters 2 and 5 covered the ways in which you can locate legislation and case law. However, as you will appreciate from the explanation provided in chapter 7, there are a range of important sources of law beyond legislation and case law. These are materials that provide information on the content, meaning, and operation of the law and which will assist you in your quest to understand the law. This chapter will complete your portfolio of 'finding' skills by explaining how to find these important supplementary resources, both in the library and online. It will cover books, journals, official publications, *Halsbury's Laws of England*, Bills and *Hansard*.

    The ability to find supplementary legal resources will give you a fully-rounded set of skills by which you can find the most useful sources of law. The use of supplementary resources will give you a much greater depth of knowledge than can easily be acquired from statutes and cases alone. There is a wealth of legal literature available, so without the ability to find it you will find yourself unable to benefit from the learned commentary of others—all of whom will (usually) have much more legal experience that you.

LEARNING OUTCOMES

After studying this chapter, you will be able to:

- Use online library catalogues and legal bibliographies to find books on a particular topic

- Understand journal citations

- Recognize the more common journal abbreviations

- Find journals in a library and online

- Distinguish between the various series of Command Papers

- Locate official publications in both paper and electronic form

- Use *Halsbury's Laws of England* to find the law on a specific topic

- Find Parliamentary Bills

- Use *Hansard* to find and follow debates in the House of Commons and House of Lords

8.1 Finding books

The ability to find books, either a specific title or a range of books on a particular topic, is important. Even if you purchase the set textbook for each of your subjects, there will still come a time when you need to find out what other books are available. You might, for instance, find that the set text is too complex, in which case you will want to find a more straightforward alternative. Conversely, if you are researching for a tutorial, a moot, or a piece of coursework, you may want to find books that go into more detail than the textbook that you have purchased.

8.1.1 Library catalogues

The first place to start looking for books on a particular topic is in your own library's catalogue as this will enable you to find which books are held at your own institution. However, there are also catalogues that provide information about the holdings of other libraries. This will be useful information if you want to know whether the university near your home town has sufficient books for your purposes during the vacation, for example, or enable you to locate a particular book that you need and order it from another library.

Most libraries provide an electronic facility by which you can search by author, title or subject area.

It is clearly impossible to provide details of how the catalogue works at every library. You should take time to familiarize yourself with the catalogue at your own institution. Your library will have instructions on how to use its catalogue. However, the experience of trial and error is also useful. Pick an area of law and try a few searches.

8.1.1.1 COPAC (www.copac.ac.uk)

COPAC is a free consolidated catalogue produced by the University of Manchester. It gives access to the online catalogues of the twenty-seven member institutions in the Consortium of Research Libraries (CURL) and contains over 31 million records. It includes the British Library, the National Library of Scotland, and the National Library of Wales/Llyfrgell Genedlaethol Cymru. There are also special collections from a small number of non-CURL libraries.

With information on the holdings of this range of libraries, this can be a useful means of locating less common books such as specialist monographs that may not be available at your own library.

8.1.1.2 HERO (www.hero.ac.uk)

HERO aims to be 'the primary internet portal for academic research and higher education in the UK'. It is another free resource which contains a complete listing of all University library catalogues available electronically as well as links to public library catalogues, archives and manuscripts and overseas library catalogues.

By using HERO, you should be able to locate any book that is of interest to you during your legal studies, including material that is published overseas.

8.1.2 Legal bibliographies

Whilst the ability to locate books using the library catalogue and the Internet are useful skills, you should not overlook the importance of 'paper-based' research skills. It may be, for example, that you are using a library that does not have computer terminals in the area that you are using and you want to be able to locate material without constantly trotting backwards and forwards between the library catalogue and the area where the books are shelved. Equally, it can be very frustrating to have to wait in a queue to use a catalogue or online search facility when you are in a hurry and want to find a book. At such times, the ability to locate materials using an alternative method may be invaluable.

8.1.2.1 *Lawyer's Law Books*

Lawyer's Law Books: A Practical Guide to Legal Literature[1] is an extremely useful reference that can be used to find books that have been written on a particular topic. It also lists useful Government publications by topic. However, the most recent edition is now around ten years out of date.

To find books on a topic, look in the list of subject headings and cross-references at the front of the book. Have a look at this extract:

DRAINS AND SEWERS 205
   see also Local Government; Public . . . .
   Health; Waters and Watercourses. . . . .
DRAMA— . . . .
   see Theatres. . . . .
DRAMATIC COPYRIGHT—. . . . .
   see Copyright. . . . .
DRINKING AND DRIVING. 206
   see also Blood Tests; Road Traffic. . . . .
DRUG MISUSE. 207
   see also Food and Drugs. . . . .
DRUNKENNESS— . . . .
   see Alcohol/Alcoholism; Drinking . . . . . .
   and Driving.

ENGINEERING CONTRACTS—
   see Building and Engineering Contracts
ENGINEERING LAW—
   see Architects and Surveyors, Building
   and Engineering Law.
ENGLISH LEGAL SYSTEM. 220
   see also Constitutional Law; Courts;
   Jurisprudence and Legal Philosophy.
ENTAIL—
   see Real Property.
ENTERTAINMENT 221
   see also Films; Radio and Television;
Sport; Theatres.

Extract 8.1 Subject headings and cross-references

You can see that this provides details of the broad reference categories and any that are related. For example, if you wanted to find if there were any books relating to drinking and driving, then this index would direct you to p. 206 where a list of texts can be found. (See Extract 8.2 overleaf.)

Lawyer's Law Books has the advantage of listing only the major legal reference works and therefore provides a manageable number of sources. You will see here that it lists fourteen texts that are directly relevant to the law in the area; a search for 'drinking and driving' on COPAC returns 143 matches (including illustrated poetry about drinking and driving which probably adds little value to your legal research).

1. Raistrick, D. (1997) *Lawyer's Law Books: A practical guide to legal literature* (3rd edn), East Grinstead: Bowker-Saur.

DRINKING AND DRIVING

See also Blood Tests; Road Traffic.

Encyclopaedias

Statutes in Force. Group: Road Traffic. Sub group 1.

Halsbury's Laws of England. 4ed. vol. 40.

Halsbury's Statutes of England and Wales. 4ed. vol. 38.

Texts

BROWN, F.
Drinking and driving: a pocket guide. Police Review, 1984.

DE BLACAM, M.
Drunken driving and the law. Round Hall Press, 1986 (Ireland).

ENVIRONMENT, DEPARTMENT OF THE
Drinking and driving: report of the Departmental Committee (Blennerhasset). HMSO, 1976.

HALNAN, P.
Drunk-driving; the new law. Oyez Longman, 1984.

HAMILTON, K.R.
Impaired driving and breathalyzer law: recent case law. Butterworths (Canada). Looseleaf

HOMMEL, R.
Policing and punishing the drunken driver: a study of specific deterrence. Springer, 1988 (Germany).

LAW REFORM COMMISSION OF CANADA
Report on investigative tests: alcohol, drugs and driving offences. 1983.

LEY, N.J.
Drink driving law and practice. Sweet & Maxwell, 1993.

McLEOD, R.M.
Criminal code driving offences: breathalizer law in Canada. Carswell, 1988. 3 vols. Looseleaf.

MITCHELS, B.
Road traffic. Longman, 1988. (Practice notes).

STONE's Justices' manual. Butterworths. Annual.

STRACHAN, B.
The drinking driver and the law. 3ed. Shaw, 1982.

WALLS, H.J. & BROWNLIE, A.D.
Drinks, drugs and driving. 2ed. Sweet & Maxwell, 1985.

WATKINS, D.
Drinking and driving: the decided cases, Police Review, 1987.

Extract 8.2 Lawyer's Law Books

Note that this entry also provides references to *Halsbury's Statutes of England and Wales* (which is covered in section 2.1) and *Halsbury's Laws of England* which can be found later in section 8.4.

8.1.2.2 *Current Law Monthly Digest*

The *Current Law Monthly Digest* contains a list of new books published during the month. At the end of the year these lists are reprinted in the *Current Law Year Book*.

This is useful to check for current books which might have been published in a particular area very recently, although it can be cumbersome to use when looking for books over more than one or two years, since the list is not cumulative and the subject headings uses are broader than those found in *Lawyer's Law Books*.

8.1.2.3 Specialist legal bibliographies

As well as *Lawyer's Law Books* and *Current Law* there are a number of other legal bibliographies which provide listings of books for particular areas of law. These are too numerous to list here, but a 'bibliography of bibliographies' can be found in *Lawyer's Law Books* under the subject heading of 'Bibliographies'!

8.1.2.4 References in textbooks

Never underestimate the value of simple strategies for locating secondary sources. All good-quality textbooks contain references to further secondary sources such as books and articles, either in the footnotes, additional reading sections, or in the bibliography. Not only do these provide the bibliographic details of books but they may give you an indication of why they are valuable sources. For example, if your textbook touches on a particular topic but not in any great detail—perhaps the point is too marginal for any great coverage in a textbook—it may provide details of the leading work(s) on that topic.

8.2 Finding journals

It is inevitable that you will need to locate journal articles at some point during your studies. Your tutorial reading is likely to contain references to publications in journals and, of course, you will want to demonstrate your research skills in your coursework essays by making reference to relevant journal articles.

See chapters 10 (writing skills) and 11 (essay skills) for a more detailed discussion of the value of journal articles in coursework.

The approach that is needed to locate journal articles will depend upon whether you are looking for a particular article that you know exists or whether you are having a speculative search to determine whether there are any articles on a particular topic.

8.2.1 Making sense of journal citations

Journal citations are used as a convenient shorthand means of pinpointing the location of a particular article. In other words, if you want to find a particular journal, you will need its 'address' in order to track it down.

Journal citations work in a similar way to citations for law reports. These were covered in section 5.1.2.

For example, if you wish to find the article cited as:

Fafinski, S. (2006) 'Access Denied: Computer Misuse in an Era of Technological Change' 70 (5) JCL 424–442.

you need to extract the key elements from the citation, so that you may find it easily in a library or online.

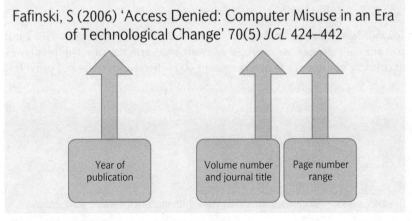

Figure 8.1 Journal citation

The year of publication and page number are self-explanatory. However, unlike the various series of law reports, there is unfortunately no single standard way of abbreviating journal titles. There are sometimes a couple of options for each journal.

Sometimes journal titles are written out in full rather than being abbreviated. This makes the task of finding them much easier!

An extremely useful guide to deciphering the multitude of journal abbreviations is the *Index to Legal Citations and Abbreviations*,[2] which provides almost 500 pages of abbreviations from '**a:** accession' to '**Zululand:** Zululand Commissioner's Court Cases (S. Afr.)'.

An alternative electronic source is the *Cardiff Index to Legal Abbreviations* available online at http://www.legalabbrevs.cardiff.ac.uk/

There may or may not be a volume number. Some journal series are just referenced by their year of publication. In others, there may be an issue number as well as a volume number. This is given either in brackets after the volume number, or after a full-stop following the volume number. In the example above the issue reference 70(5) could be shown as 70.5.

Breaking down the elements of the citation, you should see that it refers to:

- An article by S. Fafinski
- In volume 70, issue 5
- Of the *Journal of Criminal Law*
- Which was published in 2006
- Called 'Access Denied: Computer Misuse in an Era of Technological Change'
- Starting on p. 424
- And continuing until p. 442

This should be all the information you need to find the article, either in the library or online.

8.2.2 In a library

If you have the citation of the article, it should be a relatively straightforward task to find it in your library. Check the library catalogue or ask your librarian to make sure that the library carries the particular series of journals covering the date and/or volume that you need. Not all libraries carry all journals. To make matters even more complicated, even if your library *does* carry the series you need, there is no guarantee that it will have the particular volume you want. The library may have begun its subscription after the date you are looking for or cancelled its subscription before the date you require.

8.2.2.1 *Legal Journals Index*

The *Legal Journals Index* has been published monthly since September 1986 with cumulative monthly and annual volumes. It covers all relevant legal articles, case commentaries, book reviews and editorial comments. It covers around 400 different journals and provides indexing by:

- subject
- author

---

2.   Raistrick, D. (1993) *Index to Legal Citations and Abbreviations* (2nd edn), East Grinstead: Bowker-Saur.

- case
- legislation
- book reviews.

Here is an extract from the *Legal Journals Index*:

COMPUTER CRIME Companies. Fraud
Netting the fraudster. (Need for companies to develop fraud risk management strategy to prevent unauthorised access to computer systems and options faced by companies whose IT systems have been compromised, advocating use of forensic computer experts).
  Legal Week 1999, 1(7), 88

COMPUTER CRIME. Companies. Fraud. Internet
Computer fraud: Part 1: the risk to business (Definition of computer fraud, importance of businesses taking such fraud seriously, and threats to businesses through employee fraud. Web site hacking and fraud committed through use of web sites). Simon Dawson
  C.T.L.R. 1999, 5(3), 70–73

COMPUTER CRIME. Criminal evidence. Fraud
Computer-based crime preserving the evidence (Difficulties of combating computer fraud, concern that companies fail to report crime and private investigation procedures to preserve evidence and increase chances of identifying perpetrators). Nick Day.
  F. I. 1999, 14(Mar). 8–9

COMPUTER CRIME. Criminal evidence. Fraud. Internet
Computer fraud: Part 2: prevention and detection (Advice on reducing internal and external risk of computer fraud, detection techniques including disk imaging and analysis and problems relating to computer evidence). Simon Dawson
  C.T.L.R. 1999, 5(4), 114–117

Extract 8.3 *Legal Journals Index*

You will see that each subject area is broken down into categories. Each entry also gives the title of the article and its abstract or a brief description, the author's name (if available), and the journal citation.

 Practical exercise

Using the *Index to Legal Citations* or the *Cardiff Index to Legal Abbreviations* identify the journal in which Simon Dawson's two articles on Internet computer fraud were published. Try to find the two articles in your library.

The main drawback with the paper version of the Legal Journals Index is that the most recent volume (volume 14) was published in 1999. Since then it has only been available online. Therefore it is of limited use in finding current journal articles on a topic but is still of some interest for historical purposes.

8.2.3 Online

There are a number of online databases devoted to legal publications that you will find useful when searching for journal articles. You should, however, be aware that each database will only list articles in journals that are published by an organization that subscribes to that particular database. This means that you may find that the results of your search in any one database will not necessarily elicit information about all the articles that have been published on a particular topic, only the articles that have been published in journals that have paid to be listed in that database. Therefore, you may need to make reference to more than one database in order to find the article that you want or to obtain a complete list of all available articles.

For example, Westlaw lists articles published in the *Criminal Law Review* whilst LexisNexis publishes articles published in the *Journal of Criminal Law*. As the two leading journals on criminal law are covered by different databases, you would need to use both to ensure that you had been thorough in your search for articles on a topic in criminal law. By way of example, a search for articles using the search term 'intoxicated consent in rape' found twenty-eight relevant articles in Westlaw, two in Lawtel, and eight in LexisNexis.

8.2.3.1 Which database?

You may find this table useful if you wish to search for a particular journal online. Where no database is shown, this indicates that the journal is not available through the common online databases. You will either have to find the journal in the library or see if your library or institution provides alternative online means of access. For example, some institutions may have a direct subscription to the electronic form of the journal (Table 8.1).

Table 8.1 Journals, abbreviations, and databases

Journal	Abbreviation	Database
British Journal of Criminology	BJ Crim	Westlaw
Cambridge Law Journal	CLJ	
Child and Family Law Quarterly	CFLQ	LexisNexis
Civil Justice Quarterly	CJQ	Westlaw
Computer & Telecommunications Law Review	CTLR	Westlaw
Conveyancer and Property Lawyer	Conv	Lawtel
Counsel	*Counsel*	Lawtel
Criminal Law Review	Crim LR	Westlaw, Lawtel
Employment Law Bulletin	ELB	Westlaw
Employment Law Journal	ELJ	Lawtel
Estates Gazette	EG	Lawtel, LexisNexis
European Human Rights Law Review	EHRLR	Westlaw
Family Law	Fam Law	Lawtel, LexisNexis
Human Rights Law Review	HRLR	Westlaw
Industrial Law Journal	ILJ	Westlaw, LexisNexis
International and Comparative Law Quarterly	ICLQ	Westlaw
International Journal of Law and Information Technology	IJLT	LexisNexis
IT & Communications Law Journal	ITC	Lawtel
Journal of Business Law	JBL	
Journal of Criminal Law	JCL	LexisNexis

Table 8.1 *(Cont.)*

Journal	Abbreviation	Database
Journal of Environmental Law	JEnvL	Westlaw, LexisNexis
Journal of Information, Law & Technology	JILT	Lawtel
Journal of Law and Society	JLS	
Journal of Planning and Environment Law	JPL	
Justice of the Peace	JP	
Landlord and Tenant Review	LTR	Lawtel, Westlaw
Law Quarterly Review	LQR	Westlaw
Law Society's Gazette	*Gazette*	Lawtel, LexisNexis
Legal Studies	LS	
Litigation	*Litigation*	Lawtel
Medical Law Review	Med LR	Westlaw, LexisNexis
Modern Law Review	MLR	Lawtel
New Law Journal	NLJ	Lawtel, LexisNexis
Oxford Journal of Legal Studies	OJLS	Westlaw, LexisNexis
Police Journal	Police J	LexisNexis
Property Law Journal	PLJ	Lawtel
Public Law	PL	Westlaw, Lawtel
Solicitors Journal	SJ	Lawtel
Statute Law Review	SLR	Westlaw
The Guardian (Legal Section)	*Guardian*	Lawtel
The Independent (Legal Section)	*Independent*	Lawtel
The Times (Legal Section)	*Times*	Lawtel
Web Journal of Current Legal Issues	WebJCLI	Lawtel

8.2.3.2 Westlaw

Westlaw is a database owned by the publisher Sweet & Maxwell. It lists all articles that appear in their own journals as well as a selection of those owned by other publishers such as Oxford University Press. It is a well-maintained database that is updated on a daily basis, so it is a good way of locating articles that have just been published. It has the advantage of being a full-text database in relation to approximately sixty of its journals which means that it not only finds the article but also provides it in full for you to read on screen or print out. This can be a real asset if the article that you want is in a journal that is not held in your own library.

Westlaw has a 'quick search' page which enables you to get straight on with a search of journals, case law, or legislation as well as more detailed search facilities. The *Legal Journals Index* database is also available via Westlaw.

(Cont.)

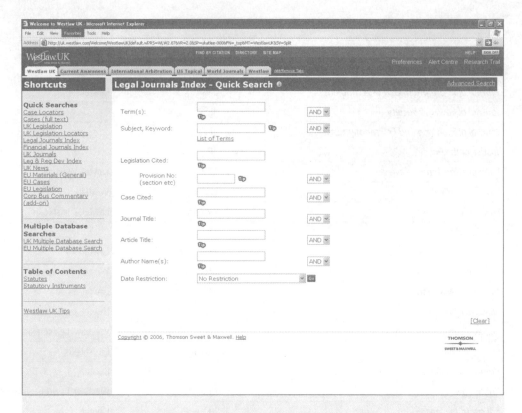

This provides an up-to-date index of legal journals which may be searched by:

- general terms, subject area, or keyword
- legislation cited (all articles which refer to a particular section of an Act)
- case cited (all articles which refer to a particular case)
- journal or article title
- name of the author(s).

If you are looking for an article that you know exists, it is likely that you will have sufficient information to find it without a great deal of difficulty by using the title of the article or the name of the author in combination with a keyword as the basis of the search.

For example, if you wanted to find an article by Stefan Fafinski that dealt with consent to injuries sustained during the course of sporting activities, you would locate the relevant article by typing 'Fafinski' in the author box (articles by authors with unusual surnames tend to lead to fewer matches) and 'consent' in the subject box: this would find the details of the relevant article.

However, it will often be the case that you are looking for articles on a topic and are not sure whether any have been written. Here, you will need to use keyword searching and it may take a fair amount of experimentation with search terms to find material that is useful to you.

8.2.3.3 Lawtel

Lawtel provides a search facility for seventy-two different UK legal publications. It is also owned by Sweet & Maxwell so you may find that there is a fair degree of overlap with Westlaw in terms of its coverage. Lawtel also includes a number of practitioner-focused journals such as the *Solicitors Journal* and *Counsel* as well as more academic titles. Practitioner journals can be particularly useful as they are published far more frequently than academic journals—the *Solicitors Journal*, for example, is a weekly publication—so it often has comment on recent cases and events. Lawtel also provides access to newspaper law reports from *The Times, The Independent* and *The Guardian*.

8.2.3.4 LexisNexis

LexisNexis is owned by the publisher Butterworths and contains the full text of articles published in around eighty-five journals and summaries of the articles found in many more journals. It is also updated regularly. In addition to academic journals, LexisNexis covers a range of practitioner titles such as the *New Law Journal*.

As with Westlaw and Lawtel, it provides the ability to search by title, author, or general search terms but it has the additional benefit of providing a drop-down list of the journals covered which can facilitate a more focused search of a particular publication. For example, if you were looking for articles on a topic within criminal law and did not want to trawl through a long list of results, you could search exclusively within the *Journal of Criminal Law*. This can be useful in speeding up your search and eliminating unwanted materials from the outset. You should be wary, however, of being overly selective in your searching as general journals, such as the *Oxford Journal of Legal Studies*, cover articles on any topic within the law, so searching in a particular specialist journal would automatically exclude relevant articles published in general journals.

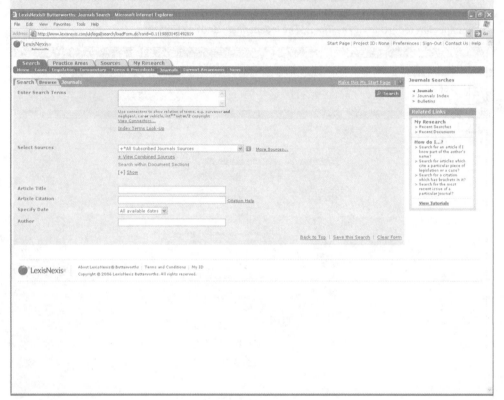

8.2.3.5 HeinOnline (www.heinonline.org)

HeinOnline was introduced in 2000 by William S. Hein & Co., an American legal publisher. It contains full text resources from a large number of journals. Unlike the other full-text services, it provides exact page images. This means that you can see all the pages as they originally appeared in print. However, as you might expect from an American service, the journal coverage is predominantly American, although it does cover certain volumes of a number of the major UK journals including:

- *Modern Law Review* (1937–2001)

- *Law Quarterly Review* (1885–1925)

- *Cambridge Law Journal* (1921–2001)

- *Legal Studies* (1981–2004)

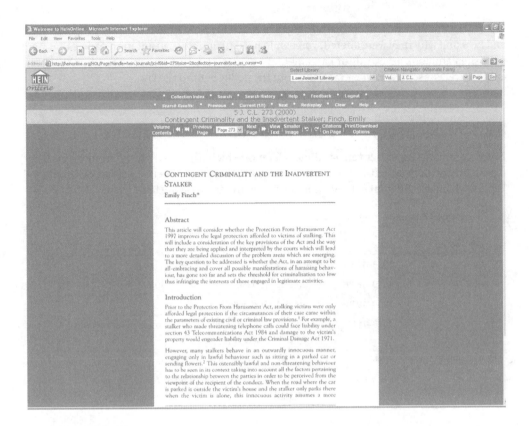

Practical exercise

Try to find the following articles online and in the library:

1. Walker, C. 'Terrorism and criminal justice' [2004] *Criminal Law Review* 311–27.

2. Slapper, G. J. 'Civil liability and corporate crime: litigation using the a fortiori principle' (1997) 1(4) *Journal of Personal Injury Litigation* 220.

3. Macdonald, E. 'Scope and Fairness of the Unfair Terms in Consumer Contracts Regulations' (2002) 65 *Modern Law Review* 763.

8.3 Finding official publications

Government department and other official organizations conduct a great deal of research prior to recommending changes to the law and their findings may be an incredibly rich source of information. If you need to understand the priorities that shaped the content of the current law or the reason why an Act of Parliament covers certain issues but not others, it is likely that you will find the answer in an official publication. For example, the Sexual Offences Act 2003 was enacted after a prolonged period of consultation over a period of years and the final statute was very different to the original proposals. If you wanted to know what the earlier proposals were and how and why they were altered, you would need to find the consultation papers that were published and look at records of Parliamentary debates. For this reason, official publications can be excellent sources of information about the policy behind the law.

8.3.1 Making sense of Command Paper abbreviations

Every Command Paper is given a unique reference which is printed on the front cover of the report (in the bottom left-hand corner). However, there have been six series of Command Papers, which use different abbreviations as shown in the following table:

Table 8.2 Series of Command Papers

Series	Dates	Abbreviation
1	1833–1869	[1]–[4222]
2	1870–1899	[C. 1]–[C. 9550]
3	1900–1918	[Cd. 1]–[Cd. 9329]
4	1919–1956	[Cmd. 1]–Cmd. 9889 (the use of square brackets was discontinued in 1922)
5	1956–1986	Cmnd. 1–Cmnd. 9927
6	1986–date	Cm. 1–(series 6 contains around 7000 Command Papers as at 2006)

It is important to look at the style of abbreviation. This will give you an indication of the date of the Command Paper—remember that there is a thirty-year gap between Cmnd. 1 and Cm. 1 for example.

8.3.2 In a library

Most libraries will contain a collection of Command Papers. These will either be arranged by series and number, in which case it is a very straightforward task to find the paper you want. However, some libraries organize their Parliamentary materials in *sessional sets*: in other words bound together in volumes for a particular session of Parliament. These will therefore be organized by year. If your library organizes its Command Papers in this way, you will need to have some idea of the year of the paper as well as its abbreviated reference.

Unfortunately, as should be clear from the table, it is virtually impossible to determine the year from the Command Paper reference (unless it is right at the start or end of the range for a particular series). However, Command Papers until 1972 are indexed by year in *British Official Publications*:[3] the relevant section is called the *Concordance of Command Papers 1833–1972*.

---

3. Pemberton J. (1973) *British Official Publications* (2nd edn) Oxford: Pergamon Press.

8.3.3 Online

8.3.3.1 *Official Documents*

Official Documents is the official reference facility for Command Papers, Departmentally Sponsored House of Commons Papers, and key Departmental Papers. It is a free service available at www.official-documents.co.uk. It contains all documents from the 2005/2006 Parliamentary session onwards in chronological order. Documents are divided by document type, and then by year or, for House of Commons Papers, Parliamentary session. A selection of papers published since 1994 are also available.

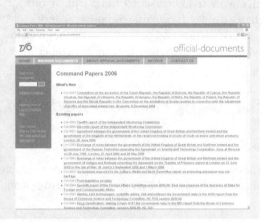

8.3.3.2 Office of Public Sector Information

The Office of Public Sector Information website www.opsi.gov.uk/official-publications/index.htm contains a list of Command Papers from 2001 by number and alphabetically by department with links to the papers on Government Departmental websites where possible.

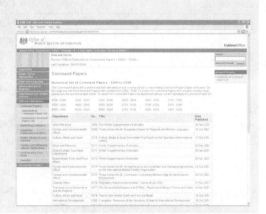

8.3.3.3 BOPCRIS

BOPCRIS (British Official Publications Collaborative Reader Information Service) is a free online database which provides British Official Publications from 1688 to 1995. It can be found at www.bopcris.ac.uk. It enables you to search and browse for relevant documents, read abstracts, read the digitized full-text version of a limited number of documents, and provides the nearest location of the documents if full-text is not available.

However, if you are searching for Official Publications after 1995 you will need to use the subscription service UKOP.

8.3.3.4 UKOP

UKOP (www.ukop.co.uk) is a subscription service provided by TSO (the Stationery Office). It is the official catalogue of UK official publications since 1980. It contains around 450,000 records from over 2,000 public bodies. It provides full search facilities and an alphabetical list of issuing bodies and departments. It provides the full text of over 30,000 documents. Where the full text is not available it provides details of where you can obtain a printed copy. It is updated daily.

8.3.3.5 *House of Commons Parliamentary Papers*

House of Commons Parliamentary Papers is a commercially-available service (http://parlipapers. chadwyck.co.uk/marketing/index.jsp). It provides a searchable full-text facility as well as a detailed index. It currently comprises an index for 1801 to 2004, full text for the entire nineteenth century, and for 1901 to 1945. Two further instalments complete the twentieth century, starting with coverage to the mid-1970s in November 2006, to be followed by a final release in Spring 2007.

8.4 Using *Halsbury's Laws of England*

8.4.1 In a library

Halsbury's Laws of England aims to provide a complete statement of English law, derived from all sources. As you can imagine, this is a massive work. It comprises sixty volumes in several parts.

Table 8.3 The volumes comprising *Halsbury's Laws of England*

Component	Content
Main volumes	*Halsbury's Laws of England* comprises fifty main volumes, arranged alphabetically by subject from 'Administrative Law' to 'Wills'. There are also two additional volumes entitled *European Communities* which deal with European law in so far as it relates to the UK.
Annual Abridgement	The *Annual Abridgment* is published each year (as a new volume rather than a cumulative volume) and includes changes to the law which have not yet been published in the main volumes
Consolidated Table of Statutes, Statutory Instruments and Tables of European Communities Materials	This volume (Volume 53) brings together references to statutory materials from all the main volumes
Consolidated Table of Cases and Chronological Table of Cases in the European Court of Justice	Volume 54 provides a list of all cases referred to in *Halsbury's Laws* including cases in the European Court of Justice.
Consolidated Index	These two volumes index the main volumes by subject matter
Cumulative Supplement	An annually published two-volume set which brings all text volumes up to date as at 31 October of the preceding year. This will include all developments which arose during the previous Parliamentary session.
Current Service Binder 1 Monthly Review	This is a loose-leaf binder which contains the most recent changes to the main volumes and the *Annual Abridgement.*
Current Service Binder 2 Noter-Up Service	This loose-leaf binder contains the latest annotations to the main volumes and the *Annual Abridgement.*

The information listed in the main volumes is brought up-to-date annually via the *Cumulative Supplement* with more recent (i.e. this year's) developments being available via the *Noter-Up Service*. Therefore, whenever using *Halsbury's Laws* you should always consult the main volumes, *Cumulative Supplement* and *Noter-Up Service* in that order:

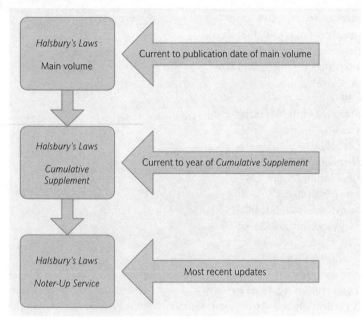

Figure 8.2 *Halsbury's Laws*

The best place to start when trying to find the law on a particular topic is the *Consolidated Index*. By way of example, imagine that a client has just come to you for advice. He lives near the site of the 2012 Olympic Park in London and is thinking of opening a greasy spoon café to sell hot bacon rolls to the construction workers that will be there to build the facilities for the Games. He is convinced that he will have a largely captive and hungry clientele and is confident that he will make a substantial profit. He (somewhat unimaginatively) wants to call his establishment the *Olympic Café* and would like to use the five-ring Olympic symbol on his shopfront and advertising material. One of his friends has told him that he might not be allowed to do that, so he wants to know what he is legally allowed to do.

You could start by looking up the subject in the *Consolidated Index* under 'Olympics':

OLYMPICS ASSOCIATION RIGHT
    controlled representation—
        meaning, **48**, 135n[4]
        forfeiture of counterfeit goods bearing, **48**, 135
        offences relating to, **48**, 133
        unauthorised use of, **48**, 141
        use of—
            meaning, **48**, 151
            not constituting infringement, **48**, 152
            onus of proof, **48**, 153
    creation of, **48**, 150
    infringement, **48**, 86n[1], 141, 151

infringement proceedings—
   proprietor's right, **48**, 153
   remedies, **48**, 153
   threat of, groundless, **48**, 154
infringing articles: meaning, **48**, 153n[3]
infringing goods: meaning, **48**, 152n[13]
infringing material: meaning, **48**, 153n[3]
judicial proceedings, meaning, **48**, 152n[22]
jurisdiction, **48**, 394n[2]
limitation, **48**, 152
Olympic motto: meaning, **48**, 151n[3]
Olympic symbol—
   meaning, **48**, 151n[2]
   counterfeit goods, **48**, 135n[2]
   offences relating to, **48**, 133, 134
   protection of, 9(2), 494n[9]
   unauthorised use of, **48**, 141, 487
parliamentary proceedings 152n[22]
proprietor, **48**, 151n[7]
protected words, **48**, 151n[4], 152
scope of right, **48**, 151
statutory inquiry: meaning, **48**, 152n[22]
vesting of, in British Olympic Association, **48**, 150

Extract 8.4 *Consolidated Index*

Notice the section headed OLYMPICS ASSOCIATION RIGHT. There are various subcategories under this heading, some of which are to do with the Olympic symbol.

Your client is particularly concerned with whether or not his use of the Olympic symbol is allowed. First, you can check the meaning of the term 'Olympic symbol'. The reference given is '*meaning*, **48**, 151n[2]'.

Each entry in the *Consolidated Index* shows the main volume number (in bold) and paragraph number of *Halsbury's Laws* where you will find the information you require. Therefore, the meaning of 'Olympic symbol' can be found in vol. 48 at para. 151. The 'n[2]' signifies that the particular information is one of the footnotes; in this case footnote 2 as denoted by the superscript 2.

If you then turn to the footnotes following para. 151 in vol. 48 you will find:

151. Scope of the Olympics association right. The Olympics association right[1] confers exclusive rights in relation to the use of the Olympic symbol[2], the Olympic motto[3] and the protected words[4]. The rights so conferred are infringed by any act done in the United Kingdom which constitutes infringement[5] and is done without the consent of the person for the time being appointed[6] by the Secretary of State ('the proprietor')[7]. The proprietor may exploit the rights conferred, but may not make any disposition of, or of any interest in or over, them[8].

A person infringes the Olympics association right if in the course of trade he uses a representation of the Olympic symbol, the Olympic motto or a protected word, or a representation of something so similar to the Olympic symbol or the Olympic motto as to be likely to create in the public mind an association with it ('a controlled representation')[9].

A person uses a controlled representation if, in particular, he:

(1) affixes it to goods or the packaging thereof[10];
(2) incorporates it in a flag or banner[11];

(3) offers or exposes for sale, puts on the market or stocks for those purposes goods which bear it or whose packaging bears it[12];

(4) imports or exports goods which bear it or whose packaging bears it[13];

(5) offers or supplies services under a sign which consists of or contains it[14]; or

(6) uses it on business papers or in advertising[15].

1. Is the light created by the Olympic Symbol etc (Protection) Act 1995s 1(1): see para 150 ante. The right carries with it the rights and remedies provided by the Olympic Symbol etc (Protection) Act 1995, which are exercisable by the proprietor. s 1(2). As to the proprietor see not 8 infra.

2. Is the symbol of the International Olympic Committee, consisting of five interlocking rings ibid s 18(1)

Extract 8.5 Scope of the Olympics association right

Therefore the Olympic symbol is 'the symbol of the International Olympic Committee, consisting of five interlocking rings'. The statutory reference to this is s. 18(1) of the Olympic Symbol etc (Protection) Act 1995.

You will also see that a person infringes the Olympic association right if in the course of trade he uses an representation of the Olympic symbol, including supplying services under a sign which contains it and using it on business papers or in advertising without the rights conferred by the Olympic Symbol, etc. (Protection) Act 1995.

Therefore, your client is not allowed to use the symbol without permission. If he does so, you can also advise him of the potential outcome by looking under 'infringement proceedings—proprietor's right, **48**, 153':

153. Infringement of the Olympics association right; proceedings and remedies. An infringement of the Olympics association right[1] is actionable by the proprietor[2]. In an action for infringement, all such relief by way of damages, injunctions, accounts or otherwise is available to the proprietor as is available in respect of the infringement of a property right[3].

If in any civil proceedings a question arises as to the use to which a controlled representation has been put, it is for the proprietor to show what use was made of it[4]. If in any civil proceedings a question arises as to the application of any of the provisions relating to the circumstances in which the Olympic association right is not infringed[5], it is for the person who alleges that the provision applies to show that it does[6].

Extract 8.6 Infringement of the Olympics association right—proceedings and remedies

Therefore, if your client proceeds, he may be sued by the owner of the right and be liable in damages (compensation) or subject to an injunction (a court order prohibiting from using the symbol). Overall, you should advise him that his plan is a bad idea!

With any search in *Halsbury's Laws* you must *always* check the *Cumulative Supplement* and the *Noter-Up Service* for any recent changes to the law since publication of the main volumes.

8.4.2 Online

Halsbury's Laws of England is available online via LexisNexis under the 'Commentary' tab.

This allows you to search the database by particular terms, or to browse each volume individually. The text displayed for a particular volume is identical to that in the paper version: there is an update section online which is the equivalent to the *Cumulative Supplement* and *Noter-Up*. The online version has the useful addition of hyperlinks to relevant legislation which you can consult if you wish. This is obviously much quicker than looking up the statute in a library or on a separate database. Take a look at the electronic version of vol. 48, para. 151 here (see following page).

The flexible search facilities and use of hyperlinks to other materials generally makes the electronic version of *Halsbury's Laws* easier to use than the bound paper edition.

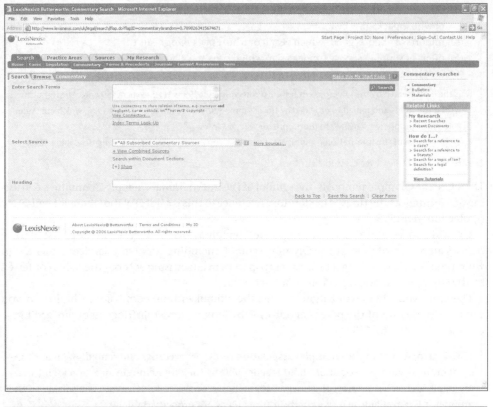

8.5 Finding Bills

8.5.1 Making sense of Bill citations

The role of Bills in the Parliamentary process is covered in chapter 1.

Public Bills carry a serial number in the bottom left-hand corner of the first page of the Bill. For example, the 2006 Video Games Bill is Bill 136.

A

BILL

TO

Amend the Video Recordings Act 1984 to extend certain provisions of that Act to video games and to make provision about the labelling of video games.

B E IT ENACTED by the Queen's most Excellent Majesty, by and with the advice and consent of the Lords Spiritual and Temporal, and Commons, in this present Parliament assembled, and by the authority of the same, as follows:—

1 **Amendment of the Video Recordings Act 1984**

  (1) The Video Recordings Act 1984 (c. 39) is amended as follows.

  (2) In section 2 (exempted works), subsection (1)(c) shall cease to have effect.

  (3) In section 8 (requirements as to labelling, etc.), after subsection (2), insert—

    "(2A) Regulations under this section shall, in particular, make provision—

        (a) about the size of a label on any spool, case or other thing in which a video game is kept,

        (b) about the prominence to be accorded to the classification in relation to age of the video game on such a label,

        (c) requiring the inclusion in such a label in relation to a video game to which subsection (2B) applies of such textual information as may be prescribed in the regulations.

Bill 136

Extract 8.7 Video Games Bill 2006

This Bill would be cited as shown in Figure 8.3.

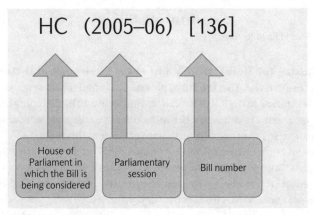

Figure 8.3 Bill citation

The convention for citing Bills therefore begins with HC (for House of Commons) or HL (for House of Lords). Since Bill numbering restarts at 1 with every new Parliamentary session, the dates of that session must be given to identify the Bill precisely. Finally, the citation provides the number of the Bill.

Traditionally, Bills in the House of Commons had a number in square brackets, and Bills in the House of Lords had a number in round brackets. You may still see this convention used in relation to Commons Bills, but Lords Bill numbers have now lost their brackets.

8.5.2 In a library

The *House of Commons Weekly Information Bulletin* gives details of Bills that are before Parliament in the current session. Bills are listed alphabetically by title. The *Bulletin* also provides details of the Parliamentary history of each Bill including the dates of each reading in the House of Commons and House of Lords and any proceedings in Standing Committee.

8.5.3 Online

Details of the Bills before Parliament in the current session can be found on the UK Parliament website www.publications.parliament.uk/pa/pabills.htm.

8.6 Finding Parliamentary debates

Remember that the Official Reports of Parliamentary Debates are generally referred to as Hansard *after one of its earliest (although not the earliest) printers. See chapter 3.*

8.6.1 In a library

Hansard is published daily and reprinted each week as *Weekly Hansard*. An index to the debates is also published every two weeks.

At the end of each parliamentary session *Hansard* is republished as a set of bound volumes with a corresponding index. These volumes are numbered sequentially—there are over 400 of them.

Here is an extract from the printed *Hansard* showing the start of the second reading of the Hunting Bill in the House of Commons:

---

15 SEPTEMBER 2004   1326

Orders of the Day

Hunting Bill

Order for Second Reading read.

3.47 pm

The Minister for Rural Affairs and Local Environmental Quality (Alun Michael): I beg to move, That the Bill be now read a Second time.

This Bill is identical to the Bill to which this House gave a Third Reading on 9 July 2003. There will be a separate debate on the motion for the suggested amendment to defer commencement, so I shall not refer further to that issue at this stage.

The House of Lords did not complete its proceedings on the Bill before the end of the previous Session, although it had the time to do so. The Government are now bringing the Bill back to enable this House, if it so chooses, to insist on the Bill and, if it is again rejected by the House of Lords, to pass it under the Parliament Act.

Extract 8.8 *Hansard*

Note that *Hansard* is printed in a two-column format. References to *Hansard* quote column numbers rather than page numbers. Therefore, the reference to the order for second reading of the Hunting Bill in the House of Commons would be 'Vol. 424 Col. 1326'.

8.6.2 Online

Hansard is available online free of charge online on the UK Parliament website at

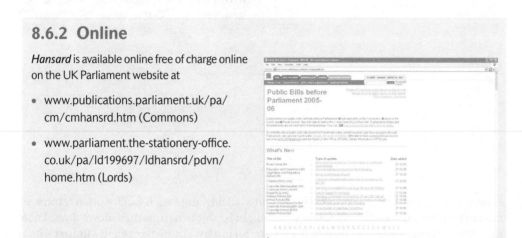

- www.publications.parliament.uk/pa/ cm/cmhansrd.htm (Commons)

- www.parliament.the-stationery-office. co.uk/pa/ld199697/ldhansrd/pdvn/ home.htm (Lords)

The format of the House of Lords pages is slightly different to that of the House of Commons.

Hansard online covers debates in the House of Commons since 1988–9 and the House of Lords since 1994–5. If you need to find earlier debates, then you will have to use the bound paper volumes.

It does not present the text in the same two-column format as the printed version. It does, however, mark the breaks in the text where new columns start in the printed volumes. If you are looking for a specific column within an online report, it is often easier to search for the column number from within the browser itself (Ctrl-F or Edit > Find (on this page)) rather than scrolling down through a mass of text.

A comprehensive search facility is also provided at

www.publications.parliament.uk/cgi-bin/semaphoreserver?DB=semukparl&FILE=search.

However, given the vast amount of information available, the search facility often returns an unmanageably large number of matches. You might be able to narrow these down if you know the names of the principal speakers in the debate; for instance the Government Minister who is sponsoring a particular Bill. The search facility allows you to put in a number of filters, which you should be prepared to do if overwhelmed by the volume of responses.

 Practical exercise

Try to find the debates in both the House of Commons and the House of Lords leading to the enactment of the Computer Misuse Act 1990 and the Hunting Act 2004.

 CHAPTER SUMMARY

Books

- Your own library's catalogue is the first place to start looking for books

- COPAC is a free consolidated online catalogue covering the libraries of twenty-seven institutions

- HERO also provides free online links to a number of library catalogues

- *Lawyer's Law Books* arranges books by topic, although it is now around ten years out of date

- The *Current Law Monthly Digest* and *Current Law Year Book* provide lists of new books published during a specific month or year, although it can be difficult to use

- Specialist legal bibliographies also exist and can be found listed in *Lawyer's Law Books*

Journals

- There is no single standard way of citing journal articles

- The *Cardiff Index to Legal Abbreviations* is a useful free online resource to help you decipher unfamiliar journal abbreviations

- *Legal Journals Index* contains lists of articles by topic, but it has not been published in print since 1999.

- Westlaw contains an up-to-date *Legal Journal Index* database

- Lawtel indexes across seventy-two different UK publications

- LexisNexis indexes around eighty-five journals

- HeinOnline is an American database, with sporadic coverage of major UK journals. It has a good selection of historical material and provides page images of the journals

Official publications

- Most libraries carry a range of official publications in print

- *Official Publications* is the official free online reference facility for Command Papers containing all from 2005/6 and a selection from 1994 onwards

- OPSI provides a list of all Command Papers since 2001 by number and department with links to some, but not all

- BOPCRIS is a free database of official publications from to 1688 to 1995

- UKOP is a commercial service from the Stationery Office. It is the official catalogue of UK official publications from 1980 onwards with the full text of over 30,000 documents

- *House of Commons Parliamentary Papers* is a commercial service with searchable full text and an index for papers since 1801

Halsbury's Laws of England

- *Halsbury's Laws of England* is an immense legal encyclopedia which aims to provide a complete statement of English law derived from all sources

- It provides indices by statute, case, and topic

- It is much easier to use online via LexisNexis than in print

Bills

- Details of Bills can be found either in the *House of Commons Weekly Information Bulletin* or online via the UK Parliament website

Hansard

- *Hansard* provides a verbatim transcript of all Parliamentary debate

- It is freely available online on the UK Parliament website which also provides comprehensive search facilities

- The online service covers Commons debates from 1988 to 1989 and Lords debates since 1994–5. You will need to find older debates in a library

PART II
Academic legal skills

This part of the book covers the skills that you will need to get to grips with the academic requirements of legal study. It begins by covering some general skills in the first two chapters on study and writing skills. The remaining chapters build on these general skills with a focus on the particular skills necessary to address both essay questions and problem questions. Each of these chapters will demonstrate various ways by which you will be able to strengthen your essay writing and problem-solving technique. In particular these chapters contain specific research-focused material to give you help with the particular research requirements of essays and problems, whilst demonstrating that the research process must always be tailored to the task in hand. Finally this part of the book will close with a chapter covering the skills required to revise effectively and to translate that revision into success in examinations.

Study skills

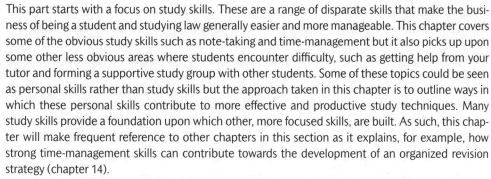

9

INTRODUCTION

This part starts with a focus on study skills. These are a range of disparate skills that make the business of being a student and studying law generally easier and more manageable. This chapter covers some of the obvious study skills such as note-taking and time-management but it also picks up upon some other less obvious areas where students encounter difficulty, such as getting help from your tutor and forming a supportive study group with other students. Some of these topics could be seen as personal skills rather than study skills but the approach taken in this chapter is to outline ways in which these personal skills contribute to more effective and productive study techniques. Many study skills provide a foundation upon which other, more focused skills, are built. As such, this chapter will make frequent reference to other chapters in this section as it explains, for example, how strong time-management skills can contribute towards the development of an organized revision strategy (chapter 14).

Resist any temptation to dismiss study skills as unimportant or to assume that they are something that you must already possess as you have enjoyed sufficient success in your studies to take you to university. Study skills are important as they underpin the whole process of learning a new subject and acquiring knowledge. If you think that you are already good at this, perhaps you are but why would you not want to improve and to find ways to make study an even smoother process? Moreover, study at degree level is bound to be different and require more from you than your previous studies so it is important to adapt and develop your existing skills to ensure that you are able to work successfully at this higher level. Finally, study skills should be seen as something that evolve and mature all the time that you study. Hopefully, you will complete your degree not only with a comprehensive mastery of the law but also with an increased confidence in your ability to engage in self-supported independent study.

LEARNING OUTCOMES

After studying this chapter, you will be able to:

- Appreciate the contribution made by personal skills of communication and organization to the evolution of effective study habits and practices

- Recognize the value of lectures and seminars and find ways to gain maximum benefit from these activities

- Develop an efficient and effective method of recording and organizing your notes

- Reflect upon your ability to manage your time and adopt some useful strategies to help you to organize your studies more effectively

- Deal with lecturers in a polite and professional manner and recognize the potential for making study more effective and enjoyable by working with other students

9.1 Lectures

Students tend to like lectures. They involve the unidirectional communication of information, they usually involve the circulation of a handout with the key points noted upon it and, unlike seminars or tutorials, lectures involve no risk that participation from the student will be required (unless your lecturer favours Socratic method in which questions are directed at students during the lecture but this is not a popular method of lecturing in this country).

What is the purpose of a lecture? Opinions on this vary amongst lecturers but there are three dominant schools of thought:

1. To outline the basic aspects of a topic in order to provide students with a foundation of knowledge upon which to build by undertaking tutorial preparation and independent reading;

2. To cover an aspect of the topic in an engaging manner in order to capture the interest of the students and encourage them to carry out thorough reading on the topic;

3. To build upon basic knowledge acquired through private study undertaken prior to the lecture and to explain complex concepts that the students will have encountered in their reading.

The common theme is the communication of information to the audience. If the job of the lecturer is to give out information, it must be the task of the student to receive it but what does this suggest about the most effective approach to lectures for students? (Figure 9.1)

9.1.1 Methods of recording information

Different strategies work for different people. Many students adopt a traditional linear approach to note-taking that records the information in words and sentences as it is presented, sometimes using headings and subheadings to identify particular topics. However, consider alternative techniques such as flow diagrams and arrows (excellent for those who like to see the logical relationships between different points) or mind maps (suited to students who have strong visualization skills). You will find examples of each of these methods in the section below on note-taking.

You may wish to make a tape-recording of the lectures. Although this may seem reasonable to you, some lecturers will object to this and some institutions have a 'no recording without prior permission' policy that is relaxed only for students with a disability that makes recording a necessity. If you would like to record the lecture, investigate the policy at your institution and always approach each individual lecturer and seek permission.

TIPS FOR GETTING VALUE OUT OF LECTURES	
DO	DON'T
Listen and think about what the lecturer is saying. It is more important to understand what is said than it is to capture every word in note form.	Write everything that is said without thought. Try to be selective and note only key points. This will make your notes more manageable.
Review your notes after the lecture. Make a note of anything that you do not understand and follow up any points that are not clear to you by using a good text book and supplement your notes with independent reading.	Rely on the lecture to give you all the information that you need about a subject. A lecture gives you a framework of information and you should supplement this with your own reading to build a more complete picture of the subject.
Develop a system of abbreviations to speed up the process of taking notes.	Talk to other students during the lecture. It is discourteous (to other students and to the lecturer), it will disrupt the concentration of those around you who are trying to listen and it may even result in your being asked to leave the lecture.
Develop a structured approach to note-taking (see below at 9.3) to ensure that your notes are organised and easy to use for reference.	
Take paper. It is a mistake to think that there will be enough room for your notes on the handout.	Arrive late, leave early, eat food, read a newspaper, play 'noughts and crosses' or text your friends.

Figure 9.1 Tips for getting value from lectures

9.1.2 Asking questions in lectures

Lecturers will vary in terms of how receptive they are to being asked questions about the substance of the topic during lectures. It is usual for the lecturer to have a clear plan of the information that is to be covered in that session so dealing with questions can interfere with that plan and lead to insufficient time to deal with the material that needs to be covered. Some lecturers, however, are perfectly amenable to being asked questions and will usually tell you this at the start of the course.

However, as the main aim of the lecture is to transmit information, it is essential that the audience are able to hear and understand, so it is perfectly acceptable to ask questions that relate to these sorts of issues even if the lecturer has made it clear that they do not usually welcome questions:

- I'm afraid I didn't catch that last point, could you repeat it?
- Could you please speak more slowly; I'm find it difficult to keep up?
- Could you please speak up a bit; it is hard to hear at the back?
- I didn't understand that point, could you explain it again?
- I'm struggling to understand this. Do you have an example that might make it clearer?

These suggestions demonstrate an effective way to phrase the question by combining the request with the explanation for its existence; this is generally viewed as a softer approach than a request on its own. If the request is for elaboration rather than repetition or a change of speed/volume, you may find that the lecturer responds by telling you to bring up the question in the seminar, in which case you should make a note of your question so that you remember to do so.

In essence, it is important that you develop an approach to lectures that enables you to make the most of the information communicated. One possible approach is to adopt a three-stage process that uses the content of the lecture as the basis upon which a more detailed and comprehensive understanding of the topic is developed (Figure 9.2).

---

1. At the lecture

Listen, think and note what seems to be the main points made by the lecturer. Check the handout and supplement this with your own notes rather than rewriting what is provided. Highlight anything that the lecturer identifies as a particularly important point.

↓

2. After the lecture

Read through your notes to ensure that they make sense and that they are complete. Make a list of key cases that you need to read, key commentators whose views you need to discover and note anything that puzzles you as an issue to follow up in your own reading.

↓

3. Before the next lecture

Find the relevant chapter in your textbook that covers the material covered in the previous lecture and use this to supplement and expand your lecture notes. Read cases and articles to gain a greater depth of understanding. If possible, glance over the subject matter of the next lecture so that you have a chance to think about how this links to the material that you have already covered.

Figure 9.2 Three-stage lecture process

 Practical exercise

 Watch the video clip of the lecture on the Online Resource Centre and take notes.

Compare your notes to the three examples of notes taken from the lecture that are also on the Online Resource Centre and see whether you feel that they are more or less useful than those that you took. Which of the three sets of notes do you prefer? Think about why this is the case and consider whether there are any techniques that you could use to improve your own approach to note-taking during lectures.

9.2 Seminars and tutorials

Seminars and tutorials are terms used to describe a method of small-group teaching. It is usual for students to be given work to do in advance of the tutorial. This may involve reading a particular case or a section of a textbook and either making notes or answering particular questions. This will often relate to an issue covered in the lecture, thus giving the students an opportunity to explore that issue in greater depth and ask questions or offer opinions about that issue in order to improve their understanding. Unlike lectures, which tend to involve a one-way process of communication from lecturer to student, seminars and tutorials are based upon group communication so that each member of the group should make a contribution to the discussion. It is useful to view a small-group session as an opportunity to voice your thoughts about the topic rather than expecting to receive information from the lecturer.

9.2.1 Preparation

You will derive far more benefit from seminars and tutorials if you undertake the required preparation. The background reading will help to familiarize you with the topic and make it more likely that you will understand and be able to contribute to the group discussion whilst answering any questions that have been set will enable you to check your understanding by comparing your answers with those suggested by others in the seminar group.

When you are carrying out the required reading prior to the seminar, make sure that you make a note of any issues that you find difficult. This will enable you to compile a list of questions that you would like answered by the seminar. This does not mean that you need to ask all these questions yourself; it is likely that the answers will emerge as the seminar discussion progresses and other students make comments or ask questions. It can be a useful technique to make a list of numbered questions on a separate sheet of paper and leave a sufficient gap in between each question so that you can make a note of the answer when it comes up in the discussion. This will give you a clear method for recording information so that your seminar notes do not get confused with the problem areas that you have identified and it will also enable you to see at a glance whether all your questions have been answered during the session. If you feel that you lack confidence to contribute to the group discussion by answering a question, you can ask one of the questions that you have noted. Not only will this clarify your understanding, it will help you to feel more involved with the group discussion and this should help you build up your confidence to make more frequent contributions to the debate. This issue is explored in greater detail in the next section.

Preparation for a seminar usually involves a combination of reading and some other activity whether this is answering a series of questions about the reading or writing an answer to a problem question. It is important to actually do the activities as well as the reading. Some students are particularly reluctant to attempt to answer a problem question on the basis that they are not sure about the correct answer. That does not matter; the value of the activity will not be negated by some errors of law and it is only by attempting to tackle the problem that you will be able to identify whether or not you understand the law in question.

One technique that can be useful is to prepare an answer by dividing your paper in half down the middle, noting the points that you are confident about on the left-hand side and those of which you are unsure on the right-hand side. As the answer builds up in the seminar, mark off each correct point and make a note of the correct answer in relation to points where you were not correct. By using this technique, you will have tackled everything and you will be able to see at a glance which points you had answered correctly. It can be very encouraging to see a line of ticks against points that you felt may have been wrong.

9.2.2 Participation

Many students are reluctant to participate in seminar discussion. Students give a range of explanations for this but several of these have a common theme relating to their lack of confidence, either to speak out or about the accuracy of their legal knowledge (Table 9.1).

Table 9.1 Common fears concerning participation in seminars

I'm not confident that I know the right answer.	Many of the other students in the group may feel the same way so at least if you get the wrong answer out of the way, the group as a whole will be closer to finding the correct answer. Anyway, you may be right and, even if you are not, at least you tried.
I don't understand the question so how can I give an answer?	You can't answer a question if you don't understand what it is asking but you can (and should) tell the lecturer that you don't understand the question so that he can explain it to you in a different way. Once you do understand the question, you may realize that you know the answer after all.

Table 9.1 (*Cont.*)

I don't like speaking out in front of others in the group.	This is generally linked to a fear of giving the wrong answer but it can be a more general anxiety about speaking in front of others. This is something that you really should try to overcome, particularly if you aim to practise law as this tends to require the ability to express yourself orally as well as on paper. Try volunteering an answer to one of the easier questions that you feel confident to answer. This should help you find your voice.
I've got a question but I don't want to ask it in case I look stupid.	If you don't ask your question, you will never know the answer. In any case, it is extremely likely that other students in the group are stuck on exactly the same point but won't ask for exactly the same reason. Try to be supportive; if someone else asks a question, say 'yes, I was wondering that too' and even that will help you to feel that you've played an active part in the tutorial.
There are some really talkative people in my group and I'm not sure how to involve myself in the discussion.	It can be a problem that a couple of confident students make a great deal of voluntary contribution to discussion which causes less confident students to feel as if they cannot chip in too. Try not to let that stop you making a comment or asking/answering a question because it is your seminar too and you need to make sure that it serves its purpose of strengthening your grasp of the topic. It can be useful to wait for a gap in the discussion to interject or to raise your hand slightly and make eye contact with your lecturer, who will then spot this and draw you into the discussion. If you feel that it is a major problem, raise this with your lecturer, in person or by email, so that they are aware that you want to speak but are a little shy; once they are aware of this, they will be able to ensure that you have a chance to contribute.

These concerns are perfectly natural, particularly at the earlier stages of your studies. Most people are reluctant to put themselves in a position where there is a risk of being wrong in public. One of the most effective ways of bolstering your confidence is with thorough preparation so that the chance of you actually giving an incorrect answer is minimized. It can be useful to volunteer an answer to an easy question at an early stage in the seminar as the initial questions tend to be more straightforward. Not only will it boost your confidence to give a correct answer but it reduces the risk that the lecturer will direct a question towards you when the voluntary contributions start to dwindle as the seminar progresses and the questions get harder.

Overall, the message with seminars and tutorials is that the more effort that you put into them in terms of preparation and participation, the more value you will derive from attendance. There are always some students who are enthusiastic about making contributions to group discussion and these are the people who are deriving the best value out of the tutorials. Remember, that is it your tutorial too but that you can only claim your share of the value by taking part.

Practical exercise

Think about your feelings about seminar participation. Do you take part enough (or at all)? What would help you to play a more active role in seminars? Are you more active in some seminars than others? If so, try to identify what factor it is that makes you feel more or less able to speak out: is it the lecturer, the subject, your grasp of the subject, or even the room layout? Reflect upon these questions and try and list three things that (a) encourage and (b) deter your participation. This can be the basis upon which you build to strengthen your level of participation in seminars.

9.3 Note-taking

Reading and taking notes is a significant part of studying the law. You will take notes in lectures and as part of your preparation for seminars, coursework, and revision as well as in the course of your own private study and reading. In fact, it is likely that a great deal of your time will be spent making notes so it is important that you are able to do so in an effective manner that enables you to make use of your notes when you come to consult them.

9.3.1 Recording information

The following examples demonstrate the variation in methods of recording the same informa-tion. It is worth experimenting with different approaches to recording your notes to find one that is most effective for the way that you think and organize your ideas.

9.3.1.1 Linear notes

This traditional approach to note-taking uses blocks of text, often separated by headings or bullet points. Key points can be emphasized by highlighting or underlining.

When using this method to take notes from an article or textbook, do try to note only the key points rather than copying out huge chunks of text. Students who do the latter tend to find that it rapidly evolves into a hand-writing exercise in which a mass of notes is accumulated without a great deal of thought being directed towards what has been written. It would be more useful to spend the time reading the chapter or article with a view to listing the five main points that are raised.

BLACKMAIL is an offence contrary to *section 21 of the Theft Act 1968*. It requires an unwarranted demand with menaces made with a view to gain or intent to cause loss.

A **demand** may be made by letter or orally and must be such that a reasonable man would consider that a demand was being made: *R* v. *Collister and Warhurst*.

Menaces must be such that an ordinary person of normal stability and courage would accede unwillingly: *R* v. *Clear*

An unlawful act can never be warranted: *R* v. *Harvey*

There is no need to establish an intention to permanently deprive.

Figure 9.3 Linear notes

9.3.1.2 Flow diagram

This approach to recording information seeks to include an indication of the relationship that different points have to each other. You might find it a particularly useful way of noting the elements of an offence.

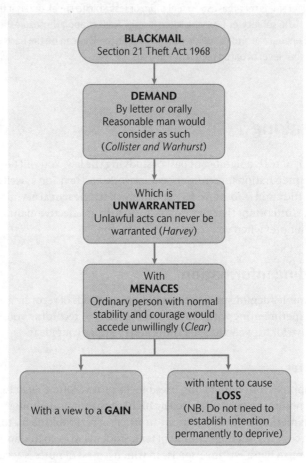

Figure 9.4 Flow diagram

9.3.1.3 Mind maps

This technique also enables you to reflect associations between topics and can be a useful means of depicting the framework of an entire topic. There is software available that will help you to produce mind maps or it can be done in a simpler way with a pen and paper. Many people who use this technique like to use a system of symbols to add meaning to the mind map; here, for example, that statutory provisions are marked with a book and cases denoted by scales (see Figure 9.5 opposite).

9.3.2 Signposting your notes

Remember that the main purpose of making notes is so that you can refer to the information recorded again in the future. This means that you need to be able to understand not only the content of what you have written but also its significance. Try to develop a system to remind yourself of the importance of the points that you have made and why they were significant.

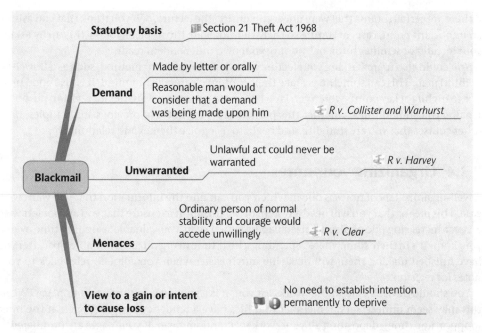

Figure 9.5 Mind map

Some students annotate in the margin with comments such as 'important argument', 'leading case', or 'look this up' whilst others use colour highlighting or symbols to draw attention to particular points and to act as reminders. If you use a system based upon colour or symbols, make sure that it is consistent so that you know what it means; it would be most unfortunate to revisit your notes at a later stage and not to be able remember whether purple highlighting meant 'important point' or 'I didn't understand this'.

9.3.3 Reviewing your notes

The best time to review your lecture notes is immediately following the lecture. However, this may not always be possible. You should try, therefore, to review your notes as soon as possible after the lecture so that the material is still relatively fresh in your mind. It is very hard trying to make sense of a set of notes a few days after they have been written.

Many students think that reviewing their notes simply involves copying them out again neatly. This is not the case. You should try to take an active approach to reviewing your notes and there are a number of practical steps you can take to maximize the value that you get from them.

Practical exercise

After a lecture, swap your set of lecture notes for a friend's . Check the accuracy of each other's notes and your understanding of the key points of the lecture. Look to see if your friend uses any note-taking techniques that might be useful to you in future lectures.

If there are certain points that were uncertain during the lecture, or if you think that you missed an important point, case, or statute so that your notes are incomplete, follow this up by asking your lecturer or seminar tutor, or by doing your own independent reading.

You could also try reworking your lecture notes using a different method, such as a flowchart or mind map. This can sometimes make their content clearer in your mind. It is also good practice to highlight key points which can later be used to produce summaries for revision purposes. Finally, you should think whether this particular topic relates to previous study topics, or to other courses that you are studying, and begin to recognize themes and relationships.

9.3.4 Organizing your notes

A well-organized set of notes is one in which you can find the information that you want with ease. This means that you will need a system of organization to ensure that you are not left with an ever-increasing pile of disorganized papers which costs you valuable searching time even if you 'know it's in there somewhere'. Spending a little time in organizing your notes just after you have finished making them will make life much easier when you come to refer back to your notes for revision.

You should devise a system that works for you. It is a good idea to number your pages. While this may seem unnecessary, remember that files have a tendency to spring open at the most inopportune times, depositing all your work in a random heap. If your pages are numbered, it will make reordering them much simpler. You may like to try using different colours of paper for different subjects, making a contents page for each of your files or using dividers in your files. These are all methods that can be used greatly to improve the accessibility of your notes.

9.4 Working with others

It is important to your success as a student that you are able to interact effectively with others. Communication and other interpersonal skills are extremely attractive to employers so you should take advantage of the opportunities available during your time at university to develop this set of skills. More than this, the ability to work with others could be viewed as a study skill, as proficiency in this area will make a significant contribution to the ease with which you are able to work through difficult areas of your studies.

9.4.1 Lecturers

This section might seem like an unusual topic to include in this chapter as it seems to be tackling an issue of personal communication rather than study skills but the ability to interact effectively with your lecturers can play an important role in your studies. It is also something that many students find difficult. The student/lecturer relationship is not like any other relationship that you will have encountered because the lecturer does not view you in the same way that you were viewed by your teachers at school. It is a difficult relationship in some respects because you are simultaneously an adult who is attending university by choice and a student who is subject to the rules of the institution. As such, you are dealing with your lecturer as an adult which suggests that the relationship is one of equals but you are nonetheless subject to their authority as they are obliged to enforce certain rules and to follow university procedures. To this extent, the relationship is not equal and, in any case, it is not quite the same as any relationship you will have encountered previously and that can create difficulties for the student. This difficulty is exacerbated by the fact that there is a lack of uniformity of approach amongst lecturers, so it is no easy matter to work out the best approach to dealing with them.

9.4.1.1 Form of address

One area where this is immediately apparent is in the tricky issue of what mode of address to adopt with your lecturer. Do they like to be addressed by their title and surname (Professor Smith) or by their Christian name (Henley)? Many lecturers adopt the 'equals/adults' approach and encourage students to address them by their Christian name whilst other lecturers prefer a more formal approach and like to be addressed by their title and surname. Some institutions have a policy on this whilst others leave it to the individual (the lecturer, not the student) as a matter of personal choice. A good rule of thumb is to err on the side of formality initially using the lecturer's title and surname; if your lecturer prefers to be addressed by their Christian name, they will soon let you know.

9.4.1.2 Email etiquette

It does not matter how informal your language when emailing your friends, your email to your lecturer should be constructed in a more formal manner. This should go without saying but it is surprising how many students send incomprehensible or inappropriate emails to their lecturers. Writing 'hello, I want a place on the minibus, cheers' is not good practice.

- **Salutation**: do not just start writing but preface your email with a salutation such as Dear Professor Jones or by their Christian name if that is how you would address them in person. Students often start their emails without a saluation when they do not know what to call the lecturer, but this is no reason to be impolite so use their title and surname if you are uncertain. Make sure that you use the correct title; this will not be difficult for you to find out and it is only courteous to take the trouble to use the correct form of address.

- **Identify yourself**: do not assume that they know who you are just because you know them. Lecturers see a large number of students and it is difficult to keep up with names and faces, so explaining who you are will smooth your communications along. Something like 'I am one of your personal tutees' or 'I am in your seminar on Thursday morning' will suffice.

- **Use clear and concise language**: the lecturer has to understand your communication so using abbreviations or text-speak may hamper this. Equally, rambling on in excess detail may blur the content of your email. Think about what it is you want to achieve—an appointment, advice on course content, an extension for an essay, to participate in an extra-curricular activity—and make sure that this is made clear in the email.

- **Be polite**: again, this should go without saying but you should not send an email that is offensive or abrasive even if you are very upset.

- **End with your name**: many students, having logged in using their university user name, think that this will suffice to identify them but the lecturer is likely to have no idea who you are if they see W8381325 under sender details or have the means of finding out easily so it makes sense to add your name at the end of the email.

If you followed this advice, the email above would read:

> Dear Professor Smith, I was in the lecture today when you announced that there were still places available on the minibus to attend the Law Fair. Please could you reserve a place for me. Thank you, Abigail (Harris)—from your Friday 5 p.m. contract tutorial.

9.4.1.3 Office hours

Institutional practice on office hours various enormously but it is usual for lecturers to set aside a period of time each week to see students. This may be by appointment, in which case you will have to sign up using the list provided on the door or email to book a time (giving the lecturer some indication of the nature of your problem so that they can work out how long to allocate to you) or on a 'drop in' or 'open door' basis which means that students can turn up without an appointment. The open door system is less formal but it does mean that you may have to wait if another student is already inside with the lecturer. If this is the case, wait patiently; it is extremely rude to keep banging on the door when you are aware that people are inside having a meeting. Equally, if you make an appointment, it would be rude and selfish (other people might have wanted it) not to keep it. If you are delayed or cannot attend, you should contact the lecturer to explain and apologize.

Do make use of office hours to go and see your lecturers. Most lecturers spend the entire time waiting for someone to turn up so do not feel that you are being a nuisance or taking up their time. Office hours are allocated so that students can go and ask questions, so do take advantage of this. However, you should not assume that lecturers will be free to see you outside the allocated hours and it is also not reasonable to assume that they have to see you because they are in their office and you want to see them.

9.4.2 Students

It is likely that you will need to work collaboratively with other students at some point during your studies. This may be a voluntary decision based upon a shared enthusiasm for mooting or a desire to share the work involved in revision or it may be imposed upon you by a requirement that you produce a presentation or an essay as a group. The ability to work effectively with other people is also important, owing to the value placed upon it by prospective employers, so it is worth devoting some time to the development of team work skills, both in a work and leisure context.

9.4.2.1 Compulsory group work

Many institutions, conscious of the emphasis placed upon the ability to work as part of team by employers, create group activities that form a compulsory, sometimes assessed, part of the syllabus of a particular module. It is also becoming increasingly common for one of the first-year subjects to involve a compulsory moot. It is also not unusual for compulsory group activities to allocate students to a group rather than allowing the groups to be self-selecting. Students tend to dislike the latter situation as it involves working with a different group of people who they may not know or may dislike. However, the ability to work effectively alongside a whole range of people is an important one, hence the popularity of this strategy.

If you have free choice and agree to work with your friends, it can be useful to establish boundaries for their task. In other words, try not to let your working arrangement interfere with your social relationships, otherwise there is a risk that acrimony will arise on a personal level if the working relationship does not run smoothly. It can be very difficult to work with your friends as resolving disputes and dealing with unequal contributions to the task can be challenging. These issues, of course, can arise when working with strangers but at least there is no existing friendship at stake if all does not go according to plan.

A first meeting that establishes ground rules can be a valuable way to avoid conflict. There is not usually any need to elect a group leader; in fact, doing so tends to create more problems than it resolves. The sorts of ground rules that will be useful involve the frequency and duration of meetings, the need for each person to complete any task that they undertake, and the importance of good communication between group members.

Ensure that everybody is clear about what the group's goal is and when it needs to be achieved. The task can then be sliced into segments, allocated to individual group members, and agreement reached about what should be achieved by the next meeting.

9.4.2.2 Study groups

Working with others can be a fantastic way to strengthen your own performance so it is worthwhile to consider forming a study group with other students. A group with between four and six members seems to be the most effective but smaller or larger groups can also work; a great deal depends on the personality of the group members and their contribution to the group.

Discussions with others can really help to clarify your own ideas and understanding. The most effective way to test whether you truly understand a particular concept is to explain it to someone else and ask them to report back to you what they have grasped as a result of your explanation. It can be a useful way of generating ideas or sharing the work load; for example, each group member undertakes to find one article of relevance to a forthcoming essay and summarize it for the group. Discussion can also help to fix information in your mind, making group work of particular value at revision time.

You will find a range of suggestions for group activities that will aid revision in chapter 13.

Many students report difficulties in getting started in writing coursework because they have done some research but they are not sure if they have understood the material that they have read or interpreted the requirements of the question correctly. This can be a real problem, particularly if it causes you to delay the start of writing so long that you end up having to rush the work and submit it in a less than satisfactory state. Group work can help here. A brainstorming session that analyses an essay title or unpicks the facts of a problem question can give you confidence to tackle the question. Be sure that you do not take collaboration too far though; preliminary discussion is fine but you must produce your answer independently or there is a risk that you will be vulnerable to accusations of plagiarism.

You will find more detailed discussion of plagiarism in chapter 10.

9.5 Time management

For those of you that have come to university directly from school, you will quickly discover that university life is very different from school life: there is a great deal more freedom. Therefore, although this freedom might seem liberating at first, you now have to take responsibility for your learning. You must self-manage your studies and research the topics yourself. Such autonomous learning requires good time-management and self-discipline, both to meet deadlines and to make sure you do not become overloaded or stressed in the process.

9.5.1 Planning

There are a range of planning techniques that you can use in order to manage your time more effectively. This section will outline one simple method of planning, but you should feel free to adapt it to your own particular way of learning. Effective planning requires some knowledge of the way in which you work—this is a very personal thing. It should also be an iterative process. The first time you work through the planning cycle, you may not know how long certain things will take. However, it is still better to have some sort of plan based on best guesses rather than no plan at all.

GOALS FOR THIS YEAR

Pass Legal Foundations
Pass Criminal Law
Pass Land Law

Figure 9.6 'Big goals'

At the beginning of the academic year, consider what is expected from you. Draw up a list of the 'big goals' for the year (Figure 9.6).

Once you have established the 'big picture' you will now be able to cascade these goals into a series of smaller goals. In our example, the big goals are passing the courses in Legal Foundations, Criminal Law, and Contract Law. To break these down to the next level, you must become familiar as quickly as possible at the start of each course with any handbooks or guides that are provided for that course. These will give you the requirements of each course, without which you will not be able to plan properly. The next-level goals will most likely be the various assessment components for these courses. Write these down.

GOALS FOR THIS YEAR Pass Legal Foundations Pass Criminal Law Pass Land Law		
PASS LEGAL FOUNDATIONS	PASS CRIMINAL LAW	PASS LAND LAW
1. Coursework essay 1 due 1 December	1. Coursework problem questions due 7 December	1. Coursework essay due 1 December
2. Coursework library exercise due 31 January	2. Coursework essay due 15 January	2. Coursework problem questions due 15 January
3. Exam sometime in May	3. Exam sometime in May	3. Exam sometime in late May

Figure 9.7 Sub-goals

You should now draw up a good timetable that shows all your lectures, seminars, free periods for extra study, and basic time out for having a life for yourself beyond study. This will give you an indication of how much spare time you have available week by week to allocate to these particular goals.

Now that you have the individual deadlines set out, and the number of hours you have available, give some thought to the amount of time that you think each of them might take. You should think in terms of actual time spent towards each task rather than in elapsed time: in other words 'I think my criminal law problem questions will take about 15 hours' work' rather than 'I think my criminal law problems will take me a month to get done'. Armed with an idea of the number of hours each task might take and the number of hours you have available per week, you can start to work backwards and decide when you are going to start working towards each goal: whether it is starting a piece of assessed work, or starting revision towards an examinable component. You will probably find that you need to start sooner than you thought—particularly if, as in this example, you find that you have concurrent deadlines!

Finally, you should embed your plan into your weekly timetable so that you can see, for any given week, not only the lectures and seminars you have to attend but what and when you need to do so in furtherance of your goals.

Proper planning will mean that you stand less chance of ending up with a mass of work at the end of the semester. Leaving things until the last minute will make the entire process more stressful and unpleasant. If you, like many students, tend to do most of your work in marathon sessions near deadlines you will also have lost the opportunity to make appropriate use of various study aids and support that might have been available earlier in the semester. Make sure you use all the facilities that are available to you.

Make sure that you have allowed time in your plans for each task to do some reading and thinking. Every assignment will always require you to read some material—and if you want to do well, you must not take shortcuts with the recommended reading—so always incorporate reading time into your overall plan. You should plan to go to the library as soon as you can, particularly if the books needed have limited availability. This will give you a better chance of accessing a good selection of books rather than running the risk of important resources being unavailable. You should also build in time for breaks. You will work much more effectively if you allow yourself time to rest—even for a short period—and you will be able to derive the maximum benefit from your non-work time in the knowledge that you have planned to take it and that not working should not affect your ability to complete your task.

By planning so that you finish a little earlier—before the deadline—you can look back at your work and correct any problems. You will also have some flexibility to deal with unforeseen last-minute catastrophes, such as computer crashes and network errors (if you are required to submit your work electronically) or printer failures and empty ink cartridges (for work on paper).

9.5.2 Dealing with procrastination

Research suggests that up to 40 per cent of university students experience procrastination—that is, the constant postponing of work till another day—as a problem.[1] Therefore, if you suffer from procrastination, you are not unusual. The tendency for procrastination in the world of study is hardly surprising. Students are required to meet deadlines for assignments and examinations in an environment which is full of events and activities competing for time and attention, many of which are less stressful than actually getting on with the work. Therefore, procrastination can be a result of the natural inclination to avoid stressful activities: students often spend more time on tasks which they themselves consider to be easy rather than on those that they think will be difficult. Many students struggle with procrastination owing to a lack of time-management or study skills, stress, or being overwhelmed with the volume of work.

However, prolonged procrastination can lead to even more stress since delaying tasks will only allow them to mount up. Proper planning is therefore very important. Dealing with the underlying stressful aspects of the activities can assist in reducing the extent of procrastination.

Practical exercise

If you are feeling overwhelmed by the amount of work that you have on your 'to do' list, then try making a 'one item' list. In other words, write the one item from your long list on a blank sheet of paper and work on that one item until you are done. This will help you to focus on the one task at hand without being distracted by easier or more enjoyable items on your list.

1.   O'Brien, W.K. (2002) 'Applying the transtheoretical model to academic procrastination,' *Dissertation Abstracts International. Section B: The Sciences and Engineering* 62(11-B): 5359.

Even when you have only one task on your to-do list, it can still be difficult to start working. Most of the time, not starting seems to be related to fear of poor results or other negative feelings than to the actual difficulty of the work. Taking the plunge is the important thing. If you start work when your ideas are fresh, you will keep your sense of purpose, and your piece of work will begin to take some shape. This shape will allow you to identify the points you need to work on and—since you started early—you will still have time left to plan your work on these points.

Practical exercise

Subdivide your single task into smaller steps that you think will take no more than, say, ten minutes to do. Start on one of these 10 minute steps. You will often find that once the 10 minutes have passed you will have engaged with the bigger task and will be able to continue productively.

9.5.3 Plan, plan, and plan again

As has already been mentioned, time-management is meant to be an iterative process; that is, one which needs to be repeated, ideally taking the results of the previous cycle into account. Do not be discouraged if your first plans proved to be wildly over-optimistic. Every time you plan afresh, you will be basing your new plan on your increased experience—you will grow more accurate at estimating how long certain things take and how much rest time you need in order to work effectively. Therefore, as you repeat the planning cycle, your awareness of the particular ways in which you study and use time will improve and so will your ability to make a workable and realistic plan.

This will lead to increased confidence in your planning ability, particularly if you are able to meet the goals that you set for yourself. You must however remain flexible to replanning as you face the day-to-day realities of student life. You will have to learn from your experiences and tweak and adjust your plans.

Time management is not only a study skill; indeed, time management and self-management are transferable skills that may be applied in all aspects of life.

CHAPTER SUMMARY

Lectures

- Lectures give a framework of information which should be supplemented by your own reading

- Listen and think instead of writing down everything that is said

- Always seek permission before recording a lecture

- Find out your lecturer's view on responding to questions in lectures and respect it

Seminars and tutorials

- Prepare thoroughly for seminars and tutorials to maximize your benefit

- Make notes of any difficult topics before the seminar and draw up a list of questions

- Participate in seminar discussions as fully as you can

Note taking

- Try different styles of note-taking—linear, flow diagrams, and mind maps—to see what works best for you

- Always review your notes as soon as you can after a lecture or seminar

- Devise a system of organizing your notes so that you can find them again quickly and easily whenever you need to

Working with others

- Find out how your lecturers prefer to be addressed

- Be polite in email correspondence

- Make the most of office hours but do abide by the system in use at your institution

- Try not to let work arrangements interfere with social arrangements

- Study groups help to clarify your ideas and understanding

Time management

- Establish clear goals

- Try to set a realistic plan to achieve those goals. Remember to include time for yourself, for research, and for unexpected emergencies

- If you are struggling to get started, work on smaller tasks first

- Adjust your plans continuously as you learn by experience

Writing skills

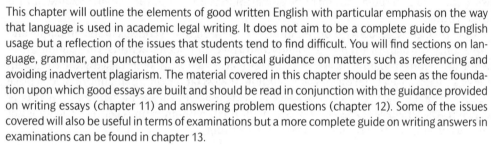

10

INTRODUCTION

This chapter will outline the elements of good written English with particular emphasis on the way that language is used in academic legal writing. It does not aim to be a complete guide to English usage but a reflection of the issues that students tend to find difficult. You will find sections on language, grammar, and punctuation as well as practical guidance on matters such as referencing and avoiding inadvertent plagiarism. The material covered in this chapter should be seen as the foundation upon which good essays are built and should be read in conjunction with the guidance provided on writing essays (chapter 11) and answering problem questions (chapter 12). Some of the issues covered will also be useful in terms of examinations but a more complete guide on writing answers in examinations can be found in chapter 13.

The ability to use language, orally and in writing, is one of the key 'tools of the trade' for a lawyer, so it is essential that you are able to use language correctly and prepare precise and accurate written documents. Many cases turn on the interpretation of a particular word or phrase so it is essential that you have the skills to appreciate the implications of the choice of particular words and that you are able to communicate the precise meaning of the law. On a more pragmatic level, you need good writing skills to demonstrate your understanding of the law to your lecturers in your coursework and examinations. This requires that you adopt the styles and conventions of language used in the law. It is a mistake to think that an essay that is accurate in terms of its legal content will succeed irrespective of the language used to express the arguments or the way in which the essay is structured. Content is important but the way that a piece of writing is organized and expressed can be equally fundamental to its success or failure. You would not like this book if it were written in ungrammatical language so that you could not readily make sense of it or if it were so poorly structured that you could not locate the information that you needed. This means that you recognize the value of good writing skills so you should strive to ensure that your own work reaches the standards that you expect in the work of others.

LEARNING OUTCOMES

After studying this chapter, you should be able to:

- Make reasoned choices about the language and written style that you use in the preparation of coursework

- Produce a polished and thoroughly referenced piece of work that is free of common grammatical errors

- Avoid inadvertent plagiarism and be aware of the risks associated with deliberate plagiarism

10.1 Language

It is important that you adopt an appropriate level of formality in your written style. The best way to gauge the appropriate level is to read a good-quality textbook that is written in language that you understand and to emulate that style.

10.1.1 Too formal or too informal?

Some students err on the side of excessive formality, believing this to be appropriate to legal writing, peppering their writing with words such as 'hereinafter' and 'henceforth'. Whilst there is nothing wrong with this as such, there is an increasing move towards the use of plain English within the legal profession, so it can be preferable to use words which are more readily understood. Moreover, using unfamiliar words raises the possibility that they will be misused, which will detract from the polished and professional impression that you are striving to present with your writing.

More frequently, students adopt an informal approach that is conversational in nature and more suited to a diary or an email to friends than a piece of academic writing. For example, there is nothing wrong in grammatical terms with sentences such as '[h]aving talked about the meaning of x we now need to take a look at y' it is nonetheless rather chatty and informal for a piece of coursework. Equally, the recent seepage of 'text-speak' into academic writing is a matter of concern. The language that is appropriate in informal communications between friends is not the sort of language that should be used in legal writing.

10.1.2 Appropriate legal writing style

As these examples make clear, there is not a constant 'correct' style that can be applied to all forms of written communication. In essence, 'correct' means 'appropriate' so you should strive to develop a written style that is appropriate for communication in academic law and that is one that is relatively formal and which uses language in an accurate and precise manner. There are a few other matters that require particular consideration before the discussion of language is concluded.

10.1.2.1 Use of the first person

First person The grammatical person is a way of referring to the participant role of the speaker or the writer. Accordingly, when a person writes as 'I', they are writing in the first person. This is entirely appropriate in informal communications and in other situations in which it is necessary to express a personal viewpoint but it is not appropriate in objective academic writing. This does not mean that it is appropriate to revert to the second person (you) or the third person (one) as an alternative.

Most lecturers regard use of the first person as inappropriate and are not receptive to essays that are written in the first person. Some students, lacking a grasp of the complexities of English grammar, try to get around the prohibition on writing in the first person by switching to 'we' or even 'one' as a result, not realizing that these are equally unacceptable.

Not only is it inappropriate to write in the first person in a piece of objective academic writing; many lecturers fear that it encourages students to assert their own views on the topic when it would be more appropriate to present the views of writers, judges, and other experts. If you appreciate that it is not appropriate to write 'I think' or 'I would argue', then you will never be tempted to express your own opinion on the state of the law and you will have to resort to repeating the views of more experienced writers and commentators.

If you are accustomed to writing in the first person and struggle to find a form of words to use, then table 10.1 should give you some ideas for alternative phraseology to get you started.

Table 10.1 First person writing and objective altenatives

First Person	Objective Alternative
In this essay, I am going to outline the elements necessary to establish that a defendant is liable for negligence.	This essay will outline the elements necessary to establish that a defendant is liable for negligence.
Alternatively, one could argue that . . .	Alternatively, it could be argued that . . .
In conclusion, I do not think that there is a need for reform in this area.	In conclusion, the majority of writers do not see a need for reform in this area.

10.1.2.2 Gender neutral language

It is accepted convention in legal writing to use the masculine word forms to encompass the feminine: section 6, Interpretation Act 1978. In other words, 'he' means 'he or she' and 'his' means 'his or hers'. Some academics frown upon this approach, believing that the prevalence of male-orientated references is exclusionary and inappropriate. This is a matter of personal preference but do be aware of the need not to cause offence in your choice of language. It would be worth checking if your institution, department, or lecturer has any strong views on the subject and adapting your use of language accordingly.

10.1.2.3 Latin

In recent years, there has been a move away from the use of Latin words and phrases within the legal profession. Certain Latin legal terms have been renamed, for example, an order of *certiori* is now known as a quashing order whilst an *ex parte* application has been renamed an application without notice.

However, there are areas of law in which the continued use of Latin is accepted; the conduct element of a crime is still known as the *actus reus*, for example, whilst it is accepted that phrases such as *res ipsa loquitur* are terms of art with an express legal meaning.

Be aware of the decline in the use of Latin and be sure to check both your textbooks and course materials for the appropriate approach to terminology. If you do have cause to use Latin words or phrases, remember that they should always be italicized.

10.1.2.4 Legal words

As you will become increasingly aware as your studies progress, many words in everyday usage also have particular legal meanings that differ significantly from their ordinary dictionary definitions: intention, consideration, assault, nuisance, appropriation, land, property, consent, and negligence, for example. As these words hold a particular legal significance, you should avoid using them in their ordinary sense within the subject area where they have a specialist meaning.

For example, if you write that 'the defendant's assault caused the victim's death', this could be confusing as it will not be clear to your lecturer whether you are using the word in the legal sense or whether you intend the word to have its everyday meaning (Figure 10.1).

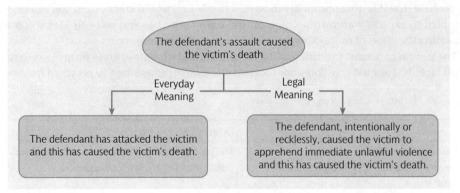

Figure 10.1 Everyday and legal meanings

To avoid any confusion, especially when it carries the risk that your lecturer will think that you misunderstand the law, it is advisable to find a synonym to use in place of any word that has a clear legal meaning.

10.2 Grammar and punctuation

Good writing is about more than just words on paper; the words need to be arranged in such a way that they make proper sense to the reader. It is grammar and punctuation that transforms a collection of words into meaningful sentences that can be understood by the reader. This is a particularly important factor in legal education as the ability to communicate precise and accurate meaning is crucial, and correct grammar and punctuation is central to this. Without grammatical expression and grammatical accuracy, the meaning of words can change as the following two sentences demonstrate:

> The panda eats, shoots and leaves (he has his dinner, kills another panda with his shotgun and moves on to a new territory); or,
>
> The panda eats shoots and leaves (the diet of the panda is shoots and leaves).[1]

If this seems like a trivial example, remember that the interpretation of statutory provisions can hinge on the meaning of one word or even on the positioning of punctuation; it is often said that Roger Casement was 'hanged on a comma', meaning that his execution was inevitable if he was convicted of the offence of which he was charged. His liability for this offence hinged upon the interpretation of the statute which was, in turn, contingent on the positioning of the comma.

Unfortunately, not all students are able to construct a grammatical and well-punctuated essay by the time they arrive at university. This problem is compounded by the fact that many of these students will be unaware that there is any problem with their grammar and punctuation. You will find that the extent to which lecturers will (a) draw attention to grammatical deficiencies and (b) offer guidance on improvement varies enormously. Some lecturers will not mention problems at all, merely deducting marks for the lack of clarity of expression without giving any indication that there is a problem with grammar and/or punctuation. Some lecturers will comment that the grammar and/or punctuation if the essay were weak or could be

---

1.   Truss, L. (2003) *Eats Shoots and Leaves: the Zero Tolerance Approach to Punctuation*, London: Profile Books Ltd.

strengthened but will not actually correct any inaccuracies. Finally, some lecturers will correct every inaccuracy and/or explain the correct approach on your essay so that you can understand the problem and how to rectify it. Although the first approach may seem very unhelpful, it is actually a throwback to the days when students that reached university were, in general, much better able to construct a grammatical essay and there was little need for lecturers to comment on this aspect of a student's work.

This is not the place to engage in a discussion of the perceived decline in educational standards or the response of university lecturers to this problem. The aim of this chapter is to emphasize the importance of good written skills such as grammar and punctuation and to provide a practical guide to strengthening these skills. In relation to grammar and punctuation, given that a comprehensive account of all the rules involved is beyond the scope of this book, the aim is to enable the student to identify any problems in this area and to equip them to seek help from appropriate sources.

10.2.1 Spotting the problem

As discussed above, not all lecturers will point out the problem so you will need to be alert for the signs that there may be a problem with your grammar and/or punctuation.

Poor grades are a good sign that *something* is wrong. If you are receiving marks that are lower than you would hope or expect (remembering to be realistic), then it may be that you are not expressing yourself with sufficient clarity or precision. Poor grammar and punctuation frequently result in a lack of clarity as the words that you have written simply do not do the job that you want them to do.

If your marks are less than you hoped, have a close look at the feedback that has been provided, both on the feedback sheet and the script itself. Are there any comments, however vague, about the quality of your written style? Comments on the script such as 'lacks clarity', 'poorly expressed', or 'vague' can also indicate that the problem is not with your understanding of the law but with the way that it is expressed. Some lecturers will simply underline phrases that they cannot understand and put a question mark in the margin whilst others will correct errors so do keep a look out for changes that have been made on your essay by your lecturer.

Some feedback sheets have categories of skills that the lecturers can tick to indicate your level of competence. The categories used will obviously vary between institutions but there will usually be some that refer to the technical aspects of the construction of the essay as well as to the use of the law itself. Have a look at the feedback form when you receive it. Do any of the categories refer to written style generally or to grammar or punctuation in particular? Anything less than 'good' could indicate a problem as 'satisfactory' is another way of saying 'could be improved'.

10.2.2 Getting help

Once you are aware that there is a problem, finding sources of assistance with strengthening your grammar and punctuation should be straightforward. Even if they cannot help you themselves, your lecturer or your personal tutor will be able to point you towards sources of assistance, whether this is a specialist skills adviser in your department or a study skills or student support service elsewhere in the university. You should not hesitate to seek help if you (or the person marking your work) feel that it is necessary; many writing problems result from a lack of understanding of the correct way to go about things and these can be corrected very easily with a little specialist assistance. Although the rules of grammar may seem complex and impenetrable, once they have been explained to you clearly and you have examples of correct usage, you will probably find that it is not difficulty to adjust your written style to take these rules into account.

An alternative source of assistance is one of the many works on correct English usage. These can be found in the library and are increasingly available online. You could, of course, purchase a concise guide to English grammar and make reference to it as you write an essay.

A final, and frequently overlooked, source of guidance is the written work of others. Whether this is the work of your fellow students or the work of experienced academics in articles and textbooks, you should scrutinize the way that others write in order to gain experience of good writing practice. It is often the case that students who read a great deal have a better grasp of grammar and punctuation as they acquire an appreciation of the rule by virtue of encountering them more frequently in the writing of others. Ideally, you should aim to improve your written style on each piece of work that you submit and one really effective way of doing this is to evaluate the way that others write with a view to adopting examples of good practice that you encounter.

10.2.3 Common problems

One of the difficulties with choosing an appropriate approach to language is that there is a difference of opinion regarding the application of the rules. Some academics consider that particular rules of grammar are outdated or overly pedantic whilst others fear that failure to adhere to these rules is part of a larger picture of declining standards of literacy. This book does not intend to engage in that debate but rather to offer students advice on how to avoid falling foul of the debate.

It seems that those with a preference for traditional approaches to grammar are likely to take issue with its absence whereas it is unlikely that a lecturer with a more relaxed attitude is going to correct your work with a comment 'this is a technically correct approach to grammar but a little bit out-of-date'! For example, the paragraph below would offend a lecturer with traditional views about grammatical written English:

> There may be a difference of opinion as to the relevance of certain rules of grammar in today's society. But, in order to ensure that nobody is offended by your writing, it is a sensible idea to adhere to the correct approach wherever possible.

However, if this paragraph was presented as a single sentence (using 'but' in the correct manner), it is unlikely that anybody would object. Lecturers who take a more progressive approach to grammar tend to believe that certain of the rules of grammar are unnecessary but they do not tend to intervene if students use them. This is because the modern view is not that the traditional approach is incorrect, just that it is outdated. This is contrary to the traditional viewpoint, which holds that the modern stance is inaccurate, hence should be corrected.

It is for this reason that it is advisable to take a formal approach to grammar wherever possible in order to avoid any question of incorrect usage.

The following is a list of some widespread errors that are easily resolved: they are a good place to start in terms of strengthening your written style.

- **Do not start a sentence with a conjunction.** A conjunction is a word that joins two parts of a sentence together such as 'and', 'but', 'or', and 'because'. As such, they should only appear in the midst of a sentence, never at the beginning.
- **Do not end a sentence with a preposition.** For example, 'I was told to find a case that I had never heard of' should be rephrased so read 'I was told to find a case of which I had never heard'. The latter is more grammatically correct but may sound odd; if so, rephrase entirely to avoid the dilemma, e.g. 'I had never heard of the case that I was told to find'.

- **The use of contractions/elisions is not appropriate.** This is the practice of shortening two words into a single form by using an apostrophe to replace the missing words such as shouldn't, couldn't and doesn't. This is too informal for academic writing and should be avoided. It is tempting to resort to elisions when trying to fit an essay within the word limit but many institutions would simply count it as two words in any case, so it does not achieve its purpose.

- **Apostrophes should be used with care.** An apostrophe either denotes a missing letter (as above) or signifies possession, e.g. that is Susan's book, the judge's decision is final. As it is clear that there is no place for elisions in academic writing, you should only be using an apostrophe to indicate possession. Remember that the positioning of the apostrophe is important; in the example given above, the position of the apostrophe shows that there is one judge making a decision—if it was the decision of a panel of judges that was in question, the apostrophe would be placed at the end of the word: the judges' decision is final. The greatest problems arise in student essays with regard to the word 'its' in its possessive sense; the court delivered its judgment. This requires no apostrophe to signify possession as it is the abstract equivalent of 'his' or 'hers' and you would not consider using an apostrophe with those words. Possessive 'its' is distinct from 'it's' which is the shortened form of 'it is'. Further problems arise in relation to years; it is a common mistake to see 'in the 1990's' as if it were possessive whereas it is actually a way of describing a collection of years so is plural and should be expressed without the apostrophe as 'in the 1990s'.

- **There is no such thing as primary and secondary paragraphing.** Each new idea should be contained in a fresh paragraph. The recent proliferation of primary and secondary paragraphing to denote the strength of the relationship between a paragraph and the one that follows by the size of the space between them is nonsense. There are sentences and there are paragraphs. If a sentence is closely related to the previous sentence, it belongs in the same paragraph; if it is not closely related, it belongs in the following paragraph.

 You will find further examples of these rules and their application on the Online Resource Centre.

10.3 Plagiarism

In the following section, you will find what might seem a surprising volume of material on referencing. There are two reasons why this level of detail is provided. First, referencing is something that many students struggle to do properly, even in the later stage of their studies, so it is important that this book provides a clear and detailed explanation of techniques that can be used. Secondly, a thorough and accurate approach to referencing should help to prevent inadvertent plagiarism.

It is commonplace to think of plagiarism as a deliberate copying from an unacknowledged source with the intention to deceive, but this is not the case as plagiarism covers all instances in which the work of another is used without sufficient acknowledgement.

....

Plagiarism The *Oxford English Dictionary* defines plagiarism as 'the action or practice of taking someone else's work, idea, etc., and passing it off as one's own; literary theft'.

....

As you see from the definition, the essence of plagiarism is the failure to give an indication of the source of material upon which reliance has been placed in a piece of work. This may be deliberate, such as in situations where a student copies material from the Internet and passes it off as their own, but it is more often inadvertent, arising as a consequence of poor or lazy referencing or from a lack of understanding about the need to provide a reference.

10.3.1 Inadvertent plagiarism

The most effective means of avoiding inadvertent plagiarism is to ensure that every piece of work that you produce is thoroughly and correctly referenced. This raises two issues: *when* to reference and *how* to reference. The latter issue will be addressed in the referencing section below whilst the remainder of this section will deal with the question of when a reference must be provided.

10.3.1.1 When to reference

Certain situations are straightforward. Most students would appreciate that a reference to the source of the following should be provided:

- **Statements of law** should be attributed to the relevant case or statutory provision
- **Direct quotations** should be attributed to their source in a book, article, case, or other material
- **Factual material** such as statistics or the findings of a research study should be attributed to their source, whether this is an official report or an academic or commercial study
- **Definitions** of legal concepts or any other matter should be attributed to the appropriate source in a dictionary, case law, statute, article, or other material

An essay is an accumulation of a number of different things. It is composed largely of the writer's own words and thoughts, which need no reference, but may be interspersed with other material from the four categories outlined above that add the weight of authority to these words and thoughts. Definitions and quotations are the direct use of another's words, hence must be acknowledged as such, whilst factual material and statements of law need to be referenced to their source in order to substantiate their authoritative status.

A more difficult situation exists in relation to material that has been read during the production of an essay but which is not referred to specifically within the text. This includes materials such as books and articles that have influenced your thinking about the topic or which has shaped the points that you have raised in your essay. It is in relation to this that greatest uncertainty about whether to reference exists. There are two general rules that can be used as guidance:

1. If you are using your own words to express an idea that is specific to a particular writer, e.g. something that a judge has stated in a case or the views of the author of an article, then a reference to the source of the idea should be provided even though you have used your own words to explain that idea. If, however, you have read several textbooks to gain an overview of a topic and the same issue is expressed in each book, then you are free to use your own words without providing a reference. This is because the mention of the idea in several places demonstrates that it is a general issue of common knowledge, so it does not need to be attributed to a particular source.

2. If in doubt, reference. It is preferable to provide too many references in your essay rather than to face an accusation of plagiarism or receive a deduction of marks for providing insufficient references. If you receive a comment from a lecturer that a piece of work contained too many unnecessary references, you should make a point of asking them to

point out to you which references were unnecessary and why this was the case so that you can make adjustments in subsequent pieces of work.

10.3.2 Deliberate plagiarism

If inadvertent plagiarism arises from lack of clarity about referencing requirements, deliberate plagiarism arises when students make a deliberate decision to try and pass off the work of others as their own. Deliberate plagiarism is almost never successful, so why do students try to plagiarize and what are the reasons that such behaviour is unwise?

10.3.2.1 Why do students plagiarize?

There are many reasons why students may make a conscious decision to take words from a source and seek to pass it off as their own work. Plagiarism can arise from a failure to understand what the coursework requires, a desperate desire to obtain a good mark, an unwillingness to interfere with the way that an idea has been expressed, or simply from the pressure of time as a deadline is looming. Ultimately, these are all manifestations of a lack of confidence in one's own ability to provide an answer to the question. Alternatively, students may resort to plagiarism because they cannot be bothered to produce their own work, they believe that everyone else is doing it, or because they feel that their course was badly taught and therefore does not merit the effort that it would take to write an original piece of work. None of these reasons are a justification for plagiarism and, certainly, none of them will provide a defence when the plagiarism is detected and you are called to account by your institution.

10.3.2.2 Reasons to avoid plagiarism

Plagiarism detection mechanisms are in place in most institutions, irrespective of whether or not this fact is advertised to the students, and these mechanisms are becoming increasingly more sophisticated. They have the ability to check the work submitted against the work of other students, at the same institution and elsewhere, as well as against all Internet resources including essay banks and paper resources. Overall, it is impossible to copy from a source of material that cannot be detected, therefore the resort to plagiarism in an attempt to acquire a good mark will ultimately be unsuccessful. Such is the battle against plagiarism that many institutions annotate degree transcripts to include an explanation that a mark in the relevant subject was amended following a finding of plagiarism; something which is hardly going to impress future employers. Moreover, the Law Society and the Bar Council require universities to notify them of proven cases of plagiarism as this is indicative of dishonesty which, of course, suggests that the person concerned is not of good character for the purposes of a career in the legal profession.

More than this, plagiarism is actually counter-productive as it deprives the student of the opportunity to test what they do know and how well they are able to express this. In other words, the learning opportunity provided by the coursework is wholly negated and the student learns nothing as a result. You will never improve your legal skills if you are not prepared to try and receive feedback on your ability. There is nowhere else in the progression of becoming a lawyer that you will be able to learn these skills and the later stages of qualification as a lawyer will expect that you are able to identify, explain, and analyse the law, so you need to acquire these skills now by a process of trial and error.

Finally, there is no guarantee that the source that you plagiarize will be good. This is particularly true of material taken from the Internet. Anyone can post anything on the Internet; there is no quality control or mechanism of checking, amending, or removing inaccurate material.

Essay banks are equally unreliable and cost vast sums of money. Think about the rationale behind it. Students sell essays that they have written to the essay bank who have no expertise in the subject at all. Essays with higher marks sell for a higher price, so students are likely to exaggerate the mark in order to gain maximum profit, so there is nothing to say that the essay that you buy as a first did not actually receive a lower second-class mark. Irrespective of this, that essay may be on the same subject matter but it does not answer the same question as that set as your coursework, so there is no point in submitting it. All you are doing is paying a vast amount of money for a piece of work of questionable quality that does not answer the question that you have been set and which is likely to be detected, as plagiarism detection software is able to access essay bank material (even if the essay bank says that this is impossible).

Ultimately, plagiarism achieves nothing and will attract negative consequences when it is detected. Do not do it.

10.4 Referencing

It is essential that your written work is fully and correctly referenced otherwise you will be vulnerable to accusations of plagiarism and all the consequences that follow on from this. The previous section discussed the situations in which referencing should be provided whilst this section considers the correct approach to referencing.

10.4.1 House style

The starting point for deciding how to reference should be the 'house style' of your department or institution; that is, the official guidance that you have been given about how to provide references within your work. If you have not yet found this, make sure that you track it down as you will need to consult it in order to ensure that your coursework is correctly referenced. The level of guidance varies enormously between institutions so you may find that you are provided with detailed instructions with examples or, alternatively, that you are merely told 'footnotes must be used' or 'your work must be fully referenced'.

If you have been given instructions as to what style to use, it is imperative that you use this and not some other style of your own making or that you have used previously. Even if you are being given some examples as guidance rather than as part of a mandatory policy, you would be wise to follow the house style because it is likely to be correct and complete, whereas any approach to referencing that you have used previously was (presumably) not one that was specifically tailored to undergraduate law.

If you have not been given any detailed guidelines, you may find the following suggestions useful. Remember, however, that there is more than one way to reference the same material, so there are likely to be other equally valid approaches. The key to good referencing is completeness and consistency so keep these principles in mind when deciding which style of referencing to use.

The sections that follow contain examples of different referencing techniques to add to the clarity of the explanations. Do take time to read the information contained in the footnotes as these will help you to understand why a particular approach to referencing has been taken.

10.4.2 Harvard referencing

One method of referencing that you may encounter is called Harvard (or 'in text') referencing. Here, an abbreviated reference that is sufficient to identify the author and year of publication is incorporated into the text as follows (Finch and Fafinski, 2007) with the addition of a specific page number (or numbers) if the reference is for a quotation or a particular idea (Finch and Fafinski, 2007: 235). This alters slightly if the name of the author is mentioned in the text of your essay; as Finch and Fafinski (2007: 235) argue in their clear and succinct explanation of referencing!

The other variation upon this that you may need to use occurs if the same author has written more than one book or article in that particular year, in which case you use letters to differentiate between them both in the in-text reference and the list of references that you provide at the end of your essay. In the text, the first reference would appear with the letter 'a' appended (Finch and Fafinski, 2007a) whilst the second would be distinguished by the addition of a letter 'b' (Finch and Fafinski, 2007b).

If you are citing a work that has more than two authors, the correct approach is to do this in full on the first occasion that the work is mentioned (Smith, Jones, Collins, and Ryan, 1990) but to use a shortened form of this on subsequent occasions that denotes that the work is by multiple authors (Smith *et al.*, 1990). This shortened form of referencing is only used if there are at least three authors. In works with two authors, both should always be cited; this book, for example, should be cited as Finch and Fafinski (2007) and not Finch *et al.* (2007).

10.4.2.1 List of references

As Harvard referencing uses only the author's name and the date of publication in the text, either a list of references or a bibliography must be provided at the end of the essay that provides full details of the publications referred to in the text. This must include any letters that you added to differentiate between publications by the same author:

A **bibliography** (see below) is a list of all materials that have been consulted during the preparation of your work. By contrast, a **list of references** is provided with work that has used Harvard referencing to provide the full details of any materials that have been referenced in the text but does not include materials that have not been cited. As such, a bibliography is a fuller record and will include all materials that would appear in a list of references plus anything else that has been read.

10.4.2.2 Referencing cases

Harvard referencing does not seem to have any hard-and-fast rules regarding the referencing of cases within the text of an essay. There are two options; first, include only the case name in the text but ensure that a list of cases with full citations is provided at the end of your essay, or, secondly, include the full case citation in the text of your essay. If you take the latter approach, remember that you should only provide the full citation the first time that the case is mentioned; after that, the case name alone (or its shortened form) will suffice:

Recently, the Court of Appeal declined to follow the House of Lords decision in *Smith (Morgan)* [2000] 3 WLR 654, preferring the reasoning of the Privy Council in *A-G for Jersey* v *Holley* [2005] 3 All ER 371. Of course, this is problematic in terms of the doctrine of precedent as, strictly speaking, *Smith* was binding upon the Court of Appeal and should have been applied in preference to *Holley*.

This approach would be correct if footnotes were used in place of Harvard referencing except that, instead of the case citations appearing in the text the first time that the case was mentioned, they would appear as footnote references.

10.4.3 Footnotes

Most legal writing uses footnotes (sometimes called Roman, Oxford, or numerical referencing). This is the system of referencing used in this book whereby the details are provided at the bottom of the same page and their position in the text is denoted by a small raised (superscript) number.[2]

10.4.3.1 Positioning

Footnotes generally appear outside of punctuation.[3] However, placing footnotes inside punctuation is becoming increasingly acceptable[4]. Whichever approach to positioning of footnotes that you decide to adopt, ensure that you stick to it as a combination of inside and outside of punctuation is regarded as poor practice. It is perfectly permissible to include a footnote within a sentence at the point where the material to which the reference refers appears, although this can just as readily appear at the end of the sentence as these two examples illustrate:

> As Finch and Fafinski[5] explain, it is perfectly permissible to provide a reference for a particular book or journal at the point in which you mention the name of the author or the title of the work.
>
> Alternatively, as Finch and Fafinski also note, it is equally correct to provide a reference to material at the end of the sentence in which it is mentioned.[6]

Providing a reference within a sentence can be particularly useful if you need to provide a case citation and another reference within a single sentence:

> In *case*,[7] it was argued that *x* and this point has been explored in detail by someone.[8]

10.4.3.2 Content and precision

When using footnotes, you should provide a complete reference. This should include page references in respect of books, articles, and cases if the reference is for a direct quotation or if the reference is for an idea that is located on a particular page (or pages) rather than in the article in general:

> Finch and Fafinski emphasize the importance of the ability to identify, locate and understand the law as well as the ability to use this effectively within an essay.[9]
>
> It is essential that precise and detailed references are provided for all materials that are used in the construction of an essay.[10]

This level of precision should also be applied to the referencing of cases. If a case is used as an authority for a specific point of law or to demonstrate the application of the law in a particular factual scenario, a general reference to the case will suffice:

> The objective approach to recklessness was finally laid to rest in *R* v *G*.[11]

---

2. This is a footnote. It may contain a short note of relevance that would break the text if it were included or, more usually, a reference to source material.

3. The superscript number appears outside of the full stop.

4. The superscript number appears inside the full stop.

5. Finch, E. and Fafinski, S. (2007) *Legal Skills*, Oxford: Oxford University Press, p. 236.

6. Finch, E. and Fafinski, S. (2007) *Legal Skills*, Oxford: Oxford University Press, p. 236. (Note, this footnote could, of course, simply have read 'ibid'. as the exact reference occurred immediately before it. If, however, footnote 4 had been on the previous page, the correct cross-reference would have been loc. cit. as it referred to the same book *and* the same page number.

7. Case citation.

8. Discussion citation.

9. Finch, E. and Fafinski, S. (2007) *Legal Skills*, Oxford: Oxford University Press. As the sentence in the text refers to the overall theme of the book rather than a particular page or section, the footnote reference need not specify a chapter or page number.

10. Finch, E. and Fafinski, S. (2007) *Legal Skills*, Oxford: Oxford University Press, pp. 234–40. Here, the sentence in the text concerns a specific issue, so reference is needed to the particular pages of the book that address that issue.

11. *R* v *G* [2003] UKHL 50.

However, if you want to draw attention to a particular argument or if you provide a quotation from the case, you should include a page reference/paragraph number and state the name of the judge concerned:

> The House of Lords held that it was not 'not addressing the meaning of "reckless" in any other statutory or common law context'.[12]

In relation to statutes and statutory provisions, you should take a consistent approach throughout your essay, taking care in particular with the following:

- **Do not change the order of referencing.** For example, if you refer to the section number first in one reference,[13] make sure you do not reverse the order in subsequent references.[14]

- **Do not fluctuate between abbreviations[15] and full statute names;[16]** use one or the other. The only exception to this occurs if you use the full name on the first mention and note the abbreviation that will be used in subsequent references.[17]

10.4.3.3 Cross-referencing and abbreviations

You must never mix different referencing styles together in the same piece of work. This means that there must be no in-text references if you use footnotes and no footnotes if you use Harvard referencing. Equally, if you are using footnotes, you *must* provide the complete reference rather than the shortened 'name, date' approach used in Harvard referencing.[18] Students sometimes resort to abbreviated references in footnotes to avoid having to type the full reference to a particular book or journal on each occasion. Not only is this a lazy (and unacceptable) approach to referencing, it can be readily avoided by using the following techniques for referring to material that has already been referenced elsewhere. You should note that these referencing conventions are sometimes misused, so you should be careful to select the correct one (Table 10.2).

By convention, these phrases are always written in lower case (no capital initial letter) and are italicized (as they are Latin phrases or abbreviations of Latin phrases). Many lecturers

Table 10.2 Latin referencing conventions

Abbreviation	Meaning
ibid.	Short for *ibidem* which means 'in the same place'. This is used to refer to immediately preceding reference provided that it is identical in every respect. Strictly speaking, it should not be used for the first reference that appears on a new page as there is no immediately preceding reference.
op. cit.	This means 'the work previously cited', so it is used to refer to a book, article, or case that has already been referenced in the essay.
loc. cit.	This means 'the page previously cited in the book previously cited' so it is a more specific reference than *op. cit.* and should only be used to refer to a particular page.

12. *R v G* [2003] UKHL 50 *per* Lord Bingham at para. 28.
13. Section 2(1)(a) Theft Act 1968.
14. Theft Act 1968, s. 2(1)(a)
15. OAPA 1861, s. 18
16. Offences against the Person Act 1861, s. 20
17. Offences against the Person Act 1861 (OAPA), s. 47. Having noted the abbreviation in the first reference, it is now permissible to use OAPA in all subsequent references as you have informed the reader how this shortened form of the statute name will appear.
18. Finch and Fafinski, 2007. This approach effectively uses Harvard referencing style in a footnote. As such, it provides insufficient information for a proper footnote; full information or an appropriate cross-reference to full information should be provided in a footnote.

object to the continued use of Latin in legal writing so it would be worth checking if your institution/lecturer prefers the more straightforward 'see note 9' approach to cross-referencing.

It is sometimes acceptable to include a short note in a footnote if this relates to something explanatory that would interest the reader or assist their understanding but which would break the flow of the argument if included in the main body of the text.[19] You should, however, exercise caution when including anything other than a reference in your footnotes as this is sometimes viewed with suspicion by lecturers, who recognize that it is an attempt to circumvent the word limit by including material in the footnotes that should rightly be in the body of the essay. Do avoid doing this; not only is it poor academic practice, it may result in the deduction of marks from your lecturer for poor referencing. As always, it is advisable to check the rules of your department to determine whether there are any proscriptions as to what can be included in a footnote.

10.4.4 Referencing Internet sources

A high proportion of plagiarism cases seem to involve material taken from the Internet that is not acknowledged as such. It is possible that at least some of these cases arise from a lack of understanding as to how to reference such material or, indeed, a lack of awareness that material derived from the Internet requires a reference.

A distinction can be made between material that is published solely on the Internet and that which is available in hard copy elsewhere and has simply been accessed online in the interests of convenience. In the case of the former, as it is only available on the Internet, it is essential that adequate information is provided to enable the reader to locate the same material. As such, it has become the convention to state the title of the material and the author (if it is possible to do so—not all online material will enable you to identify the author) and provide the URL (web address) where the material can be found as well as the date upon which this was accessed:

> Hedges have historically not been controlled by planning law. However, it has finally been recognised that the height and intrusiveness of a neighbour's hedge can blight an adjoining property (http://www.sprattendicott.co.uk/news/0507-high-hedges.html accessed on 3rd November 2006).

It is important to include the date that the material was accessed as Internet content is frequently changed and updated, so there may be no permanent record of the material that you have referenced, unlike the situation in relation to printed material. It is for this reason that it can be useful to print out material found online that is not available elsewhere to ensure that you do have a permanent record that you can produce if the integrity or accuracy of your research is ever questioned.

In relation to material that is accessed online but is available elsewhere, such as a Home Office report, some might say that there is no need to include any mention of the Internet as the report can be referenced without it in a way that enables the reader to identify the source material and locate it themselves should they wish to do so. From this perspective, the fact that the report was found online is irrelevant, so to include the URL upon which the report can be found would be the equivalent of adding 'as read in the Bodleian library on 3 November 2006' in the footnote in relation to a hard copy.

---

19.   For example, if your essay discusses a particular line of authority, you may want to add some interesting information about it or draw attention to an article that takes a critical approach to the law that you are outlining. This draws the reader's attention to it at the appropriate point of the essay but ensures that the flow of your argument is not broken. In many respects, notes provided in footnotes can be regarded as interesting asides.

Whilst there is some sense in this view, it can never hurt to note the use of the Internet in relation to such material just to indicate that you have not actually read the report in the original, so a reference would look like this:

> A Home Office report (year) HMSO: London (www.homeoffice.co.uk/specificreport, accessed on 3 November 2006).

Strictly speaking, you should only do this if you have used an online version because the hard copy was not available to you. It is not necessary, for example, to provide case citations followed by 'accessed on Westlaw on 3 November 2006'.

When referencing Internet sources, it is essential that you are accurate in recording the URL as this enables the reader to find the material. You can increase accuracy by using the 'cut and paste' option to eliminate the possibility of typing errors; this can be particularly useful in relation to long and technical URLs. It is important to remember, however, to ensure that the pasted URL matches your text: blue hyperlinks in the midst of your essay give a very poor impression of the care you have taken with presentation.

10.4.5 Bibliography

You should provide a bibliography at the end of your work which details all the materials that you have used in the preparation of your essay, irrespective of whether you have made specific reference to them in your answer. In other words, the bibliography should contain everything that you have referenced (whether by a footnote or Harvard referencing) plus anything that you read or consulted but did not mention specifically in your text, for example, books that you used for background reading.

You should ensure that you provide full details of all the material listed in the bibliography. The following are examples of the approach that you could use in relation to the various materials that you may have used in your writing. Again, be aware that there are various styles that you can use to do this and that this will differ in terms of the positioning of particular information but the essence of the information will remain the same.

- **Book**: (1) name(s) of author(s) (2) year of publication (3) title (in italics, bold or underlined) (4) edition number (if any) (5) place of publication (6) name of publisher:

  Finch, E. and Fafinski, S. (2007) *Legal Skills*, Oxford: Oxford University Press.

- **Chapter in edited collection**: (1) name(s) of author(s) (2) title of chapter (3) name(s) of editor(s) (4) 'eds.' (5) year of publication (6) title (in italics, bold or underlined) (7) edition number (if any) (8) place of publication (9) name of publisher (10) pages on which the chapter appears:

  Finch, E. 'The Problem of Stolen Identity and the Internet', in Jewkes, Y. (2006) *Crime Online*, Cullompton: Willan Publishing, pp. 29–45.

- **Article**: (1) name(s) of author(s) (2) title of article (3) name of the journal (in italics, bold or underlined) (4) year (5) volume number (if any) (6) pages on which the chapter appears:

  Fafinski, S. 'Consent and the Rules of the Game: The Interplay of Civil and Criminal Liability for Sporting Injuries', *Journal of Criminal Law* (2005) vol. 69(5), pp. 414—26.

You will find more information on the way in which secondary resources are cited in chapter 6 and this can be used to assist you in ensuring that you provide full bibliographic references. Remember in particular that journals with volume numbers (such as the Journal of Criminal Law*) should have round brackets around the year whilst journals without volume numbers (such as the* Criminal Law Review*) should have square brackets.*

10.4.6 Quotations

Quotations can add authority to your work as you are, in effect, using the words of someone with far more legal expertise than yourself to support your argument. They should not, however, be overused; some students make the mistake of submitting an essay which is little more than a series of linked quotations. This is not the way to demonstrate your own understanding of the topic. The general rule is that you should not use a quotation to make a point that could be made in your own words.

Short quotations should be incorporated within the body of your essay 'using quotation marks' whilst longer quotations (more than a couple of lines or sentences) should be indented in a separate paragraph:

> This is because a short quotation will not break the flow of the argument and will generally be readily distinguishable from your own words whereas longer quotations, more than a few lines or sentences, should be set out separately as they are sufficiently long to stand alone as a self-contained idea. Do not forget that a long quotation does not need any additional punctuation marks as its separation into a distinct paragraph is sufficient to identify it as a quotation.

This is called a 'block quotation'. Not only does it not require quotation marks, it is usual to space it differently to the rest of the essay in order to differentiate it from your own words. For example, if you were using double or one-and-a-half line spacing for your essay, you would use single line spacing for your block quotations.

You can add or delete words from a quotation provided that you indicate that you have done so and the final result is not misleading and the changes are shown. Omitted material is indicated by the use of ellipses (. . .) whilst additional material is surrounded by square brackets. Square brackets can also be used to indicate a change of from upper to lower case (or vice versa). For example, if you wish to take a fragment of a quotation and use it as a complete sentence, you will need to change the initial letter of the first word from lower to upper case as demonstrated in the first example in the diagram (Figure 10.2).

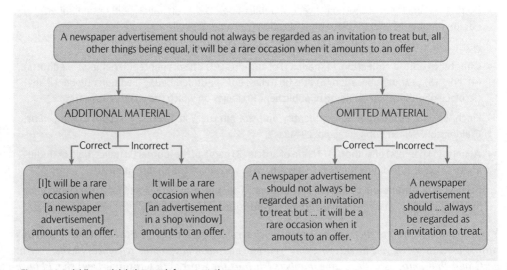

Figure 10.2 Adding and deleting words from quotations

10.5 Word limits

It is likely that most, if not all, pieces of coursework that you complete during your legal studies will have a word limit. Although students almost universally rail against these, protesting that they are too restrictive to enable them to answer the question properly or to enable them to say all that they want to say, essays and problem questions are carefully written to fit within the specified word limit. As such, it *is* possible to write a good answer within the constraints of the word limit.

10.5.1 Why is the word limit a problem?

If you are struggling, consider whether any of the following are applicable:

- **Too much irrelevant information.** Check whether you have understood the question correctly and evaluate how relevant each point that you want to include in the essay is to the question. Have you gone off at a tangent?

- **Too much descriptive detail.** Are you including lengthy explanations of the facts of cases when less, or even no, detail would suffice?

- **Too long-winded in your written language.** Some people have an aptitude for concise expression whereas others use far more words than are necessary to express even the simplest of ideas.

Alternatively, you may find that you have said everything you want to say and have not yet reached the word limit. This may be because you have an admirable concise written style and that you have ensured that you have only included relevant material. Unfortunately, it is more likely to mean that you have

- **Left out some relevant material.** If you are significantly short of the word limit, you have missed out something that should be included. Revisit the question and review your reading to see if there is something that you have overlooked.

- **Failed to provide sufficient detail.** This may arise because you have tried to keep description to a minimum and have gone too far and excluded some necessary explanation or because you have misjudged the complexity of a particular issue and provided only a simplistic explanation.

You will find more detailed advice on interpreting questions, selecting relevant material and keeping a strong focus on the question in chapter 11.

10.5.2 Why stick to the word limit?

It is essential that you do adhere to the word limit, however challenging that may seem, as most institutions impose a penalty for failure to do so. This may be a deduction of marks or a refusal to read any words that go over the specified limit. Either type of penalty will reduce the mark that your work receives. In some institutions that have a cumulative deduction policy, i.e. a deduction of two marks for every ten words over the limit; an essay which was too far over the limit could end up with a mark that was lower than the pass mark once all the deductions have been taken into account.

Do not make the mistake of misstating the word limit—quoting that you have used 1495 words in a 1500 limit when you have really used 1743—as this generally attracts an even more severe penalty, sometimes zero and a requirement that the coursework be repeated.

10.5.3 What counts towards the word limit?

Always check your department's regulations to determine how the word count is calculated. Some institutions exclude references to statute and case law from the word count, for example, so all statutory references and case citations can be deducted from the overall limit. This is likely to apply only to actual references rather than all discussion of case or statute law, so make sure that you make an accurate deduction. Equally, some departments will state that all references are included in the word count (which makes checking that you have made an accurate declaration of the word limit easier) whereas others exclude footnotes from the word count but specify that they must only be used to reference and not to introduce any additional text. There are many other potential policies on counting words that may arise at different institutions. This chapter does not aim to outline all the possibilities, rather just to orientate you to the existence of the different methods of counting words. It highlights the need to check the rules in order to ensure that you are adhering to the requirements of the word limit in force at your institution.

10.6 Presentation

Presentation of coursework, or how it looks on the page, is important. If you look at several pieces of work with identical content, you will probably find that you make instinctive evaluations about their quality on the basis of their visual appearance (you will find some examples of good and bad presentation in the Online Resource Centre if you want to test this theory). A well-presented piece of work that complies with any institutional requirements with regard to font choice or formatting, for example, will create a good first impression with the marker. Whilst this may not necessarily contribute to the grade that the essay receives (unless your department awards marks for presentation), it cannot do any harm to ensure that the person marking your work feels favourably disposed towards it from the outset.

10.6.1 Formatting

If there is a house style with regard to presentation, use it even if you do not like the style chosen. Most people have a font style or pattern of layout that they favour but that is no reason not to adhere to the specifications that you have been given. Some departments even impose an automatic deduction of marks for failure to comply with the presentation requirements of assessed coursework, so it is always advisable to find out what the requirements are and follow them to the letter. In the absence of any specifications as to style, you may like to bear the following in mind when choosing how to present your work:

- **Font and font size:** choose a relatively straightforward font that is easy for the marker to read. It would generally be unnecessary to have a font size larger than 12-point in the main body of your text.
- **Line spacing:** double or one-and-a-half line spacing is advisable as it is easier to read in large quantities than single-spaced text. Moreover, wider line spacing ensures that your work covers more pages and gives the marker more space to write comments in the margin.

- **Margins:** as with line spacing, wide margins allow the marker space to write comments. The default settings should give sufficient space.

- **Paragraphing:** using a double space between paragraphs creates more 'white space' that makes the page easier on the marker's eye and gives additional space for comment.

Overall, these guidelines are aimed at ensuring that the page is not too crowded so that the words look squashed onto the page.

10.6.2 Statutes and cases

It is usual to use different formatting to ensure that statutory references and case names stand out from the bulk of the text. Your institution may have particular requirements in this respect but, if not, choose a style and stick to it throughout your essay. As with so many aspects of presentation, consistency is the key to success. If you decide to underline statute names, for example, make sure that you do this all the way through your essay rather than switching to bold on page 3 and then forgetting altogether on the final page.

It is usual to italicize case names but not the full citation. Moreover, the 'v' should be in ordinary font and not italics. As such, the correct way to present a case is as follows:

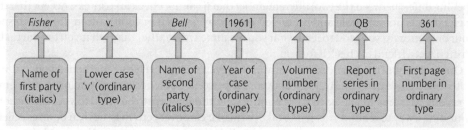

Figure 10.3 Case presentation

10.6.3 Headings

This section address issues of the presentation of headings rather than their use in essays (which can be found in chapter 11). If you are using headings in your work, make sure that you use an appropriate and consistent approach to formatting them. For example, if you use two levels of heading (main headings and subheadings), make sure that the style you use for the main heading is more prominent than that of the subheading and that you use the same style throughout your work. Finally, do make sure that something follows the heading; leaving a heading 'hanging' as the final words on the bottom of the page whilst the text follows on the next is not an effective approach to the use of headings.

10.6.4 Page numbers

It is useful to ensure that the pages of your work are numbered. If your marker drops your essay, it might be difficult to reorder them if they are not numbered. Equally, if you staple the pages in the incorrect order (it happens!) and they are not numbered, your lecturer may not realize that the pages are not in order and merely assume that the flow of your argument is not logical.

10.6.5 Capital letters

There is an unfortunate tendency amongst students to capitalize every word that seems significant, such as Judge, Court, Case, and Law, or any phrases that seem sufficiently important, for example, Rule of Law, *Actus Reus* or Invitation to Treat. This is incorrect and should be avoided. The use of capital letters should be reserved for the word at the start of a sentence and proper nouns only.

10.6.6 Checking for errors

Although the aim is to allow the marker plenty of space to write comments, you really want to attract feedback about the content of your legal argument rather than technicalities of presentation, so do ensure that the spelling, grammar, and punctuation is correct. There are few things more disheartening for a student than the return of an essay that is covered in corrections, so avoid this by ensuring that you do not give the marker a great deal to correct. It should go without saying that the work should be meticulously checked for basic errors prior to submission, but far too many students submit work that looks suspiciously like a first draft in that it is peppered with the sorts of error that should have been corrected prior to submission.

The solution is to leave sufficient time prior to submission to check your essay thoroughly for accuracy. Use the spell check, making sure that it is set to UK English rather than US English (the spelling differs between the two) but remember that it cannot check for context. Accept that the spell check is not infallible and proofread your essay yourself or, as it is often difficult to spot your own errors as you tend to read what you meant to write rather than what you have actually written, get a friend to check it for you.

One technique that can be particularly useful, even after you have strengthened your writing skills through years of study, is to compose a personalized checklist of potential problems. Everyone has some weakness in their writing style and it is easy to be blind to your own errors, so finding a way to remind yourself to take particular care over certain issues can be an excellent way of ensuring that you produce a polished and accurate piece of work. You could start with quite a general checklist in the early stages of your studies that reminds you to check such basics as spelling or the technicalities of presenting case names and citations correctly. As your written style strengthens, some of the basics will become second nature whilst other, more specific problems, will inevitably emerge. For example, perhaps you find the distinction between plural and possessive 'its' confusing or you are unclear about the difference between 'affect' and

Check spelling and grammar	☐	Are footnotes on the right page?	☐
Check 'its' and 'it's'	☐	References: complete and correct?	☐
Does it look right on paper?	☐	Underline statutes	☐
Any hanging headings?	☐	Italics for case names	☐
Check use of capitals	☐	Does it make sense?	☐

Figure 10.4 Checklist

'effect'. Irrespective of the nature of your problem, your checklist can evolve to reflect this as you progress.

 This is just one example of the sorts of points that you could include on your checklist (Figure 10.4). You will find a downloadable template of this on the online resource centre, with some suggestions of categories that you might like to use at the start but which can be altered to suit your own requirements.

CHAPTER SUMMARY

Language

- Strive for an appropriate level of formality in your written style; the approach used in good textbooks and articles will provide a useful example

- Avoid casual language such as text speak and the use of the first person

- Be alert for the conventions relating to gender-neutral language and the use of Latin

- Be aware that words that have legal and non-legal meanings, such as assault, can confuse the reader

Grammar and punctuation

- Take care to ensure that your work is grammatical as this contributes towards accuracy and precision

- Look for evidence that would suggest that there is a problem with your grammar and punctuation and ensure you seek appropriate assistance if it appears necessary

- Take note of the common problems that arise and strive to eliminate them from your writing

Plagiarism and referencing

- Plagiarism is a form of academic dishonesty that is readily detected and attracts negative consequences both within your institution and in the professional world

- Bear in mind that a thorough and precise approach to references will avoid accusations of inadvertent plagiarism. If in doubt, reference

- Note the situations outlined in this chapter in which a reference should be provided, taking particular care to ensure that ideas are attributed to their source

- Find out whether your institution or department has a 'house style' and, if so, ensure that you follow it

- Never combine footnotes and in-text references

- Familiarize yourself with the conventions for referencing and cross-referencing

- Take particular care with Internet sources

- Always provide a complete bibliography

Quotations

- Incorporating quotations into your work can add strength to your arguments but you must ensure that you do not use it out of context or misrepresent its meaning

- If you add or remove words or emphasis, this must be noted in the quotation or its reference as appropriate. Ensure that any changes do not alter the meaning of the quotation

- Do not overuse quotations. The bulk of your essay should be expressed in your words as opposed to merely joining together a string of quotations. Equally, do not use quotations, particularly from textbooks, to express concepts that could be expressed in your own words; your ability to explain legal concepts will attract more credit than your ability to select an appropriate quotation

Presentation

- Discover whether there are any mandatory requirements for the presentation of coursework and, if so, ensure that you adhere to them

- Ensure that you leave sufficient time prior to the deadline for submission to check your work thoroughly for presentational errors

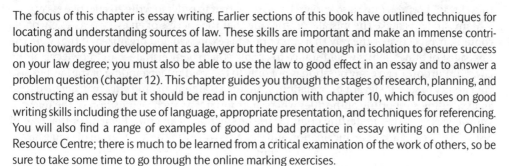

Essay skills

11

INTRODUCTION

The focus of this chapter is essay writing. Earlier sections of this book have outlined techniques for locating and understanding sources of law. These skills are important and make an immense contribution towards your development as a lawyer but they are not enough in isolation to ensure success on your law degree; you must also be able to use the law to good effect in an essay and to answer a problem question (chapter 12). This chapter guides you through the stages of research, planning, and constructing an essay but it should be read in conjunction with chapter 10, which focuses on good writing skills including the use of language, appropriate presentation, and techniques for referencing. You will also find a range of examples of good and bad practice in essay writing on the Online Resource Centre; there is much to be learned from a critical examination of the work of others, so be sure to take some time to go through the online marking exercises.

The production of an essay involves a combination of writing skills and legal knowledge. As such, several other chapters in this book will provide useful information that contributes to the process of writing a successful essay. For example, you must know how to find the relevant law (chapters 2, 5, and 8), use it (chapters 3 and 6) and how to express your understanding in good written English following the practices and conventions of legal writing (chapter 10). In addition to these important factors, you must also understand how to tailor your knowledge to the particular essay and how to construct a focused, flowing, and analytical essay. Mastering the art of essay writing is essential as, together with problem questions, essays are the dominant means of assessment that you will encounter, both as coursework and examinations, on your law degree. This chapter guides you through the stages of producing an essay from analysing the question, conducting the research, selecting material, and structuring the answer. These stages of the essay-writing process are illustrated by examples and suggestions of ways to make your essay stand out to the marker.

LEARNING OUTCOMES

After studying this chapter, you should be able to:

- Analyse an essay question in order to identify its scope and requirements

- Prepare to write the essay by engaging in effective research and planning

- Structure an argument and select supporting material

- Identify the skills that are being assessed in the essay and tailor your essay to ensure that these skills are demonstrated

- Evaluate the essay that you have written to ensure that it demonstrates the relevant skills and knowledge and that it adheres to the necessary style and referencing requirements

11.1 What is a good essay?

This is an important question as you cannot be expected to produce a good essay until you know what features combine together to create a good essay. In essence, a good essay is one that answers the question and, in doing so, demonstrates a range of written and analytical skills. It is important to emphasize that a good essay requires as much thought to be given to the way that the essay is constructed as is given to its content. In other words, it is not enough that you know the relevant law; you must also know what to do with it in order to write an effective essay.

Many students make the mistake of thinking that the success of an essay rests solely on its content, irrespective of the way that this content is expressed and organized. If that were the case, a list of bullet points would suffice to enable you to demonstrate your knowledge of the law. The purpose of an essay question is not only to test your understanding of the law but also your ability to select relevant information, structure an argument, and engage in detailed legal analysis using supporting authorities where appropriate. As such, acquisition of the relevant knowledge is merely the starting point for the production of an essay. Remember that careful research will elicit accurate information and that this will form the foundation of your essay.

Students often state that they have not started their essay but mean that they have thought about it and conducted some research but that there are no actual words on paper yet. Equally, the essay is often regarded as finished as soon as the last word is typed. It is a mistake to prioritize the actual writing of the essay as this is only one stage in the four-stage process of producing a good essay (Figure 11.1).

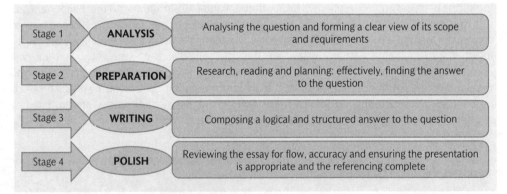

Stage 1	ANALYSIS	Analysing the question and forming a clear view of its scope and requirements
Stage 2	PREPARATION	Research, reading and planning: effectively, finding the answer to the question
Stage 3	WRITING	Composing a logical and structured answer to the question
Stage 4	POLISH	Reviewing the essay for flow, accuracy and ensuring the presentation is appropriate and the referencing complete

Figure 11.1 The four stages of essay writing

This chapter will provide a detailed account of the requirements of each of these stages in order to assist you with the production of an essay that answers the question set, demonstrates appropriate skills, and which meets with the approval of your marker. Remember, though, that it may be necessary to move backwards and forwards through the stages: you may, for example, find that you need to do more research once you have moved into the writing stage or that you need to reconsider what the essay means during the research stage, but that is not a problem.

This chapter does not intend to suggest that there is a rigid progression through the stages but to ensure that each stage is given adequate attention to help you with the production of your essays.

11.2 Analysing the question

It is important to take time to analyse the question in order to work out what it requires. This is a fundamental first step as you cannot hope to answer the question unless you are clear about what it is asking. Even your initial research should be undertaken with a firm eye on the requirements of the question; you do not have to know what the answer is in order to work out what the question is asking. In fact, analysis of the question will help the research process as you will be more able to eliminate irrelevant or peripheral information if you are clear about what it is the question requires.

11.2.1 What does the question ask?

It is essential to the success of every stage of the essay-writing process that you focus on what the essay asks rather than the broader issue of what the essay is about. This distinction should become clearer if you consider the following essay title:

> To what extent does the Sexual Offences Act 2003 achieve its aim of 'simplifying the law' and 'strengthening the protection afforded to victims of [rape]'?

Give some thought for a moment to these questions:

- What is the essay about?
- What does the essay ask?

The answer to the first question is relatively straightforward; the essay is about, variously, sexual offences, rape, or the Sexual Offences Act 2003. However, you could write an essay on any of these topics that would wholly fail to address the issue at the heart of the question which is whether the recent reforms to rape law have achieved their stated objectives.

Far too many students limit their prospects of success by answering the first question rather than the second. This can be a particular problem in examinations as many students tend to feel pressured and latch on to the most obvious aspect of the question with a sense a relief that they have encountered something familiar which suggests that it is a question that they can answer. This is a mistake because the broad topic 'sexual offences' covers a whole range of issues that are simply irrelevant to this question and, as such, attract absolutely no marks whatsoever. For example, a discussion of grooming—a measure introduced by SOA 2003 to deal with those who use the Internet to lure children into sexual activity—falls within the broad category 'about the SOA 2003' but has just as little relevance to this question as a consideration of:

- manslaughter—a different criminal offence
- resulting trusts—a different area of law, or
- agricultural policy in the 1950s—a non-law topic.

11.2.2 Reword the question

One of the most effective ways to work out what the question asks is to rewrite it in your own words with the aim of discovering one or two clear questions that you understand. For example, the following two questions simplify the SOA title and make it far easier to keep its core issues in mind when researching and writing the essay:

- Is the offence of rape simpler to understand than it was under the previous law?
- Are victims of rape better protected under the new law?

By focusing on what the question asks rather than on the broader question of what it is about, you will find it much easier to identify relevant material for inclusion in your essay and to eliminate material which, although *about* the general issue of rape, has no relevance to the particular question *asked* by the essay.

Practical exercise

It is a good idea to practise analysing essay titles by rewording them as this will give you the confidence to do it with your own work. Try and identify the questions that are being asked in the following essay titles. You should be able to do this even if you have little knowledge or understanding of the topic of the essay:

1. The postal rule is outdated and has no place in modern contract law. Discuss.

2. If the United Kingdom has a constitution at all, its central pillar is parliamentary sovereignty. Discuss this statement with particular reference to the European Community.

3. Explain how charitable purposes are defined and consider whether the current approach is satisfactory.

4. Outline the approaches that a judge may take to statutory interpretation and consider their relevance following the enactment of the Human Rights Act 1998.

 You will find suggested answers to these questions on the Online Resource Centre where there is also explanation of how the answers were reached.

Remember that you are rewording the question to enhance your understanding of what it requires. You must take the utmost care to ensure that you are not rewording it in a way that changes its sense or meaning. When your essay is marked, it will only attract credit for material that is relevant to the question that was asked and not for other points, however interesting or clever, that are not pertinent.

11.3 Research and planning

These preparatory stages should take at least as much time as the actual writing of the essay. This is the stage at which you find the answer to the question, select material for inclusion in your essay, and engage in some preliminary planning of the structure of your argument. Taking care with these preparatory stages does make the writing of the essay less troublesome, as many of the difficult issues will have already been resolved.

11.3.1 Focus on the question(s)

The aim of the preceding section is to emphasize the importance of working out what the question wants prior to starting the process of research, planning, and writing that will produce the essay. This is because you cannot answer a question unless you know what it is asking. Students sometimes think that research is the first stage and certainly it can be but you will be so much more effective in your research if you start with a clear idea of what you are trying to find out which you will be able to do if you have analysed your question as the first stage prior to commencing research. Try to remember that you do not need to know the answer in order to conduct research: after all, that is what research is all about—finding answers. Of course, you are likely to discover information during your research that assists you to reach a more informed understanding of the questions but your research will be more effective if you have given thought to what it is you are trying to find before you start to research.

11.3.2 Brainstorming

One method of exploring what you already know about a topic is brainstorming. This involves writing down everything that you can think of about a topic in the order it comes into your mind. This technique has been a really useful way of finding out just how much you do know about a topic as part of the revision process (see chapter 13) but it can also be helpful in essay writing as it is a way to establish a list of potential topics for inclusion in your essay so that you can make some preliminary decisions about relevance and thus direct the focus of your research and reading.

You might find it useful (and more enjoyable) to work with a friend at this stage. Write the topic at the top of a piece of paper and give yourself a set period of time—two minutes should be ample—to write all that you can think of about that topic. At the end of the time, reflect upon the points that you have listed and note your preliminary thoughts about their relevance to the question. Of course, it may be that you are not sure how relevant they are until you find out more about the law but at least you should have eliminated some material and identified some further questions that need to be answered as part of your research, i.e. how relevant is this issue to my essay.

This example is based upon a brainstorming session about rape that generated a diverse selection of points about rape. Once you have all your ideas recorded, you can evaluate how relevant each issue is to the question asked. This example shows the relevance of each of the issues to (a) the question about the SOA 2003 provided earlier in the chapter and (b) 'Outline the role of consent in the offence of rape and consider whether recent legislative changes have improved the law' (Figure 11.2).

RAPE	Q1 RELEVANCE?	Q2 RELEVANCE?
Definition (old law, new law)	Yes	Yes
Consent	? Has it changed?	Yes
Penetration—vagina, anus, mouth	Yes, new law	Probably not
Male defendant—new offence of penetration (s2) by either sex	Yes, new law	Probably not
Transsexual rape—what sex is the victim?	? Unsure?	No
Cases under old law—would they be different under new law?	Some cases	Consent cases
Marital exemption—R v. R	Probably not	No
Conviction rates	New law, improved?	Possibly
Intoxication and consent	? Unsure?	Yes
Stranger rape, date rape, drug-assisted rape	? Unsure?	Possibly
Rape of children—rape by children	Probably not	No

Figure 11.2 Evaluating a brainstorming session

By dealing with a single brainstorming session about the broad topic of rape and then testing the relevance of the points which emerged against two different questions, it is hoped to emphasize the importance of considering the particular question (what the question asks) rather than the general topic (what the question is about).

 Practical exercise

Try this technique with the four essay titles provided in the practical exercise on p. 250. The topics for brainstorming in relation to each essay are listed below. Remember that the first stage is to brainstorm the topic and the second stage is to evaluate the relevance of each point that this has identified in relation to the particular question.

1. Contract: offer and acceptance.
2. Constitutional law: parliamentary sovereignty/European law.
3. Trusts: charitable purposes.
4. English Legal Systems: statutory interpretation/HRA

 You will find suggested answers to these questions on the Online Resource Centre where there is also an explanation of how the answers were reached.

11.3.3 Getting started

It can be extremely difficult to make a start on the research and planning of an essay just because it all seems such an immense task, particularly if you feel that you are overwhelmed from the start because you are faced with a topic that you do not understand. This section outlines some of the early steps that can be taken that will help you to make a start on your preparation.

11.3.3.1 Gathering information

Earlier chapters in this book have provided in-depth coverage of a range of legal sources, how to find them, and how to make effective use of them. This chapter will not repeat that information but will merely highlight a few key points of particular relevance to conducting research for an essay. You will probably find that you need to make reference to earlier chapters to help you with the research process.

The most sensible starting point for your research is the relevant chapter in a good textbook. You may find it useful to read the chapter in its entirety without making any notes, just so that you get a feel for the topic. It can be helpful to see the complete picture prior to any attempt to extrapolate particular information. If you find that there is a great deal of material in the chapter that you cannot understand, it would be advisable to find an alternative textbook, even if the one you were reading is the recommended book for the course. If you are struggling with the topic, it may be that a more straightforward coverage of the same material will help you to get to grips with it. This is particularly important when you are conducting research for an essay because you need to be able to understand the basics of a topic in order to be able to write about it. There is little to be gained by persevering with a book if you feel that you do not understand what it is saying.

You should not restrict yourself to a single textbook. Each book will present the core information on a topic in a different way and will inevitably choose different cases and examples to illustrate the law that is outlined. Reading a variety of textbooks will help you gain a broader perspective of the topic in question. You can also use textbooks to identify other sources of information, such as articles and cases, and reading a range of books will increase the amount of additional sources that you discover.

A textbook is a good source of basic information that should be used to give you a solid understanding of the topic. However, quoting extensively from a textbook in your essay or using textbooks as the sole point of reference for your arguments will not impress your lecturers. You need to demonstrate the ability to move beyond a textbook and engage with this sort of analysis that you will find in articles and monographs. These sources of information will supplement the framework of knowledge that you have acquired from textbooks and enable you to engage in some more sophisticated analysis of the issues raised by your essay.

11.3.3.2 Organizing your research

Once you feel that you have a good picture of a topic in your mind, it will be useful to start taking notes of issues that are of relevance to your essay.

During the course of your research, you will use a variety of sources and you will want to keep a record of the relevant information that you have found. The most common method of recording information is, unfortunately, also the least effective in terms of organization. Most people organize their research findings according to their sources; in other words, they will read an article or book chapter, make a notice of the relevant information that they find, and then repeat this process with the next source of information. The disadvantage of this system is that you end up with a number of condensed versions of each source that you have read. This usually means that you end up writing out the same information several times as you encounter the same point in a number of different sources.

It is also very easy to become distracted from the purpose of the note-taking, i.e. extrapolating information pertinent to a particular essay question, and instead to note all the information that seems to be important to the writer of the article. The unfortunate consequence of this is that you are devoting time to noting down information that has no relevance whatsoever to the essay without really thinking about what it is that you want to achieve, so that ultimately the situation becomes nothing more than an exercise in handwriting.

The best way to avoid this and to make the research process more effective is to evolve a system of organizing your notes that is based on the issue or question that you want to address. If you have analysed your question and brainstormed your topic as suggested above, you will already have identified specific questions that you want to answer. Write each of these questions at the top of a separate sheet of paper and note any information which you locate that is relevant to these questions on the appropriate sheet of paper. The advantage of this is that your notes are organized by issue, which will enable you to see at a glance how much information you have on each of the points. This will be useful when you come to plan the structure of your essay.

Figure 11.3 illustrates the way that notes organized by issue could appear. You will see that there is no need to spend time copying out reams of detail from the books as you can note the key piece of information and the page on which it appears so that you know where to find it. The notes also record any additional sources that have been identified from your reading.

Remember that you should keep a note of all the sources that you have used during your research for inclusion in your bibliography; it is infuriating to feel that the essay is complete and then have to spend hours tracking down details of books and articles so that your referencing is complete.

It is also a good idea to keep a record of any ideas, thoughts, or questions that occur to you during the course of your research. It is often the case that inspiration will strike whilst you are reading: you might think of a clever point or argument or else see a link with other information or cases that needs to be followed up elsewhere.

You will find some information on effective note-taking techniques in the chapter on study skills: see chapter 9.

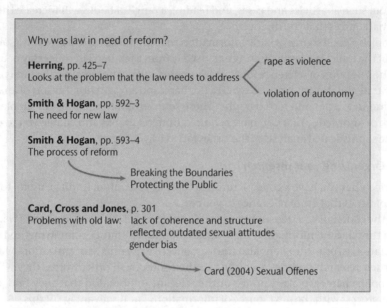

Figure 11.3 Organizing your research by issue

11.3.4 Structuring the argument

It is not enough to ask the right questions and find relevant material, it is also necessary to organize that information into a coherent and logical essay. This is one of the stages in the process that students tend to find difficult.

As your research progresses, you should acquire an increasingly detailed set of notes and develop an idea of the sorts of points that you could include in your essay. If you have used the issue-based method of organizing your research illustrated in Figure 11.3, you will find that your notes are already arranged in categories and this may help you to structure your essay; this is a good starting point but you should not accept the strategy that your notes suggest without giving the matter further thought.

It is important that you remember that there should be a clear line of argument that develops in your essay; in other words, your essay should be going somewhere and developing with a purpose. It can be informative here to refer back to your initial analysis of the essay: what question(s) did you identify that needed to be answered? Your essay should be structured around those questions, taking into account the material that you have identified during your research as being necessary to answer those questions (Figure 11.4).

Of course, this is just one way in which the sample essay could be structured. It would be equally accepted, for example, to take each of the questions that comprise the essay and deal with them individually, picking up on examples from the *actus reus* and *mens rea* of rape that are appropriate to an evaluation of whether the SOA 2003 (1) simplifies the law and (2) offers more protection to victims.

If you experience difficulty in deciding on a structure, try writing down all the points that you would like to include on separate scraps of paper and then moving them about, trying out different structures. Some points will have an obvious place in the essay; for example, it would not make sense in the above example to start the essay with a discussion of consent and then move on to define the offence of rape in the second paragraph.

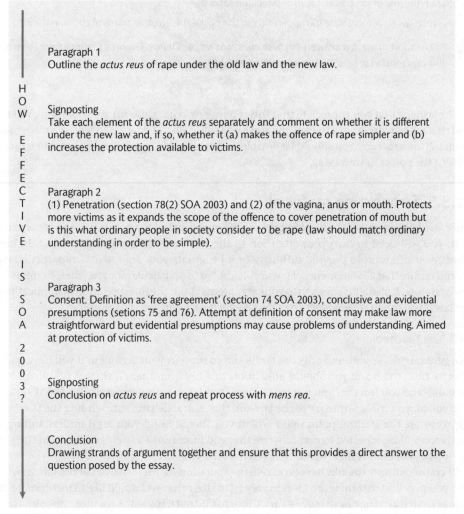

Paragraph 1
Outline the *actus reus* of rape under the old law and the new law.

Signposting
Take each element of the *actus reus* separately and comment on whether it is different under the new law and, if so, whether it (a) makes the offence of rape simpler and (b) increases the protection available to victims.

Paragraph 2
(1) Penetration (section 78(2) SOA 2003) and (2) of the vagina, anus or mouth. Protects more victims as it expands the scope of the offence to cover penetration of mouth but is this what ordinary people in society consider to be rape (law should match ordinary understanding in order to be simple).

Paragraph 3
Consent. Definition as 'free agreement' (section 74 SOA 2003), conclusive and evidential presumptions (setions 75 and 76). Attempt at definition of consent may make law more straightforward but evidential presumptions may cause problems of understanding. Aimed at protection of victims.

Signposting
Conclusion on *actus reus* and repeat process with *mens rea*.

Conclusion
Drawing strands of argument together and ensure that this provides a direct answer to the question posed by the essay.

HOW EFFECTIVE IS SOA 2003?

Figure 11.4 Structuring the argument

Practical exercise

Have a try at constructing a working structure for the essay on the postal rule that was used in the earlier practical exercises. Think about the line of argument that you would need to present in that essay and then put the following points in the order that you think that they would occur in an essay.

1. Outline the difficulties of applying the postal rule to modern commercial transactions.

2. Define the postal rule.

3. Outline the role of offer and acceptance.

4. Comment on whether the postal rule achieves its original purpose.

5. Explain contract formation

6. Provide examples of the traditional operation of the postal rule.

7. Explain the role of the postal rule in contract formation.

8. Use case law to demonstrate the application of the postal rule to other forms of communication.

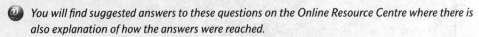 *You will find suggested answers to these questions on the Online Resource Centre where there is also explanation of how the answers were reached.*

It is important that you appreciate that this is only a working structure for your essay. You may find that when you come to the writing stage your ideas do not flow when you try and organize them in this structure. You should be flexible and prepared to reconsider the order in which to present the points in your essay.

11.3.5 Supporting material

Once you have an idea of the basic framework of your essay and the points that you want to raise in it, you will need to turn your attention to the selection of supporting material. In other words, you will want to provide authority to substantiate your arguments. In particular, you should ensure that all statements of law are attributed to a particular source, whether this is case law or statute. It also adds strength to your arguments about the interpretation or application of the law if you can make reference to material which backs up your position.

11.3.5.1 Textbooks

As a general rule, you should only use textbooks to support your argument if you have quoted directly from them and you should only quote directly from them if there is no other source available and you feel that you cannot express the idea in your own words. Textbooks exist to give you an accessible summary of the law and the central debates surrounding the law; basically, they are the starting point upon which you should build your legal understanding. As such, you will be expected to demonstrate that you have read a variety of sources in the preparation of your essay rather than simply relying on textbooks.

Of course, some textbooks have an excellent reputation for their analysis of the law, in which case you may find that there are ideas expressed in there that you would like to incorporate into your essay. If this is the case, it may be a good idea to find out if the author of the textbook has elaborated on this point in an article or monograph and, if so, are to rely on this to support your argument instead. Overall, it is advisable to be sparing in your reliance on textbooks in your essay.

11.3.5.2 Statutory provisions

The position regarding statutory provisions is straightforward. If you are referring to a particular piece of legislation, you should always indicate the name of the statute and, if appropriate, the section or subsection number. This does not necessarily mean that you should quote the full wording of the section itself; it will often be more appropriate to paraphrase the statutory provision or to select a segment of the section.

11.3.5.3 Case law

There are three main ways in which you might want to use case law in your essay to support your answer.

- **The course of a legal principle:** if a legal rule, definition, or test has evolved in case law, you should attribute it to its source in the same way that you would if the area of law was governed by statute. For example, in criminal law, the test for oblique intention was formulated by the House of Lords in *R* v *Woollin* [1999] 1 AC 82.

- **An elaboration on the meaning of a word or phrase:** case law is a major source of interpretation of the meaning and application of words and phrases used in law. For example, the phrase 'ethnic origin' as found in the Race Relations Act 1976 was subjected to in-depth interpretation in *Mandla* v *Lee* [1983] 2 AC 548.

- **The operation of the law:** if you want to ascertain the scope of the law and how it applies in particular situations, you can look at how it has taken effect in case law. For example, if you were addressing the tort of defamation in relation to media coverage of the private lives of celebrities, you could use the cases involving the right to freedom of expression to determine the scope of the law. You can also use case law to demonstrate the impact of changes in the law as you can show how the outcome of a decided case would differ; this can be an especially powerful way to support your arguments for or against a particular interpretation of the law. For example, in relation to the sample essay, you could use cases decided under the old law and, in order to demonstrate its impact explain how they would have a different outcome under the new law.

11.3.5.4 Academic commentary

Sources such as journal articles and monographs can provide valuable support for the arguments made in your essay. It is suggested that you should also strive to include at the very least two, preferably opposing or contradictory, academic viewpoints within your essay to demonstrate the different perspectives that exist in relation to the issue under consideration.

This approach is much stronger than merely asserting your own opinion of the law, although it is perfectly permissible to produce academic arguments that concur with your own preferences. Remember, though, that there is a need for balance and objectivity; whatever your preferred view, you should ensure that an alternative stance is at least acknowledged in your essay. From a pragmatic point of view, identifying two different standpoints is likely to attract greater credit from the marker than reliance on a single view, plus you are also demonstrating your research skills in identifying more than one opinion on the same issue, thus showing evidence of wide reading.

11.3.5.5 Internet sources

Students tend to like the Internet as a research tool because it is a quick and easy source of information: type in a word or phrase and you will be presented with a whole host of results within a split second. However, traditional legal resources are reliable and accurate whereas the quality of material found on the Internet cannot be guaranteed. It is acceptable to use the Internet to access official publications, such as those found on the Home Office website, but you should use material of uncertain origin with great caution.

You will find some guidance on evaluating the value of material found on the Internet in chapter 7. It is important that you take note of this and limit yourself to the use of material that has objective academic merit.

When selecting supporting material, bear in mind the following guidelines:

- Statements of law need to be supported by reference to their source in either statute or case law.

- Factual statements should be attributed to their source, e.g. over 5000 women are killed by their partners each year in England and Wales.

- Analysis, discussion, and speculation about the law are strengthened by reference to supporting material.
- A balanced argument is more effective than a one-sided stance, so select supporting material that takes into account a range of perspectives on the issue under consideration.
- Be cautious in your use of textbooks, using them only if you can find no other supporting material for a particular argument, example, or opinion and never as a reference point for a statement of law that is contained in a case or statute.

Remember that all supporting material must be fully and appropriately referenced in your essay. Failure to do so carries a risk that you will be accused of plagiarism. You will find detailed information on the correct approach to referencing in chapter 10.

11.4 Writing the essay

Once you have researched the topic, gathered your material, and put together a preliminary plan of your essay, it is time to start writing. This section of the chapter will outline the skills that are necessary to produce an effective and analytical essay and it will then move on to cover some of the key issues that arise in relation to the process of writing.

11.4.1 What skills does the question require?

It is essential to the success of your essay that you realize that it is a means of assessing skills as well as knowledge. With this in mind, it is important that you are able to tailor your answer to ensure that you demonstrate the appropriate skills.

Benjamin Bloom, an educational psychologist, conducted research into the skills demonstrated by students in their essays and was concerned to note that there was insufficient evidence of what he termed 'higher-order' skills. He divided skills into six categories and arranged them in a hierarchy, depicted in the Figure 11.5, to demonstrate their importance and complexity.

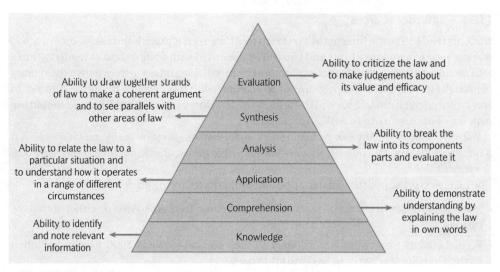

Figure 11.5 Bloom's taxonomy

Higher-order skills are those identified by Bloom as demonstrating a stronger grasp of a subject as evidenced by the ability to *use* knowledge rather than merely to acquire and repeat it. To take a very basic example, you would be able to demonstrate *knowledge* by finding a map of the area, *understanding* by explaining the route to another person, but *application* by actually reaching your destination. Once there, you might want to *analyse* how useful the route was and, ultimately, decide whether to use it again or to find an alternative. In legal studies, you may hear the distinction between higher and lower-order skills summarized as description (knowledge, comprehension) and analysis (application, analysis, synthesis, evaluation).

Bloom's taxonomy demonstrates the point made earlier that a successful essay rests upon more than mere identification and explanation of the relevant law. The lower-order skills are considered to be more straightforward and easier to demonstrate thus an essay which moves beyond knowledge and comprehension to demonstrate higher-order skills is likely to be more successful. That does not mean that the lower-order skills are unimportant or should be omitted, merely that they should be considered the foundation upon which a demonstration of higher-order skills is based. In other words, you need to be able to describe the law in order to analyse it.

The words in an essay question that describe the skills required are sometimes called **process words**.

You can identify the skills that are important within an essay by the process words that are used in the question. The table below identifies some of the process words commonly associated

Table 11.1 Higher-order and lower-order skills

Skill	Indicated by . . .	Example
Knowledge	Words that invite a factual or descriptive response or a straightforward statement of law	Describe, define, outline, state, identify, list, what, how, when, which
Comprehension	Words that require an explanation of the law, interpretation, or the ability to extrapolate key information	Explain, use examples, summarize, paraphrase, interpret
Application	Words that suggest the need to apply the law to different circumstances or to predict how the law would react to a new situation	Apply, demonstrate, advise, predict
Analysis	Words that indicate that a case or legal principle should be broken down into its component parts and subjected to close scrutiny	Analyse, assess, consider, measure, quantify, how far
Synthesis	Words that indicate that the ability to draw together strands of an argument and to identify similarities and differences	Justify, compare, contrast, distinguish
Evaluation	Words that indicate that the law should be measured to determine whether it is effective, consistent, moral, desirable, better than before or a useful solution to a particular problem	Appraise, criticize, evaluate, comment, reflect, discuss, how effective

with each of the categories of skills and provides some elaboration upon what each of these requires from the writer of the essay.

This is an indication only; never think that the absence of an 'evaluation' word in the title of an essay indicates that it is inappropriate to engage in evaluation. The use of a particular word in an essay title is more likely to emphasize a particular skill that your lecturer is interested in rather than indicating that it should be demonstrated to the exclusion of all other skills. A good essay should contain a combination of higher- and lower-order skills.

The most effective way to ensure that you cover a range of lower and higher-order skills in your essay is to consider from the outset how these might be demonstrated. This example is based upon the question about the SOA 2003 (Figure 11.6).

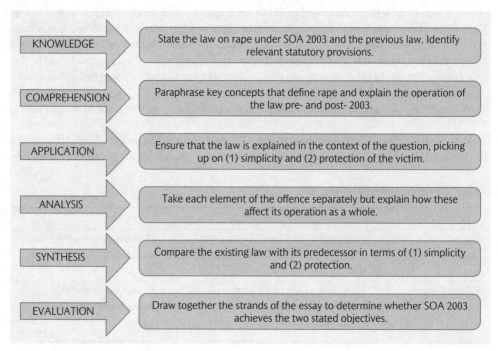

Figure 11.6 Covering higher and lower-order skills

 Practical exercise

Look back at the four essay questions that were given in the first practical exercise in this chapter and work out how you would demonstrate skills from each of the six categories in relation to them.

 You will find suggested answers to these questions on the Online Resource Centre where there is also explanation of how the answers were reached.

You can use process words to help you to understand the priorities of the lecturer with respect to the different aspects of the essay. For example, if part of the question uses lower-order words and part of the question uses higher-order words, this could be a good indication of where the complexity in the question lies. You might find it helpful to use the 'do what to what' technique: this asks 'what does this essay require me to do (skill) and to what piece of law (information) (Figure 11.7).

Outline the methods used to record crime in England and Wales and comment upon whether this provides an accurate measure of the amount of violent crime that occurs.

Figure 11.7 'Do what to what'?

Applying the 'do what to what' approach to this question, it is clear that there is a description aspect to the essay and an analysis aspect:

Do what? Outline (lower-order skill)
To what? Methods of recording crime

Do what? Comment (higher-order skill)
To what? The accuracy of the measurement of violent crime

It is essential that you remember that a successful essay requires an appropriate balance between description and analysis. An essay that is heavily descriptive does not demonstrate sufficient higher-order skills to achieve a high mark whilst an essay which contains insufficient description will also struggle because analysis needs to be based upon a foundation of description in order to make sense. For example, you cannot analyse the impact of the redefinition of rape contained in SOA 2003 unless you describe how the law is now and how it was prior to the enactment of the legislation; therefore, a certain degree of description is a necessary ingredient of a successful essay.

Achieving the right balance between the two is a difficult task as there is no magic formula that sets out the appropriate contribution of each to an essay as this will vary according to the question. The most effective rule to apply is to include sufficient description to support the analysis; in other words, describe things that need to be understood so that the discussion will make sense to the reader.

11.4.2 What do lecturers want?

You have an audience of one for your essay (the person marking it) so it makes sense to keep the requirements of that audience to the forefront of your mind when writing your essay.

11.4.2.1 Course outline

This is a document that provides an overview of the subject that you are studying. You will find that your institution has one for each of the subjects, core subjects and options, which will provide information that may help you to understand the requirements of that subject and also to give you some insight into the priorities of the lecturer responsible for that subject. The information included on the course outline will vary between institutions but you could usually expect to find:

- the subject broken down into the topics that will be studied, possibly with an indication of the weeks in which this will take place
- the assessment method used on the course (exam, coursework, presentation, research paper) and the weight given to each component
- information about non-assessed or voluntary coursework
- a breakdown of the number of lectures and tutorials that will take place and possibly some information regarding the amount of private study that is expected

- details of recommended reading
- learning objectives.

This information not only gives you an idea of what to expect on your course but can also help you to appreciate the requirements of your coursework. For example, if an essay is due for submission in Week 7, it will not relate to material covered later on in the syllabus and is unlikely to cover material that has not been covered by the start of Week 6, possibly earlier depending on the practice in your institution. Moreover, the reading list may be useful in pointing you towards some material that is relevant to the essay.

Learning objectives are a statement of the subject-specific knowledge and skills that students are supposed to have acquired by the end of the course. They may provide a good insight into the skills which are important to the subject that you are studying so you can ensure these are demonstrated in your essay.

11.4.2.2 Assessment criteria

These have an obvious importance to your essay as they are the criteria against which it will be marked. Assessment criteria tend to be agreed on a department-wide basis and identify the factors that your lecturer will be looking for in your essay. You may find these on the assessment feedback form that is attached to your work when it is returned to you and it is often the case that the relevant criteria are listed and accompanied by a series of tick boxes in which the lecturer can indicate your competency in each area.

	Weak	Below Average	Satisfactory	Good	Excellent
Knowledge of the relevant law	☐	☐	☐	☐	☐
Application to the question	☐	☐	☐	☐	☐
Use of supporting authority	☐	☐	☐	☐	☐
Written style, grammar and punctuation	☐	☐	☐	☐	☐

Figure 11.8 Sample assessment criteria

By looking at the categories that are listed on the form, you can identify what skills are being evaluated in your work and try to ensure that these are demonstrated. Another approach that is used to communicate the assessment criteria to students is to categorize the level of skills that are expected in work that falls within a particular classification. This is demonstrated in the example below (Figure 11.9).

There are, therefore, various methods that can be used to ascertain what skills and competences you need to demonstrate to impress your lecturers with the quality of your essay. For some reason, students often fail to take these matters into account and continue to produce essays that comply with their own personal view of a good essay. This can be extremely costly in terms of lost marks if their view does not coincide with what the lecturer considers to be a good essay. Lecturers are looking for a combination of legal knowledge and an ability to use it and thus are likely to consider the following factors to be important:

- The relevance of the material included and the arguments put forward to the question
- Evidence of comprehension and an ability to analyse the law
- A strong structure and clear and logical organization of material
- Evidence of research and incorporation of wider reading into the essay
- An appropriate written style with good grammar and punctuation
- Full and accurate referencing including a bibliography
- Good presentation.

FAIL: Less than 40%
A weak answer that fails to address the question posed and which shows inadequate understanding of the subject area. Little or no evidence of reading or research and reference to irrelevant materials. Significant weakness in presentation and organization as well as numerous errors of grammar and punctuation.

PASS, THIRD CLASS: 40–49%
A fair answer that provides some material of relevance to the question posed and which shows some limited understanding of the subject area. There may be some reference to supporting materials but little, if any, attempt at analysis; a highly descriptive answer with some errors and omissions. Presentation and organization is likely to be poor and there may be significant errors of grammar and punctuation.

LOWER SECOND CLASS: 50–59%
A satisfactory answer that covers a fair degree of the material of relevance to the question albeit it in largely descriptive detail. There may be an attempt an analysis that is either ineffective or fails to get to grips with the issue at the heart of the question. There should be evidence of a reasonable level of understanding and an ability to incorporate some supporting materials into the answer. There may be some grammatical and presentational errors but these should not be widespread.

Figure 11.9 Example assessment criteria by classification

11.4.3 Common problems

Although insufficient research and planning can have a detrimental impact on the overall success of the essay, it is the writing stage that offers the greatest potential for problems to arise that will have a negative effect on the quality of the essay. After all, it is the words on the page that are actually assessed, so problems at this stage can make or break the essay. This section covers a range of things that could go wrong, with some suggestions as to how to anticipate and avoid these common problems.

11.4.3.1 Insufficient time to write

Make sure that you leave yourself enough time to write your essay and to reflect upon what you have written. Many students delay the start of the writing process and, as a consequence, have insufficient time available to review the first draft of their essay and make necessary changes. This delay may be due to poor time management, to a conviction that the research process is not complete, or to anxiety concerning a lack of understanding of the subject matter.

Understanding the reason for the delay in starting to write is half the battle in overcoming the problem. Some students find it hard to let go of the research process, always thinking there is an elusive piece of information which, if found, would guarantee the success of their essay. There has to be a point at which you let go and start writing with the information that you have found. If you think you do not understand the law, try consulting a more basic textbook. Ultimately, if there is something that you feel you cannot grasp, you will have to write the essay as best you can despite that lack of knowledge. Misunderstanding one aspect of the law will not necessarily condemn your essay to failure and it may be that you actually have a far better grasp of the law than you realize.

Time-management skills are discussed in chapter 9.

11.4.3.2 Inability to write

It can be the case that you have a good grasp of what needs to go into the essay but find it difficult to start writing. The best way to overcome problems with writing is to write. Choose something quite simple, such as the definition of a key concept or an explanation of a leading case: it does not really matter what it is, provided that you write something to overcome the feeling that you cannot write. Alternatively, free-flow writing in which you complete a writing task within a set period of time, such as one minute, can be a good way to put down your ideas on paper without worrying about using any particular form of words. The following are some suggestions for free-flow writing tasks:

- The aim of this essay is to . . .
- In the first paragraph, I will explain . . .
- The first argument in the essay is that . . .

Remember that once your ideas are out on paper, you will need to refine their expression so that you are using an appropriate written style for your essay. Further guidance on this can be found in chapter 10.

11.4.3.3 Poor structure and flow

There should be a logical flow to your essay so that one point follows another in a logical and coherent manner. Poor structure will interrupt this flow and make your essay disjointed and difficult to read. If you cannot tell whether your structure is sufficiently strong from reading your essay through, try inserting some signposting to see whether the organization of your material seems logical.

. . . .

Signposting refers to the phrases that you use in an essay to guide the reader through your arguments. Sentences such as 'having discussed *x*, this essay will now consider *y*' and 'although it may seem that this case resolves the problem, it is also important to take into account *z*' are examples of signposting.

. . . .

If your signposting between paragraphs does not make logical sense, this is good evidence that your structure needs to be rethought. Remember, that you can signpost your essay quite simply: 'however' indicates that you are putting an opposing view to the point that preceded the sentence or paragraph whereas words such as 'furthermore' or 'in addition' indicate to the reader that the next point substantiates or consolidates the prior argument.

Lack of planning can lead to a weak structure, so effort put in at the preparations stages can pay dividends in avoiding this problem. Of course, you may find that the structure that you planned to follow no longer works once the points are expressed in detail. One way to tackle structural problems is to label each paragraph on the basis of its purpose and then look at the skeleton of the essay that emerges to see if the points raised are arranged in a logical order (Figure 11.10).

1	Introduction	This is part of the structure of the sample question once its paragraphs have been named according to their purpose. Initially, this structure seems perfectly logical. It starts by defining the offence and then takes the *actus reus* elements before the *mens rea* elements. The problem arises because consent has a role in both the *actus reus* and *mens rea* of rape so it interferes with the structure of the essay, making it repetitious. The most effective way to resolve this is to replace Paragraph 5 with a discussion of the dual role of consent in rape and then go on to elaborate upon its operation in terms of the *actus reus* and *mens rea* in the paragraphs that follow.
2	Definition of rape	
3	Identification of the *actus reus* elements	
4	Discussion of penetration of the vagina, anus and mouth	
5	Discussion of consent	
6	Identification of *mens rea* elements	
7	Discussion of consent	

Figure 11.10 Ordering paragraphs

You should always be prepared to reorganize your essay if it seems that the structure that you have initially chosen is not working effectively.

11.4.3.4 Weak focus and irrelevant points

An essay with a weak focus is one in which the points raised are not linked back to the question with sufficient frequency or clarity. Remember the point made at the outset of this chapter that there is a difference between what the essay is about and what it asks. If you fail to explain the material that you have included with reference to the title of the essay, you are in danger of falling into the 'about' rather than the 'asks' category.

This is easily resolved. At the end of each paragraph, ask yourself what its content contributes towards addressing the question posed by the essay and then make sure that this is made explicit in your answer. For example, in the sample essay, you would want to make sure that every paragraph furthered your discussion of whether the SOA 2003 enhanced the protection available to victims of rape or clarified the law, so you would need to explain how, if at all, each element of the offence achieved one or both of these objectives.

This technique can also help you to filter out irrelevant material: if you cannot find a way to link a particular point to the question posed, then it has no place in the essay.

11.4.3.5 Word limits

It should be possible to write a detailed and analytical answer within the specified word limit but students often find this a struggle. If you are having difficulties with the word limit, it is likely that you have one of the following problems:

- **Relevance:** inclusion of unnecessary material, irrelevant points, too much descriptive detail, long quotations, too many examples.
- **Written style:** insufficiently concise, too conversational, rambling.

The solution is to examine your essay sentence by sentence and ask whether each one (a) has a valuable role to play within the essay (relevance) or (b) could be expressed in a more concise manner (written style).

You will find a detailed consideration of issues associated with appropriate written style in chapter 10. The remainder of this section will focus on issues of relevance.

When deciding whether a particular point is relevant to your essay, question what role it plays and why you originally chose to include it. Sometimes material that seems important at the early stages of research becomes less relevant as you gain a stronger understanding of the topic. For example, the historical background to a particular piece of legislation may have helped you understand the subject on first reading but its contribution to your understanding of the subject need not be expressed in words in your essay, it will be implicit in the way that your understanding is reflected. Make sure that every point that you include makes a contribution not to your understanding of the topic but to your answer to the question raised in the essay.

Think carefully about the level of description that you include, remembering that there should be sufficient description to support the analysis. Consider the following questions:

- Is it necessary to describe the facts of a case (a) in so much detail or (b) at all?
- Do you need to include two examples to demonstrate the same point?
- Could you paraphrase a quotation or definition of a statutory provision rather than using the complete wording?

Students sometimes develop a strong commitment to a particular point that they have included because they remember how much work went into finding it and working it into the essay or because they think it is a particularly clever or interesting point. Try to bear in mind that if it is not relevant to this particular essay, then it will attract little or no credit, irrespective of how clever or interesting it is or how much work is behind it. You may have to be brutal in cutting material out of your essay but, hopefully, the piece of work as a whole will be stronger for it.

11.4.3.6 Introduction and conclusion

Many essays that are submitted by students have neither an introduction nor a conclusion. Some students believe that because nothing of substance is written in these parts of the essay, they attract no marks and are therefore a waste of words. This mistaken belief is based upon a conviction—one that hopefully has been dispelled by this chapter—that only legal knowledge and understanding gains credits and that written style counts for nothing.

The introduction is important because it identifies the issue that will be discussed and sets out the structure that the essay will follow. It is also the first thing that your lecturer reads and so gives him an initial impression of the quality of your essay; clearly, then, it is beneficial to you that the lecturer's first impression is a good one.

A good introduction will:

(a) reword the issue at the heart of the question to establish it as the focus of the essay;

(b) explain the steps that will be taken to explore this issue, thus giving some indication of the structure and content of the essay.

Practical exercise

The following is an example of an introduction that would be appropriate for the sample essay on sexual offences. Do you think that it is an effective introduction? What, if any, features would you change?

The Sexual Offences Act 2003 was introduced in order to simplify the law and to give greater protection to victims of rape. This essay explores the extent to which the Act has achieved these objectives by outlining the elements of the definition of rape and comparing these with the previous law in order to assess whether its terms are more straightforward, its reach extended to a greater range of victims, and its provisions more likely to result in the conviction of the guilty.

Try writing an introduction for one of the four essay titles used previously in the practical exercises. You will find some suggestions on the Online Resource Centre where there is also an opportunity to rate sample introductions.

The conclusion is also often overlooked as students simply stop writing with no attempt to draw together the strands of their argument or to reflect upon the issue that was at the heart of the question.

Remember that the purpose of the conclusion is to take the points that you have made in the body of your answer and to use these to provide a concise answer to the question posed. Therefore, as a general rule, no new information should be introduced into the conclusion. Equally, your conclusion should answer the question using points from your essay rather than summarizing all the arguments that you have made.

11.5 The final stages

It is a mistake to think that once the final word is written, the essay is finished. However much effort you have expended in the production of the first draft, the essay will still benefit from further consideration to ensure that the points are expressed with clarity and precision, the arguments flow smoothly, and sufficient attention has been paid to all aspects of presentation.

Ideally, you should aim to complete your essay at least one day prior to the deadline for handing it in. Not only does this give you some leeway should you encounter an unexpected emergency, such as a broken printer, it also gives you space in which to put aside your essay so it you can read it the following day with fresh eyes. This distance should enable you to read what you have written rather than what you think you have written; errors are invisible whilst you are still close to your work.

Make sure that you view your work with a critical eye; look for errors, inconsistency, and other areas where the essay could be improved with a little more work. Try never to think 'this is good enough' or 'this will do' if you can see ways in which your essay could be better. Remember that the difference between 59 per cent and 60 per cent is one mark, so you could, in effect, improve your essay by a whole classification by taking care at this stage.

It is worth taking particular care with presentation; you want your lecturer to think that you have spent time and effort on the production of your essay. Shoddy presentation gives a poor impression. It may be the case that there are marks available for the presentation of the essay, in which case failing to take trouble with the way that the essay looks is simply throwing away easy marks. Check whether your institution, department, or lecturer has any particular style requirements and, if they have, make sure that you adhere to them.

Now is also the time to check and double-check that your referencing is thorough and accurate. Failure to provide references may leave you vulnerable to accusations of plagiarism. Make sure that every reference to work of another person is attributed to its source and take particular care to ensure that quotations are fully referenced; this means including the page number upon which the words can be found and, if the quotation is from a case, the name of the judge whose words are being used. Finally, make sure that a full bibliography is appended to the essay.

You'll find more detailed discussion of referencing, plagiarism, and other points relevant to the presentation of the essay in chapter 10.

Practical exercise

 1. Now that you have read this chapter, you should have all the skills necessary to write an effective and successful essay. Have a look at the examples on the Online Resource Centre for further guidance on strategies and techniques for writing an essay that will impress your lecturers.

 2. You may also want to test your ability to spot weaknesses in an essay by marking some of the essays that you will find on the Online Resource Centre. This will help you to appreciate what lecturers are looking for and will make excellent practice for reviewing your own work.

 CHAPTER SUMMARY

Preliminary analysis

- Make sure that you take time at the outset to analyse the essay rather than starting research or, worse still, writing without having identified the focus of the essay

- Rewrite the question(s) at the heart of the essay in your own words to make sure that you have a simple and clear grasp of what is required, taking care not to change the meaning of the essay

Research and planning

- Start by consulting a textbook to ensure that you have a clear understanding of the area of law but make sure that you move on to consider other materials such as cases and articles; an essay written solely on the basis of textbook research will probably lack depth of analysis and certainly will not demonstrate impressive research skills or width of reading

- Keep careful note of the sources used in your research but try to avoid excessive note-taking that can degenerate into compulsive writing that is not accompanied by sufficient thought. Remember, you are looking for answers to a particular question, not producing a summary of all the material that you locate

- Plan a working structure for your essay that can be used as a framework for your writing. Make sure that you think about the way that your arguments will flow and never forget the importance of keeping a firm focus on the central issue of the question

- Give careful consideration to the selection of supporting materials, remembering that it is important to present a balanced argument that acknowledges different perspectives on the issue at hand

Writing the essay

- Make sure that you give yourself sufficient time to write the essay and bear in mind that the structure you have planned may not work in practice, in which case you may need to start from scratch and reorganize your arguments

- Take care to ensure that every paragraph does something to further your argument and give thought to the balance between description and analysis in your essay

- Keep a firm focus on the question; if you cannot see how a point relates to the question, it may be that it has no place in your essay. Remember, you are answering a specific question rather than merely writing about a particular topic

- The purpose of an essay is to test knowledge and understanding of the law but also to assess the level of skill that you have in using the law. Ensure that your essay strikes an appropriate balance between description and analysis

- Check the materials that you have been given in order to identify what skills and abilities are being assessed and make sure that your essay demonstrates them

- Write an effective introduction and conclusion. The introduction is the first impression that your lecturer receives of the quality of your work whilst the conclusion is the last thing that they read, so may stick in their mind as indicative of the overall quality of your essay whilst they are marking

Polish and presentation

- Allow plenty of time to check your essay for coherence, accuracy, and consistency

- Find out what the requirements are for the presentation of essays and ensure that you adhere to these requirements to the letter. Easy marks can be lost for failing to do so and it gives to the marker a poor impression of your essay if you have not troubled to follow the rules regarding the submission of coursework

- Check the presentation of your essay and, in particular, check that the referencing and bibliography are immaculate

Problem skills

12

INTRODUCTION

This chapter builds upon the earlier sections in the book that outlined how to locate and understand the law by explaining how to use your legal knowledge. Chapter 11 provided guidance on how to use this knowledge to construct a focused and analytical essay and this chapter will concentrate on the very different set of skills that are needed to use the law to answer a problem question. This chapter will guide you through the process of analysing a scenario in order to identify the relevant issues to ensure that your answer is comprehensive and does not miss any important points. It will outline strategies to use to ensure that the law is applied effectively and that good use is made of supporting authorities. This chapter should be read in conjunction with chapter 10 that covers writing skills, as this will ensure that your problem answer is well-written, presented in an appropriate manner, and is thoroughly referenced.

The ability to use the law to determine the outcome of a dispute is one of the most important skills that a lawyer must develop. An abstract understanding of the law based upon how it has been used in decided cases is not enough; you must be able to apply the principles of the law to new and unusual factual situations. Remember, a client who comes to you for advice does not want an explanation of how the law has been used in other cases; he wants to know how it applies to his situation. It is also an important skill because problem questions are a popular means of assessing knowledge and skills in both coursework and examinations but, unfortunately, many students limit their success because they have not developed an effective problem-solving technique. This step-by-step guide to problem solving aims to help with this by explaining how to tackle problem questions and by demonstrating the steps with examples to ensure that you have a clear picture of what is required.

LEARNING OUTCOMES

After studying this chapter, you should be able to:

- Differentiate between the skills needed to answer a problem question and those required for the construction of an effective essay

- Analyse a problem question in order to identify the legal issues that need to be resolved

- Prepare to answer the question by engaging in effective research and planning

- Structure the answer in a logical and organized manner

- Provide concise and well-supported statements of law that are applied to the facts of the question in an effective manner

- Evaluate the answer that you have written to ensure that it demonstrates the relevant skills and knowledge and that it adheres to the necessary style and referencing requirements

12.1 All about problem questions

Before launching into an explanation of how to deal with problem questions, it seems sensible to take a little time to describe what problem questions are and what they seek to achieve. If you appreciate what it is that they aim to assess, this will help you to understand how to set about dealing with them in a way that is likely to meet with the approval of your lecturers.

12.1.1 What is a problem question?

A problem question involves a set of hypothetical facts that raises at least one question, usually more, that needs to be answered by reference to the law.

In other words, it is a short story about events that give rise to potential legal responsibility about which you are expected to offer advice to one or more of the parties or to otherwise comment on the legal position that arises from the facts. This is sometimes called a fact pattern.

Problem questions tend to end with a question or instruction so that you are clear about the task:

- Does Stuart have a claim in negligence?
- Can the contract be enforced?
- Advise Linda as to the extent of her liability for property offences.
- Do John's actions amount to a breach of Article 11 of the European Convention on Human Rights?

The facts of the problem will be constructed with care so that the answer to the question is not clear but needs to be puzzled out. You are unlikely to encounter a problem question that reads:

'Jack hates Charlie so he shoots him in the head at point-blank range shouting "I want you to die"'.

This is because there is no complexity to the issue: both elements of the offence of murder are so readily established that the question could be answered in a few lines.

This demonstrates a major characteristic of problem questions: they are designed to raise issues that do not have an obvious and straightforward answer so that you have to explore the intricacies of the law and speculate a little in order to reach a conclusion.

You will find an example of a problem question in section 12.3. This will be used in this chapter to demonstrate the process of building an answer that demonstrates both a good grasp of the relevant law and of the legal skills that are being assessed.

12.1.2 It is not an essay!

It is essential that you appreciate that the distinction between an essay and a problem question is not solely one of presentation; they require something qualitatively different from the student in terms of the skills used and the nature of the answer produced.

In general terms, an essay involves an exploration and analysis of a particular topic whilst a problem question requires the student to apply the law to a set of facts and reach a conclusion about the legal responsibility of the parties involved.

If you take the same approach to answering a problem question that you do to writing an essay, your problem answers will be weak and will not achieve high marks.

12.1.3 What skills are required?

There are a range of skills involved in dissecting and answering a problem question. As you will see, although legal knowledge is important, you will need to be able to do more than merely outline the relevant law; you must also be able to use it to reach a conclusion about the legal liability of the parties. This involves:

- The ability to sift through the mass of facts to identify those that are relevant, those that set the scene, and to oust any potential red herrings
- Sufficient knowledge of the area of law to be able to identify a potential basis for legal action, to establish a starting point for research and to be able to understand the law that is uncovered during the research process
- Research skills that enable you to investigate the area of law and to locate statutory provisions and cases that are relevant to the facts of the problem
- Writing skills that enable you to structure an answer, to organize its content in a clear and logical manner, and to incorporate authority into your answer
- The ability to apply the law to the facts of the question in order to determine the extent of the parties' legal liability

Although all of these skills are important and play a role in constructing an effective answer to a problem question, it is the last of these—application of the law to the facts—that is crucial to the success of your answer.

In chapter 10, you will find a section which examines Bloom's taxonomy of skills and discusses these in the context of legal writing. The higher-order skills of application and analysis are particularly important to problem solving.

12.2 Problem-solving technique

The key to success in problem solving is to develop an effective technique. This is something that will be invaluable in both coursework and examinations and which is transferable between the different topics that you study; in other words, a good problem-solving technique is equally applicable to criminal law, equity, and trusts, employment law or any of the other subjects on the law curriculum that use problem solving as a means of assessment.

Your own institution may provide guidelines on problem solving. If this is the case, you should study this carefully and take note of the information provided. Alternatively, there are well-publicized techniques that you may find useful; these have different names but share a common basis in their approach to breaking down the tasks involved in problem solving (Figure 12.1).

Despite the difference of terminology, each of the four stages used in each method is the same:

1. Identify the question that needs to be answered.
2. State the law that enables the question to be answered.
3. Work out how the law would operate in relation to the question identified.
4. Reach a conclusion that answers the question.

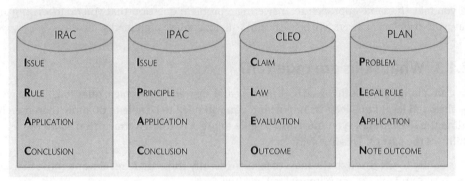

Figure 12.1 Some mnemonics for problem solving

You might find it easier to understand this process in relation to a non-law example.

Imagine that your university has a policy regarding the late submission of coursework that states that the penalty for submission up to one day after the deadline without good cause or prior permission attracts a deduction of 10 marks. Furthermore, work that is submitted more than one day late but within a week of the deadline attracts a deduction of 25 marks and work that is submitted more than one week late receives a mark of zero. The essays are stamped with the time and date of submission upon receipt in the general office. The submission deadline for your essay is 4 p.m. on Friday. Your essay is submitted at 4.02 p.m.

This is a very simple example but it demonstrates the process that is involved in problem solving.

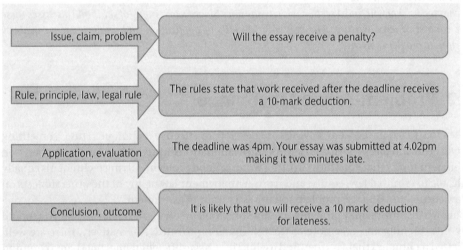

Figure 12.2 The problem-solving process

It is ironic that the method involved in problem solving causes so many headaches for students but, in reality and stripped of its legal content, the process of identifying a question to be answered, the applicable rule, and combining the two to reach a conclusion is one that we all do, all of the time, as part of everyday life: eligibility for a discount, complying with a shop's refund policy, nightclub opening hours, and even reading a train timetable all involve a similar process of the identification and application of a general rule to a particular factual situation.

Of course, your concern is to take this technique and apply it to legal problems. There are also other factors to take into account such as the level of detail needed, the correct approach to incorporating case law, and the difficulties of a factual situation that does not have a determinative answer and all of these points will be addressed in the course of this chapter. However, quite apart from these complexities that are particular to law, it is reassuring to know that the technique that is the cornerstone of effective problem solving is one that is familiar.

With this in mind, why not try the technique outlined above in relation to the following non-law examples:

Practical exercise

These examples are designed to help you develop a methodical approach to problem solving. As such, they are very simple so you could reach a conclusion without going through the steps outlined above but that would defeat the purpose of the exercise. Try to follow the four-stage procedure with these simple facts to build up your confidence and expertise ready for solving more complex problems as the chapter progresses.

1. The Post Office has introduced a new system of calculating the cost of postage based upon weight and size. A small letter is one which weighs less than 50g and is no thicker than 5mm. This costs 35p postage. A letter that weighs more than 50g or is thicker than 5mm is a large letter and costs 72p postage. You wish to post a package that weighs 40g and is 10mm thick. How much will this cost?

2. Your grandmother offers you a cash incentive to encourage you to study for your exams. She agrees to pay you £10 for every exam that you pass and £50 extra if you pass all five exams. You only pass four exams. How much money can you expect to receive?

3. You notice an advertisement for an essay-writing competition on the law school noticeboard. The first prize is £500 so you would like to enter. The competition rules state that the essay must be written by an undergraduate student under the age of 21 at the closing date (31 March this year) who has not yet studied European law. Do you qualify to enter the competition (based on your own circumstances)?

 You will find suggested answers to these questions on the Online Resource Centre where there is also explanation of how the answers were reached.

You probably found it easy to work through these exercises and you should take heart from this because it means that you have already grasped the essential skills that you need to succeed in answering problem questions in law. These skills will need to be honed and developed and you will find help and guidance on this in the remainder of this chapter. The following sections explore each aspect of problem solving in greater depth in order to help you develop your understanding of what is required.

12.2.1 Warning

It is of fundamental importance that you separate the question into a series of issues and deal with each of these separately. The IRAC, IPAC, CLEO, and PLAN techniques will not work if you try and apply them to the question as a whole. It is a common mistake for students who first encounter this technique to use it as a means of dividing their answer into four sections and dividing the content as follows:

1. Issues: all the issues from the question as a whole are identified and listed.

2. Rules: an abstract discussion of all the law that is raised by the issues, all amalgamated together.

3. Application: a short section that is usually extremely weak because it is detached from the law and it does not break the question down into sufficiently small issues.

4. Conclusion: a short factual paragraph that summarizes the findings.

If you make the mistake of dividing the whole answer into sections as explained above, rather than slicing it up into a series of issues and subissues as explained in the following section, it is extremely likely that your answer will fail as you will not have demonstrated an effective problem-solving technique to the marker.

 You will find an example of an answer to a problem question that demonstrates this fundamental failing on the Online Resource Centre as well as an example of how the technique should be used to produce an effective answer to the same question.

12.3 Issues, claims, and problems

The first stage in the problem-solving process is to identify the question that needs to be answered. In the example given above on p. 274, this was quite simple: will the essay receive a penalty? However, it is not always a straightforward matter to identify the issue within a problem question; indeed, it is likely that there will be multiple issues within a single question that need to be extrapolated from the mass of detail. This is an important stage in the process as if you do not isolate the correct question to ask, you cannot hope to reach the right conclusion.

This is an example of a typical problem question that you might encounter. As you see, it involves a series of events that involve several different parties. This tort problem about injuries sustained by visitors to a donkey rescue centre will be used throughout this chapter to demonstrate the process of building up an answer to a problem question.

Gerald runs a small donkey rescue centre in South Oxfordshire. Tess and her granddaughter, Diana (7) visit the centre. They go into the stable yard where there are large signs that read 'donkeys may bite, so mind your fingers' and 'please do not feed the donkeys—they may confuse your finger for a carrot'. Tess sees the signs but has left her glasses in the car so cannot read what they say. She feeds slices of apple that she has brought with her to several donkeys and receives a nasty bite from Firethorn Mulan, the centre's temperamental stallion. There used to be a sign on his door that warned that stallions are unpredictable but it had fallen off the previous day and not yet been replaced. Upset by her experience, Tess goes into the cafeteria. She tells Diana not to wander off but Diana ignores Tess and goes into the exhibition of farm equipment. Two of the rarest machines are roped off to protect them from the public. Diana climbs over the ropes and starts to climb on one of the machines but receives a deep laceration from one of the exposed cutting blades. In the cafeteria, employee Wendy is making a pot of tea for Tess. The cafeteria is newly refurbished. The work was done by local handyman, John, who is an excellent carpenter but who lacks expertise is electrical fitting. As a result, some of the wiring is incorrect and this causes a massive power surge during which the tea urn explodes, showering Wendy with boiling water and causing her to suffer serious burns.

Advise Gerald as to the extent of his liability, considering Occupiers' Liability only and not any potential claims in Negligence.

12.3.1 Analysing the question

The most effective means of identifying the issues in a problem question is to analyse the facts that you have been given and take a note of relevant facts relating to the two key variables: parties and events. This will help you to address the key question: who has done what to whom?

12.3.1.1 Parties

It will be at least one party in the problem, probably more in many subject areas. You may encounter a single party in problem questions on public law topics, such as constitutional and administrative law and criminal law, as these areas of law involve the liability of an individual in relation to the State. Of course, it is possible for public law topics nonetheless to involve other parties; there may be multiple applicants in a judicial review problem, for example, or several defendants or a range of victims in a criminal law problem. Problem questions in areas of private law, such as contract and tort, will involve at least one party making a claim against another, so it is important that you identify both the claimant(s) and the defendant(s).

Make a list of the people in the question and determine whether they are parties who have a claim or parties who face liability. It may be that there are other people in the question who fall into neither of these categories. If this is the case, do not simply ignore them but consider why they have been included. It is likely that they are there for a reason.

The instructions that accompany the problem facts are often an excellent source of information that will assist you in the identification of the roles of the various parties. In the example given in this chapter, you are told to advise Gerald about the strength of the claims against him, so it is a straightforward matter to identity him as the defendant.

Table 12.1 Parties in the problem question

Claimant	Defendant	Other Parties
Tess	Gerald	
Diana	Gerald	Tess (child's mother)
Wendy	Gerald	John (the handyman)

12.3.1.2 Events

It is also important to work out what has happened to the parties as this provides the necessary information to ascertain what area of law is relevant to the topic. It is extremely useful to establish these facts at the outset as this will act as a reminder that precise reference needs to be made to them at some point in your answer. As you will see in the discussion of application below, one of the more common weaknesses in a problem answer is the failure to make reference to precise facts, therefore having a list to hand from the outset may help to overcome this problem (Figure 12.3).

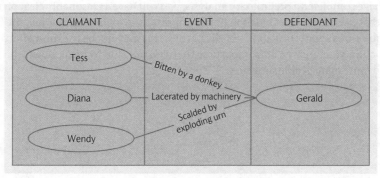

Figure 12.3 Claimants, events, and defendants

This diagram depicts the answer to the 'who did what to whom' question in the sample question and this gives three potential situations in which Gerald may be liable. In a question involving several parties, the obvious structure for your answer is to consider each party in turn, particularly if the basis for liability is the same for each of them as it is here (the issue is Occupiers' Liability in each case).

It is important to be methodical and thorough. Start at the beginning of the question and work through each sentence in turn, making a note of potentially relevant information. It may not be clear at this stage how each piece of information is relevant but this should become apparent as you become more familiar with the legal issues raised by the question during the course of your research.

It is important to devote time and attention to this early stage of the problem solving process as it is the cornerstone of the success of your answer. If you fail to identify issues at this stage or omit relevant facts, it is inevitable that the remainder of your answer will have gaps. You should bear in mind that it is not always straightforward to identify the issues in a problem question.

 Practical exercise

Use the techniques outlined above to identify the issues in this problem question. Do not worry if you cannot make an exact identification of the relevant offences; focus on framing the issues at this stage. It is perfectly permissible to identify a range of potential offences, i.e. burglary/theft, or to go for a general topic, i.e. one of the non-fatal offences against the person, at this stage as the research that you go on to conduct will help you to narrow down the possibilities.

Stuart is short of money and hopes to borrow £500 from his brother, Neil. In order to get into Neil's good books, Stuart decides to take him a bottle of whisky that he plans to steal from the local supermarket. Once inside the supermarket, Stuart loses his nerve and leaves without going near the alcohol aisle. Instead, he goes into a department store and uses his credit card to buy Neil an expensive sweater, knowing that he is over his credit limit. Neil is thrilled with the sweater but refuses to lend Stuart any money. Stuart punches Neil in the face causing a cut which requires stitches. Neil sets fire to the sweater and leaves it burning on Stuart's doorstep the following day. Discuss the criminal liability of the parties.

 You will find suggested answers to these questions on the Online Resource Centre where there is also explanation of how the answers were reached. You will find further practical exercises online so that you can practise identifying the issues in a range of subject areas.

Once you have completed a preliminary analysis, you will have a reasonably clear picture of the questions that need to be asked. Although it is important to identify and frame the 'big' issues that raise questions about the liability of the parties, this may not be the most effective way for you to structure your answer. It is important that you are able to break down the topic into smaller and more manageable subissues.

12.3.2 Finding the subissues

At this stage of the analysis of the sample problem, we have three 'big' issues which were identified by concentrating on the parties and the events:

1. Can Tess hold Gerald liable for her injuries after she was bitten by a donkey?

2. Can Diana hold Gerald liable for the lacerations caused by his machinery?

3. Can Wendy hold Gerald liable for the burns she received when the urn exploded?

In order to break this down into more manageable subissues, more information is needed about the basis upon which Gerald may be liable. In this particular example, the instructions that accompany the facts make it clear that the relevant area of law is Occupiers' Liability. This makes it an extremely straightforward matter to break each of the big issues down into subissues on the basis of the elements that have to be established in order to establish Occupiers' Liability (Figure 12.4).

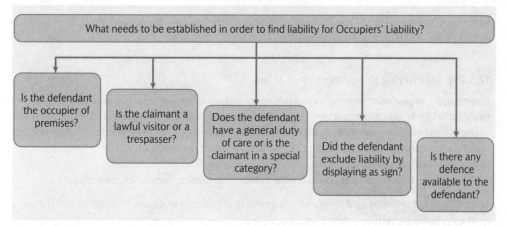

Figure 12.4 Subissues

By exploring the subissues within the big issue, you are effectively breaking the answer down into a series of mini problem questions, so the techniques outlined above can be used in relation to each subissue. As such, it will be a succession of IRACs (or whichever of the acronyms you prefer).

By taking each subissue in turn and subjecting it to a methodical analysis, you will give the answer a strong structure and it should help to ensure that you are thorough and do not omit any important points from consideration.

ISSUE 1: Is Gerald liable under Occupiers' Liability for the injury sustained by Tess when she is bitten by his donkey?

- **Subissue 1.1** Is Gerald an occupier of premises?

  - State the law
  - Apply it to the facts
  - Conclusion

- **Subissue 1.2** Is Tess a lawful visitor or a trespasser?

  - State the law
  - Apply it to the facts
  - Conclusion

- **Subissue 1.3** Is there a general duty of care or does Tess fall into a special category?
  - State the law
  - Apply it to the facts
  - Conclusion
- **Subissue 1.4** Has Gerald excluded his liability by displaying a sign?
  - State the law
  - Apply it to the facts
  - Conclusion
- **Subissue 1.5** Is there any defence available to Gerald?
  - State the law
  - Apply it to the facts
  - Conclusion

Conclusion on the big issue by drawing together the strands of argument presented in the subissues.

You would then repeat this technique with the additional two big issues (see p. 279) and this would provide a structure for your answer.

12.3.2.1 Identifying the correct area of law

However, if the problem question does not specify the particular basis of liability, you will have to identify this from the nature of the question. Imagine that the sample question merely asked 'Advise Gerald of the extent of his tortious liability'. This would require you to identify the relevant basis of liability and this makes the problem question more challenging as inaccuracy here can put the entire answer off course.

There are various steps that you can take to help you identify the relevant topic(s):

1. Look at your syllabus and eliminate all topics that you will not have covered by the time that the coursework is due to submission.

2. Make a list of topics covered on your course so far and summarize them in a few words that capture their essential nature. If you do that with topics which are likely to be found on a tort course, you will see that some of the topics covered have no relevance at all to the sample problem. For example, if you used this technique on the sample question, you would soon conclude that only Negligence, Occupiers' Liability, and Employers' Liability (in relation to Wendy) could possibly have any relevance to the question:

   - Negligence: breach of duty of care leading to harm
   - Special duties: particular type of negligence
   - Nuisance: interference with quiet enjoyment of one's property
   - Employers' liability: duty towards employees
   - Occupiers' liability: duty of landowner to visitors and trespassers
   - Defamation: harm to person's reputation

3. If all else fails, ask for guidance. You can share information with other students (remembering not to take this too far for fear of contravening plagiarism regulations: see chapter 10) but you could also check with your lecturer. They will not be prepared to give you too much specific guidance but a quick (and polite: see chapter 9 for guidance on how to get help from lecturers) email saying 'I was planning to cover Negligence, Employers' Liability, and Occupiers'

Liability, in my answer but am concerned that this may be too broad and perhaps I should focus exclusively on Occupiers' Liability' should elicit a helpful response.

Practical exercise

 This approach to isolating potential areas of law by summarizing the key characteristics of each topic can be extremely effective. Why not try it with the problem involving Stuart and Neil and see how you get on by comparing your answers with those on the Online Resource Centre? You will find other problem questions there that you can try in a range of subject areas.

12.3.2.2 Multiple areas of law

Many problem questions will involve several different legal topics within a problem question. One of the reasons for this is that it enables the lecturer to assess your knowledge of more than one topic but, more importantly, it tests your ability to differentiate between different topics.

This is an important facet of learning a topic. It is a relatively straightforward matter to look up the relevant law and apply it to the facts if you are told what topic needs to be considered, but it is far more difficult to work out from the facts what the relevant topic is in the first place. Imagine how much harder the question about Gerald and his donkey rescue centre would have been if it had not been specified that the relevant area of law was Occupiers' Liability and not negligence.

If you are confident that a particular issue raises potential liability in more than one area of law, you will need to discuss both and this will require some careful thought in terms of the structure of the answer. You will, however, be able to gain additional credit by evaluating which area is the most suitable basis for liability.

12.4 Rules, principles, and law

The first stage of the problem-solving process is to identify the question that needs to be answered. Once that is identified, the next stage is to provide a statement of law that will enable that question to be answered.

12.4.1 Researching the law

In order to identify and state the law as part of your answer to the problem question, you will need to undertake research to ensure that you have a good understanding of the relevant law.

The following suggestions should help you to carry out effective research:

- Start with a textbook and read the entire chapter or section of the chapter that is relevant to your legal issue. This will give you a solid overview of the topic.

- Once you have a grasp of the topic, you should have a clearer appreciation of how accurate you have been in framing your issues and subissues. Review these now and make any changes that are necessary in light of your initial research.

- Take each subissue individually, using a separate sheet of paper for each if this helps you to organize your thoughts. Make a note of any material in the textbook that seems pertinent to each issue, paying particular attention to statutory provisions and case law.

- If you feel that you are struggling to understand the law, try consulting a different textbook to see if that makes the issues clearer. Different authors explain the same concepts in different ways so you may be more able to follow the explanations in an alternative textbook.

- Make sure that you are precise in noting the wording of statutory provisions and in recording full case citations; you will need these when you come to write your answer.

- Be prepared to follow up references contained in the footnotes of your textbook. For example, if a case is cited in the footnote in relation to the definition of an occupier but there is nothing in the text that elaborates upon this, you will need to find the case to discover whether it says anything that is relevant to your question.

- Remember that a problem question is concerned with the current law and its interpretation. Concentrate on finding this and do not be distracted by discussion of how the law used to be or how it came to be as it is today. This sort of historical background is relevant to an essay question and to your broader understanding of the topic but it has no place in an answer to a problem question.

- Bear in mind that problem questions are designed to assess your ability to apply the law to new and novel situations, so do not expect to find an exact answer to all the issues raised in your question in the textbook. It is likely that some of the issues are framed so that you have to look at what law there is and speculate upon how that might apply. With this in mind, try to find cases that state general principles that can be applied to your issue or which deal with similar, although not identical, situations.

Taking these points into account, you should aim to have a series of notes that gives you the basis to make statements of law in relation to each of the issues raised on the facts of the problem. You might want to note your thoughts about the way that the issue is likely to be decided as you go, as this will make the job of applying the law to the facts much easier (Figure 12.5).

DEFINITION OF OCCUPIER

No statutory definition although Occupiers' Liabilty Acts 1957 (visitors) and 1984 (trespassers) deal with liability in general.

Defined in *Wheat* v. *E.Lacon & Co Ltd* [1966] 1 All ER 582 (seems to be leading case) as person who exercises an element of control over premises.

This includes physical control of premises and legal control of premises—*Harris* v. *Birkenhead Corporation* [1976] 1 All ER 341

THOUGHTS: seems straightforward as Q says that Gerald runs the donkey rescue centre so presumably has physical control of the centre even if he is not the legal owner.

Figure 12.5 Thoughtful research with notes organized by issue

12.4.2 Stating the law

This is a crucial part of the problem-solving process and what is required is an initial abstract statement of a legal principle (from statute or case law) and, if necessary in relation to the issue at hand, some further elaboration on aspects of that principle.

This can be quite difficult to understand so the first subissue from the sample question will be used to demonstrate this technique in practice:

ISSUE 1: Is Gerald liable under Occupiers' Liability for the injury sustained by Tess when she is bitten by his donkey?

- Sub-issue 1.1 Is Gerald an occupier of premises?
  - **State the law:** There is no statutory definition of 'occupier' under the Occupiers' Liability Acts 1957 and 1984 but an occupier is defined in *Wheat* v *E. Lacan & Co Ltd* [1966] 1 All ER 582 as a person who exercises an element of control over premises.
  - Apply it to the facts
  - Conclusion

This demonstrates an initial statement of a relevant legal principle which could be applied to the facts as they stand. However, it might be useful to elaborate on this by reference to case law that provides further clarification of the meaning of this definition, as this will facilitate more precise application:

- Sub-issue 1.1 Is Gerald an occupier of premises?
  - **State the law:** There is no statutory definition of 'occupier' under the Occupiers' Liability Acts 1957 and 1984 but an occupier is defined in *Wheat* v *E. Lacan & Co Ltd* [1966] 1 All ER 582 as a person who exercises an element of control over premises. In *Harris* v *Birkenhead Corporation* [1976] 1 All ER 341, it was held that this meant physical control over the premises as well as legal control.
  - Apply it to the facts
  - Conclusion

It is always a question of judgement as to how much law to state in relation to any particular point. In the sample problem, the issue of occupier of premises is not particularly complicated but needs to be established with sufficient clarify because it is the foundation of Gerald's liability in this area of tort law. There are other issues in the problem that will require more detailed exploration with reference being made to different statements of law.

As a general rule, the more uncertain the area of law and the more complicated the issue, the more legal principles you will need to include within your answer.

12.4.3 Common problems

This stage of the problem-solving process is relatively straightforward and does not pose as great a challenge for the student as breaking the problem question down into appropriate issues and the application of the law. However, there are problems that do arise with a fair degree of frequency in relation to this stage of the process that are worthy of mention.

12.4.3.1 Law in large chunks

Success in problem-solving is dependent on breaking the law down into small chunks and dealing with each chunk individually. Therefore, an answer which deals with a clump of legal issues together is going to be weaker than one that separates them out for individual attention. It is essential to remember that once you have sliced up each issue into a series of subissues, each one of these should have some statement of law, however brief.

Three certainties are required for the existence of a valid trust. There must be certainty of intention, certainty of subject matter and certainty of objects. Certainty of intention requires . . . Certainty of subject matter requires . . . Certainty of objects requires . . . The first of these is satisfied by . . .

This example starts well by identifying the main issue and breaking it down into three subissues, but then it provides a statement of law for each of these without any application. This provides a block of legal statements pertaining to three separate subissues. A preferable approach would be to complete the discussion of each subissue by providing a statement of law, applying it to the facts, and reaching a conclusion before moving on to state the law relevant to the next subissue, as the example below illustrates:

> Three certainties are required for the existence of a valid trust. There must be certainty of intention, certainty of subject matter and certainty of objects. Certainty of intention requires that there is evidence that the testator intended to create a trust rather than disposing of his property as an outright gift. The testator has (application and conclusion). Certainty of subject matter requires . . . This is established by . . .

12.4.3.2 No abstract statement of the law

This stage of the problem-solving process is concerned with providing an accurate and concise statement of the current law. It does not require that this law is explained in the context of the particular facts of the problem; that is an issue of application which is important at the next stage of the process.

If you combine the statement of law and its application, you are failing to demonstrate an appropriate problem-solving technique *and* omitting to demonstrate your knowledge of the law. However, it is common for students to provide an explanation of the law in the context of the facts. If you do not understand what is meant by this, the following examples should demonstrate the point:

Table 12.2 Examples of abstract statements of law

Explanation of law in context of the facts	Abstract statement of the law
The *actus reus* of theft is putting the cuff-links in his pocket.	The *actus reus* of theft is the appropriation of property belonging to another.
The relevant standard of care is that of a qualified and experienced doctor.	The relevant standard of care is that of the reasonably competent professional.
The applicant will have standing to bring a claim for judicial review because the grant of planning permission will have an effect on his everyday life.	The applicant will have standing to bring a claim for judicial review if he has sufficient interest in the issue.

The statements in the first column are **not** accurate statements of the law; they are explanations of how the requirements of the law are satisfied in relation to a particular set of the facts. As such, they are *applying* the law rather than *stating* it.

Students sometimes take the combined approach as a deliberate ploy to conserve words. This is a mistake: it may save words but it loses marks.

12.4.3.3 Too much detail

A further factor that can weaken a problem answer is the inclusion of an excessive level of detail when providing a statement of law. This tends to take two forms:

- Too much descriptive detail, e.g. the detailed facts of a case.

- Inclusion of irrelevant material, e.g. issues not raised by the facts.

Both of these problems can be addressed by use of the 'so what' test. This involves asking 'so what does this contribute to my answer' in relation to each sentence included in your answer. If the answer is 'nothing', the sentence should be removed. It is seeking to identify material that is not directly relevant to the issue at hand.

Practical exercise

Use the 'so what' technique to eliminate the unnecessary material from these sample answers based upon examples used earlier in the chapter.

1. Wendy has submitted her essay at 9.15 a.m. the day after the deadline for submission. The rules state that there is a 10 mark penalty for submission up to one day after the deadline. An essay which is more than one day late will receive a 25 mark penalty if it is within one week of the deadline but after that it will receive zero. It is likely that Wendy will receive a 10 mark penalty unless she can establish that she had good cause for late submission.

2. Stuart has punched Neil in the face causing a cut which required stitches so may be liable under section 20 of the Offences against the Person Act 1861. The *actus reus* requires a wound or the infliction of grievous bodily harm. Grievous bodily harm is defined as 'really serious harm' and, according to the CPS Charging Standards includes serious injuries such as broken limbs. Moreover, it has been held by the House of Lords that psychological injury can amount to grievous bodily harm if it is sufficiently serious and is established as a matter of expert evidence. It does not include mere emotions such as distress or fear but requires an established psychiatry injury. A wound is defined as a break in the continuity of the skin and will be satisfied as a cut that requires stitches must have broken Neil's skin.

 These are quite straightforward examples to demonstrate the point, but you will find some more challenging exercises on the Online Resource Centre that you may find useful in helping you to identify unnecessary material.

12.5 Application and evaluation

It is this stage of the process that is at the heart of problem solving. The first stage enabled you to identify the questions that needed to be answered; the second stage involved identification of the law needed to answer these question, but it is this third stage that involves combining the issue and the law and actually answering the question.

This is the aspect of problem solving with which students struggle the most and yet it is quite straightforward, as the following example demonstrates:

- Subissue 1.1 Is Gerald an occupier of premises?
- State the law: There is no statutory definition of 'occupier' under the Occupiers' Liability Acts 1957 and 1984 but an occupier is defined in *Wheat* v *E. Lacan & Co Ltd* [1966] 1 All ER 582 as a person who exercises an element of control over premises. In *Harris* v *Birkenhead Corporation* [1976] 1 All ER 341, it was held that this meant physical control over the premises as well as legal control.
- **Apply it to the facts:** As Gerald is described as the person who runs the donkey centre, this implies that he has physical control over the premises even if he is not the legal owner of the centre.
- Conclusion

As you see in this example, the essence of application/evaluation is to draw upon the facts provided to demonstrate how the requirements of law are satisfied.

Here, the law defines an occupier as a person who exercises a degree of control over the property so the application/evaluation stage of problem-solving picks up on evidence from the scenario that demonstrates that Gerald exercises control over the donkey centre.

The application stage is sometimes said to require the greatest level of skill and understanding of the law as it requires the student to look at the facts and select the ones that fulfil the requirements of the law. This is not something that can be cribbed from a textbook, remembered from a lecture, or looked up on the Internet; it requires actual understanding of the requirements of the law and an ability to recognize them amongst a mass of facts.

Practical exercise

It is a good idea to practise with some simple examples to gain confidence in identifying the relevant facts. Have a look back at the donkey sanctuary scenario and pick out the facts that satisfy the following requirements:

1. If the definition of 'premises' includes land and buildings, what facts suggest that the injuries sustained by Tess, Diana, and Wendy occurred on premises?

2. To fall within the provisions of the Occupiers' Liability Act 1957, the person who is harmed must be a lawful visitor to the premises, ie someone with express or implied permission from the occupier to be on the premises or whose presence is known to the occupier. What facts suggest that Tess, Diana, and Wendy are visitors?

3. An occupier will not be liable for a visitor's injury if he has given sufficient warning to enable the visitor to be reasonably safe. Are there any facts that suggest that any of those who have been injured have been given a warning and, if so, was it sufficient to enable them to be reasonably safe?

4. An occupier may have to take additional measures to protect children from harm, especially if there are allurements on the premises, but the law strives to seek a balance between the duty of an occupier and the responsibility of parents for the safety of their children. In this scenario, what might act as an allurement to a child, what measures has Gerald taken to protect against this, and what factors might suggest some element of parental responsibility?

 You will find answers to these questions on the Online Resource Centre along with an explanation of how the answers were reached. You will also find further practical exercises which will test your ability to identify relevant facts from the question that will demonstrate that the requirements of law are satisfied. This is an important area, so it will be worth taking some time to ensure that you are able to apply the law effectively to the facts.

12.5.1 Common problems

This stage of application/evaluation does hold a range of pitfalls that can lead students astray. The following is an outline of some of the problems that seem to arise frequently, with some suggestions for their avoidance.

12.5.1.1 Lazy application

This is a phrase that can be used to describe situations when students have made some mention of the facts but in such a general way that it is not really application at all as it does nothing to resolve the issue at hand. Phrases such as 'this requirement is satisfied on the facts' or 'it is clear from the facts that this is satisfied'. This may well be so, but there is no credit available for application that does not refer to *specific* facts from the problem to establish that the requirements of the law are satisfied.

It also describes the situation when the student abdicates responsibility for application by delegating it to someone else, usually 'the court' or 'the jury'. Here, the student is acknowledging that a decision will have to be made about whether the requirements of the law are satisfied but strives to find a way to avoid doing this themselves. To be clear, even if the issue is one of fact that will be decided in court by the jury, that is not a useful stance to take in a problem question. Imagine if a client says to you 'am I going to be convicted of murder?'. He will not be in the least impressed if your advice is that this will be a question of fact for the jury! Accordingly, you must extrapolate evidence from the facts that give an indication of how the issue is likely to be decided. You might find that speculative application (see section 12.5.2.1) helps to overcome this problem.

The following example demonstrates both of these flawed approaches to application as well as some illustrations of a more effective approach to application (Figure 12.6).

Sound application

On the basis of what facts? If it is that clear, you should be able to refer to specific facts to support this conclusion

John has taken Linda's watch and put it in his pocket so may be liable for theft. Theft is defined in section 1(1) of the Theft Act 1968 as the dishonest appropriation of property belonging to another with intention to permanently deprive. The *actus reus* of theft is the appropriation of property belonging to another. Appropriation is defined in section 3(1) as the assumption of the rights of the owner. John has picked up the watch and placed it in his pocket which is an exercise of the rights of ownership. The watch is personal property as required by section 4 and it belongs to Linda (section 5). The *mens rea* of theft is intention to permanently deprive and dishonesty. The intention to permanently deprive is clearly established. Situations in which a person is not dishonest are outlined in section 2 and do not seem to be relevant here so the *Ghosh* test would need to be applied. This is a two-stage test which asks firstly whether the defendant's actions would be considered dishonest according to the ordinary standards of reasonable and honest people and, secondly, whether the defendant realised that his conduct was dishonest by those standards. This is a question of fact to be determined by the jury.

This is fine despite the lack of detail as this is an unproblematic issue that does not need in-depth consideration

The test needs to be applied in order to reach a conclusion, even a tentative one, about the defendant's dishonesty and his liablility for theft. Leaving an issue to the jury is not application of the law.

Figure 12.6 Lazy and effective application

12.5.1.2 Essays in disguise

Another weakness which limits the success of many answers is a greater resemblance to an essay than to a problem question. This arises when students engage in detailed discussion of the law raised by the question that strays further and further away from the issue at hand.

Try to remember that essays and problem questions have very different requirements. A problem question requires a concise and focused statement of the relevant law. Exploration of how the law used to be, how it might be in the future, or what it is in other jurisdictions are only rarely relevant in a problem question.

Students also have a tendency to include far too much descriptive detail of the law and this gives their answer the feel of an essay (see section 12.4.3.3 above). Try not to test relevance by asking 'is this point relevant?' as this question will be answered in relation to the topic in general. 'Is this point necessary to establish this part of the law?' is a far better question and one that will keep your answer focused and prevent it from turning into an essay on the general issue.

Another useful way of keeping the answer to the point is to ensure that every paragraph includes a mention of the name of one of the parties and at least some mention of specific facts from the problem. By doing this, you will force yourself to link up with the question and this should stop you from straying too far into abstract discussion.

12.5.2 Strengthening application

In addition to avoiding these common problems, there are a variety of techniques that can be used to improve the quality of your answer by strengthening the application of the law to the facts.

12.5.2.1 Speculative application

As you have doubtless realized by now, problem questions do not provide all the facts that you need to reach a determinative answer to all the issues raised. You will often encounter a situation in which you have worked through the subissues and need to establish just one more point to reach a conclusion about liability, only to find that the information you need in order to do so is simply not included in the question.

When this situation arises, it is perfectly permissible to engage in a little speculative application. This means that you can explore some hypothetical situations in order to engage in some conjecture: if X then Y. This is demonstrated in the following example (Figure 12.7).

Huw has submitted his essay after the 4pm deadline. The rules state that essays submitted after the deadline that are up to one day late will receive a 10 mark penalty.

> Application of the general rule could be followed by a conclusion that Huw will receive a penalty but there are exceptions to the rule so it is reasonable to speculate about whether Huw might fall within them.

There are some exceptions to this noted in the rules. For example, if Huw had been granted an extension by a lecturer, there would be no penalty. There is nothing in the facts to suggest that this is the case.

> This is straightforward situation to discuss as Huw either has an extension or he does not so there is little more to be said on this point.

Equally, the rule states that a person who has good cause for late submission will not be penalised. If Huw was late because his printer broke, this is unlikely to be regarded as a good reason as it is such a commonplace occurrence that he should have contemplated that it could happen and have planned for it. However, if Huw was late because he was knocked off his bicycle on the way to submit his essay and delayed by the need to seek medical treatment, this is likely to be regarded as a good cause for lateness.

> This situation can involve more detailed speculation as it revolves around interpretation of 'good cause'. Inclusion of hypothetical possibilities to illustrate understanding of the scope of the exception add further strength to the answer. This approach can be used when case law has considered the interpretation of a particular word or phrase.

There is no evidence to suggest that Huw has received an extension or has good cause to submit his essay late thus, in the absence of such circumstances, it seems that Huw will receive a 10 mark deduction for late submission.

> The conclusion that follows speculative application should always draw reference to its contingent nature by noting that it is the best conclusion possible on the known facts but may alter if further facts come to light or a particular interpretation is preferred and applied.

Figure 12.7 Speculative application

12.5.2.2 Taking a balanced approach

The central premise of the legal system is that claims are tested against each other in order to establish which of the opposing arguments between private parties (in civil cases) or between the State and an individual (in criminal law) is the stronger. As such, it is important that you demonstrate this objectivity in your answers by considering both sides to the argument when exploring liability. Moreover, from a pragmatic perspective, if you present one argument, you will get credit for that but if you provide a second argument to counter that initial point, there is additional credit available.

Therefore, it is important to scrutinize every issue to determine whether there is a viable counter-argument that needs to be considered. There will not always be a counter-argument; in the scenario involving theft of Linda's watch, it is a straightforward matter to determine that the watch is personal property, so there is no counter-argument to consider. However, moving on to consider the issue of intention to deprive permanently, although it is reasonable to assume that this is John's intention as he has surreptitiously placed the watch in his pocket, it may be that he only wants to borrow it because, moving to consider the issue of dishonesty, he wants to have it cleaned and repaired as a surprise for Linda. If the facts are silent on an issue, it may be necessary to engage in speculative application in order to explore both sides of the argument (see section 12.5.2.1).

Equally, if the issue involves interpretation of a particular word or phrase, do not be content with finding one case on the issue and assuming that this provides the answer. You should research the issue and see if there is any conflicting authority that suggests an alternative outcome is possible.

12.5.2.3 Supporting authority

The inclusion of authority to support your application of the law is a real strength but it is also something that is not always done very effectively by students. All too often, an argument is raised that requires support which is either not provided at all, or the relevant case is added on in brackets at the end of the sentence or in a footnote reference with no indication how it supports the proposition asserted.

> Although Diana is a lawful visitor to the donkey centre, she may have become a trespasser by climbing on the roped-off machinery (*The Calgarth* [1927] P 93).
>
> Although Diana is a lawful visitor to the donkey centre, she may have become a trespasser by climbing on the machinery as it was roped off to prevent the public approaching it. This issue was discussed in *The Calgarth* [1927] P 93.

Neither of these examples make effective use of the authority; in fact, the second is misleading as it could be read as meaning that the issue of moving into a roped-off area was discussed in *The Calgarth*. A better approach is one that explains the principle from the case:

> Although Diana is a lawful visitor to the centre, she may have become a trepasser by entering the roped-off area. It was said in *The Calgarth* [1927] P 93 that a person who is given permission to enter a house is not necessarily given permission to slide down the banisters, so it may be that Diana has exceeded the permission given to her by entering the roped-off area.

One way to ensure that you use authority effectively is to make sure that you have linked the case to the facts in some way. This requires you to explain how it is relevant and consider how it might impact on the outcome of the case.

12.6 Conclusion and outcome

The final stage of the process involves reaching a conclusion on the basis of the preceding application of the law as is demonstrated by reference to the sample question:

- Subissue 1.1 Is Gerald an occupier of premises?
  - State the law: There is no statutory definition of 'occupier' under the Occupiers' Liability Acts 1957 and 1984 but an occupier is defined in *Wheat* v *E. Lacan & Co Ltd* [1966] 1 All ER 582 as a person who exercises an element of control over premises. In *Harris* v *Birkenhead Corporation* [1976] 1 All ER 341, it was held that this meant physical control over the premises as well as legal control.
  - Apply it to the facts: as Gerald is described as the person who runs the donkey centre, this implies that he has physical control over the premises even if he is not the legal owner of the centre.
  - **Conclusion**: Therefore, Gerald will be regarded as the occupier of the donkey centre for the purposes of establishing Occupiers' Liability.

You will need to reach a conclusion for each subissue and then draw these together to reach a conclusion for the main issue. If you consider the issue of Gerald's liability for the injury sustained by Tess, you will see that it contained a series of subissues that combine to provide an answer to that main issue. Each of these—whether Gerald is an occupier, whether the stable yard is premises, whether Tess is a visitor, and so on—will be considered and a conclusion reached and these can then be considered cumulatively to reach a conclusion on liability.

Of course, it may be that it is not possible to reach a definite conclusion. It is a mistake to think that there is always an answer in law: it is not usually a case of right and wrong but of strong and weak arguments, so you should remember that you are not looking for the 'right' answer but for the conclusion that is likely to be reached based upon which argument is the strongest.

Take the following factors into account when reaching a conclusion:

- **There are three different levels of conclusion:** (a) a conclusion for each subissue; (b) a cumulative conclusion that draws upon each of these to reach a conclusion for each issue; and (c) an overall conclusion to the problem question. This should outline the liability of the party or parties for each issue that was raised by the question. In essence, the end conclusion is a summary of your findings.

- **Make sure that your final conclusion is consistent with your earlier discussion.** It would be unfortunate if, in the early stages of the essay, you concluded that Gerald had given sufficient warning of the dangers posed by feeding the donkeys only to state in your final conclusion that he was liable for the injury sustained by Tess. Thorough checking once the answer is complete should help you to spot any inconsistencies.

- **Do not be afraid to reach an 'it depends' conclusion.** As stated earlier, it is not always a case of finding the right answer but of exploring the possibility of liability, so it is perfectly acceptable to reach a conclusion that says 'it seems that Gerald may be liable for the injury sustained by Tess but this depends upon whether his notices are regarded as adequate warning of the dangers inherent in feeding the donkeys'. Making a note of the contingencies will strengthen your answer.

- **Do provide an overall conclusion.** Given the constraints of the word limit, students are sometimes tempted to stop writing after dealing with the final issue and leave the marker to pick out the conclusions for each issue that are distributed throughout the answer. This is poor practice and will weaken your answer. The question will require that you discuss someone's liability and your conclusion should always provide a concise and focused answer to the question posed, so it is important that you draw together all the strands of your argument here.

12.7 Tips for success in problem questions

There are a range of points to bear in mind that will help you to strengthen your problem-solving technique.

12.7.1 Follow the instructions

This is an obvious but frequently overlooked point. If the instructions tell you to discuss the liability of a particular party and to consider liability in a particular area of law, this is all that you should cover in your answer. There is no credit available for discussing other issues that are raised on the facts but which are excluded by the instructions.

For example, if a problem stated that Jack had smashed his way into Charlie's house and injected him forcibly with a lethal dose of heroin and you were asked to discuss Jack's liability for homicide offences, there would be no point whatsoever in establishing that Jack is liable for criminal damage to Charlie's door.

Consideration of irrelevant issues will not give you any marks and it will weaken the quality of your answer because it will either cost you words that could be used to discuss a relevant issue (in a piece of coursework) or time that could be devoted to a relevant issue (in an examination).

Students sometimes think that discussing points that are outside the scope of the instructions will attract additional credit from the marker, particularly if this means covering an area of law that is not covered on the course syllabus, because this will demonstrate their research skills. This is generally not the case, so avoid the temptation to do this and concentrate on the instructions that you have been given and the areas of law covered on your syllabus.

12.7.2 Methodical approach

If you follow the guidance given in this chapter, you should be able to work through each of the issues in turn in a methodical manner. This should ensure that you do not miss any important issues and that your answer is thorough and systematic. These are essential features of a strong answer. Students are often tempted to 'jump in' and deal with the most obvious issue first—usually something that they can recall discussing in a seminar or which bears a strong resemblance to a decided case—but this makes the answer weak because you are failing to deal with the other issues that are also raised by the question but may be less obvious, and you are also not demonstrating a thorough and methodical approach to problem solving.

12.7.3 Check and polish the final answer

You should never submit the first draft of your answer. It is important that you take the time to check every aspect of the answer prior to submission: the formatting, spelling, and grammar, the referencing and, of course, the accuracy of the content. Try to leave sufficient time before submission to have a break from the answer and come back to read it with fresh eyes otherwise it is all too easy to read what you think you have written rather than what you have actually written, so mistakes could be overlooked. It might help to read your answer on paper rather than on the computer screen as mistakes can seem more visible in print.

You will find more detailed guidance on writing skills in chapter 10 that will help you to ensure that you submit a well-written and thoroughly referenced piece of work.

Practical exercise

 Reflect upon the guidance provided in this chapter and use it to evaluate an answer to a problem question that you have written either as part of your coursework or in preparation for a seminar. Make a list of its strengths and weaknesses to identify areas where improvement can be made in subsequent pieces of work. As the chapter on study skills suggests, reflecting on your own work can be an excellent way to improve your performance. However, if you would like to use the points raised in this chapter to evaluate answers written by others, have a look at the Online Resource Centre where you can find some practical marking activities that you might find useful.

 CHAPTER SUMMARY

Finding the issues

- Take time to analyse the facts of the problem question in terms of the parties and events so that you know 'who has done what to whom' as this provides a good basis for structuring your answer

- Break an issue down into a series of subissues so that each can be considered in turn. It is essential that the issues are sliced up into manageable chunks, so that the law can be stated and applied to the facts

Stating the law

- Start by consulting a textbook to ensure that you have a clear understanding of the area of law but make sure that you move on to consider case law as this will ensure that your answer has sufficient depth of understanding

- Provide concise and abstract statements of the law that can be applied to the facts. Avoid reams of descriptive detail such as lengthy explanations of the facts of cases

- Make sure that there is some supporting authority—either statute or case law—for each statement of law that is made

- Remember to look at both sides of the argument for complicated issues. It may be necessary to search for cases that give alternative outcomes or different definitions of key words or phrases

- Keep careful notes to record your research. It is very frustrating to arrive at the writing stage and not be able to find details of a case you need because you thought you would remember. A systematic approach to note-keeping is a real asset and can save a great deal of time

Application of the law

- Look at the facts and extrapolate specific information that demonstrates that the requirements of the law are satisfied

- Never rely on lazy application such as 'this is clearly established on the facts'. If the facts are that clear, it should be easy for you to identify them and include them in your answer! Equally, never abdicate responsibility for application of the law to the fictitious jury

- Speculative application that considers hypothetical situations can be a useful way of increasing the depth of analysis in your answer and demonstrating your understanding of the law, but do not stray too far away from the facts provided in the answer

- Support your application with case law wherever possible but make sure that this is done effectively by stating the principle and incorporating it into your answer. Case names tacked onto the end of a sentence add nothing to the quality of your answer

- Present a balanced and objective answer by looking at both sides of the argument

Conclusion

- Reach a conclusion on each subissue, issue, and the overall liability of the parties and make sure that there is consistency between these different levels of conclusion

- Do not be afraid to reach a conclusion that is not determinative. Problem questions are written to raise difficult issues, so it may be that the best answer is one that says 'it depends' and then notes the contingent factor

- Make sure that the final conclusion draws together all the strands of your answer and provides a concise summary of your findings as to the liability of the parties

- Do not be tempted to omit the final conclusion in the interests of the word limit

Revision and examination skills

13

INTRODUCTION

The earlier chapters in this part of the book have been aimed at helping you to develop the skills that you need to succeed as your course progresses. Chapter 9 outlined a range of study skills whilst chapter 10 provided a detailed examination of writing skills and chapters 11 and 12 contained detailed guidelines on writing essays and answering problem questions. This chapter focuses on the skills needed to ensure that your revision is effective in preparing you for the examinations that you will need to pass at the end of each year (or twice-yearly, depending upon how your course is structured). Unlike many other resources that abandon the student at the door of the examination room, this chapter will not only guide you though the revision process but also beyond this to the examination itself by outlining various strategies that can be used to ensure that your knowledge is used to good effect in the examination room.

Revision and exam skills are important and yet they are not always covered by lecturers or in text-books dealing with study skills. Perhaps this omission is due to an assumption that students who have worked steadily throughout the course will have all that they need to succeed in the exams without any additional advice on revision and exam preparation. This is a misconception and one that can leave students ill-equipped for success in the exams, particularly as the approach to revision that is favoured by students—rereading and rewriting notes—is not particularly effective. This chapter provides a selection of practical tips on formulating an effective revision strategy from planning and organization through to a series of practical tasks that can be undertaken alone or in groups. The overall aim of the chapter is to provide some insight into the variety of ways that revision can be made more variable, engaging, and effective.

LEARNING OUTCOMES

After studying this chapter, you should be able to:

- Formulate a realistic plan of revision appropriate to your circumstances

- Review your syllabus to identify appropriate topics for revision

- Use a range of different strategies to engage in active revision

- Acknowledge the value of practice answers and incorporate these into your revision strategy

- Recognize the different requirements of essays and problem questions and take account of these in your revision and in the exam

- Plan and produce focused and successful answers to exam questions

- Avoid some of the common problems that limit exam success

13.1 Preparing to revise

Planning and preparation are the key to successful revision. Too many students dive straight into the revision process without any clear idea of what they are trying to achieve. It is worth taking time to organize your thoughts at the outset and devise a workable and effective revision strategy, taking the factors outlined in the following sections into account.

13.1.1 Timing and structure of the exams

In order to plan your revision, it is essential that you have a clear picture of the task ahead of you. A vague knowledge that you have to sit five papers in five weeks' time is not sufficient information upon which to base an effective revision strategy. Try to ensure that you can answer the following questions as your first step in the revision process.

13.1.1.1 When do your examinations take place?

This question is of immediate importance because it defines how long you have available for revision. The time available for revision varies enormously between institutions. Count how many days, including weekends, there are from the first day of your revision to the first day of the exam period. If you divide each day into two study periods, you can also give yourself half-day breaks that will give you some relief from studying. Once you have a clear idea of how many days of revision there are, you can start to plan how to break those days down into study periods for the various subjects.

13.1.1.2 How much time is there between papers?

Again, this various enormously, not only between institutions but from year-to-year within the same institution. You may be fortunate and have exams evenly spaced out over a period of two weeks or you could be unlucky and face four papers in two days. Irrespective of the time between papers, it is not a good idea to take these gap days into account when calculating the number of revision days available for the following reasons:

- You could be tempted to use all the pre-exam revision time for the first subject and then slot the remaining revision into the gap days which will give disproportionate attention to the subject of the first exam and leave you short of time to deal with the other subjects.

- If you are reliant on gap days to revise a particular subject, you will be in difficulties if something interferes with that plan such as illness or some unexpected setback.

It is a much better strategy to count only the days before the first exam as full revision days and then to use gap days to generally refresh your memory, confident in the knowledge that the bulk of the work is already done.

13.1.1.3 How many papers will you be sitting?

With a wide range of optional subjects on offer and a more diverse range of methods of assessment, it is impossible to make generalizations about the 'usual' number of papers that any student will sit. Some students prefer to opt for subjects that are assessed exclusively by coursework, so may be facing few (or no) examinations whilst others, particularly students taking 'half credit' subjects, will have more examinations.

Your revision time should be spread fairly evenly across the number of subjects that you are studying. It is one of the unfortunate facts of student life that half-credit subjects carry less weight towards your degree than full-credit subjects but tend to involve just as much work in terms of revision. As such, it is probably not a good idea to differentiate between full and half-credit subjects when allocating revision time.

With these details in mind, you can get a good general idea of the number of days available to revise each subject. If you have 42 days until the first examination, this gives you potentially 84 half-day study periods to allocate to five subjects. Rather than dividing 75 half-days (remember to factor in rest days) by five to allocate fifteen study periods to each subject, you may want to take other factors into account in the allocation process; for example, you may have found some subjects particularly difficult or they may be assessed solely by examination so that more is at stake (Table 13.1).

Table 13.1 Allocating revision time

Subject	Percentage of exam	Difficulty	Number of sessions
Family	50	4	10
Medical	50	3	17
Company	100	1	22
International	60	2	18
Criminology	25	5	8

It is a good idea to draw up a revision calendar and mark the subjects on it so that you have an immediate visual reminder of where you are in the revision process (it is also very satisfying to be able to cross out completed tasks, giving a real feeling of progress). There are two ways in which you could allocate time by subject in your revision timetable:

1. **Clustered:** consecutive study periods are allocated to the same subject. This allows a concentrated focus on each subject but does mean that the first revision topic is rather distant by the time that the exam period starts. Some people who use this method start with their revision with the final exam subject and work towards their first subject so that this is revised immediately prior to the start of the exam period. In this way, the gap days can be used to work back through the revision topics.

2. **Dispersed:** this method allocates days on a revolving basis so that there are no concentrated periods of study and no subject becomes stale. It can make the revision process more interesting, particularly if some of the options were not as enjoyable as you had hoped, but there is a lack of continuity of thought, especially if you have chosen a diverse range of options (Figure 13.1).

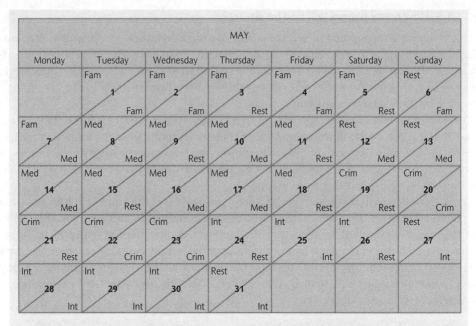

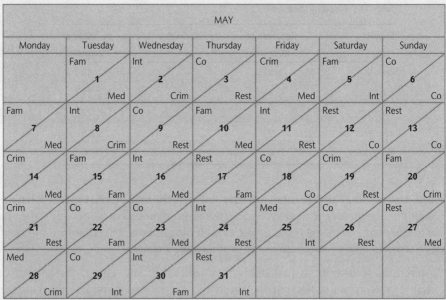

Family		Fam				
Criminology		Crim				
Medical		Med				
Company		Co				
International		Int				
Time Off!		Rest				

Figure 13.1 Clustered and dispersed revision timetables

13.2 Reviewing each subject

Once you have worked out how much time to devote to each subject, you need to spend time evaluating each subject on which you will be examined so that you have a plain understanding of how much work is to be done.

13.2.1 Study the syllabus

The syllabus will provide details of the areas that have been studied in that particular subject, so should be the starting point for your revision from which you can make a list of topics to revise. Think carefully about any advice you have been given by your lecturers: were you told that any topics were not going to be examined, for example? Many students use revision books to help them at this stage of their studies, but it is important to remember that these are generic guides, so may contain material that is not on your syllabus or may omit altogether topics that were studied in depth on your course. The aim is to produce a list of topics that were covered in the course so that you can use this to ensure you select a sufficient range of revision topics. Ideally, you should try to revise the entirety of the course but, failing that, aim to cover at least three-quarters of the topics covered by your syllabus, taking into account the following points.

13.2.1.1 Avoid question spotting

This involves making predictions about exam content on the basis of past papers. Just because there has not been a question on a particular topic for a few years does not mean that is it likely to appear on your paper. Equally, the fact that a particular topic has appeared on the exam paper for the past three years does not mean that it is any more or less likely to appear this year. Finally, do not make assumptions about the content of the exam on the basis of the topic of any course-work that has been set; again, this does not eliminate it as a potential exam topic nor make it more likely to appear.

Avoid this unreliable (but popular) method of selecting revision topics in favour of aiming to cover as much of the syllabus as possible.

13.2.1.2 How prominent was each topic?

The emphasis given to a topic by your lecturers can give some insight into its overall importance to the subject, hence the likelihood that it will feature in the exam. For example, if five out of the twelve weeks in tort were given to the study of negligence, it does not make sense to disregard it as a revision topic.

13.2.1.3 How complete was your coverage of the topic?

In a perfect world, you would have a complete and comprehensive set of notes taken at the lectures, supplemented by your tutorial preparation and further reading upon which to base your revision. Although some gaps can be filled in at this stage, it is not useful to spend your revision time learning topics for the first time. Equally, if there is a topic that has always been a struggle for you, now is probably not the best time to try and master it.

Once you have a list of topics to revise in each subject, you can start to slot these into your revision timetable. Do bear in mind that you will need to be realistic in allocating time to any particular topic; it would be unrealistic to expect to cover all of negligence in a single half-day session. Setting yourself unrealistic goals means that you will struggle to meet them, which can lead you to lose motivation and to feel overwhelmed by the whole revision and examination process. It is better to overestimate the amount of time that it will take to revise a particular topic and then give yourself a reward when you finish with time to spare.

13.2.2 What is the format of the exam in each subject?

Some institutions have a single universal format for examination papers which means that they are always the same length and involve the same number of questions. If your institution does not adopt this approach, make sure that you find out the length and format of the exam in each subject you are sitting. This is essential information to have during the revision period because it can give an indication of the level of detail that is expected in each answer and the breadth of revision of the subject as a whole that is needed.

Make sure you know the answers to the following questions in relation to each subject that you are sitting.

13.2.2.1 How long is the exam?

This can be a good indicator of the depth of analysis expected in each answer when considered in conjunction with the number of questions that must be answered. For example, if there is a requirement to answer two questions in a two-hour exam paper, more detail will be needed to answer the questions than would be the case if there was a requirement to answer four questions in the same time period. It is also useful to know how much time to allocate to each question so that you use your time in the exam room effectively and can practise writing answers within the relevant timeframe as part of the revision process (see below at 13.3.4).

13.2.2.2 How many questions are there?

It is also important to know how much choice there is in terms of questions: a paper that requires you to answer four questions out of six is likely to be far more challenging than one that requires you to answer four out of ten. It is also the case that a smaller choice of questions implies either that the entirety of the syllabus will not be examined or that a range of topics will be combined in a single question. You can obtain a good idea of the approach taken at your institution by looking at a range of past papers.

13.2.2.3 Are there any compulsory questions?

Compulsory questions are can be a gift or a curse. Some institutions include compulsory questions on important issues within a subject but advise students in advance what this will be, so that they know to include it in their revision. Other institutions include compulsory questions but give no guidance as to the subject matter, which means that thorough revision of the entire syllabus is essential.

13.2.2.4 What type of paper is it?

Closed-book examinations are traditional but many institutions are moving towards alternative methods such as open-book exams (where certain textbooks or other materials may be taken into the examination room) or seen papers (where some or all of the questions are released to the students in advance).

Each type of paper requires a slightly different approach to revision. In general, it is advisable to revise open-book exams as if they were closed-book but with the additional requirement that you are familiar with the layout of the book, as you do not want to waste valuable exam time fumbling around the index.

13.2.2.5 What is the format of the paper?

Some exam papers give the student a free choice, e.g. answer any four questions from eight, whereas others are divided into sections with a requirement that at least one question is answered from each section. This latter approach needs to be taken into account in the revision process, so it is important that you determine the basis upon which the two sections are categorized. It might be that one half of the paper is essays whilst the other half is problem questions (quite a common practice). If so, you will have to ensure that your revision of each topic is sufficient to enable you to deal with both types of question (the revision process is different for essays and problems as will be discussed below at 13.3.6). Alternatively, the paper may be divided into sections on the basis of subject matter. For example, some tort courses have a two-part examination paper with one part dealing with negligence and the other with the remainder of the torts. In such a case, a student who was unaware of this fact may give insufficient attention to negligence as a revision topic and be significantly disadvantaged as a result.

13.2.2.6 What can you take into the exam room?

This is an issue at the planning stages of revision because you will need to make sure that you have the appropriate materials. For example, many institutions allow students to take a statute book into the exam room but place restrictions either upon which series of statute book can be used or require that the book be free from annotation.

Find out what the regulations are and ensure that you adhere to them (it is very off-putting for students to have their material removed in the exam room because of non-compliance). If you can take materials into the exam room, make sure that you familiarize yourself with them as part of the revision process to avoid any waste of time fumbling around the book in the examination.

All this information should be readily available to you. If you are not sure, it is worth asking your lecturer, tutor, or course leader to ensure that you have clear and accurate information.

13.2.3 Your strengths and weaknesses

It is a good idea to tailor your revision plan to suit your own ability and preferences. On a basic level, some people work well in the morning whilst others find it difficult to get started. Just before the exam is not the time to try and force new study habits upon yourself, so ensure that you devise a revision plan that fits within your usual working preferences provided, of course, that this gives you an appropriate timeframe within which to work.

You should also be aware of your strengths and weaknesses, both in terms of the topics that you study and your preparation for essays and problem questions. Some students have a strong preference for essays whilst others favour problem questions but all students will need to answer a mix of both in the examinations, so do give thought to strengthening your technique if you are weak in one or other answer style. Honing the quality of your answers should be an integral part of the revision process; remember, success in exams is not attributable exclusively to what you know/can remember but also to how you use it.

13.3 Revision strategies

It is not only the organization of revision into manageable chunks that can cause difficulties; once the structure for revision is established, it can often be hard for students to know what to do in that structure.

In other words, whilst everyone knows that they must revise, not everyone is clear on what exactly this involves. This lack of certainty leads many students to read and re-read their notes in the hope that the information contained therein will stick in their minds whilst other students take this further and write and rewrite their notes. These strategies may lead to a greater familiarity with the relevant information, but it is not nearly as effective as some other revision techniques that involve more active engagement with the material.

Rather than viewing the purpose of revision as fixing information in the mind, it is preferable to see it as a process that prepares you for the exam. This involves recollection of information and the ability to use it in an effective manner. Simply re-reading or rewriting notes in isolation is not sufficient to achieve the first aim and does nothing whatsoever towards the second. An active approach to revision is far more effective in achieving both of these aims.

13.3.1 Consolidating notes

Although note-making alone is not an effective revision strategy, a good set of notes is the foundation of successful revision. Ideally, these will have been produced incrementally as the course has progressed; it is not useful to start the revision process with a blank sheet of paper and nothing to revise. You should aim to take the notes that you have made during lectures, in preparation for seminars, and as part of your private study and condense them into a more concise and memorable set of key points.

Condensing your notes is an important part of the revision process. Not only does it produce a set of concise points that can be committed to memory, the actual process of filtering and recording information will contribute to your understanding of the material as you make decisions about the significance of different points and the relationship between them.

13.3.2 Recalling information

It is essential that you find a way to make the material memorable.

The first point to note is that it is much easier to recall things you have understood. This is why it is useful to review the syllabus and weed out topics that have never made any sense to you. If you have not grasped them by the time the revision period starts, it will probably require far too great an investment in time to get to grips with them now. In fact, you should only really try to incorporate topics that have always mystified you into your revision if it is absolutely necessary, e.g. the topic is the subject of a compulsory question or you have been puzzled by so much of the course that dealing with some difficult topics is essential.

Memory is triggered by association so it can really help the revision process if you vary your strategies so that each topic is somehow associated with something in particular. If you sit in the same place, doing the same thing for all the topics that you revise, there is nothing for your memory to latch onto in order to differentiate it from all the other legal information milling around inside your head. Try varying the following factors to create an association.

13.3.2.1 What you do to revise

If you vary the activity in which you engage when revising, this can aid recollection by linking a particular topic to a particular activity. For example, you might decide to use a topic map to revise theft, a quiz for homicide offences, and flashcards for defences. Remember that many people remember images more readily than words which could be another reason to incorporate diagrams into your revision.

13.3.2.2 Where you revise

If you vary the location where you revise, you may be able to picture the place that you were and use this to link to the information. For example, you could revise negligence in your room, damages sitting in the park, and remedies in the library. This is an effective aid to recollection, particularly if you can link this to other senses such as a particular type of music or the smell of flowers if you revised a particular topic in the park. You can also use visualization of the location to take you back to a particular lecture or tutorial where a specific topic was discussed.

13.3.2.3 Others involved in your revision

If you get other people involved in your revision, not only will you be engaging in more active revision, but you may be able to make links between the topic and the person concerned that will facilitate recollection. For example, your mother could quiz you on offer and acceptance, you could engage in collaborative revision of exclusion clauses with a friend, and explain the finer points of misrepresentation to your partner.

13.3.2.4 Use numbers, rhymes, and pictures

Make use of numbers, rhymes, and pictures to help you remember.

- For example, the elements of theft are defined in the sections which follow in the order that the words appear in the definition of theft:
- Section 1 defines theft as the dishonest (section 2) appropriation (section 3) of property (section 4) belonging to another (section 5) with the intention of permanently depriving the other of it (section 6) so if you learn the definition in section 1, this will help you to remember the section numbers of its elements.
- Rhyming techniques are also useful: burglary is fine (section 9) but robbery is great (section 8).
- Pictorial techniques are particularly good in relation to case law (Figure 13.2).

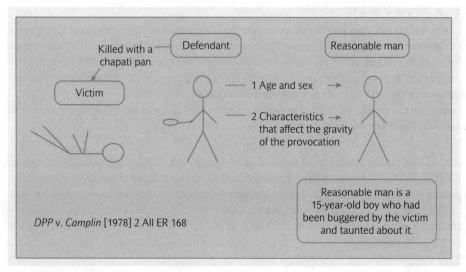

Figure 13.2 Using pictures to remember case law

13.3.3 Active revision

Reading notes can become monotonous and even the best attempts at concentration can end with the eye gliding over the paper without taking in anything, whilst copying out reams of notes can end up as nothing more than an exercise in handwriting. One of the most effective ways to activate the brain is to ask it to do something so try to devise strategies that are more engaging.

13.3.3.1 Revision flashcards

There are small cards that have a question or piece of information to be recalled on the front and the answer on the back. Preparing these can be useful revision in itself as it requires you to identify and note key issues. They are particularly popular as a means of revising cases, but remember that you are concerned with the facts *and* the legal principle from the case.

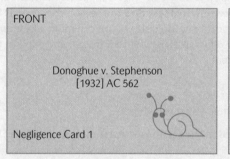

FRONT	BACK
Donoghue v. Stephenson [1932] AC 562 Negligence Card 1	Facts: D found remains of decomposed snail in bottle of ginger beer purchased for her by a friend. Suffered gastro-enteritis. Held that D could sue the manufacturer. Principle: Established the 'neighbour principle' as basis for duty of care in negligence. See Card 2.

Figure 13.3 A revision flashcard

These cards limit the amount of information that can be recorded so should help you to keep your points brief, which will make them easier to remember. They are portable so you can carry them with you to revise in spare moments and they contain the answers, so make it easy for others to help you with your revision by testing you even if they know nothing about the law.

13.3.3.2 Templates and quizzes

Activities which test your recollection are a particularly valuable part of revision as they enable you to assess how much you do know and how much work you still have to do. These are both activities that you can do as part of your revision and are particularly useful for testing how much you can remember from one session to the next if you use the first session to prepare a template or quiz that you will complete in the session that follows.

A template is a paragraph which explains a particular case, principle, or concept but which leaves out certain key words and phrases.

JUDICAL REVIEW is a process by which the ... court exercises its ... jurisdiction to review the decisions of ... In order to bring an action for judical review, an applicant must have ..., meaning that he must have a ... interest in the case, and bring the claim ... and at least within ... months. There are three grounds for judicial review which were identified by Lord ... in the ... case: these grounds are (1) ... (2) ... and (3) ...

Figure 13.4 A template for judicial review revision

The preparation of a template is as much a part of the revision process as the test of recollection that it offers once it is completed, as preparation requires the student to consider what information is essential about a topic and to omit appropriate key words. Equally, the preparation of a quiz requires that you give thought to the construction of sensible questions. You might find quizzes a useful way to engage in collaborative revision with other students.

13.3.3.3 Diagrams and flow charts

Visual representations of information can be a great asset during revision in terms of enabling you to see the entirety of a large topic at a glance. This can be useful in helping you to understand and remember the relationships between the elements of an offence or a set of offences. The preparation of a flow chart or diagram will make you really think about these relationships and, once in the exam room, you should be able to visualize the diagram which is an excellent way of jogging your memory as to its contents. You could scribble the diagram down from memory in the rough notes areas of your exam booklet (Figure 13.5).

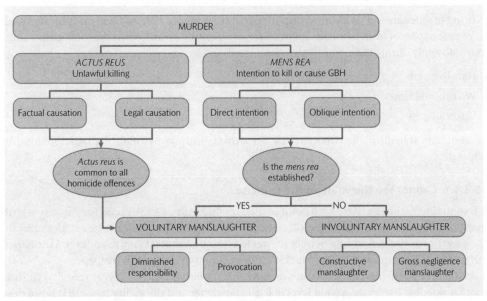

Figure 13.5 A murder flowchart

13.3.3.4 Recorded notes

Making a recording of your notes that you can play back can be a good way of adding variety to the way in which your mind receives information and can help you to make effective use of spare periods of time, such as when travelling by car or train, sitting in the bath, or lying in bed at night (although the merits of playing recordings through the night are hotly debated—do make sure that you have proper rest during the busy revision period).

A variation upon this theme is to record a group of friends discussing a revision topic and listen to this, bearing in mind that you have less control over the accuracy of the content.

13.3.3.5 Free-flow writing

Free-flow writing is a fantastic way to generate ideas and you will often be surprised by how much you do actually know. You make a note of a word or phrase at the top of a blank sheet of paper or fresh document and allow yourself a set period of time in which to write absolutely everything that comes to mind about this topic without any concern for structure, order, or grammatical sense. Any period of time from one to five minutes will work well for revision and it might be an idea to start short and build up to longer periods of time as your knowledge increases. It can be a useful starting point for revision, so that you can identify what you know and, more importantly, what you do not know by comparing your free-flowing writing with your notes.

Remember that although free-flow writing can be a useful way of unlocking information stored in the brain, it is not necessarily a useful technique to use if you become stuck in the exam itself as this could encourage you to spill all sorts of unrelated information onto the page when what is required is that you provide a focused answer to the question. It is a good technique to use for revision and could help if your mind goes blank during the exam, provided that you do this as part of your rough work and extrapolate relevant points to use in your actual answer.

13.3.4 Practice answers

Writing practice answers is *the* most important part of revision. This involves finding questions from past papers or from tutorials, for example, and writing an answer in the same constraints as would apply during the exam:

- Hand-written
- Within a set time
- Without notes.

Students are often disinclined to write practice answers and give two main explanations for this reluctance.

13.3.4.1 Cannot see the value of the exercise

It is sometimes said that there is no point in using revision time to write practice answers to past questions because those questions will not come up on the paper. This is true but the value of the exercise lies not in finding a perfect answer to a question that is likely to appear on the paper but in strengthening your ability to tackle any question that appears on the paper.

As stated earlier in this chapter, exams do not just test *what* you know, they also test *how* you use that knowledge. Therefore, a good level of legal knowledge and the ability to recall it is not desperately useful unless you can use it to construct a coherent essay or produce a balanced answer to a problem question. These are inherently practical skills which require practice to get them right. You would not expect to be able to drive a car after having read a book about how to do so; you need to practise actual driving on the road. The same applies to essays and problem questions; you cannot expect to be able to produce effective answers in the exam without practice.

Even if you have written essays and answered problem questions as part of your coursework, this is not the same as doing so in the exam room without notes and within tight time-constraints. Writing practice answers, in conditions that are as close as possible to those that you will encounter in the exam, enables you to test, review, and refine your technique and is the key to producing effective and successful exams in the exam room.

13.3.4.2 No feedback on the accuracy of the answer

Some students question the value of the exercise if there is no means of determining whether the content is correct or of receiving comment on the quality of the answer and what needs to be improved. In other words, it does not seem to be a useful exercise unless the end result is marked.

This is a misguided standpoint. Part of the value of the exercise lies in familiarizing yourself with the amount that you can write within the given timeframe and it gets you used to the requirement to engage with a question and formulate a focused answer under pressure. Unlike coursework, you do not have time in the exam to think about what the question means, to ask lecturers for guidance, or to talk it through with your friends, so writing an exam answer is an unfamiliar skill and one that needs practice.

Moreover, it is not true that there is no feedback available on the content and quality of your answers. If you ask, you may find that your lecturers are prepared to offer comment on at least one practice answer and, of course, there is nothing to stop you evaluating your own answer. In fact, the ability to engage in critical evaluation of one's own work is a key skill that you should be striving to develop and this is a perfect opportunity to put it into practice. You can compare the content with your notes to spot any material that you have left out and reflect upon aspects of the answer such as structure, clarity, language, and detail.

This exercise may be more effective if you enlist some other students to take part. Several students could attempt the same question and then exchange answers in order to comment on each other's work. This will be particularly useful if it generates some discussion of the legal issues that are relevant to the answer, e.g. it could lead to a debate about whether or not a particular point should have been included in the answer or which of the range of cases used was the most effective. Never underestimate the contribution to improving your own essay writing or problem-solving skills that is made by engaging in constructive criticism of the work of others.

Overall, then, the benefits of writing practice answers are:

- Getting the 'feel' of how much can be written within 45 minutes (or however much time is available per question in your examination)

- Testing how much information you are able to recall about a particular topic

- Practising the skills that are necessary to use the information effectively: essays require analytical skills whilst problem questions need application of the law to the facts

- Enhancing your knowledge and understanding of a topic by reviewing your own answers or those written by others.

13.3.5 Collaborative revision

One of the best ways to make revision more effective and more enjoyable is to work with others. There are a range of ways that have already been mentioned earlier in this chapter in which you can involve others in your revision, but the following are a few more suggestions of things that other students have found particularly useful.

13.3.5.1 Study groups

If you form a study group with other students, you will be able to share the workload of revision amongst the members of the group. You could:

- Agree that each person will prepare a set of revision notes on a particular topic and distribute these amongst the group. With four people in a group, you would have notes on eight topics even though you had only prepared two sets of notes yourself. Obviously, you are dependent on the work of others, so it is useful to choose students that you trust to do the work and to do it to a reasonable quality.

- Select a topic for discussion or a task to complete as a group and either record the activity or nominate someone to take notes, so that you have a record of what was said and done. For example, you could agree to spend an hour working out what the key elements of negligence are and what cases should be used to support the main principles.

- Prepare templates and quizzes to share with the group or write practice answers and compare them with the rest of the group. One group once spent a great deal of time making a version of Trivial Pursuit that replaced the usual categories with the six subjects that they were studying in their second year which they then played at every opportunity. It was so good that other students offered to pay to take part! This shows that you can make revision into an enjoyable activity but do be wary of devising activities that take too much time to set up and organize. These students came up with the idea at Christmas and spread the writing of questions across several months.

Not only do these activities split the workload of revision, they all encourage you to talk to others about the law and this can be one of the more effective methods of gaining an understanding of the material.

13.3.5.2 Talking to others

Some people say that you can only be sure that you understand something fully if you are able to explain it to someone else in a way that they understand. As such, this can be a useful factor to take into account with your revision. Take a concept such as oblique intention and explain it to a friend or family member who does not have any background in the law. Try and make it as clear as possible but without unnecessary detail. Give them an opportunity to ask questions to clarify any points that are unclear and then ask them to explain oblique intention back to you. If they are able to give you a relatively clear and detailed account, then your explanation to them was a good one.

13.3.6 Essays and problem questions

A key factor to take into account as part of your revision strategy is whether you are revising a particular topic in preparation to answer an essay or a problem question. Many students fail to take this into account and just tackle each topic of their revision in the same way. However, as essays and problem questions have different requirements, both in terms of the nature of the content and the type of skills involved in their production, it stands to reason that the approach to revision in preparation for each type of question would be qualitatively different.

13.3.6.1 Problem questions

These assess your ability to disentangle a mass of interwoven facts in order to make a determination about the legal liability of the parties by applying the current law to the factual situation. As such, it requires knowledge of the current law and an awareness of the variety of ways in which it could be applied as demonstrated in case law.

13.3.6.2 Essays

Essays involve a greater depth of knowledge about the topic which might include historical information about the evolution of the law and the ability to comment on future developments by way of evaluation of proposals for reform. The emphasis here is on the ability to consider the law in depth, to address policy considerations, and to engage in critical evaluation of the efficacy of the law (Figure 13.6).

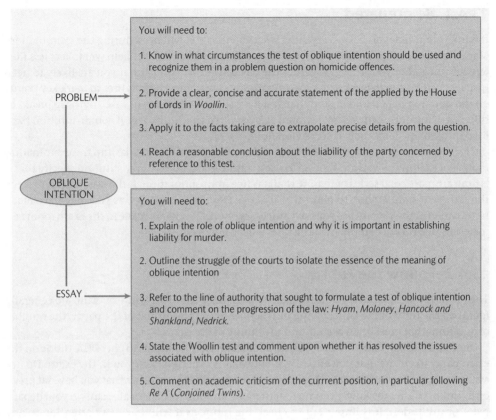

Figure 13.6 The different requirements of essays and problem questions

You will find a more detailed consideration of the requirements of essays and problem questions in chapters 11 and 12. There will also be some discussion of factors that are important in tackling each of these types of question in the sections that follow.

13.4 The exam

It is probably true to say that however much revision you have done and however diligently you have followed the advice in the earlier section of this chapter, you will probably still quail at the thought of the exam itself. Most people dislike exams and suffer from varying degrees of nerves. The following sections are designed to address a range of issues related to the exam with a view to ensuring that you are able to put in a good performance that makes the most of your hard work during the revision period and throughout the year.

It is important that you realize there is not an expectation that you will produce coursework quality answers during exam conditions. Naturally, you will be able to produce less detailed answers during the exam but that does not mean that there should be any sacrifice of the other elements that contribute towards the final answer. Although the primary purpose of the exam is to test knowledge and understanding, it also assesses your ability to use the law to produce structured and discursive essays and methodical answers to problem questions, so it is important to use the exam as an opportunity to demonstrate your legal skills as well as your legal knowledge.

13.4.1 Be prepared

It is important that you have everything with you that you will need during the examination. Many students feel quite stressed on the day of the exam, so it might help you to feel less flustered if you gather your things together the day before. Work out what you are likely to need (pens, pencil for rough work, ruler for underlining case names, highlighter to mark key points on the question paper) and ensure that you have spares as back-up in case anything breaks or runs out of ink during the exam. It would also be worth checking to see if your institution has a list of prohibited items such as correction fluid.

Give some advance thought to any materials you are permitted to take into the examination room. For example, if you are allowed to use a statute book, does your institution specify that it is from any particular series or require that it is free from annotation. If the latter applies, check through your statute book to make sure it is free from any markings, as you may have made notes earlier in the course that you have since forgotten. Checks are made in the exam room and materials that do not comply with the rules will be removed.

13.4.2 Follow the rubric

The rubric is the explanatory notes or instructions that accompany the exam and are generally found on the front of the paper giving instructions about the format of the paper, the number of questions that must be answered, and the timing of the exam.

Once in the exam room, it will be important to take a few moments to check the rubric on the exam paper to ensure that you are clear about what is expected from you in the exam. Do not assume that the requirements of this exam will be the same as any other that you have sat previously unless you are absolutely certain that there is a uniform format for all exams in your department or institution. It is important to check the rubric as it will draw your attention to any compulsory questions or any requirements to answer questions for a particular part of the paper.

13.4.3 Read the paper

Some institutions give you a short period of reading time at the beginning of the exam, during which you can read the paper but you cannot start writing your answers. If your institution does not have this policy, make sure you take a few minutes to read the paper carefully; it does not matter if everyone else has started writing straight away. A few minutes spent analysing the paper and thinking about the requirements of each question and whether or not you would be able to answer it will save you time overall.

It can be useful to make notes about the questions, either on the paper itself (if this is permitted), or on rough paper (if it is provided) or at the back of your answer booklet, to ensure that you have a clear idea of the scope of the questions. This will enable you to make an informed decision about which question to answer. You may find this technique useful for analysing the paper:

1. Write the question numbers on a sheet of paper, leaving a gap of a few lines between each number and note the main topic of the question and whether it is an essay or problem question.

2. On the basis of this information, eliminate any questions that you feel you would prefer not to answer. For example, if there is an essay on misrepresentation and you have a preference for problem questions and did not revise misrepresentation, you can probably rule out the possibility of answering that question from the outset.

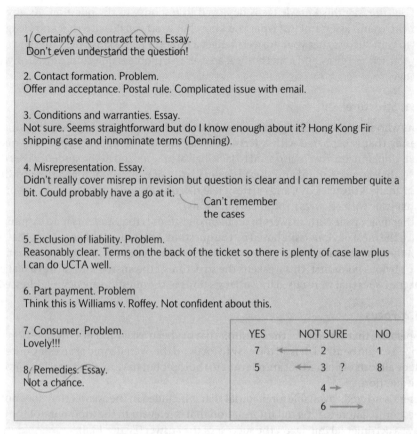

1. Certainty and contract terms. Essay.
Don't even understand the question!

2. Contact formation. Problem.
Offer and acceptance. Postal rule. Complicated issue with email.

3. Conditions and warranties. Essay.
Not sure. Seems straightforward but do I know enough about it? Hong Kong Fir shipping case and innominate terms (Denning).

4. Misrepresentation. Essay.
Didn't really cover misrep in revision but question is clear and I can remember quite a bit. Could probably have a go at it.
— Can't remember the cases

5. Exclusion of liability. Problem.
Reasonably clear. Terms on the back of the ticket so there is plenty of case law plus I can do UCTA well.

6. Part payment. Problem
Think this is Williams v. Roffey. Not confident about this.

7. Consumer. Problem.
Lovely!!!

8. Remedies. Essay.
Not a chance.

YES	NOT SURE	NO
7 ← 2		1
5 ← 3 ?		8
	4 →	
	6 →	

Figure 13.7 Analysing the question paper

3. For the remaining possibilities, look at the questions again and note a few more details about them that might help you to appreciate what they require and whether you might want to tackle them. Bear in mind that it is not enough to know a lot about the topic, you have to be able to answer that particular question.

4. If you are not sure whether or not you would be able to answer a particular question, try making a quick list of the issues you think are raised by the question to see how much information you can generate.

5. Make a note of the questions you feel you could definitely answer. Hopefully this will be sufficient to tackle the paper. If you have ticked more questions than are needed, you will have to make a judgement about which of these to tackle based upon your preferences for the subject matter. If you have not ticked sufficient questions to complete the paper, you will have to revisit some of those that you have crossed off and reconsider whether you could attempt an answer (Figure 13.7).

13.4.4 Plan each answer

It does not take a great deal of time out of the overall time available to write an answer plan and this investment of time tends to pay immense dividends as it leads to a stronger and more focused answer. It is important that you realize it is not just knowledge that attracts marks in the exams, but the way this knowledge is deployed in response to the question. As any form of assessment, exams assess not just what you know but what you do with that knowledge, so it is crucial to your success that your answers reflect a range of legal skills, including the construction of a structured essay and a methodical answer to a problem question, as well as your legal knowledge.

13.4.4.1 Structure

Students who start writing straight away without making a plan often produce a poorly structured essay that is peppered with asterisks and arrows denoting paragraphs that need to be inserted. Unplanned answers also tend to lack logical progression as the student raises different points as they come to mind and this impedes clarity of expression, limits the possibility for depth of analysis (in an essay), and carries a real risk that important material will be omitted (a particular issue with answers to problem questions).

Another major issue with answers to problem questions is that students tend to 'jump in' and deal with the most obvious issue raised by the question. This is usually something that reminds them of the facts of a case or they can remember the issue being discussed in a seminar. By tackling the obvious point first, this weakens the structure of the answer and carries a real possibility that the issues that were raised by earlier sections of the question are never addressed.

13.4.4.2 Focus

It is imperative that you answer the question that has been asked and not the question that you had hoped would be asked. It is all too easy to focus on the overall topic of an essay question and to include all sorts of points that are relevant to the topic but have no bearing whatsoever on the specific question.

As there is no credit available for material that is included in the answer that does not answer the question, a failure to filter out information that is relevant to the topic but not the question can have a detrimental impact on the success of the answer (Figure 13.8).

Question
Critically assess how developments in the past ten years have impacted on the traditional notion of Parliamentary sovereignty expounded by Dicey.

Introduction
The development which has had the most dramatic effect on Dicey's traditional notion of Parliamentary sovereignty is membership of the European Community. This essay will outline the elements of Dicey's traditional view of sovereignty and move on to consider how this has been eroded by the provision of the European Communities Act 1972.

Figure 13.8 Focus on the question

As should be immediately obvious, this essay is going to encounter difficulties as the question specifies a focus on developments in the past ten years, such as the enactment of the Human Rights Act 1998 and devolution, whilst the introduction to the answer makes it clear that the focus is going to be on earlier developments concerning membership of the European Community.

This may be a result of a misreading of the question; it is common for questions on sovereignty to involve a consideration of the impact of the European Communities Act 1972, so it is possible that the student has not paid sufficient attention to the actual question but has made assumptions about its requirements. Alternatively, it may be the case that the student has only revised sovereignty in relation to membership of the European Community, so cannot comment on the Human Rights Act or devolution and is adapting the question to cover material with which he is familiar.

Although these situations are common, they are both the result of bad exam practice and will result in a weak mark for this question as there will be little relevant material.

Such problems can be avoided if care is taken at the planning stage. Write the key words from the question in capitals at the top of your planning page or highlight them on the exam paper so that they are to the forefront of your mind and make a list of points for inclusion that are relevant only to this particular topic within the broader topic.

13.4.5 Writing the answer

This final section will address a range of factors that you need to take into account when writing your exam answers and will conclude with a list of 'top tips' for success in exams.

13.4.5.1 Timing

It is relatively common for students to run out of time and fail to complete the requisite number of questions. Avoid this by dividing the time available by the number of questions to determine how much time is available to answer each question. Factor into this the five minutes that is needed to plan each answer and make yourself a time plan for the exam. Write this down and note the time at which you need to start a fresh question and make sure that you stick to it. In a three-hour paper that requires that you answer four questions, your time plan might look something like this:

Question	Plan	Answer	Finish
7	2pm	2.05	2.45
5	2.45	2.50	3.30
2	3.30	3.35	4.15
3	4.15	4.20	5pm

Figure 13.9 Planning your time

It can also help to write the starting time alongside the relevant question on the exam paper as this might help you to keep to it. It is important that you allocate equal amounts of time for each question (unless there is not an equal weighting between them). There is always a temptation to devote more time to the questions that you feel you can answer more proficiently but this is not a good practice.

In this example, there are four questions to be answered in three-hours. Each carries equal marks, so it would be a mistake to spend the first hour-and-a-half answering your first question, the next hour answering the second, twenty minutes on the third and then having a frantic scribble for the last ten minutes to try to put something down for the final question, and yet this is exactly how many students end up allocating their time. Some students try and avoid doing this by answering the question they feel will be their weakest first on the basis that it will probably not take up so much of their time. This can be a useful strategy but it can also be dispiriting if you are disappointed with the quality of your answer. It is preferable to start with a presumption that each question will take the same amount of time and move on as soon as your chunk of time for a question has finished, irrespective of whether or not your answer is complete. You can always go back and complete the answer if you have time spare at the end.

13.4.5.2 Stick to the plan

If you have taken the time to write a plan, you should try to stick to it. If a fresh idea occurs to you whilst you are writing, rather than putting it straight into your answer, make a note of it in your rough work area and then take a moment to consider where this additional point fits within your plan, what that will do to the structure of your essay, and how it will impact on the other points that you had planned to raise. There is nothing wrong with finding fresh points to include as your answer progresses—sometimes writing out one point jogs your memory about another—but do bear in mind the need for an organized and flowing answer.

13.4.5.3 Incorporate authority

The use of authority in the exam is an issue that tends to trouble students. It is true that your answer will appear more polished and knowledgeable if you are able to incorporate some reference to authority into your answer but it is important that the use of authority demonstrates understanding rather than appearing as if a random selection of case names have been sprinkled over your exam paper.

It may seem as if there is an immense amount of case law to learn and remember but try to identify a few key cases in relation to each topic, with particular emphasis on those that demonstrate essential principles. Remember that it is more important that you know the legal principle from the case rather than the facts but that the facts might help you to demonstrate the operation of the law. Equally, do not trouble your memory with lists of case citations: the name and, if possible, the year will suffice. If you cannot call the case name to mind, draw reference to it by the use of key facts:

> In a reported case in which a tramp dropped his cigarette and failed to deal with the smouldering mattress, it was held that . . .

13.4.5.4 Essays and problem questions

It is important to remember your essay writing and problem-solving skills. It is unfortunate that many students concentrate on putting words on paper in the exam and give insufficient attention to the construction of effective essays and methodical problem answers.

You may like to consult the chapters on essays (chapter 11), problem questions (chapter 12), and writing skills (chapter 10) to remind yourself of the core characteristics that should be presented in a good answer.

The following list draws attention to points that are of particular relevance in an exam context:

- Your essay should have an introduction that identifies the central issue and sets out the structure and content of the essay. This is important as it is the first impression the marker receives of the quality of your answer, so it is worth taking trouble to ensure that the impression conveyed is good.

- Although there is not a requirement of the same level of detail in an essay in an exam as there would be if the same essay were set as coursework, there is still a need for analysis. A wholly descriptive answer will meet with limited success, so remember the need to present an objective and analytical discussion as part of your essay.

- The key to success in problem questions lies with a methodical approach to untangling the facts and identifying the issues that need to be resolved.

- Remember that the key task when answering a problem question is to reach conclusions, even tentative or contingent conclusions, about the liability of the parties. Keep your focus on this and do not become distracted into a lengthy abstract discussion of the law. If you turn the problem question into an essay, you will get very little credit.

- Do not include lengthy outlines of the facts of cases in either an essay or a problem question. It may be appropriate to include some discussion of the facts but make sure this is done in a way that supports, rather than destracts from, the main thrust of your essay or your analysis of a party's liability.

13.4.6 Top tips for exam success

The chapter concludes with some general pointers that should help to strengthen your exam performance.

1. **Answer the correct number of questions.** Some students tackle an extra question if they have done the required number and there is time remaining but you would be better advised to use that time to improve one of your existing answers as you cannot have credit for five questions if the exam requires that you answer four. Equally, some students find that they are struggling to find a question to answer and give up without completing the required number of questions. Always try a last question, even if you feel that your answer will be weak. You will know *something* of relevance to the question—perhaps more than you realize—and it will at least attract some marks whereas making no attempt will attract no marks at all.

2. **Make sure that your script is legible.** You cannot be credited for work that cannot be deciphered. There are various policies on illegibility, so it is impossible to make a generalization about what will happen if your writing cannot be read by the examiners, but options include discounting illegible material altogether, or requiring the student to pay for the script to be typed out so that it can be read.

3. **Stay until the end of the exam.** If you think that you have finished but there is an hour of the exam remaining, it is likely that you have not written enough, so it is important to revisit each of your answers and read them through carefully to see if anything can be added to improve their quality. Have you missed out an important issue in a problem question or omitted a key point in an essay? If you can spend that hour adding material to your answers that increases the grade of each question by two marks, that will give your paper an additional eight marks, which is almost a whole classification.

4. **Follow the instructions.** There is no credit available for material that is outside the scope of the question, so it is essential you read the question carefully and do exactly what is asked. For example, if a problem question in criminal law sets out a series of events and then instructs you to 'discuss Dave's liability for homicide offences', you will receive no marks whatsoever for discussing Kate's liability for murder, or Dave's liability for theft or non-fatal offences. Irrelevant material attracts no credit and takes up time that could be spent writing material that would gain marks.

5. **Keep calm.** Many students find exams stressful and get into such a keyed-up state that they are not functioning properly in the exam. This is counter-productive as it interferes with their performance and this leads to a self-perpetuating cycle as they receive poor exam results, so become even more anxious in the next set of exams. If you are aware that you suffer in this way, take steps to deal with this prior to the exam. There are some excellent courses on dealing with exam nerves and it may be that some are on offer at your institution. Investigate what help is available and take advantage of it.

Practical exercise

 Unlike the other chapters in this book, this chapter has not included any practical exercises or self-test questions. There are, however, a range of practical activities on the Online Resource Centre that are relevant to the material covered in this chapter, including some exercises in marking exam answers written by other students to help you to identify the good and to learn from their mistakes! You will also find a host of sample material that you may find useful in your revision.

CHAPTER SUMMARY

Preparing to revise

- Take time to reflect on the requirements of the exams and the content of each subject to be examined in order to prepare an effective revision timetable

- Tailor your programme of revision to your own strengths and weaknesses as a student

Revision strategies

- Try to avoid exclusive reliance on reading and rewriting notes as a revision strategy as this is a passive approach which does not test your ability to use the material effectively

- Vary the activities that you use as part of your revision. This is to help you to remain engaged and interested in the process and it will aid recollection in the exam

- Consider using a range of methods to record information: written notes, diagrams, pictures, and tape-recordings all engage the brain in a different way

- Involving others in your revision distributes the workload and enriches the revision process

- Writing sample answers is the most effective revision activity as it orientates you to the amount of writing that can be done in the timeframe and enables you to make your mistakes prior to the exam and learn from them in order to strengthen your exam performance

Exam technique

- Make sure you are fully equipped for the exam with writing equipment, any materials that you are entitled to take into the exam room, and a clear knowledge of where and when the exam will take place

- Read the question paper carefully, including the rubric, and analyse each question to determine its requirements so that you can make decisions about which questions to answer at the outset

- Allocate your time equally between the questions and remember to include a five-minute period of planning and, preferably, time at the end to read through your answers, making any necessary amendments

- Do not forget that the ordinary requirements of structure, language, analysis, and application that are applicable to essays and problem questions are still needed in the exam. Answers that demonstrate legal skills as well as legal knowledge tend to be more successful

- Remember to include reference to authority to support your answer

- Answer the required number of questions—no more and no less—in legible handwriting using all of the time available. Pay particular attention to any instructions that accompany the question as there are no marks available for moving outside the requirements of the question

PART III
Practical legal skills

This final part of the book covers some practical legal skills: namely presentations, mooting, and negotiation. These will help you move beyond online and written study to give you a broader range of real-life legal skills. The first chapter in this part will give you the skills you need in order to prepare and deliver an effective oral presentation, covering the issues of content as well as those relating to timing, combating nerves, and engaging the interest of your audience. The second chapter moves on to discuss mooting, which offers unparalleled opportunities for the development of the skills associated with the delivery of a comprehensive and persuasive oral argument as well as providing an opportunity to develop your research skills and enhance your ability to construct and organize a coherent legal argument. Finally, this part will conclude with an introduction to negotiation, which will give you an opportunity to develop a feel for how the law operates in practice and how it affects the lives of real people.

Presentation skills

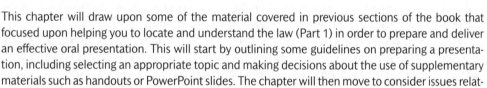

14

This chapter will draw upon some of the material covered in previous sections of the book that focused upon helping you to locate and understand the law (Part 1) in order to prepare and deliver an effective oral presentation. This will start by outlining some guidelines on preparing a presentation, including selecting an appropriate topic and making decisions about the use of supplementary materials such as handouts or PowerPoint slides. The chapter will then move to consider issues relating to the delivery of the presentation, including matters such as timing, combating nerves, and engaging the interest of the audience.

Many students are reluctant to give an oral presentation. For some students, this aversion is so extreme that they will avoid taking optional subjects that include a compulsory presentation element, even if the subject is otherwise one that they would like to study. These feelings are entirely natural; an oral presentation focuses the attention of many people on a single person which makes it a very nerve-wracking situation even for otherwise confident students. However, the ability to present information orally is a core skill for most professionals, not just those working within the law, so it is essential that you overcome any qualms about addressing others. Like anything else, the prospect of giving a presentation is daunting only until you know that you can do it proficiently. Many people are not natural speakers and will always quail at the thought of addressing even a small audience, but the fear does recede with practice so it would be extremely valuable if part of your university development included some attempts to overcome your anxiety about public speaking. This is particularly important given the growing tendency amongst prospective employers to require a presentation from applicants for work placements and training contracts. This chapter aims to equip you to prepare and deliver an easy-to-follow and engaging presentations.

After studying this chapter, you should be able to:

- Select an appropriate topic that fits within the constraints of your course

- Conduct effective research into your presentation topic

- Construct an organized and flowing presentation

- Prepare some appropriate visual aids and use them effectively

- Understand the importance of practising the presentation

- Deal with common problems associated with nerves

- Deliver a comprehensive and engaging presentation

- Take questions from the audience with confidence

- Reflect upon your performance in order to strengthen future presentations

14.1 The presentation process

For most people faced with the need to deliver a presentation, the focus is on the actual delivery of the material. It is usual to think of 'the presentation' as the time-slot in which the material is communicated to the audience. Whilst this is clearly an important time, most of the work required for an effective presentation will be complete before you get to your feet in front of your audience. Planning and preparation are essential prerequisites of a good presentation and yet this 'behind the scenes' activity tends to receive very little attention.

Most students accept that they have to do *something* before standing up and speaking, but there seems to be general uncertainty as to what form this preparation might take and how exactly it prepares you to speak for the required amount of time.

One of the problems seems to be that students omit an essential stage of presentation preparation, treating it as a two-stage process.

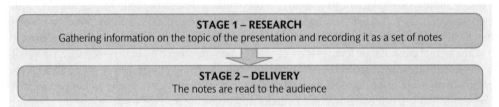

Figure 14.1 Two-stage presentation process

Although this approach does serve the purpose of transmitting the information to the audience, this is not necessarily packaged in a particularly palatable form. In fact, many student presentations are extremely boring because of the way in which the material is delivered: listening to someone read their notes for 10 minutes is not in the least engaging for the audience and it can be very off-putting for the presenter to look around and see a distracted and bored audience.

To overcome these problems, it is valuable to insert a further stage in between research and delivery (Figure 14.2).

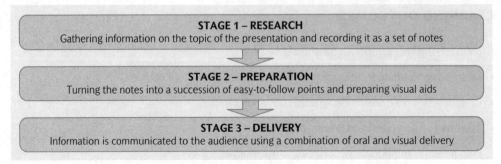

Figure 14.2 Three-stage presentation process

As you will see, by inserting a middle step in the process, the end stage is also different and as a result the presentation is far more engaging for the audience.

It is important to consider a fourth stage that takes place after the presentation is complete. This stage involves a period of review in which the presenter takes stock of the way in which the presentation was received and seeks to identify examples of good and bad practice. The reflection stage maximizes the learning impact of the presentation and should enable you to strengthen future performances (Figure 14.3).

STAGE 4 – REFLECTION
Critical evaluation of the performance in order to improve future presentations

Figure 14.3 The reflection stage

Each of these stages will now be considered in turn to guide you through the process of preparing, constructing, and delivering a presentation as well as providing comment on the reflection stage.

14.2 Research stage

It is always tempting to see the delivery of the presentation itself—the end product—as being of primary importance. After all, it is this that determines the success (or otherwise) of the presentation, irrespective of whether success is measured in terms of the response of the audience or, in the case of an assessed presentation, the mark awarded. However, an effective end product is only possible if the groundwork has been done properly; it is for this reason that the 'five Ps' are often used to emphasize the importance of the pre-delivery stages of a presentation (Figure 14.4).

Proper Planning Prevents Poor Performance!

Figure 14.4 The 'five Ps'

14.2.1 Choosing a topic

In some instances, particularly if the presentation is part of assessed coursework or is a compulsory non-assessed part of a course, the topic of the presentation will be allocated to you. Although this gives you no scope to choose your subject matter, it does ensure that you have a workable presentation topic that gives you a clear direction for your research. This means the topic 'fits' within the time allocated (or is capable of 'fitting' within it), that there is sufficient material available for you to research the topic, and that it is sufficiently linked to the relevant course material.

In the absence of a predetermined topic, you will have to choose an area of law upon which to base your presentation. This can be a tricky business as the success or otherwise of your presentation may depend upon the choice of subject matter, so give it some serious thought and take the following factors into account.

14.2.1.1 Time frame

Choosing an appropriate topic will depend upon the time frame available for your presentation: obviously, a greater level of detail is expected in a 45-minute presentation than would be the case in a 10-minute slot at the start of a tutorial. Never try to cram too much information into the time available. Content overload is a major weakness in a presentation as it tends to leave the audience reeling; it is better to leave material out than to overload your audience with too much information delivered at high speed.

For example, if you have to deliver a 35-minute presentation on employment law, your initial decision might be to focus on sex discrimination. After some preliminary research, you are likely to discover that this is too broad to cover in this time frame. You will therefore need to select a smaller issue such as pregnancy-related dismissals or discrimination on the basis of sexual orientation. It may help to phrase your presentation title as a question — for example, 'how effective is English law in protecting postoperative transsexuals from discrimination?' and ask your lecturer if they feel that the topic will fit within the time frame of the presentation. If your lecturer offers an opinion on the breadth of your topic, do take this into account; they have a clearer idea of the material available and the amount of detail that is appropriate for the time frame of the presentation. Setting the boundaries of your presentation too wide or too narrow can have adverse consequences on its overall success.

- **Too wide:** you will struggle to fit all the information into the time available, so will end up either rushing your delivery, leaving out relevant material, or taking too superficial an approach
- **Too narrow:** you will run out of things to say or fill up time by repeating points or including superfluous material that weakens the focus of the presentation

14.2.1.2 Assessment criteria

If the presentation is assessed, students should check the assessment criteria to determine what attributes are regarded as important and what weight is given to them. Is there an equal emphasis between content and presentation style, for example, and is there any credit available for the use of visual aids?

This can be useful in helping you to select a topic. For example, if credit is available for demonstrating independent research skills, selecting a topic that is covered in detail in the textbook is not going to enable you to demonstrate this skill, so your presentation will not attract a great deal of credit for this element. It may help to make a list of the desirable characteristics of a successful presentation from the assessment criteria and note how your topic will satisfy these characteristics.

It is essential that you know what you are aiming to do and even if it feels as if the answer is to 'survive the presentation,' the ultimate answer will probably be to 'get a good mark in the presentation'; the latter is more likely if you have the assessment criteria in mind from the outset.

14.2.1.3 Aim

Make sure that you are clear about what you are trying to achieve in your presentation. If you have been given a title, what does it suggest about the aim of your presentation? Is it to introduce the topic, to give an overview, or to deal with a particular issue in depth? If you are unclear, seek clarification from your course materials or by asking your lecturer.

If you have free reign to select your own topic, it will add focus to your presentation and make the preparation process easier if you identify a clear aim to be achieved by your presentation. Keep this to the forefront of your mind when researching and planning your presentation and ensure that you inform the audience of this aim from the outset as this will orientate them to what to expect from your presentation.

14.2.1.4 Audience

Although you may have subjective aims in mind when delivering a presentation, such as obtaining a good mark, not looking foolish in front of your friends, or impressing a prospective employer, the predominant aim of any presentation is to communicate something of value to the audience. To be able to do this, you need to have some idea of what the audience want, need, or expect from your presentation. In other words, in order to choose a appropriate topic and select content at a suitable level, you need to understand how much your audience already know about the subject matter.

If you are presenting to your peer group as part of an assessment, you have the advantage of knowing exactly what level of prior knowledge they have about your topic and this will help you to select an appropriate level of depth. Equally, your assessment may specify the level of expertise of your audience by providing instructions such as 'imagine you are have been asked to deliver a 30-minute presentation to senior partners at your law firm that updates them on a recent development in employment law' which will help you to determine what sort of depth is required and this in turn will be useful in selecting an appropriate topic.

14.2.1.5 Available material

You will need to make sure that there is sufficient source material available to enable you to research your presentation topic thoroughly. This means that you need to be able to identify a range of source books, articles, reports, and cases on your chosen topic and be able to obtain them in good time to prepare for your presentation. The increasing availability of online resources may help here, but remember the importance of ensuring that material that you encounter online comes from a reputable academic or professional source.

You will find some valuable guidance on evaluating the source of online materials contained in chapter 7. Remember that anyone can post anything on the Internet, so you should not rely on material for academic purposes unless it comes from a reputable source.

14.2.1.6 Interest and popularity

If you have free choice, it is also useful to take into account any interests of your own within the subject as it is always easier to research something that interests you and your enthusiasm for the topic will communicate to the audience, making your presentation more engaging.

It can also be sensible to take into account any information you have about the choice of topic made by other students. This can be significant if there is an entirely free choice of topic for an assessed presentation as it will be difficult to make your treatment of a topic seem original and interesting if it covers the same material as ten other students have already presented. In short, overlap with topics chosen by others will make your presentation seem uninspired even if it is the result of a great deal of hard work and independent research. If you are committed to presenting on a popular topic, try to find an unusual slant on the material.

14.2.2 Researching the topic

Once you have a clear idea of the topic of the presentation, you can start with the research.

14.2.2.1 Start early

Try to leave as much time as possible to do this before the presentation date in case it is difficult to acquire of some of the material that you need. That said, it is also important to know when to stop the research and start the construction of the presentation as both take time and both make an important contribution to the finished product. Aim for a roughly equal division of the time available between research and construction; you can always go back to research if you find you have overlooked something once you start to put the presentation together.

14.2.2.2 Be focused yet flexible

Achieve a good balance between keeping your focus and being receptive to new material. If your topic was allocated to you, there is far less flexibility to pursue different avenues of research but if you have some element of choice, take some time to follow up potentially interesting side-issues as they may change for the better the slant of your presentation. Remember, however, that if you change the focus of your presentation, you will need to change the title to reflect this. If you were required to submit a title in advance, you should check to find out whether changes are permissible.

14.2.2.3 Be effective in your note-taking

Remember, there is little to be gained by copying reams of material from books and journals, but do ensure that you have a clear and complete record of the sources you have used. Although you are presenting your material orally, you may still be required to produce a bibliography or a research journal and, of course, you may wish to include quotations or extracts from these sources on any handout that you produce to accompany your presentation, in which case you will need to be able to provide full bibliographic details.

In particular, you should take care to keep a note of any ideas you have during the research process about how the material could be used in the presentation. Try to devise a note-taking strategy that allows you to differentiate between factual material and your ideas, e.g. by dividing your page into two columns or by using different coloured ink to highlight your thoughts.

You will find more information on note-taking in chapter 9 that deals with study skills.

14.3 Preparation stage

Once you have conducted your research into your presentation topic, you will probably feel somewhat overwhelmed (a) by the volume of material that you have gathered, and (b) by the prospect of turning it into a presentation. This is not unusual and it is these factors that lead to two of the key factors that limit the effectiveness of student presentations:

1. trying to cover too much information in the time available; and,
2. reading from a set of notes that are not suited to oral delivery.

Both of these problems can be resolved by judicious selection of material and by planning a structured presentation that is not exclusively reliant upon oral delivery but which makes use of visual aids.

14.3.1 Selection of material

It is always tempting, having devoted time and effort to conducting research, to try to make use of all the interesting facts that you have discovered. However, it is important to ensure that you do not exceed the time allocated for your presentation: in fact, if the presentation is assessed, you may actually lose marks for failing to work within the time frame stipulated. Equally, a hurried presentation that skims over a great deal of material is very difficult for the audience to follow and is likely to be a negative factor if your presentation is assessed.

Formulating a question that you will answer in your presentation is a good way to identify your focus and select relevant material as it tends to identify the 'job' that the presentation is trying to do. Once you are clear about what you are trying to achieve, you can sift through all the material you have gathered in order to eliminate that which is not relevant. As with essay writing, remember to judge the relevance of material in relation to the issue, not the topic: in other words, try not to think 'is this about provocation?' or even 'is this about the reasonable man in provocation?' but rather 'does this help me to explain the policy of the law towards the characteristics attributable to the reasonable man in provocation?'. The more specific you are in framing your issue, the easier you will find it to decide whether material is relevant.

Practical exercise

The following exercise can be used to help you determine the relevance of the material to your presentation.

1. Write your title at the top of a blank sheet of paper (or at the start of a new document).

2. Make a bullet point list of all the points that you could include.

3. Review the list, grouping similar points together and eliminating any repetition or overlap.

4. Draw three columns headed: essential, peripheral, and irrelevant and allocate each of your points to one of the columns, remembering that the question of relevance is determined by reference to the specific details of your presentation title and not to the general topic of the presentation.

5. Use this as guidance when determining the content of your presentation, starting with material that you have categorized as essential. If you still feel that you have too much information, you should repeat the exercise, this time using the three columns to divide up the points that you initially categorized as essential.

A worked example of this technique can be found on the Online Resource Centre. You might find it useful to take a few moments to look at this example and read the accompanying notes to ensure that you have a good insight into the prioritization of the material.

14.3.2 Organization of material

Once you have made a preliminary selection of the material to include in the presentation, you need to consider the order in which your points will be made. Bear in mind that your presentation should follow a logical progression, it should 'tell a story' and, like all good essays, it should have a beginning (introduction), middle (the bulk of the presentation, divided into a series of issues), and an end (conclusion) (Figure 14.5).

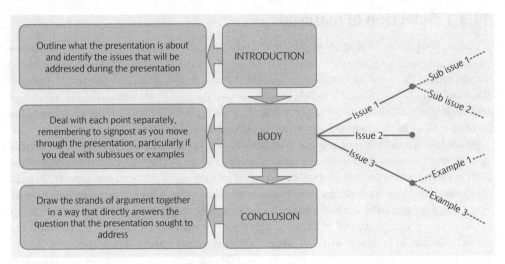

Figure 14.5 Organizing the material

14.3.2.1 Introduction

The introduction and conclusion should be succinct, clear, and straightforward. The introduction should outline the topic to be discussed, explain the structure and duration of the presentation (including any time allocated for questions at the end), and tell the audience why the topic is important and/or interesting. In essence, the introduction should give the audience an understanding of what is to follow and give them a clear and concise account of the question that the presentation will address and the reason that this is important.

14.3.2.2 Main body

The body of the presentation can be more complicated to organize, so keep in mind the argument that you are going to advance and break this down into a series of issues and subissues. Bear in mind that one point should lead into another and that you should take care to select examples that demonstrate the point you are making and do not distract from the flow of your presentation. You may want to experiment with more than one potential structure to ensure that you find the most effective way to organize your material.

For the audience listening to the presentation, there are two tasks that need to be carried out simultaneously. First, they have to digest the point you are making and, secondly, they have to slot this into the bigger picture of the topic as a whole. This can be difficult, so it is essential that you help your audience to following the structure of the presentation with clear signposting; phrases such as 'there are three points of importance here and I shall discuss each in turn' or 'this is a powerful argument but there is an equally compelling counterargument that we must now consider'. Signposting explains to the audience how each piece of information relates to that which precedes and follows it and how it fits into the broader topic, so it is an important consideration and one which can contribute to the success of your presentation.

14.3.2.3 Conclusion

The conclusion should provide a brief summary of the material covered and a direct answer to the question addressed in the presentation. Try to think of a way to make the central message of the presentation stick in the mind of the audience by identifying a maximum of three points that you want them to remember and highlighting these.

You will find some examples of possible wording for the introduction and conclusion on the Online Resource Centre where there are also suggestions for signposting phrases that can help to guide the audience through the main body of the presentation.

14.3.3 Using visual aids

Research into the psychology of effective communication has indicated that people take in more information from visual images than they do from listening. Therefore, it is a good idea to ensure that your presentation engages the eyes as well as the ears of the audience by using visual aids, whether in the form of a handout, use of an overhead projector or a PowerPoint presentation, or by writing/drawing on a whiteboard or flipchart as the presentation progresses.

Effective use of visual aids can achieve the following four objectives (Figure 14.6).

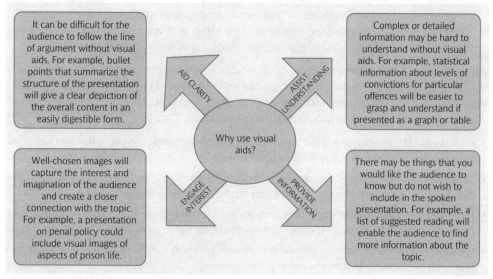

Figure 14.6 Effective use of visual aids

1. **To aid clarity:** a successful presentation is one which can be followed by the audience with ease. Visual aids can add clarity to a presentation by helping the audience to follow the line of argument and see links between the different topics. Look at the figure above which outlines the benefits of visual aids. It has immediate impact in communicating that there are four factors to be taken into account whilst Figure 14.5 on the structure of the presentation makes it apparent that there are three stages but that the second of these is the more complex and detailed. Diagrams, graphs, illustrations, flow charts, and other devices add clarity, so visual aids can have a positive impact on the comprehensibility of your presentation.

2. **To assist understanding:** an oral presentation is a series of spoken words that are constantly replaced by others. The audience has to listen, understand, and keep pace with what you are saying and this may be a struggle, particularly if your presentation is dealing with complex issues. Visual aids will provide a written or pictorial source of reference that the audience can use to help them make sense of what you are saying and to remind themselves of the key points. Equally, it is often said that 'a picture paints a thousand words', so you may find that your audience is more able to understand if you complement your words with illustrations.

3. **To engage interest:** giving the audience something to look at whilst you are speaking can be an excellent way of engaging their interest and, if the images are well-chosen, of capturing their imagination. Most people tend to take in information more readily by observation than they do by listening, so using visual images can really enhance the impact of your presentation. That said, a presentation that is littered with gratuitous illustrations that have only a tenuous link with the material in question will act as a distraction as the audience ponder the connection between the content of the presentation and the seemingly irrelevant illustration.

4. **To provide additional information:** in a limited time frame, you may not be able to cover all the information that the audience needs about a topic or you may have additional points of interest that were not directly relevant to the content of the presentation that you would nonetheless like to communicate the audience (perhaps the issues that were in the third column when you categorized your material) that could be listed on a handout as 'further thinking'. Be sure to give careful thought to including additional information on a handout, however; visual aids are supposed to supplement that spoken word and your presentation is supposed to be a self-contained exposition of a topic, so it is not good practice to use the handout as the repository for all the material that you did not have time to include.

Although there are clear benefits to using visual aids, you should do so only if you are prepared to devote effort to their preparation, as shoddy and ill-prepared visual aids will give a wholly negative impression to the audience. You must also take responsibility for ensuring that you are able to use your chosen visual aids during the presentation:

- Do not leave the production of the handout until the hour before the presentation in case you have printer problems or cannot find a photocopier

- Make sure that the room is equipped with an OHP projector or PowerPoint facilities and check prior to the presentation to make sure that they are operational

- Have a back-up plan in case anything goes wrong with the visual aids. What will you do, for example, if the bulb in the OHP projector blows during the presentation?

- Ensure that the visual aids are visible! It is all too common to find material crowded onto a handout, presumably in order to use as little paper as possible, or to see PowerPoint presentations that use a small font size that means that the audience struggle to read the content

- Consider the use of colour to enliven your presentation. Stick to two or three colours, however, as too much colour will be a distraction and make the visual aids look chaotic. It can be very effective even if you just use coloured paper for the handout

The following section will outline the main types of visual aid that you may wish to use in your presentation and comment on how they can be used to good (and bad) effect. Further on in the chapter, you will find suggestions on how to use these aids during the delivery of the presentation (see section 14.4).

14.3.3.1 Handouts

You should always prepare a handout to accompany your presentation unless you are told not to do so by your lecturer. Even if you are using one of the other visual aids such as PowerPoint, it is still a good idea to provide a handout. A good handout should enable the audience to follow the structure of your presentation and should give them a snapshot of the content that they can supplement with notes if they choose to do so. Moreover, you can include information on the handout that needs to be communicated accurately but that the audience may not be able to note down during the presentation, such as definitions, quotations, statutory references, and case citations.

As such, a handout is a guide and a source of essential information. It should not be overloaded with detail and it should never be a word-for-word copy of your presentation—why would the audience bother to listen if they have been given a transcript of the presentation? A room full of people who are clearly paying no attention when you speak is very off-putting for a presenter, so make sure that you use your visual aids to increase engagement with the audience rather than to distract them or give them an excuse not to listen. Remember, visual aids supplement, rather than replace, the spoken word.

Part of the skill in putting together a handout is thinking about how the information looks on the page. This requires that careful thought is given to the appearance and size of the font used and how the information is spaced out on the page. Think about your own views, positive and negative, of the handouts given to you by lecturers by way of guidance.

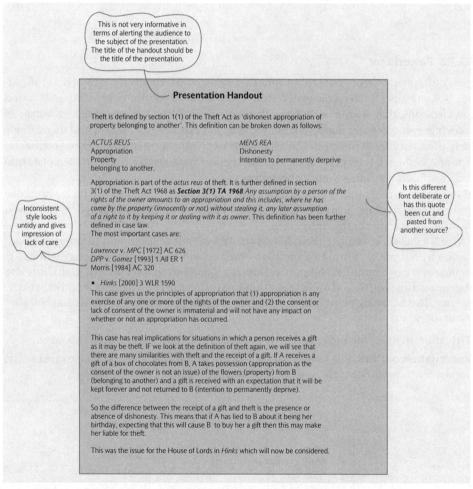

Figure 14.7 An example of a handout concerning theft

Practical exercise

The following exercise can be used to help you to appreciate the qualities that characterize a good handout and the factors that render a handout less useful to the audience.

1. Take a few minutes to read through the handout shown in Figure 14.7.

2. Make a note of the things that you consider to be the strengths and the weaknesses of the handout. You will see that three of the weaknesses have been noted already to give you a start but there are many more points to note remaining.

3. Is there anything lacking that you would want to see included?

4. How useful do you find the handout?

5. Draw out your own version of the handout with a view to making it more user-friendly.

You will find an improved version of the handout on the Online Resource Centre with some commentary on its merits that you may like to compare with your own thoughts. You will also find more examples of handouts with some interactive exercises you can complete online that will help you to evaluate the handouts.

14.3.3.2 PowerPoint

PowerPoint is an excellent visual aid and one that you should certainly try to use if it is at all possible. Not only does it have a range of features, such as the opportunity to incorporate sound and video clips, that are not available with other visual aids, it has the added advantage of improving your computer literacy skills by giving you experience of a new, and increasingly widely-used, package. If you are not familiar with PowerPoint, most institutions run courses on its use and, besides, it is very easy to pick up by experimentation as it is based on a template into which you insert text, images, and other features.

If you decide to use PowerPoint, you should ask your lecturer if the room in which you are due to present is suitable for you to do so; if not, it may be possible to arrange a change of venue if you give sufficient warning of your intentions.

There is some disagreement about how many PowerPoint slides should accompany a presentation with some suggesting an approach based on slides per minute of presentation, e.g. one slide every two minutes. Not only is this rather onerous in long presentations, it is also rather unrealistic; you should use as many slides as you need to communicate your point to the audience. The following points may help you to plan the slides you need to accompany your presentation:

- **Title slide:** this tells the audience who you are and what you are going to talk about.
- **Presentation outline:** this should be used during your introduction as you explain to the audience what points you are going to cover and in what order. For example:

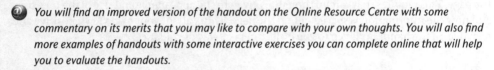

Figure 14.8 An example outline slide

- **Content slides:** the general rule is that there should be one slide for each major concept or idea that you introduce to the audience. You should be relatively sparing with the amount of words used on each slide and remember to keep the font size large: visual aids are not useful if they cannot be read by the audience.

- **Summary slides:** this corresponds with your conclusion and lists the points that you have covered to demonstrate the way that your ideas fit together. It may be spread over several slides if you want to include an 'implications' or 'future directions' section in your presentation.

- **Any questions?:** however much you hope that nobody will ask any questions, most presentations require you to allow time for questions and it is certain that your lecturer will ask something even if nobody else does.

 You will find a sample PowerPoint presentation on the companion website with some additional explanation of the choice and layout of the material.

14.3.3.3 Overhead projectors (OHP)

Until the recent growth in popularity of PowerPoint, OHPs were the main visual aid used during presentations. Most lecture and seminar rooms will have an OHP whereas the facilities to use PowerPoint may not be available in the room in which your presentation is due to take place. If you do plan to use an OHP, it is advisable to visit the room before the presentation and make sure the equipment works, as blown bulbs are a common hazard. It is also a good idea to familiarize yourself with the operation of the OHP prior to the presentation. Make sure you have enough acetate sheets and the correct pens and plan out the spacing of the content carefully: the general rule is no more than seven points of seven words on each sheet. If you are going to print the content, make sure you use a sufficiently large font (no less than point 18) and one that is relatively plain, such as Arial, as this is easier for the audience to read. If you want to include diagrams or graphs that are copies from books or other sources, make sure that these can be reproduced at an appropriate size and that any change of size does not blur the content.

14.3.3.4 Whiteboards and flipcharts

If there is a whiteboard in the room, you may like to use this to note information as the presentation progresses, because this can give quite a dynamic feel to the presentation. It can be particularly useful if you want to show the links between points, such as the overlap between the branches of State in relation to the separation of powers, or if you want to provide a visual depiction of the development of a topic such as noting a chronology, for example.

There are, however, a number of pitfalls for the unwary or inexperienced user of a whiteboard. You need to ensure that your writing is sufficiently clear to ensure that it can be read by all of the audience and you must remember that writing takes longer than speaking, so you may feel ill-at-ease with the silence whilst you are using the whiteboard. Of course, you can speak whilst writing but this means that you are facing away from your audience and you might find it hard to do two different things at once, particularly if you are finding the delivery of the presentation stressful.

Flipcharts are not used very often during student presentations, possibly because they are rarely available, but they can be very effective. Unlike a whiteboard presentation, your materials can be prepared in advance, although there is also the flexibility to write/draw as your presentation progresses. Make sure that your writing is sufficiently large and clear and do not go overboard on the use of colour: one main colour and one accent colour should be sufficient. As with handouts, do not try to crowd too much material on a single sheet of paper—it can be a good idea to plan out the content of each sheet in pencil first to see how it looks before using marker pens. One of their key advantages is that the paper can be annotated lightly in pencil to give you reminders of things to do and say that cannot be seen by the audience during the presentation.

As you can see, there are a range of visual aids available to support your presentation. Although the preparation of visual material can be quite time-consuming, the positive impact that it has on the presentation generally makes it a worthwhile exercise. Many students find that preparing a thoughtful and polished selection of visual aids makes them feel more confident about their presentation; if nothing else, it gives the audience something else to look at, so diverting attention away from the speaker.

Although there is much to be said in their favour, do not feel pressured into using visual aids if you do not feel comfortable in doing so. Some students feel that having to use an OHP, for example, makes them very self-conscious during the presentation whilst others find that worries about whether PowerPoint will work properly add to the overall anxiety that accompanies the presentation. Overall, it is preferable not to use visual aids, other than a handout, if they are going to be more of a hindrance than a help.

14.3.4 Practise

The most important element of preparation is practise. Most people are not used to speaking in public, so it is inevitably something that is going to need a little bit of practise.

14.3.4.1 Why practise?

You must practise your presentation several times over to ensure that:

- The presentation fits within the time allocated to it
- The order of the material is appropriate and one point runs smoothly into another
- There are no tricky words or phrases that trip up your tongue
- You familiarize yourself with the appropriate pace at which to speak
- You become accustomed to hearing your own voice
- You know how and when to use any visual aids
- You identify and eliminate any distracting habits

Many of these points will be more readily addressed if you practise in front of an audience. For example, you may think that your pace of delivery is appropriate but only someone who is listening can tell you whether that is the case. Equally, if you have any odd habits, such as fiddling with a pen or flicking your hair, you are likely to be unaware of this unless it is pointed out to you. Finally, a third party can give you feedback on the most important element of all: whether your presentation makes sense to the audience.

14.3.4.2 What to practise?

Although the obvious answer to this question would seem to be 'the presentation', it is not necessarily useful to devote too much practice time to the actual presentation. There are two separate facets to a good presentation: (1) the subject matter, and (2) the presentation style.

Although you will want to practise the actual presentation for the reasons noted in the preceding section, you should not neglect to practise in order to strengthen your presentation style. Until you are a seasoned public speaker, it might be an idea to practise the two separately, particularly if you are asking an audience of your peers to comment on your presentation as they may be tied up with commenting on the content rather than style.

Practical exercise

The following exercise can be used to help you to practise your presentation style. You will find that it will also help you to work on issues such as the organization of the content of the presentation and incorporating signposting.

1. Choose something that you know extremely well as the topic for a 5-minute presentation. There is no need for it to have any academic merit as the essence of a good presentation is the communication of information, irrespective of the nature of that information. Suitable topics could be (a) good pubs in your home town; (b) favourite sporting activities; or (c) your first term as an undergraduate student.

2. Prepare a presentation on the topic. The idea of the exercise is to evaluate your presentation style, but this will not work if you treat it as a freeflow speaking activity in which you spill forth thoughts without structure. Use some of the techniques suggested in this chapter to help you to structure and organize your presentation.

3. Ask a couple of friends to observe your presentation and comment upon your style. Try to emphasize to them that you want honest and constructive feedback: it is much easier for your friends to say 'that was great' as they do not want to upset you, so you may need to convince them that you want to hear an objective review of the strengths and weaknesses of your technique. It can help to give them a feedback table and ask them to write comments as they may find this easier than voicing any negative views to you in person.

4. Make a list of the strengths and weaknesses that your audience noted. Ask them for suggestions as to what they think would improve on areas of weakness. Reflect upon your own experience as a presenter: how did it feel when you were delivering the material? What things would you change in future presentations?

5. Rework the presentation taking these observations on board and ask your friends to watch it again or present to a different group of friends. The aim is to determine whether you have improved on your previous performance.

You will find some clips of students presenting on ordinary topics on the Online Resource Centre. Have a look at these and note your own comments of the strengths and weaknesses of their presentation style and compare your thoughts with the commentary that accompanies the clips.

Once you have some general insight into your presentation style, it would be useful to practise the actual presentation to work on issues associated with the content. Remember to practise with the visual aids that you plan to use to make sure that you can use these without interrupting the flow of your presentation.

Having considered the mechanics of putting together a presentation, all that remains is to consider how to deliver it to the audience with clarity and confidence.

14.4 Delivery stage

This is the stage of the process that you probably think of as *the* presentation. Having followed the steps outlined in relation to preparation, you should have a presentation in a clear and accessible form, supplemented by carefully constructed visual aids. This section will go through some of the factors that will influence the success of the actual delivery of the presentation.

14.4.1 Delivery style

Your main objective in giving a presentation is to communicate an idea to the audience. This means that they need to be able to understand you. It is your job to make sure that you deliver your presentation in such a way that it is capable of being understood and, more than that, that it is packaged so that the audience *want* to listen. As such, you will need to take the following points into account.

14.4.1.1 Engage with the audience

One of the worst ways to deliver a presentation is to read it to the audience from a prepared script. It leads to a flat and uninteresting delivery, which is very boring for the audience and it often causes the presenter to speak far too quickly. Reading a script also means that you have little or no eye contact with the audience as you have to focus your attention on the page.

The best way to avoid reading a script is not to write one in the first place. There really is no need as you will be familiar with your subject matter and you can ensure that you remind yourself of the order in which the points need to be raised by using cue cards. This frees you to look at the audience (collectively rather than any particular individual) and your delivery will be more natural as a result. Cue cards should be numbered (in case you drop them) and contain short reminders of each key point. Do not be tempted to divide your script into chunks and write these on cue cards as you will find that you merely read from those instead.

It is important also to remember that good written language and good spoken language differ dramatically. Speech tends to involve shorter sentences and more readily understood language than written communication, so if you write a script, the chances are that it will not be in language that is suited to oral delivery.

It is also easier to engage the audience if you replicate the variations in pace and tone that occur in natural speech. Try to make sure that you sound as much like yourself as possible in ordinary conversation, taking into account the need to pace your delivery. It can help to include instructions to remind yourself of these points on the cue cards. Write appropriate phrases such as 'pause', 'slow down', and 'look at the audience' on the cue cards but make sure that you do so in a different colour so that you do not confuse it for the text of your presentation. Nobody wants to engage the audience by making them laugh when you read out 'change the slide' from the cue cards!

Hopefully, you will have gained an awareness of these issues from your practice sessions.

14.4.1.2 Timing, pace, and volume

During the planning stages, you should have taken steps to ensure that your presentation fits within the time allocated to it. Remember that the audience will find it difficult to digest complicated material, so you will need to reduce your speed of delivery so that it is slower than ordinary speech. This can feel strange and it is not uncommon for speakers to start at a measured pace but to pick up speed as the presentation progresses until they are going too fast for the audience.

You will also probably find that you need to speak at a slightly louder volume than you would in ordinary conversation. Your voice will project better to those at the back of the room if you remember to face the audience. This is particularly important when using visual aids: even experienced speakers tend to look at their materials rather than the audience and this can really muffle the voice, so should be avoided.

14.4.1.3 Signpost your presentation

Telling the audience what you are doing makes it so much easier for them to follow the development of your argument. It is good practice to ensure that you start each fresh point with an explanation of how it relates to the rest of your material. If you think about it, there are only three options:

1. **It picks up on something said earlier in the presentation.** Try using phrases such as 'you may remember that I explained this at the start of the presentation' or 'referring back to the definition that I outlined earlier'.

2. **It is one of a series of points.** You can remind the audience of this by using a phrase such as 'the second point to consider here is . . . ' or simply 'secondly'.

3. **It is a move to an entirely new issue or perspective.** Advise the audience of the change by using phrases such as 'having outlined the position under English law, we now need to consider how this has been altered by membership of the EC' or 'that concludes the discussion of dishonesty so I'll move on to consider issues relating to appropriation'.

It also helps your audience to follow your presentation if you signpost your use of visual aids. Simple phrases such as 'this slide lists the four characteristics of an easement' or 'you will find the definition set out in full halfway down the first page of the handout'. Although this may seem like stating the obvious, you must realize that what is obvious to you—who is so familiar with the content and structure of your presentation—is not obvious to the audience. Moreover, it is important to remember that the audience will regard your presentation favourably if you have made life easy for them, so giving frequent clues as to the location of key information or the relevance of a particular point to the overall topic will always create a good impression.

14.4.1.4 Using visual aids

Visual aids are there to support your presentation but they can only do so if you use them effectively.

- Make sure that your handout, slides, or other materials follow the order of your presentation; if you have made last-minute changes to your content, you should check to see whether this necessitates alterations in your materials

- Practise using any equipment so that you are confident you will be able to operate it during the presentation

- Think about where you are going to stand in relation to the equipment. You do not want to block the screen or to have to keep walking across the room to change your slides

- Do not use visual aids as a substitute for speaking, by, for example, telling the audience to read a PowerPoint slide or section of a handout. One of the worst comments that could be made about your performance would be 'lousy presenter but a competent projectionist'

- Talk to the audience and not to the visual aids. Even the most experienced speakers make this mistake, as they look at their own PowerPoint slides or the material they have written on the whiteboard when they are explaining the points, rather than looking at the audience.

14.4.2 Combating nerves

Nerves are a problem for many students who are faced with the prospect of making a presentation. Even students who are confident of speaking out during group discussion in tutorials tend to find the prospect of standing in front of the group and speaking somewhat daunting. One of the best ways of overcoming nerves is to try and isolate what it is that is causing anxiety—knowing what the problem is takes you halfway towards overcoming it. Common fears include the following:

14.4.2.1 Presenting inaccurate material

This is such a common worry and yet it is one that should really not trouble you. If your research and preparation has been thorough, the content of your presentation should be accurate, so there should be no cause for anxiety on that front. Even if it is dreadfully inaccurate, it is extremely unlikely that other students will notice and even less likely that they will point it out. Your lecturer should not interrupt during the presentation, particularly if it is an assessed component of the course, although they may speak to you afterwards if they feel that you have missed the point or made mistakes regarding the law.

If you are particularly worried about inaccuracy; for example, if you feel that you may have misinterpreted the law or missed a vital point, it would be perfectly acceptable to approach your lecturer, explain your worries, and ask him to look at your planned content to ensure that there are no dreadful errors or omissions. If the presentation is assessed, your lecturer may not be able to do this, in which case you could cooperate with other students in the group, asking them to check your work for accuracy and agreeing to do the same for them in return.

14.4.2.2 Forgetting what to say

Thorough research and preparation will have made you extremely familiar with the subject matter, so, provided you have a note of the order in which you want to make points, it is extremely unlikely that you will forget what to say. You should be able to explain all the key concepts in your presentation without relying on any particular form of words. However, this fear tends to lead students to write a full script, which they intend to follow to the last word. As discussed earlier, reading a script (or reciting a memorized script) is not effective as it leads to stilted delivery, a fast delivery pace, and lack of engagement with the audience. Try making a numbered list of the points that you want to make and explaining each of them out loud without any further notes or prompts. The more you practise doing this, the more fluent you will become and this should help your fear of 'drying up' during the presentation recede.

Rather then merely forgetting what to say, you may fear that you will be incapable of speaking; that you will open your mouth but no words will come out. This is a common fear but an exceptionally rare occurrence. If you have never been incapable of speech at any time previously in your life, there is no reason to think that it will happen during your presentation. Of course, the stress of the situation may make your mouth dry—that is an entirely explicable physical response to fear—so make sure that you have some water with you to sip during the presentation. You should practise your opening sentence as often as possible—write it out on cards and pin them up at different places around your room so that you see them all the time; once the first sentence is out, the rest will follow on naturally.

14.4.2.3 Being visible and/or being judged

Probably the most frequently expressed concern arises from the visibility attached to the delivery of a presentation. Most student discussion takes part within a group where there is far less emphasis on any particular group member and where any lack of knowledge is readily concealed. A presentation removes these safety features and focuses uninterrupted attention on one person for a protracted period of time. This visibility and focus renders the speaker vulnerable to the criticism of their peers and it is probably this factor that induces the most anxiety: in fact, you could say that the three points listed above are merely specific examples of the overriding fear of looking foolish in front of others.

There are a couple of points to note here. First, do not imagine for one moment that every member of the audience is actually paying attention. The only person that you can guarantee is actually listening to what you say is the lecturer—even your friends are probably letting their minds drift whilst maintaining expressions of encouragement or polite attention. Secondly, even if people are paying attention, they are doing so out of interest in what you are saying, not because they want to criticize you. In fact, most people will be willing you on to succeed, knowing that they have either survived the experience or have their own presentation to give later that term, so it is really a mistake to assume that there is any negative judgement being directed towards you.

Overall, then, most presentation anxiety arises from a concern about looking foolish in front of others. Most of the reasons that you might feel foolish, such as inaccurate material or forgetting what to say, can be overcome with careful preparation and by practising the presentation several times beforehand. Other factors that might cause concern, such as inability to operate the equipment, can also be addressed by practice. Ultimately, most people do not have to speak in front of others very often, so a presentation is unknown territory and it is human nature to fear the unknown.

You can take various steps to minimize this prior to the presentation, such as ensuring that you become used to speaking out in front of other students by contributing to tutorial discussion. Some students find that the best way to appear confident is to pretend to be confident. They watch those who they consider to be confident presenters and emulate their behaviour. Other students take a contrasting approach by starting the presentation by confessing that they are feeling very nervous.

Practical exercise

The following exercise can be used to help you to practise your presentation style. You will find that it will also help you to work on issues such as the organization of the content of the presentation and incorporating signposting.

1. Have a think about your fears about giving a presentation. Try to articulate these as precisely as possible and note them as a list of numbered points on a sheet of paper.

2. Deal with each numbered point in turn and ask yourself (a) why you think that this will happen, and (b) what the outcome will be if it does happen. For example, you might be afraid that you will run out of time and not be able to deliver all of your presentation. This could result in loss of marks in an assessed presentation.

3. Think of at least two ways that you could stop the problem from arising. For example, you could practise the presentation several times to make sure that it fits within the time allocated and you could review the content to consider which points could be omitted if you run short of time on the actual day.

4. Consider how you will deal with the outcome of your feared situation occurring. In other words, address not just the consequence but the consequence of the consequence! For example, if you run short of time you will lose some marks as a result but it is unlikely to make the difference between a pass and fail, besides which it is unlikely that the course is assessed 100 per cent on the presentation.

By tackling your fears directly, you will be able to think of ways to prevent them from occurring and also to realize that the consequence of their occurrence is not actually as bad as you imagine. You will find some short clips on the Online Resource Centre of students talking about their presentation fears and their experiences when their fears became reality. Watch it and be reassured that your fears are not unique and that, even if the worst happens, you will survive unscathed.

14.4.3 Dealing with questions

Most presentations conclude with a period of time for the audience to ask questions. It is probably fair to say that even the most confident presenter has some qualms about dealing with questions. This is because it is actually the only part of the presentation that you cannot control. If the presentation is assessed, the ability to deal with questions assumes a particular importance because it gives the marker an indication of the depth of the speaker's background knowledge. Try to take into account the following points to help you deal with questions:

- Listen to the question. Concentrate on what the person asking the question is saying rather than worrying that you will not know the answer

- Ask them to repeat the question if you did not follow it or to reword it if you did not understand it

- Take time to think about the answer to ensure that you have something sensible to say rather than saying the first thing that pops into your head just to fill the silence

- Be honest. If you do not know the answer, say so

- Do not talk for too long in answer to any particular question. It will come across as if you are rambling which will detract from the overall impression of your oral presentation skills. Think about your answer and make a couple of succinct points.

14.5 Post-presentation stage

You may think that your task is complete as soon as the final question has been answered and you have taken your seat with a sense of relief and achievement but there is another stage of the process which is frequently overlooked in its importance and that is the post-presentation reflection.

14.5.1 Why reflect?

You should reflect upon your performance in order to ensure that you gain something from the activity, so that you would be a more effective and confident presenter on the next occasion. You may think that once was enough and that you will never be called upon to present again but you cannot be sure of that, so it will maximize the learning potential of the activity if you set aside a little time to reflect upon how the presentation went and what, if anything, you would do differently if you were able to repeat the presentation the following day.

Try and formalize this process a little by making notes so that you have a record of your thoughts whilst they are still fresh in your mind. It will not help you improve in the future if, two years down the line when you need to give a presentation as part of an application for a training contract, you have difficulties calling to mind the topic of your presentation let alone your views on its strengths or weaknesses.

14.5.2 Seek feedback

The process need not take long and you can make use of any feedback that you have been given by your lecturer and by the audience. If the lecturer gave you feedback at the time, it might well have been based as much on content as it was on style and it may have been sanitized a little if there were negative aspects to the presentation, so that you did not feel embarrassed in front of the audience. It would be worth sending the lecturer in question an email to request more tailored feedback. Remember that you will receive a specific answer if you ask a specific question, so rather than saying 'could you give me some more feedback on my presentation?' try asking your lecturer to list three things that they liked about your presentation style and three things that they think that you should change. You may also receive written feedback at some point, particularly if the presentation was assessed.

It may be useful to consider in advance how to elicit the most useful feedback from your audience. Why not prepare a form to distribute at the beginning of the presentation and ask the audience to complete the forms and leave them behind at the end of the presentation? This could take a simple format that could be quite general, to give the audience the ability to note their own thoughts, or it could ask specific questions. Remember, however, not to ask too much of the audience as they are there to listen and learn rather than to provide you with a detailed commentary on your presentation technique.

FEEDBACK FORM

Thank you for attending my presentation on 'The Evolution of Appropriation in the Offence of Theft'

Please take a few moments to note your thoughts about this presentation:

What were the good aspects of the presentation that you enjoyed or thought were useful?

1.

2.

3.

What aspects of the presentation did you think were less good and which you found unhelpful?

1.

2.

3.

Figure 14.9 An example feedback form

CHAPTER SUMMARY

The research stage

- Take care to formulate a presentation topic that takes account of the time frame within which the presentation must be delivered, the availability of material, the aim of the presentation, and the requirements of the assessment criteria

- Start your research as early as possible to ensure you have time to identify and obtain relevant material and make sure that your note-making is effective

- Strive to find an original or interesting slant on the material to ensure that the presentation is interesting, particularly if you are aware that other students are covering the same topic

Preparing the presentation

- Content overload is a major problem for many presentations. Select your topic and the content of the presentation carefully to ensure that you do not try to cram too much material into the time available

- If you are having difficulties in making decision about the content, try ranking each point on the basis of its relevance to the question that your presentation is seeking to answer

- Make sure that your presentation tells a story by giving it a clear introduction, a series of interrelated points within the body of the presentation, and a conclusion that draws together the issues raised and provides a succinct answer to the question posed by the presentation

- Always prepare a handout unless explicitly told not to do so. This should contain a skeleton of the presentation to give the audience an insight into its structure and content as well as noting any detailed information such as quotations that the audience could not be expected to note down during the presentation

- Give careful thought to the selection and presentation of visual aids to ensure that they complement, rather than replace or distract from, the presentation

- Practise, preferably in front of an audience. Present on everyday topics to practise your delivery style and then practise the actual presentation to ensure that it fits within the time frame and that everything flows smoothly

Delivering the presentation

- Try to adopt a style of delivery that is engaging for the audience to listen to and follow. Take particular care with the timing, pace, and volume of your presentation and remember that good spoken English differs enormously from good written English

- Never read from a prepared script. If to recollect the content of the presentation poses a problem, use numbered cue cards with key words and phrases noted that will jolt your memory

- Signposting is essential to enable your audience to follow the line of your argument and to understand how each point relates to others in the presentation. Use a signposting phrase in relation to each new point raised

- Anticipate issues that will cause you to feel nervous and try to formulate a means of pre-empting any problems that you fear may arise. Remember that most people suffer from presentation nerves

- Be prepared to answer questions from the audience. Listen carefully to what is being asked and take a moment to think about the answer before launching into a response

Review and reflection

- Presentations are increasingly required as part of the job application process, so take advantage of this opportunity to become a more accomplished presenter by reflecting upon your performance. Try to be honest with yourself about your limitations as a presenter and find ways to strengthen areas in which there is room for improvement

- Be active and precise in seeking feedback from others about your qualities as a presenter and remember that asking precise questions tends to elicit precise answers

- Circulating a feedback sheet and inviting the audience to complete it is a really valuable source of feedback, as written feedback tends to be more objective, hence more useful to your review of your performance, than face-to-face comment

Mooting skills

15

INTRODUCTION

The focus of this chapter is mooting. It will provide a step-by-step guide to assist students through the process of preparation and delivery of a moot argument with reference made to associated issues such as conducting legal research and production of a skeleton argument. Attention will be drawn, in particular, to aspects of mooting that students tend to find worrying or difficult, such as formulating a flowing argument, developing a confident oral presentation style, and dealing with judicial interventions. This chapter is a general guide that will be invaluable for preparation of any moot but a sample moot is used throughout as a source of specific explanation and illustration.

Participation in a moot will provide an insight into the way that the law is used in practice and also acts as an invaluable introduction to the skills that are required to present a case on appeal. Mooting offers unparalleled opportunities for the development of the skills associated with the delivery of a comprehensive and persuasive oral argument as well as providing an opportunity to develop your research skills and enhance your ability to construct and organize a coherent legal argument. It is this 'skills-richness' that makes mooting an excellent activity for demonstrating a commitment to a career in the legal profession; thus, your level of involvement with these activities should be emphasized on your curriculum vitae and in applications for a pupillage or training contract. Despite the clear benefits of taking part in these activities, many students are reluctant to do so. Although the explanation for this reluctance is usually said to be fear of standing up and presenting an argument, this fear often arises from a lack of understanding of what is required. This chapter seeks to demystify the mooting process and encourage more students to take part in this valuable and ultimately enjoyable activity.

LEARNING OUTCOMES

After studying this chapter, you will be able to:

- Analyse a moot problem and understand its requirements from the perspective of each of the mooters

- Appreciate the role of each of the mooters and be aware of the mechanics of mooting in terms of the timing and delivery of submission

- Engage in detailed and meticulous research and preparation including the production of a skeleton argument and a bundle

- Evaluate the strength of the opponent's argument and check to determine that the authorities relied upon are current and relevant

- Deliver a logical and organized moot speech with confidence and deal with judicial interventions

- Adhere to mooting conventions and the requirements of mooting etiquette including the use of appropriate terminology

15.1 The moot problem

Just as a moot point is one that could be argued either way, a moot revolves around an unsettled legal argument that could go either way depending on the skill of the mooter. It involves a fictitious factual scenario set in one of the appellate courts, generally the Court of Appeal or House of Lords. Two teams of two mooters present submissions for each party and seek to persuade the judge that theirs is the correct interpretation of the law. The example provided is a typical moot problem that demonstrates its characteristics. It is always worth devoting time to the analysis of the moot problem as it has a great deal of essential information to convey to the mooters, as you will see in the sections that follow (see Figure 15.1).

15.1.1 Level of the court (1)

There will always be an indication of the level of the court in which the moot will be heard. Take note of this and ensure that you keep it in mind when researching and constructing your legal argument. It will be influential in the way in which you use authorities and formulate your submissions owing to the doctrine of precedent.

Issues of precedent and the hierarchy of the courts are detailed in chapter 6, so you may like to revisit this and refresh your memory on the 1966 Practice Statement concerning the ability of the House of Lords to depart from its own decisions and the rule in Young v Bristol Aeroplane in relation to the status of Court of Appeal authority.

15.1.2 The case name (2)

You will have been told by the organizer of the moot whether your team represents the appellant or the defendant. Armed with this information, you need to work out which of the parties that means you are representing. In this example, this is straightforward as the first-named party (Pollard) is the appellant and the second-named party (Windsor) is the respondent.

15.1.2.1 Civil cases

In civil cases, the name of the case usually remains the same from inception to completion; a case that is listed as *Pollard* v *Windsor* at first instance would be listed in the same way on appeal, irrespective of which party initiated the appeal. There are exceptions to this general rule. For example, *Nattress* v *Tesco Supermarket* became *Tesco Supermarket* v *Nattress* [1972] 1 AC 153 upon appeal so it is advisable always to check carefully to ensure you are clear about which party you are representing in the moot.

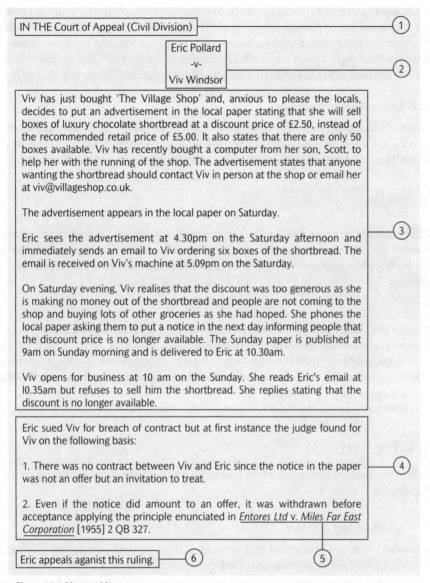

IN THE Court of Appeal (Civil Division) — ①

Eric Pollard
-v-
Viv Windsor — ②

Viv has just bought 'The Village Shop' and, anxious to please the locals, decides to put an advertisement in the local paper stating that she will sell boxes of luxury chocolate shortbread at a discount price of £2.50, instead of the recommended retail price of £5.00. It also states that there are only 50 boxes available. Viv has recently bought a computer from her son, Scott, to help her with the running of the shop. The advertisement states that anyone wanting the shortbread should contact Viv in person at the shop or email her at viv@villageshop.co.uk.

The advertisement appears in the local paper on Saturday.

Eric sees the advertisement at 4.30pm on the Saturday afternoon and immediately sends an email to Viv ordering six boxes of the shortbread. The email is received on Viv's machine at 5.09pm on the Saturday. — ③

On Saturday evening, Viv realises that the discount was too generous as she is making no money out of the shortbread and people are not coming to the shop and buying lots of other groceries as she had hoped. She phones the local paper asking them to put a notice in the next day informing people that the discount price is no longer available. The Sunday paper is published at 9am on Sunday morning and is delivered to Eric at 10.30am.

Viv opens for business at 10 am on the Sunday. She reads Eric's email at l0.35am but refuses to sell him the shortbread. She replies stating that the discount is no longer available.

Eric sued Viv for breach of contract but at first instance the judge found for Viv on the following basis:

1. There was no contract between Viv and Eric since the notice in the paper was not an offer but an invitation to treat. — ④

2. Even if the notice did amount to an offer, it was withdrawn before acceptance applying the principle enunciated in *Entores Ltd* v. *Miles Far East Corporation* [1955] 2 QB 327. — ⑤

Eric appeals aganist this ruling. — ⑥

Figure 15.1 Moot problem

15.1.2.2 Criminal cases

Criminal cases always list the Crown as the first party followed by the name of the defendant: *R* v *Smith*. If the defendant appeals against conviction, this will be listed as *R* v *Smith*. If the defendant is successful in the Court of Appeal and the prosecution appeal against this decision, the case will remain listed as *R* v *Smith*. The only exception to this occurs if the first appeal is initiated by the prosecution, i.e. the appeal is by the Crown against the defendant's acquittal, as this is listed as *DPP* (Director of Public Prosecutions) v *Smith*.

15.1.2.3 Judicial review

Judicial review cases involve a different style of case citation, appearing as either *R* v *Secretary of State for the Environment ex parte Smith* or, if the case is more recent, as *R (Smith)* v *Secretary of State for the Environment.* Irrespective of the method of citation, the parties in a judicial review case are the aggrieved individual or group (Smith) and a public body (Secretary of State for the Environment); the Crown is never an actual party to the proceedings but is named in the citation as judicial review cases are public law matters in which the Crown is notionally representing the interests of the individual or group against the public body.

15.1.2.4 Unrepresented parties

The final style of citation that you might encounter is *Re Smith*. This indicates that the proceedings involve a party who is incapable of representing themselves. This is common in probate cases (dead person), family proceedings (child), or cases involving mental incapacity.

? Self-test questions

 Have a look at the sample moots on the companion website and work out which party is the appellant and the respondent in each case. Compare your answers with those provided on the Online Resource Centre and make sure that you understand the explanations that are also provided.

Overall, the case name gives no indication of which party is the appellant and which is the respondent. It is essential to use the past history of the case and the way in which the grounds of appeal are stated to ascertain the roles of appellant and respondent. It is always painful when mistakes are made and a judge is confronted with two opposing teams who think they are representing the same party. Not only is this embarrassing for the team who made the mistake, it means elimination from the moot and a waste of all the time devoted to preparation.

15.1.3 The facts (3)

The bulk of the information provided in a moot problem is the factual background that led to the dispute.

15.1.3.1 Issues of fact and law

It is important that you remember that these facts were (hypothetically) established at first instance so cannot be changed, reinterpreted, or supplemented in any way. A moot is an argument on a point of law, so there is no scope whatsoever for a re-evaluation of the facts; you must work with the information that is provided. This means that you cannot research (or, worse still, invent) supplementary facts that support your argument. For example, in *Pollard* v *Windsor*, the respondent may want to establish 'normal business hours' for a village shop but cannot refer to figures in *Retail Weekly* that indicate that 98 per cent of small local shops open at 10 a.m. on a Sunday as this is a question of fact and not a question of law.

See chapter 6 for more detail on the distinction between issues of fact and law that will help you to determine what it is permissible to include as part of your moot argument.

15.1.3.2 Make use of the facts

Pay careful attention to the facts. Some mooters present an abstract legal argument on their ground of appeal that is too detached from the particular facts of the appeal. Remember that your job is not only to argue the niceties of the distinction between an offer and an invitation to treat but to *use* this to persuade the judge that the notice in the newspaper was an offer (if you are representing Pollard) or an invitation to treat (for Windsor). Reference to the particular facts of the moot will help you to ground your argument and, because abstraction from the facts is a common weakness, your ability to relate the law to the facts will impress the judge if it is done effectively.

15.1.4 Case history (4)

The past history of the case, i.e. how it was decided at first instance and in any previous appeals, can be useful, particularly if the problem includes details of the reasoning of the judge.

15.1.4.1 Respondent's perspective

For the respondent (who won at the earlier stage of the proceedings), it can be a powerful argument that the decision of the judge at first instance, who had all the facts before him and had the advantage of hearing oral evidence from the parties, should not be disturbed (or the jury decision if the issue involves criminal law). The respondent should pick up on the reasoning given by the judge as the starting point for their submissions.

15.1.4.2 Appellant's perspective

The reasoning of the judge can also assist the appellant as it provides insight into the sort of argument that the respondent is likely to advance, so a fair amount of effort should be devoted to refuting this argument.

Neither party should limit their submissions to the issues raised in the reasoning of the judge but should include this as only one factor to be taken into account when dealing with their point of appeal.

Practical exercise

Pollard v *Windsor* does not give detailed reasoning for the judge's decision at first instance other that to state that reliance was placed upon *Entores*. Have a look at the other moots on the Online Resource Centre that include more detailed reasoning for the earlier decisions and try to determine:

1. how the arguments raised could be used to assist the respondent;

2. how the arguments raised could be used to assist the appellant;

3. what dangers exist if either party fails to take these reasons into account?

You will find some comment on these questions on the Online Resource Centre.

15.1.5 Court authorities (5)

If a moot problem includes reference to a particular case within the facts, this acts as a court authority. This means that it can be used by both the appellants and the respondents without counting towards their allowed number of authorities. Therefore, if *Pollard* v *Windsor* was mooted and the rules stated that each mooter could rely on four cases, this means that each person may use four cases in addition to *Entores Ltd* v *Miles Far East Corporation*.

15.1.6 Grounds of appeal (6)

In *Pollard* v *Windsor*, the grounds of appeal are not specifically stated but can be taken from the two findings of the trial judge. Other moots will phrase this differently and will state 'Eric appeals on the following grounds' (you will see some examples that are differently worded on the Online Resource Centre).

Self-test questions

It is essential to mooting success that you can identify which 'way round' the arguments go—in other words, what are the appellant and respondent respectively arguing? Have a look at *Pollard* v *Windsor*. Senior counsel for the appellant is arguing that the advertisement is an offer but what are the other parties arguing?

1. Junior counsel for the appellant
2. Senior counsel for the respondent
3. Junior counsel for the respondent

 You will find the answers on the Online Resource Centre where you will find other sample moot problems. Make sure that you can identify the argument for each of the mooters in a couple of these and check your conclusions with the answers online.

It is worth noting that it is only a convention that the senior counsel deals with the first ground of appeal and that the junior counsel deals with the second. However, as it is such a well-established convention, if you intend to depart from this, it must be made clear to the judge in the opening submission of the senior counsel.

15.2 Participants

Mooting involves a simulation of an appellate hearing where the focus of the activity is the presentation of arguments on a particular point of law. This can be distinguished from a mock trial which is an enactment of a first instance trial where the focus is on the presentation of evidence and the examination of witnesses. Both activities are excellent vehicles for the development of advocacy skills but the latter is little used, largely owing to the complexities of its organization. Mooting, by contrast, is far easier to organize and can go ahead with just five people—four mooters and a judge—although it is relatively commonplace for the judge to be assisted by a clerk.

15.2.1 Layout and roles

This typical layout shows the relative positioning of the parties in the moot room. It is important to ensure that the judge can see each of the mooters clearly and that the clerk is positioned so that he can communicate easily with both the judge and the mooters (Figure 15.2).

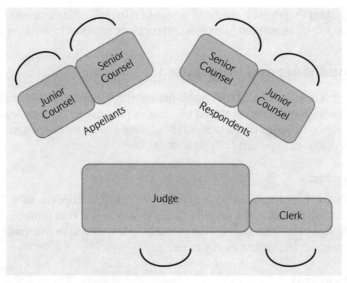

Figure 15.2 A typical moot room layout

Each participant in the moot has a particular job to do (Table 15.1).

Table 15.1 Moot participants and their roles

Participant	Role
Judge	Presides over the moot, hears arguments from counsel, asks questions during the moot, delivers a judgment on the law, and determines which team has won the moot
Clerk	Assists the judge by passing authorities and finding page references, keeps time and indicates how much time is remaining to the mooters
Senior Counsel (Appellant)	Opens the moot and introduces all the parties to the judge, presents the submissions concerning the first point of appeal on behalf of the appellant. In some instances, exercises a right to reply on behalf of himself and his junior
Junior Counsel (Appellant)	Addresses the second point of appeal on behalf of the appellant, ensures that the closing of his speech summarizes both points of appeal and invites the judge to overturn the ruling of the lower court and uphold the appeal
Senior Counsel (Respondent)	Opens the moot for the respondents, presents submissions on the first point of appeal on behalf of the respondent, taking care to address the points raised by senior counsel for the appellant
Junior Counsel (Respondent)	Deals with the second point of appeal, responds to and counters the arguments advanced by the junior counsel for the appellant and closes the submissions for the respondent

In addition to the participants, the **Master of Moot** also has a key role to play in organizing the moot, setting up the room, and overseeing the exchange of skeleton arguments and authorities as well as organizing any refreshments after the moot is complete (usually only if the moot is an internal final or part of a national competition involving teams from visiting institutions). As such, it is important that the role is held by someone reliable who is not averse to putting time into doing the spadework without getting any of the glory attached to winning a moot.

15.2.2 Appellants and Respondents

The two opposing teams are called the appellants and the respondents. Although the job of all the mooters has a strong common theme in terms of presentation of legal arguments with a view to persuading the judge that a particular outcome should be reached, there are distinctions between the job of appellant and respondent.

15.2.2.1 Appellants

The appellants are the team allocated the task of presenting the appeal, so will represent the party who was unsuccessful at the previous hearing. As the side that initiates the appeal, the appellants will set out the reasons why the previous ruling should be overturned. This means that the appellants set the agenda for the moot.

15.2.2.2 Respondents

The respondents, as the name suggests, must *respond* to the points raised by the appellants; in other words, they must tackle each of the submissions made by the appellants as to why the previous ruling should be set aside. Failure to address a submission advanced by the appellants is taken as conceding that point, i.e. accepting that the appellants are correct. Therefore, the respondents must negate the arguments of the appellants before advancing their own submissions.

15.2.2.3 How do the roles differ?

It seems from this that the respondents have a harder task before them than the appellant as they have to tackle the arguments raised by the appellant before they can present their own submissions.

This seeming advantage to the appellants is actually less beneficial than it appears at first glance. An appellant who sets out their own argument without a thought for what opposing counsel will say in response is demonstrating a narrower range of mooting skills than the respondent who has to take note of what the appellant is saying and tailor the response to address the points raised.

Stronger mooters will incorporate an anticipated response into their submissions when acting for the appellant. As the diagram (Figure 15.3) illustrates, this involves the appellant speculating about the way in which the respondent will seek to counter the appellant's submission and then explaining why the respondent's argument is unsatisfactory. By doing this, the appellant makes the work of the respondent much harder as they now not only have to get around the appellant's submission, they also have to find a way to overcome the appellant's anticipated rebuttal of their submission that has not yet been made!

This approach can be extremely effective for the appellant. Of course, it is only speculation about what the respondent *might* argue and it is always galling when the respondent actually advances a wholly different line of argument, particularly if the respondent presents this with an air of incredulity. For example, the respondent may say:

> Senior counsel for the appellant has seen fit to entertain Your Lordship with fanciful arguments based upon a strange interpretation of *Carlill*. My Lord, I would not seek to waste Your Lordship's time with such frivolous arguments based upon a manifest misunderstanding of the law.

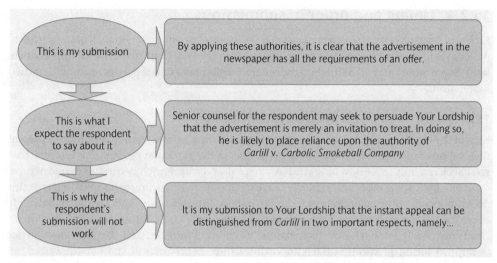

Figure 15.3 Anticipating responses

It would, of course, take a courageous respondent to make such a statement as the judge might respond by saying 'But I was quite convinced by senior counsel for the appellant's use of the authorities. Perhaps you could explain to me why you see them as erroneous'. In general, unless you are feeling exceptionally brave *and* very sure of your own interpretation of the law, it is preferable to take a less scathing approach to the submissions advanced by your opponent.

15.2.3 Senior and junior counsel

Just as it is a well-established mooting myth that it is easier to act as appellant than it is to take the role of respondent, it is also often said that it is easier to act as junior counsel.

So, how true is this?

The main advantage attached to the role of junior counsel is that senior counsel speaks first, so there is never any requirement to be the first person to stand up and speak. For this reason, it is usual that the most experienced of the pair of mooters should act as senior counsel. The allocation of the role of senior counsel to the more experienced (or less nervous) mooter is particular advantageous to the appellants as senior counsel for the appellant utters the first words of the moot and a confident start has obvious advantages. Equally, it is senior counsel for the appellant who will exercise the right to reply if this is available and it makes sense for this role to be given to someone who is less uncomfortable at voicing less practised submissions.

Having the more experienced mooter as senior counsel is less compelling for the respondents. Indeed, some teams of respondents allocate the role of junior counsel to their more experienced mooter for a number of reasons. First, the second ground of appeal is often (but not inevitably) more complex than the first, thus requiring a more adept presentation. Secondly, there is no particular need for experience attached to the role of senior counsel for the respondent. Finally, as junior counsel for the appellant will often be a less experienced or less skilful mooter than senior counsel for the appellant, it can be advantageous if the stronger respondent is pitched against the weaker appellant, particularly as senior counsel for the respondent is (in the absence of a right to reply) the last person that the judge will hear speak, leaving the judge with a favourable opinion of the advocacy skills of the respondents.

15.2.4 Timing and order of submissions

Each moot will have its own rules concerning the amount of time given to each of the parties to present their submissions, including rules relating to the way that this period of time is calculated. Some moots may also stipulate the order in which each of the parties must present their submissions.

15.2.4.1 How much time is available to each mooter?

Each of the mooters will have a particular amount of time allocated to them in which to present their submissions. This varies according to the rules of the particular moot, so it is essential that you check carefully to see how long you have to speak and what is included in this period of time.

For example, some moots may specify that each mooter has 15 minutes to speak but that this does not include time taken in responding to judicial interventions. This approach makes life easier for the mooters because the amount of time available to deliver their submissions is clearly defined. It is much harder to prepare a speech when the rules state that the clock will not be stopped during questioning as it is impossible to predict how many or how few questions the judge will ask and how much of the allocated time will be taken up with judicial questioning.

15.2.4.2 Who speaks when?

The two main options are depicted in the diagram (Figure 15.4). The first approach allows the judge to hear the entirety of the appeal case before hearing from the respondents whereas the second approach ensures that the first point of appeal is dealt with before the second is raised. The first option is more usual but some judges to prefer the second approach, particularly if the points of appeal are complex, so it is worth checking before the moot starts. If the neither the rules nor the

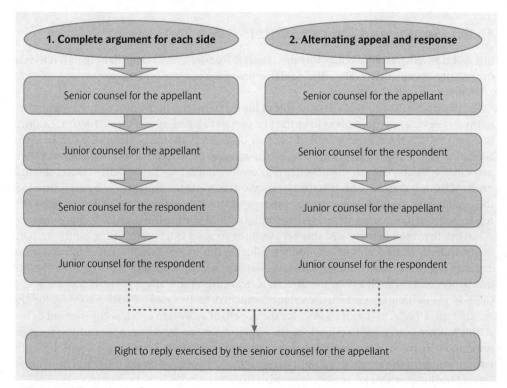

Figure 15.4 Who speaks when?

judge specify an order of play, it is courteous for the opposing teams to reach agreement prior to the commencement of the moot and to ensure that this is communicated to the judge and the clerk.

15.2.4.3 Right to reply

The right to reply gives the appellants one final opportunity to rebut the submissions made by the respondents. This is a right given solely to the appellants (and generally exercised by senior counsel for the appellant on behalf of both senior and junior counsel) because the respondents have already had an opportunity to rebut the appellant's submissions.

Not all moots include a right to reply. This is because the aim is to ensure that each of the mooters have a task of equivalent difficulty before them, hence they all speak for the same amount of time (although some moots allocate more time to senior counsel than junior). As the right to reply is only an issue for senior counsel for the appellant, some competitions take the view that this imposes a greater burden on senior counsel for the appellant.

If there is an option to reply, senior counsel is well advised to exercise it. Judges are aware that it is one of the more difficult tasks in the moot, particularly as it requires the senior to deal with the junior's grounds, plus it means that the appellants have the last word and their submissions are fresh in the judge's mind as he retires to make a decision.

15.3 Researching the moot

Although mooting is associated with advocacy skills and the ability to 'think on one's feet', the contribution of detailed research and preparation to the quality of the speech that is delivered should not be underestimated. It is true that the best mooters are able to bluff their way past any gaps in their knowledge but the thought of being lost for words during the moot is one of the greatest concerns expressed by prospective (and more experienced) mooters and the best way to avoid it is to engage in thorough and meticulous preparation.

15.3.1 Analyse the facts

The starting point for preparation should be an analysis of the moot problem itself. It is a good idea to familiarize yourself with the facts and issues before researching the law. It is true that some mooters prefer to start by researching the legal issues on the basis that a moot concerns a point of law. However, it seems preferable to know what the problem is (the facts) before investigating the answer (the law). By familiarizing yourself with the point of appeal and the relevant facts, you will be able to undertake more purposeful and effective legal research.

15.3.2 Keep focused

Make sure that your point of appeal is at the forefront of your mind at all times to focus your research and your thinking. In the sample moot, the point of appeal for senior counsel for the appellant is simple: the advertisement is an offer. As you will see from the other examples on the Online Resource Centre, this is not always the case and some points of appeal can be several sentences long. If this is the case, then try to reword your point of appeal in the simplest terms (without losing the meaning) to avoid confusion. Some mooters like to write their issue at the top of each page of their notes to help them retain their focus whilst others note it prominently at the top of their copy of the moot problem.

15.3.3 Construct a time line

It is usually useful to construct a time line of events that led to the appeal. Some moot problems span months or even years whilst others, like the sample moot used in this chapter, involve events that occur over more condensed periods of time. Irrespective of the time frame involved, sifting through the facts of the moot and forming a chronology of significant events will help you to form a clear picture of how the situation developed and can be crucial in helping you to identify key issues.

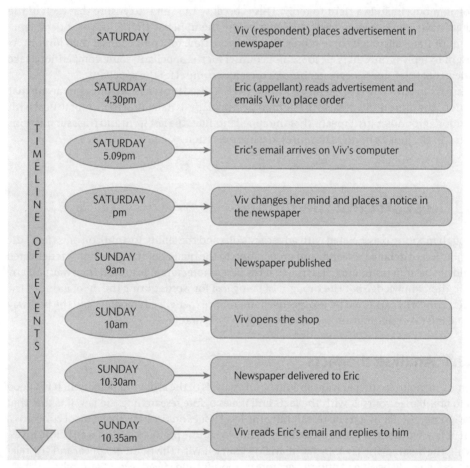

Figure 15.5 Constructing a time line

15.3.4 Search for relevance

Do not forget that each sentence holds information of relevance. You may not be able to work out why a particular fact is relevant at first reading. It may not become apparent until you have researched the law and given the facts further thought. If the relevance of a particular fact remains elusive, it can sometimes be illuminating to consider how the problem would be different if that fact was either altered or entirely absent.

For example, unless you had studied contract recently, you would probably not grasp the significance of the fact that Viv has only fifty boxes of shortbread available. Nonetheless, you should note it as a point that you do not understand and search for its relevance when researching the law. Never ignore facts merely because you do not understand them as they may be crucial to your opponent's argument.

15.3.5 Two sides to the argument

Remember that the point of appeal has been chosen because it can be argued either way, so there are probably as many facts in the problem that support your opponent's argument as there are that support your own.

Never blind yourself to your opponent's argument.

A good mooter knows the opposing argument as well as they know their own, as only if you have considered how your opponent will attack your submissions can you attempt to defend them against this. Scrutinize the facts carefully for information that supports your own stance and for facts which favour your opponent and make a note of these. For example, a preliminary evaluation of the sample moot from the stance of senior counsel for the appellant might elicit the following information.

OFFER (appellant)	INVITATION TO TREAT (respondent)
The subject matter (boxes of shortbread) and the price (£2.50) are stated so there is certainty	But is this just the same as the display of an item with a price label (*Fisher* v *Bell*)?
Viv specifies the means of accepting the offer → What further information could they need for such a simple transaction? ←	Or is she suggesting that people should contact her for further information BUT
Limited boxes are available (isn't there a case about this – something to do with wine?)	But this could mean it is an invitation to treat as she knows that she will have to refuse to sell to some people once her supply runs out
The advertisement states that she *will* sell the shortbread – is this definite language that demonstrates he intention?	Although we do not know the precise wording of the advertisement
Eric assumes Viv is bound to sell the shortbread → Both parties treat it as an offer Viv realises that she has to revoke the offer in order to avoid being bound hence the fresh notice in the newspaper →	Does that matter? Or is she just being courteous to her customers?

Figure 15.6 Evaluating both sides

15.3.6 Identify questions to be answered

Once you have a clear idea of the facts surrounding your point of appeal, you will probably find it relatively straightforward to make a list of questions that need to be answered. Of course, as you have not yet made a start with your research, your list of questions will probably be quite broad and general but it is still worth making a list, as this should identify the core issues and it is always much easier to research if you have a series of questions that need to be answered.

In relation to the sample moot, the following questions would probably appear on the list at this stage of the preparation process:

- What is the definition of an offer and what are its essential characteristics?
- What is the definition of an invitation to treat and what are its essential characteristics?
- Is there case law on advertisements in newspapers?
- What is the relevance of the finite quantity of items?
- If both parties behave as if the advertisement was an offer, does that help my argument?

Having analysed the facts and formulated some questions that need to be addressed, it is time to move on to consider the research process.

15.3.7 Research the law

As a starting point for your moot research, there are two key things that you should seek to find:

1. a concise and accurate statement of the current law, including relevant statutory provisions and case law; and,
2. a clear and relatively detailed summary of the law that provides some indication of the scope of the topic and insight into problem areas.

15.3.7.1 Halsbury's Laws

You will find the first of these in *Halsbury's Laws*, which is a multi-volume encyclopedia of the entirety of English law organized alphabetically by subject area. It is provides a statement of the law and an indication of the leading cases and statutes from which the law is derived. This can give you an excellent early pointer towards material that is relevant to your point of appeal. It is important to make *Halsbury* a starting point for your research as many judges, particularly those who are in practice, will expect you to cite *Halsbury* as a source of any definition of key concepts, particularly if there is no statutory definition, e.g. offer, invitation to treat, the postal rule.

You will find a more detailed guide to locating material using Halsbury's Laws in chapter 8.

15.3.7.2 Textbooks

Although *Halsbury* provides a definition and authority, it will not provide sufficient detail for the totality of the moot. For example, it will provide a definition of offer and invitation to treat but it will not help you to resolve the dilemma that these definitions disclosure, i.e. that the facts of the moot do not fall squarely into either category.

Make sure that you identify and use a range of the leading 'heavyweight' textbooks; a moot judge will not be impressed if you quote from a revision guide as a source of law in the moot. Select a text which goes beyond straightforward description of the law to tackle some of its complexities—you may even find some discussion of the moot point but remember that if the textbook makes your point of appeal seem simple, you need to find a more detailed and analytical text.

Moots tend to require a great depth of knowledge about a relatively narrow aspect of the law, so it will not take you long to grasp the basics from textbooks and be ready to move on to deal with more detailed sources of information. You would also expect to find references to other pertinent materials in your textbook so you should ensure that you look at those texts that offer plentiful footnotes and references to articles and specialist works that deal with the more complex points.

You will find guidance on how to identify and locate materials in chapter 8.

15.3.8 Using cases

Case law should form the bulk of your research for a moot. Starting with the core cases identified by *Halsbury's Laws* and your textbook research, you should read each case carefully, noting the points that support your point of appeal and the points that go against you. It is essential that you do not simply ignore the points that do not fit your argument, as it is likely that the judge will tackle you about this even if your opponent does not. It can be useful to use a two-column approach to organizing your notes that matches the points that favour your argument and the opposing points that favour your opponent.

There are a range of issues to take into account when dealing with case law.

15.3.8.1 Which court heard the case?

Remember the importance of the doctrine of precedent and the hierarchy of the courts. If you are in the Court of Appeal, you are likely to be bound by House of Lords decisions unless you are able to establish that the facts of the appeal are materially different to the case law. A decision of a lower court is of less assistance unless it is the only case that tackles the precise legal issue that is at the heart of your point of appeal.

15.3.8.2 What is the legal issue?

The legal issue is that question that needs to be resolved by application of the law. For example, in the sample moot, the legal issue is whether the advertisement is an offer or an invitation to treat. If you can find a case that deals with the same legal issue as your point of appeal, it is likely that it will be of some assistance to you in preparing your submissions, irrespective of whether the case supports or undermines your argument.

15.3.8.3 What was the *ratio* and what was merely *obiter*?

You should ensure that you have extrapolated the *ratio* from every case on which you seek to rely and on which your opponent places reliance as a routine part of your moot preparation. Remember that only the *ratio* of the case is binding whilst the remainder of the judgment—the *obiter dicta*—is merely persuasive. You should ensure that you can distinguish between the *ratio* and *obiter* statements. Part of your task as a mooter is to convince the judge that your submissions have more legal force than those of your opponent, so do not be afraid to draw the judge's attention to the fact that you are presenting a binding authority to the court (but do so respectfully).

*This is something that students tend to find difficult. You will find more discussion on the distinction and tips on identifying the **ratio** of a case in chapter 6, which should help you to deal with this issue.*

15.3.8.4 In what jurisdiction was the case heard?

This is important as only cases heard within your own jurisdiction—England and Wales—can be binding upon the court. This does include, however, certain decisions of the European Court of Justice (see chapter 6). Cases heard in other jurisdictions, such as Scotland, Ireland, Commonwealth jurisdictions, and other Member States of the European Community, may be persuasive authority. Privy Council decisions are also persuasive as the Judicial Committee of the Privy Council is comprised of Law Lords.

Never overlook the value of persuasive authority in mooting. If the law in this jurisdiction seems to go against you, there is much to be gained by finding overseas authority that deals with the issue in a different way; you may be able to persuade the judge to rule in your favour, particularly if you are mooting in the House of Lords. Be sure to draw the fact that you are relying on a persuasive authority to the attention of the judge rather than hoping that they will not notice and explain why it is useful to the appeal in hand. This will be addressed in more detail in the section below on constructing a moot speech.

You will find a more detailed discussion of the nature of persuasive authorities in chapter 6.

15.3.8.5 Has the case been used in subsequent cases?

Not only can awareness of this alert you to additional authorities but the way in which a case is used in the future can affect its status as an authority.

You should make it a habit to check the status of each case that you encounter; it is very embarrassing (and ultimately fatal to your prospects of success in the moot) to present an argument based upon a case that has been overruled. You should, of course, extend this practice of checking to your opponent's authorities when these are revealed to you upon exchange of skeleton arguments (discussed below at pp. 367–8).

This is a key part of your moot preparation so make sure that you are able to check the status of your cases effectively rather than leaving it to chance. The means by which you can find out how a case has been used since it was decided and the effect of this on its status as an authority are detailed in chapter 6.

 Practical exercise

1. Use one of the methods outlined in chapter 6 to find out how *Entores* has been used in subsequent cases, e.g. has it been applied, distinguished, or overruled?

2. Look at the summaries of any cases that you have identified in *Current Law* to determine whether any of those cases would be of assistance in resolving the issue at the heart of the second point of appeal in the sample moot—whether an email should be treated like a letter or a telex. It is worthwhile to get practice at checking cases in this way as it is a relatively quick and easy way of locating potentially useful resources to support your moot argument.

 Compare your findings to the answers provided on the Online Learning Resource. You will find more practical exercises that involve finding out whether any particular case is still a good authority to use in your moot.

15.3.8.6 Are the facts of the case similar to the facts of the moot?

The closer the factual match between the case and the moot, the more likely it is that you will be able to convince the judge that the case should be followed.

Even if the facts are not identical (and it is very unlikely that you will find an identical set of facts), look for parallels. Conversely, if the case is one that you want to avoid (because it favours your opponent's argument), you will need to point to how the cases differ in order to distinguish the case from the issue before the court.

In the sample moot, the issue is whether an email is more closely analogous to a letter (in which case the postal rule applies) or a telex (the rule relating to instantaneous electronic communications displaces the postal rule). As such, you would need to think what characteristics an email shares with each of the other forms of communication.

15.3.8.7 Which series of reports should be used?

Remember to use the correct version of a case that is reported in more than one set of reports. You will find details of the hierarchy of law reports in chapter 4 but you may find the diagram useful for ease of reference.

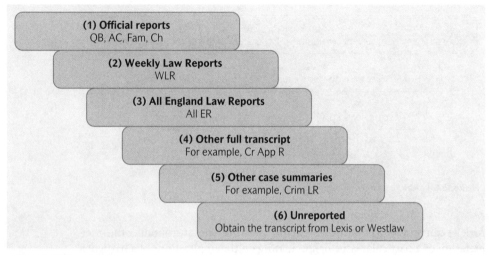

(1) Official reports
QB, AC, Fam, Ch

(2) Weekly Law Reports
WLR

(3) All England Law Reports
All ER

(4) Other full transcript
For example, Cr App R

(5) Other case summaries
For example, Crim LR

(6) Unreported
Obtain the transcript from Lexis or Westlaw

Figure 15.7 Hierarchy of law reports

It is frequently the case that mooters become so focused on the actual delivery of their speech that they forget that a whole range of other factors contribute to a thoroughly prepared and well-polished moot. Little details such as ensuring that you select the most appropriate series of reports for a particular case can go a long way to communicating an impression of professionalism and attention to detail to the judge. In the final decision as to who has won the moot, the judge can be swayed by small details like this if the parties are otherwise evenly matched: a moot can be won by a quarter of a point, so even the smallest detail can be crucial.

Practical exercise

Make sure that you are familiar with the hierarchy of law reports. It is a good idea to practise selecting the most appropriate authority so that it becomes second nature to do so.

 You will find a range of exercises on the Online Resource Centre, many of which involve some quite unusual law reports and overseas authorities as well as further guidance on choosing the appropriate reports to use.

For now, can you put these (fictitious) case citations in the correct order?

1. *R* v *Mulan* [1999] 2 Cr App R 345
2. *R* v *Mulan* [1999] Ch 345
3. *R* v *Mulan* [1998] 3 WLR 1234
4. *R* v *Mulan* [1999] 1 All ER 98
5. *R* v *Mulan* [1998] Crim LR 42

15.3.9 Articles

It can be useful to think of engaging in research for a moot as a staged process whereby you take a progressively deeper look at an increasingly narrow issue (Figure 15.8).

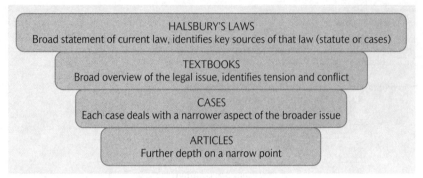

Figure 15.8 Researching a moot problem

Articles can provide a fantastic insight into the intricacies surrounding the interpretation of a particular issue or speculating on the implications of a particular case, so, in a way, can carry some of the weight of formulating your submissions for you. Articles may also provide a means to expand a particular legal principle into a new area in the absence of any case law that considers the issue. For example, the second point of appeal in the sample moot concerns whether an email should be likened to a letter or some other form of communication. As case law has yet to deal with email communications, it may be that you will find an article that looks at the existing law and postulates how it will apply to new forms of communication.

 Practical exercises

Review the methods outlined in chapter 8 for finding articles. Note that the first stage of searching concerns the selection of key words and phrases to use as search terms. What words and phrases would you use to locate articles that might provide insight into the second point of appeal in the sample moot? Using search techniques effectively is a skill that will improve with practice so have a go at finding articles on the following issues:

1. Offer and acceptance by email.

2. The *cy pres* doctrine for charitable purposes concerning animals.

3. Circumstances that render the recipient of a gift liable for theft.

4. Liability for psychiatric injury caused to rescuers.

 Compare your findings with the answers given on the Online Resource Centre. You will find an explanation of the search terms and methods used to locate the material. There are further practical exercises on the Online Resource Centre that will help you to become faster and more effective in locating relevant material.

15.3.9.1 Choosing an article

When relying on articles to support your submissions in a moot, you should bear in mind that the receptiveness of the judge to the article may depend either on the status of the journal in which it was published or the reputation of the author that wrote it. Obviously, you cannot predict the preferences of the judge with regard to articles and it is a sweeping generalization to say that practitioner judges (solicitors, barristers, judges) prefer practitioner publications such as the *New Law Journal* whilst academic judges (lecturers) favour 'heavyweight' publications such as the *Modern Law Review* or the *Criminal Law Review*. Therefore, the best approach to take when choosing articles as authority is to use the one which best supports your argument. If the judge criticizes your choice of authority or asks if you are aware of a different article, try to have a reasoned explanation for your choice:

> I am aware of the shorter piece in the *New Law Journal* but the article to which I have referred Your Lordship is a more detailed analysis of the law.

> I have read the piece to which Your Lordship refers but the article which I rely upon is a more recent consideration of the law that takes into account new case law.

Of course, it may be that there is only one publication on that particular issue, in which case you could advise the judge of this to circumvent any criticisms regarding your choice of authority:

> This is the only academic commentary on this issue, My Lord, thus is the only guidance on the interpretation of this case that is available.

Do try to find out something about the author of an article if you want to rely upon it to support your interpretation of the law. Clearly, an article written by a leading expert with twenty years' experience will be better received than a case note written by a PhD student (not that the latter has no value, far from it, but the former is more likely to carry weight with the judge). Nobody will expect you to have a detailed knowledge of the background of the author, but a general awareness of the level of expertise of the writer will help your case:

> This article was written by so-and-so who is a Professor in Contact Law at the University of *x* who specializes in *x* and is the author of the leading work in this area.

This is preferable to either of the following (both of which are real answers given by mooters in response to a question from the judge about the author of an article they had relied upon):

> I don't know, my lecturer told me to use it.

> She's my criminal law lecturer. She's sitting over there. Do you want a word with her?

15.4 Preparing to moot

Once you have conducted your research and made note of material pertinent to your point of appeal, you will be ready to move into the next stage of preparation which takes you from the research stage to the moment that you enter the moot room. Do not keep these stages too firmly delineated in your mind; it may be that you do not realize that there is a gap in your research until you are putting your submissions together, in which case you will have to do more investigation of the law. Equally, once you receive the skeleton argument from your opponents, you will need to research to find out exactly what it is that you plan to argue.

15.4.1 Constructing submissions

A submission is a strand of argument used to advance your point of appeal. In essence, your moot speech will be comprised of a series of submissions, each one dealing with a separate legal issue. There is no 'right' number of submissions and the same point of appeal could be broken up in several different ways, all of which would be perfectly acceptable. The following examples use the first point of appeal from the sample moot by way of illustration.

15.4.1.1 A single submission

In essence, this approach takes the entirety of the point of appeal and presents it as a single point:

1. The advertisement in the newspaper was an offer.

This has the merit of simplicity but it is not a particularly imaginative way to approach this point of appeal. It would be preferable if at least some information was added to substantiate this view and to make it read a little less like a straightforward 'cut' from the moot problem:

1. There is binding authority upon this court that provides that the advertisement in the newspaper must amount to an offer.

This is a brave approach as it leads the mooter with little space to manoeuvre if the judge does not accept that the authority to which he is directed is binding. A less cut-and-dried alternative might be preferable:

1. The preponderance of authority favours the construction of the advertisement in the newspaper as an offer.

There is nothing wrong with making a single submission but it is worth considering whether your argument could be broken into more digestible chunks for the judge, particularly considering that the average time allocated to each mooter is around 15–20 minutes.

15.4.1.2 Alternative submissions

This approach breaks your speech into chunks and avoids putting all your mooting eggs into a single basket as you are giving the judge two different ways of finding in your favour:

1. The preponderance of authority favours the construction of the advertisement in the newspaper as an offer.
2. Alternatively, if this interpretation is not accepted by the courts, there are compelling policy arguments to support the construction of the advertisement as an offer.

A policy argument is one which is not supported by authority (and which may actually go against authority) but which is nonetheless compelling on, for example, common sense or moral grounds. It may be the case that strict application of case law would lead to a result which seems absurd in the context of the particular facts or the moot, for example, in which case policy grounds may dictate that the letter of the law should not be followed. Policy arguments can be supported by reference to overseas authorities or academic writings as well as case law and statute.

15.4.1.3 Cumulative submissions

This approach also breaks the speech into chunks but by dividing the overall point of appeal into smaller and more manageable segments:

1. The advertisement in the newspaper was sufficiently certain in its terms to amount to an offer.

2. The inclusion of a specified quantity of goods in the advertisement removed any possibility of the vendor being contracted to supply goods that were no longer in existence.

3. The respondent's subsequent actions in placing notification in the newspaper that the goods were no longer available demonstrated that she intended the advertisement to be an offer which would be binding upon acceptance.

It is important to remember that each submission should be a self-contained legal argument that is supported by authority as well as part of a larger legal question. For example, it is true to say that the 'big' legal question in the sample moot is whether the advertisement is an offer but this does break down into a series of subquestions that form the basis of the three submissions above, each of which has been judicially considered in its own right.

15.4.1.4 Combined submissions

As the heading suggests, this approach combines cumulative and alterative submissions:

1. The advertisement in the newspaper was sufficiently certain to amount to an offer.

2. The conduct of the respondent indicated that she intended the advertisement to amount to an offer.

3. Alternatively, even if the authorities do not support these submissions, there are compelling policy arguments that favour the construction of the advertisement as an offer.

This approach is sometimes popular as a means of dividing the submissions that have some basis on legal authority into segments and then adding an alternative argument based upon policy as a 'back stop' if the earlier arguments are unsuccessful. This can be particularly useful if you feel that your arguments based upon legal principle are quite weak.

15.4.2 Preparing a speech

You will now be ready to turn your research and planning into a speech that can be delivered to the judge. Note from the outset that this section refers to the preparation of a speech rather than writing a speech. This is because writing out every word that you intend to address to the judge is one of the most counter-productive activities that you can do when preparing to moot.
There are several reasons for this:

1. **Good written English and good spoken English are not the same.** If you write a speech, you will probably use the same sort of words and phrases that you do when writing an essay, but this is not the sort of language that is best used in oral presentation. Oral communication tends to make use of more straightforward words and you may find that much of a written speech does not flow easily off the tongue when spoken out loud. Take heed of the experience from the early mooting career of one of the authors who wrote a speech that included the phrase 'these cases are clearly of distinguishable material facticity' to which the judge responded 'do you mean that the cases can be distinguished on the facts, counsel? If so, say so. And stop reading your essay and speak to me, preferably in words that I can understand'.

2. **If you write a speech, you will read it.** If you read your speech, it is highly likely that it will sound flat, stilted, and expressionless plus you will not be able to make eye-contact with the judge if you are reading from a sheet of paper. Moreover, if you read, you are likely to lose your place if you take your eyes away from your paper and this is likely to make you flustered and waste valuable time as you shuffle through your paper to find your place (plus, rustling papers tends to annoy most moot judges).

3. **Your speed of delivery will be too fast.** Mooters who read from a prepared speech almost inevitably tend to do so far too quickly for their argument to be comprehensible to the listener. Remember that it takes more time to listen and to digest what you have heard, than it does to speak. Think about your lecturers. You would probably be really infuriated if any of them delivered their material at too fast a pace because it is difficult to take in what they are saying, let alone make a note of it. If you speak rather than read, you will have to think about your words and this is likely to slow your pace of delivery.

4. **Reading does not demonstrate oral presentation skills.** Reading a prepared speech precludes the mooter from exhibiting a whole section of skills that are being evaluated by the judge. Not only does reading reduce your marks in this particular moot, it deprives you of an opportunity to improve upon your oral presentation skills.

5. **A scripted presentation is inflexible.** The judge may ask you a question that raises an issue that you had planned to address later in your speech. If you are tied to your script, you will need to find that point of your speech (more paper rustling) or, if you answer the question without reference to your script, you may find that you actually repeat the same point when you encounter it later in your speech.

That is not to say that you should not take any written material into the moot. Nobody expects you to deliver a 20-minute speech without any written notes whatsoever and you will find that most practitioners have some notes to aid their recollection of the points that they wish to make and the order in which they are to be made. The form of your notes is a matter of personal preference. Many mooters use a series of postcards (always numbered in case you drop them) each of which has a key point whilst others work from a plan that contains a list of numbered points.

You will find some examples of these approaches on the Online Resource Centre.

15.4.2.1 Remember the housekeeping

Your speech must include various issues of housekeeping such as:

- Introductions: senior counsel for the appellant introduces everyone, senior counsel for the respondent introduces himself and his junior, junior counsel introduce themselves
- Summary of the facts: senior counsel for the appellant summarizes the facts of the appeal and senior counsel for the respondent may do so if there is a discrepancy between the team's view of the facts
- Summary of submissions: all mooters must summarize their submissions at the end of their speech
- Handover to the next mooter: all mooters should pass over to the next mooter properly rather than merely stopping and sitting down
- Reminder of the desired outcome: both junior counsel should close by reminding the judge of what they would like him to do, e.g. 'I would invite Your Lordship to uphold the appeal and confirm the finding of the court at first instance'.

15.4.2.2 Practise

It is always advisable to practise your moot speech out loud, preferably to an audience of at least one person, prior to the moot itself and time your presentation. In the absence of an audience, you may have the means to record yourself delivering your speech; there is much to be learned from listening to an audio recording or watching a video recording of your performance. Try to overcome the natural reluctance to see yourself from a third-party perspective and instead take note of practical features: make sure that you are audible, that your pace of delivery is appropriate and that you do not fidget or wave your arms about, for example. Try really to evaluate your performance objectively. You could make a two-column list of good and bad points and then try and think of practical ways in which your could improve on the weaknesses; for example, pausing at the end of key points or looking up towards the judge more often. Then record your performance again and see if it has improved. Even if you have no means of recording yourself, practising will help to you accustom to the sound of your own voice and make the whole experience of standing up alone and speaking a more familiar one.

15.4.3 Skeleton arguments

A skeleton argument is an outline of the submissions to be made in furtherance of the grounds of appeal that give the opposing team and the judge an indication of the nature of your case and the authorities that you intend to rely upon.

IN THE Court of Appeal (Civil Division)

Eric Pollard

-v-

Viv Windsor

Senior counsel for the appellant:

The advertisement in the newspaper was an offer capable of immediate acceptance and not an invitation to treat as contended by the respondents.

1. The advertisement in the newspaper was sufficiently certain in its terms to amount to an offer capable of immediate acceptance.

Fisher v. *Bell* [1961] 1 QB 395
Partridge v. *Crittenden* [1968] 2 All ER 421

2. The inclusion of a specified quantity of goods in the newspaper advertisement removed any possibility that vendor could be contracted to supply goods that were no longer in existence.

Grainger v. *Gough (Surveyor of Taxes)* [1896] AC 325

Junior counsel for the appellant:

The offer contained in the newspaper advertisement had been accepted thus a binding contract was formed prior to the purported revocation by the respondent.

1. A unilateral contract is capable of acceptance by performance. The appellant followed the stipulations of the newspaper advertisement thus a binding contract was formed between the parties.

Carlill v. *Carbolic Smoke Ball Company* [1893] 1 QB 256

2. Even if the contract was not formed by performance, the respondent's revocation was not effective as the principle in *Entores Ltd* v. *Miles Far East Corporation* [1955] 2 QB 327 is not applicable to these facts.

Entores Ltd v. *Miles Far East Corporation* [1955] 2 QB 327
LJ Korbetis v. *Transgrain Shipping BV (The "Alexia M")* [2005] EWHC 1345

Senior Counsel: Mr Gerald Brown
Junior Counsel: Miss Constance Compton

Extract 15.1 Sample skeleton argument

15.4.3.1 Exchange of skeletons

The rules of most competition moots require the exchange of skeleton arguments at least 24 hours prior to the moot whilst some national competitions will require exchange up to three days in advance. This means that you must construct a skeleton argument that outlines your submissions and authorities and provide a copy for the opposing team, usually via the Master of Moots (who will generally send a copy to the judge at this time). Even in internal competitions, an exchange of skeleton arguments or at least an exchange of authorities is usual the day before the moot.

15.4.3.2 Dealing with the opponent's skeleton

Ideally, once you have received your opponent's skeleton argument, you will be able to spend time studying their submissions and reading their authorities in order to ensure familiarity with their argument. It is a grave mistake to neglect this stage of preparation but some mooters take the view that they will still present their own arguments irrespective of the plans of the opposition team. This is an extremely unfortunate attitude and one that can lead to difficulties. In mooting, you should aim to know the opposing arguments as well as you know your own as only then are you in a position to counter them, and studying the opposing team's skeleton should provide a real insight to their approach to the moot.

- Obtain a copy of the authorities upon which the opposing team intend to rely
- Read them carefully, noting the points that have the potential to support their argument and, more importantly, any points that are useful to your submissions
- Are the cases that they have selected good law or have they been doubted or overruled?
- Can the cases they have chosen be distinguished on their facts from the facts of the appeal?

Remember, you cannot alter the wording of your submissions as they appear on the skeleton that you have sent to your opponents, but you can modify the content of your submission to take into account any points that have arisen as a result of the exchange

15.4.3.3 Ethical considerations

Finally, a word about ethical considerations in the preparation of the skeleton argument: ideally, it should contain:

(a) a clear statement of the submissions that will be made; and,

(b) a corresponding list of the authorities that will be used to support these submissions.

Some mooters are reluctant to 'give away' their arguments to the opposing team in advance and try to formulate opaque or, worse still, misleading submissions. The ultimate in unethical behaviour is to include a case, usually a long and complicated one, which the mooters have no intention of using but which is listed on the skeleton to distract and confuse the opposing team. These practices are unacceptable and will be noted by the moot judge. Remember, moots are won by meticulous preparation and persuasive delivery, not by springing surprises on the opposing team.

15.4.4 Bundles

The final point to consider in preparation to moot is the construction of a bundle. A bundle is a collection of material upon which you will be placing reliance during your submissions. In practice, this is generally:

- A copy of the moot problem
- A copy of the skeleton argument

- Copies of each of the cases used by you (if you have individual bundles) or yourself and your partner (if you have a team bundle) in the order that they appear on your skeleton argument for the first time. It is good practice to use the copies of the bound law reports that you will find in the library rather than online transcripts (this is largely because of the pagination).

15.4.4.1 Bundle or no bundle?

In most moots, the preparation of a bundle is left to the discretion of the mooters. Bear in mind that it can be quite costly to prepare a bundle as it requires a fair amount of additional photocopying, so it is only worthwhile doing this if it is going to be an advantage to you.

A good bundle that is used effectively by the mooters can be a real plus but a poorly prepared or ill-used bundle is worse than no bundle at all, so it is not advisable to prepare one unless you do it properly and remember to guide the judge around it.

15.4.4.2 Preparing the bundle

If you decide to produce a bundle, you must be prepared to make full copies of each authority that you intend to use. It is poor practice to include only segments of a case. There is no need to include copies of cases that your opponent intends to use unless you plan to refer to the case in detail yourself, e.g. by quoting from it, in which case it should be included in the bundle. Make sure that you remember to signpost your use of your opponent's authorities, otherwise the judge may think that you have exceeded the number of cases permitted by the rules of the moot.

You should number each page of the bundle and some mooters use numbered dividers to separate the cases so that negotiation of the bundle is easier for the judge. Although you should take all possible measures to make the bundle easy to use, it is generally frowned upon to highlight or otherwise mark significant passages within the judgment, as you are expected to be able to guide the judge there, using appropriate words:

> I refer Your Lordship to the case of Fisher and Bell which was reported in the first volume of the Queen's Bench Reports in 1961 at page three hundred and ninety five. Your Lordship will find this case at Tab 3 of the bundle. I would like to direct Your Lordship to the words of Lord Chief Justice Parker on page three hundred and ninety seven of the judgment, which is at page 17 of the bundle, halfway down the page, paragraph C, sentence commencing 'In my opinion'.

You will find more information on the preparation of a bundle on the Online Resource Centre as well as an animated example of a completed bundle.

15.5 Delivering a moot speech

Although this can seem like the most daunting aspect of mooting, remember that you have a solid background of research and preparation to rely upon. Moreover, the majority of students who do participate in mooting avow that their nerves disappear as soon as they rise to their feet and start speaking to the judge. It can help to concentrate on the first words that you will say to the judge, as you will usually find that the words flow relatively easily once you are started.

15.5.1 Introductions, submissions, and conclusion

The starting point and conclusion of your speech will differ slightly according to the role that you have taken or been allocated in the moot (Figure 15.9).

SENIOR COUNSEL	JUNIOR COUNSEL
Introductions Senior counsel address the judge first on behalf of the appellant or respondent so are responsible for introducing the mooters and the issues to the judge. Senior counsel for the appellant should introduce the appellants and the respondents whereas senior counsel for the respondents should simply introduce themselves and their junior. **Facts** Senior counsel for the appellant should also offer the judge a summary of the facts of the appeal. Senior counsel for the respondent should only deal with the facts of the appeal if he feels that the senior counsel for the appellant has misrepresented them in some significant way. **Conclusion** Although the main responsibility for concluding for the appellant and respondent lies with junior counsel, senior counsel should summarize their submissions as they pass over to their junior.	**Introductions** As junior counsel follow on from their senior counsel, the main introduction will already have been made thus all that is needed is to remind the judge of your name. **Facts** Whilst there is no need to outline the entirety of the facts of the appeal, it is always useful to remind the judge of the key issues that comprise the second point of appeal. **Conclusion** As the last person that the judge will hear speak for either the appellant or the respondent, junior counsel must summarize the submissions of both senior and junior counsel to pull the two strands of the appeal or response together. Junior counsel should invite the judge to grant the appeal and reserve the finding of the trial judge or Court of Appeal (appellant) or dismiss the appeal and uphold the decision of the trial judge or Court of Appeal (respondent).

Figure 15.9 Structuring the speech

It is also good practice for each mooter to outline their submissions to the judge at the start in order to give a clear overview of the structure and content of the speech that will follow. The following is suggested wording for the opening and closing of senior and junior counsel arguments. Remember, there is no magic to any particular form of words; these are merely examples of the approach that could be taken.

Senior counsel for the appellant has the most information to include in the opening:

> If it pleases Your Lordship, my name is Mr Brown and I am senior counsel for Eric Pollard who is the appellant in this case. I am assisted by my junior counsel Miss Compton who will be addressing Your Lordship on the second point of appeal. My learned friends opposite Mr Nugget and Mr Mulan appear for the respondent Mrs Windsor. Would Your Lordship benefit from hearing a summary of the facts of the case? [pause to await a response, provide a brief summary if required and move on] My Lord, I shall be addressing the first point of appeal, namely that the advertisement in the newspaper was an offer and not an invitation to treat as contended by the respondents. I shall be making three submissions in furtherance of this point of appeal, namely: [list them concisely—do not provide the same level of detail that is on the skeleton argument]. My Lord, might I proceed with my first submission?

Senior counsel's closing should be brief:

> In conclusion My Lord, it is the submission of the appellant that the advertisement in the newspaper is sufficiently certain that it can amount to an offer which is capable of immediate acceptance. My learned junior will now address Your Lordship on the question as to the point in time at which the offer was accepted and a binding contract was formed. Unless I can be of further assistance to Your Lordship that concludes my submissions on the first point of appeal.

Junior counsel's opening may be equally concise:

> My Lord, as you have heard, my name is Miss Compton and I shall be addressing the second point of appeal on behalf of the appellant, Mr Pollard, namely, that the offer was accepted and a binding contract formed prior to any purported revocation of the offer by Mrs Windsor. I have two submissions to make in furtherance of this argument: firstly [concise list]. May I proceed with my first submission?

The closing will be more detailed:

> My Lord, you have heard from my learned senior that the authorities favour the construction of the advertisement in the newspaper as an offer and that reliance has been placed in particular on the attitude of the parties themselves towards the situation to support this conclusion. Your Lordship has also heard my submissions concerning the point in time at which the offer was accepted by Mr Pollard and irrespective of whether this is to be taken as the time that the email was sent, when it arrived or at the resumption of trading hours, all these events preceded the notification of revocation to Mr Pollard. Accordingly, I would invite Your Lordship to find in favour of the appellant by upholding the appeal and overturning the decision of the trial judge. Unless Your Lordship has any further questions, that concludes the case for the appellant.

15.5.2 Dealing with judicial interventions

It is almost inevitable that the judge will interrupt the delivery of your submissions to ask questions. This does not mean that your submissions are inaccurate or unclear; it is just part of the practice of mooting that enables the judge to test some of the core skills involved. For example, the judge will be able to ascertain how well you understand the issue at the heart of your point of appeal and the law that relates to it by asking questions and he will also be able to assess how you are able to depart from what you planned to say and then regain the flow of your argument after addressing the question. Keep in mind the following points.

15.5.2.1 Listen to the question

Too many mooters fail to listen to what the judge is asking as their mind is filled with thoughts along with lines of 'oh no, he's asking a question, I won't know the answer and then I'm going to look so stupid'. It is perfectly understandable that the prospect of answering questions might cause you to panic, particularly in the early days of your mooting career, but you cannot hope to give a good answer if you have not listened to the question.

15.5.2.2 Think before answering the question

Even if you have listened to and understood the question and know what to say, it is a good idea not to 'grab' at the question but to think carefully about how to present the answer to its best effect. Remember that it is better to pause and give a reasoned and coherent answer to the question rather than to gabble away with the first words that come into your head.

15.5.2.3 Ask for clarification

There is absolutely no point in trying to answer a question that you do not understand. Ask respectfully: 'I'm afraid that I didn't grasp Your Lordship's meaning' or 'My Lord, I would be obliged if Your Lordship could rephrase the question'. Alternatively, you could rephrase what you understand the question to be to check that this is correct before attempting to answer: 'Am I right in thinking that Your Lordship is asking whether . . . '

15.5.2.4 Deal with the question when it is asked

The judge will sometimes ask a question about an issue or case that you are going to address at a later point in your submissions. It is not good practice to tell the judge that you will deal with this 'later' for several reasons:

- It is impolite to make the judge wait for an answer
- The question must be relevant at this point of your submission or the judge would not have asked it
- It suggests to the judge that you are wedded to a script and cannot depart from it to answer a question

If you are really convinced that answering the question now would ruin the structure of your argument, it is permissible to seek permission to deal with the question later: 'My Lord, I was planning to address this issue at a later point of my submission but, of course, if Your Lordship prefers I will deal with it now'.

15.5.2.5 Provide a clear, concise, and confident answer

Your response to questions should have the same ring of confidence as your submissions and should be relatively concise—it is poor form to keep rambling on in the hope that you will eventually hit on the answer to the question. Check that you have answered the question to the judge's satisfaction; 'Does that address Your Lordship's question?' (never 'Is that alright?'). If you are keen to avoid the possibility that the judge might ask more questions, try asking instead: 'My Lord, might I continue with my submissions?'.

15.5.2.6 Ask for assistance

Ask the judge if you need some time/assistance to answer the question. The judge may say 'no' but there is no harm in asking: 'My Lord, might I take a moment to consult my notes/the authorities so that I am able to address your question fully?' or 'My Lord, may I consult my learned junior?' (as you may not speak to others in the moot room without seeking the permission of the judge).

15.5.2.7 Know when to give up

If you really cannot answer the question, communicate this politely to the judge, stating 'My Lord, with apologies I find that I am unable to assist you on the point, might I return to my submissions'. The judge will usually allow you to do so and will only keep you with the question if he feels that he can guide you to the answer.

 There are a series of video clips demonstrating these and other useful strategies and phrases on the Online Resource Centre.

15.5.3 Using cases

It is usual for a great deal of time to be spent during the moot on the use of cases. The general idea is that the mooter presents principles of law taken from cases and seeks to persuade the judge that they should be applied to the facts of the moot in a particular way. As such, the effective use of cases is an essential part of a polished moot performance.

15.5.3.1 Which cases can I use?

To a certain extent, this depends upon the way that the moot rules are worded. If the rules state that each team can use eight cases, then each mooter within that team can use all eight cases if they wish to do so. If, however, the rules state that each mooter may use four cases each, then you cannot rely upon the four cases used by your mooting partner. Remember that a case which is cited in the facts of the moot is a court authority which can be used in addition to the allocated number of cases. In addition to this, you may use any of the cases relied upon by your opposite number (so senior counsel for the respondent if you are senior counsel for the appellant). In addition to this, you may refer to any material whatsoever, irrespective of whether it has been included on the skeleton argument of any mooter, in response to a judicial question.

15.5.3.2 Correct citation

Just as it is important to use the appropriate series of case reports during the moot, it is also essential that you follow mooting convention when referring to a case. This is best demonstrated by way of example. You will be familiar with the way that a case citation looks on paper:

> *Fisher* v *Bell* [1961] 1 QB 395

If you read that citation out loud, you might say that it is Fisher versus Bell nineteen sixty-one one queue-bee three nine five. This is *not* the correct way to cite a case orally. The following rules apply:

- The 'v' in the case name should be read as 'and' or 'against' and never 'versus' or 'vee'
- The name of the reports is said in full; they are never called by their abbreviation
- Page and volume numbers must be spoken as words and not as numbers, e.g. two hundred and fifty five rather than two five five

Following these conventions, you will be able to read the citation for *Fisher* v *Bell* correctly:

> 'I refer Your Lordship to the case of Fisher and Bell which is reported in the first volume of the Queens Bench Reports for nineteen sixty one at page three hundred and ninety five.'

You would only provide a citation for the case the first time that it is mentioned. On subsequent occasions, it is entirely proper to refer to the case as '*Fisher* and *Bell*'. If you are the respondent and the case has already been cited to the judge, you may refer to it as '*Fisher* and *Bell* as cited by my learned friend opposite'.

15.5.3.3 Summarize the facts

You should always offer the judge a summary of the facts of the case that you seek to rely upon after you have cited it to the court:

- Is Your Lordship familiar with the facts of this case?
- Would Your Lordship like to be reminded of the facts of this case?
- Would Your Lordship like a summary of the facts?

You should prepare a summary of the facts of each case that you intend to present to the court—your own authorities, any court authorities and, if you are the appellant, your opponent's authorities if it is possible that you will refer to them during your submissions as this will be the first time that they are presented to the court.

When you offer a summary of the facts to the judge, they may ask whether the facts are relevant. You need to know the answer to this question as it will become obvious if you are wrong in your answer. The judge is asking you whether you intend to draw parallels between the case cited and the appeal in order to persuade the court to reach the same conclusion or whether you intend to distinguish the facts in order to persuade the court not to follow the case. If so, then the facts are relevant. Alternatively, the facts may have no bearing whatsoever on the issue at stake in the moot but you are merely using the case as authority for a general legal principle. For example, you would cite *Ghosh* in a criminal law moot as authority for the test to be applied to establish dishonesty; you would have no interest in the facts of the case, only the legal principle.

15.5.3.4 Quoting from a case

It is usual to quote from sections of the case. In doing so, it is your job to ensure that the judge can find the passage from which you are quoting: 'I would like to draw Your Lordship's attention to the words of Lord Diplock at page 324 of the judgment [pause for the judge to find that page; watch him, he will look up or nod when he has it] at paragraph B, halfway through the paragraph, sentence beginning 'there is no doubt' [again look at the judge and wait until he indicates that he has found that right place and then begin to quote]. You would pause at the end of the quotation to denote to the judge that you have finished and then recommence your submissions, preferably by explaining how that quotation applies to the facts of the moot.

Never quote from the headnote (anything said in the headnote will also be in the main body of the judgment) or from the speeches of counsel.

CHAPTER SUMMARY

Getting started

- Make sure that you understand the roles of the different parties involved in a moot. It is a good idea to watch a moot or look at the clips in the Online Resource Centre to ensure you are clear about what happens when and how

- Analyse the moot problem carefully to ensure that you know what party you are representing, what ground of appeal you are addressing, and what the relevant facts are that make up the issue in hand

- Take care to ensure that you are familiar with the rules of the moot in relation to such matters as the number of cases that can be used and the time available for each mooter to present their submissions

Researching the moot

- Remember that you need to start with an accurate and authoritative statement of law so *Halsbury* might be a useful port of call

- Add depth to your understanding by reference to leading textbooks, articles, and cases

- Keep a strong focus on the central issue of the point of appeal and ensure that you take a balanced approach that notes rather than ignores opposing authority

- Be thoughtful in your selection of authorities and supporting material. Be prepared to justify your choice of cases to the judge if questioned

Preparing to moot

- Experiment with different structures and vary the content of your submissions until you find an approach that feels right. Your final choice of submissions should be the result of careful planning rather than being based on the first submissions that came to mind

- Prepare your submissions and note the main points on numbered cue cards. Never write a complete script or you will be tempted to read it and this is a cardinal mooting sin

- Leave yourself sufficient time to practise on several occasions before the moot, preferably in front of an audience of at least one person who will give you honest and constructive feedback on your performance. Alternatively, watching a recording of yourself can be a good way to gain insight into your performance

- Construct a clear and concise yet open and honest skeleton argument and ensure you meet the deadline for exchange

- If you decide to use a bundle, make sure that it is meticulously presented and that you are able to use it effectively, otherwise it will do you more harm than good

- Check each authority upon which you intend to place reliance to ensure that it is still good law and that you have the correct and appropriate series of law reports

Delivering the moot speech

- Try and make a confident start however nervous you may be feeling. Most people find that they forget about the presence of anyone else other than the judge once they have started to speak so it is effectively a two-person dialogue

- Take heed of courtroom etiquette at all times. In particular, make sure you address the judge appropriately as My Lord or Your Lordship and never Judge or Your Worship

- Do not stray too far from the facts of the moot. Abstract statements of law are all very well and good but your key task is to use that law to persuade the judge to find in your favour in the moot. The judge will not do this unless you explain how the law applies to the set of facts before him

- Deal with judicial interventions when asked to do so and in a confident manner. Do not be afraid to ask for clarification or time to think

- Make sure you give the judge time to find his place in a case or in your bundle. Pause frequently and watch the judge to see if he is keeping pace with you. Do not carry on regardless and hope he catches up. There is nothing to fear in silence so stand quietly and wait until the judge looks at you as this is a sign that he is ready for you to speak

Negotiation skills

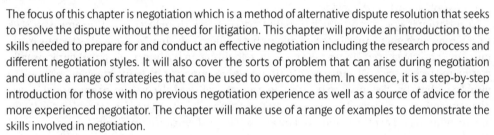

16

INTRODUCTION

The focus of this chapter is negotiation which is a method of alternative dispute resolution that seeks to resolve the dispute without the need for litigation. This chapter will provide an introduction to the skills needed to prepare for and conduct an effective negotiation including the research process and different negotiation styles. It will also cover the sorts of problem that can arise during negotiation and outline a range of strategies that can be used to overcome them. In essence, it is a step-by-step introduction for those with no previous negotiation experience as well as a source of advice for the more experienced negotiator. The chapter will make use of a range of examples to demonstrate the skills involved in negotiation.

The role of alternative dispute resolution has increased dramatically in recent years with approximately 90 per cent of civil and family disputes settled by negotiation or mediation rather than in the courtroom. It plays a role in the lives of most legal professionals and the ability to conduct an effective negotiation that reaches a settlement which is acceptable to both parties is an important legal skill. It is increasingly common for negotiation to feature in the lives of undergraduate law students, as well as those on the LPC and BVC, either as an extra-curricular activity or as part of the skills programme that is embedded within the curriculum. Participation in negotiation will give you a feel of how the law operates in practice as opposed to limiting your experience to 'law on paper' and it demonstrates a commitment to the development of legal skills that should strengthen your curriculum vitae.

LEARNING OUTCOMES

After studying this chapter, you should be able to:

- Appreciate the role of negotiation in professional practice and have some insight into skills necessary to conduct an effective negotiation

- Analyse a negotiation scenario and extrapolate information that provides insight into the aims and interests of the client

- Engage in preparation and planning for the negotiation which includes detailed research into the legal and factual issues

- Open the negotiation in a professional manner and establish a workable agenda of issues that need to be addressed during the negotiation

- Deal with each of the issues in an effective and ethical manner, eliciting information from the other team and asking questions to clarify areas of uncertainty

- Engage in critical reflection of the success of the negotiation and your performance in a way that enables you to use the experience as an opportunity for skills development

16.1 About negotiation

There are three main forms of alternative dispute resolution: negotiation, mediation, and arbitration. Greater attention has focused on ADR since emphasis was placed on their importance in the Woolf Report.[1]

Negotiation is a process by which (usually) two parties with an interest in the same issue seek to reach an agreement that is acceptable to both sides. This may be done directly but is frequently done via lawyers. It can take place by telephone, in writing, or by email but is usually conducted face-to-face. Distance negotiations give less opportunity to interpret and respond to visual cues but that distance can be preferable when dealing with complex or emotional issues. Many negotiations use combined methods; for example, an initial meeting at which the issues are introduced and explored, followed by an exchange of written communications and a final face-to-face negotiation to finalize the details of the agreement.

Agreement between the parties is the essence of negotiation. Without agreement, there is not settlement, unlike arbitration where a third party is able to impose an outcome on the parties, making it more akin to litigation. Mediation is more similar to negotiation except that, rather than the face-to-face oppositional process that characterizes negotiation, proceedings are controlled by a mediator who coordinates and facilities the discussion. Although mediators are objective, they are able to introduce issues for discussion whereas parties to negotiation have direct control over which issues are discussed.

Negotiations can occur at any stage in the proceedings and can feature in most types of dispute. Even in criminal law, there is scope for negotiation prior to court proceedings as representatives of the defendant can explore the possibilities for withdrawing or altering the charges for the CPS.

In recognition of the importance of negotiation as a legal skill, there is a national negotiation competition each year which is open to teams of undergraduate and postgraduate students and is organized by the Centre for Effective Dispute Resolution.[2]

16.1.1 Types of negotiation

It is generally accepted that there are two main types of negotiation (although the terminology used to despite these categories varies) (Figure 16.1).

---

1. Lord Woolf, *Access to Justice: Interim Report* (www.lcd.gov.uk, June 1995).
2. You can find out more about the negotiation competition and the work of CEDR more generally by visiting their website: www.cedr.co.uk.

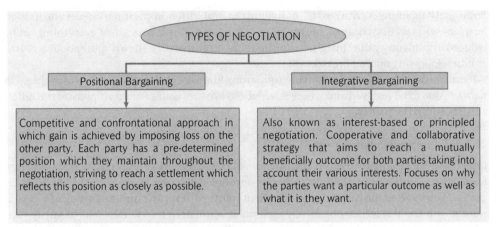

Figure 16.1 Positional and integrative bargaining

16.1.1.1 Positional bargaining

This approach is best deployed in situations where the issue is purely financial, there are no other issues to take into account, and no need to preserve amicable relations between the parties.

Jack damaged two panels of his neighbour's fence beyond repair and agrees to pay for replacements. Charlie, his neighbour, maintains that Jack should pay for the entire fence (10 panels) to be replaced as two new panels would stand out and spoil the look of the garden. He also demands top quality panels (£50 each) whilst Jack proposes to provide average quality panels (£30 each). Charlie can fit the panels himself and there are no delivery costs.

The sum payable could be calculated four different ways:

- Two panels of average quality   £60
- Two panels of high quality   £100
- Ten panels of average quality   £300
- Ten panels of high quality   £1000

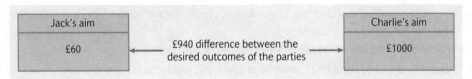

Figure 16.2 Positional bargaining

From a positional bargaining perspective, every pound gained for Charlie leaves Jack one pound worse off. This is described as a zero-sum game.

Zero-sum game describes a situation in which one party's gain is equivalent to the other party's loss. In the example above, if you calculate one party's gain and deduct the other party's loss, the total would be zero. It is useful to think of this in terms of sharing out a pie: the larger the slice taken by A, the smaller the piece remaining for B.

Positional bargaining is criticized for its inability to deal with non-pecuniary issues and its ineffectiveness in tackling complex negotiations involving multiple issues. Not everything can be reduced to monetary value: imagine using financial incentives to settle a dispute about access to children following marital breakdown.

It can be useful in negotiations involving a strong financial element or one in which there is a narrow issue to be resolved and where reference to broader issues would emphasize the differences between the parties.

16.1.1.2 Integrative bargaining

Integrative bargaining focuses on the interests of the parties. It focuses on the client's needs, fears, desires, and emotions in order to reach a negotiated outcome that is compatible with their goals. If you focus exclusively on *what* the client wants without any understanding of *why* that want it, you could reach an objectively reasonable settlement that wholly fails to satisfy your client's subjective interests as this simple example illustrates:

> Stuart and Neil are arguing over one remaining orange. Their mother, Wendy, cuts the orange in half and gives half to each child, seeing this as a perfect compromise. However, if she had asked *why* each child wanted the orange, Wendy would have discovered that each had a different assignment at school the following day that involved part of an orange: Stuart needed the juice for home economics whilst Neil needed the peel for an art class. As such, Wendy's objectively fair solution failed to meet the subjective needs of either child whereas asking *why* they wanted the orange would have led to a different basis for division that would have given each child exactly what they wanted.

As this example shows, it is not useful to make assumptions about a client's goals or to impose your interpretation of a good outcome on the client. With knowledge of the client's goals, you will be able to negotiate more flexibly to achieve these in the face of unexpected offers from the other side.

 Self-test questions

Make a note of the sorts of interests that could be at stake in the following situations for each party. Remember, you need to move beyond an identification of *what* each party might want in order to discover *why* they want it.

1. A husband and wife engaged in negotiations for his access to their children following the breakdown of the marriage.

2. Negotiations for the sale of a house between the vendor and purchaser.

3. Contract negotiations undertaken on behalf of a professional golfer and a new sponsor.

4. The owner of a hotel and a carpet fitter concerning the supply and installation of new carpets.

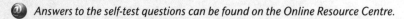 *Answers to the self-test questions can be found on the Online Resource Centre.*

Even in cases which appear to be limited to negotiations of a financial nature, integrative bargaining can be a more effective approach to adopt than positional bargaining. A client whose instruction is to obtain the highest financial settlement possible may actually want money for a number of reasons. Asking *why* should provide insight into the issues motivating the client and therefore give you greater flexibility in achieving a favourable settlement.

Asking *why* may be useful even in situations that appear to be exclusively financial and may give greater flexibility and creativity in reaching a favourable settlement that fulfils the client's needs.

> Gerald agreed to renovate Diane's classic car by the end of March but fell behind schedule and is in breach of contract. Gerald has completed most of the work and has purchased some expensive parts but Diane wants her money refunded in full.

This seems straightforward but further insight is provided by enquiring into Diane's goals. She needs the money to pay Bruno who has agreed to fix the car within a week. Diane needs the car within this time so that it can be used at her sister's wedding. Awareness of this goal gives more flexibility to negotiate with Gerald on non-financial terms as Gerald is able to offer Diane a choice of three classic cars to use for her sister's wedding if she agrees to allow him to complete work on her car and keep the payment that has been made.

This should go some way to demonstrating the benefits of looking beyond the seemingly straightforward financial aspects of a dispute in order to find a more creative solution.

16.2 Negotiation skills

It is likely that you have a great many of the skills needed to negotiate already. Most people do as we learn how to make bargains from a very early age. Think of the sorts of deal that are struck between parents and children.

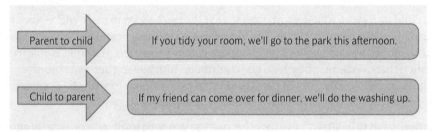

Figure 16.3 Deals between parent and child

Various factors will influence the success of the negotiation. For example, the child may think that a trip to the park does not justify the effort of tidying his room whilst the parent may feel that the responsibility of feeding and entertaining another child is too onerous to be repaid by washing-up.

Experience teaches us to deal with more complex negotiations in which more accurate predictions are made about factors that will act as an incentive to the other party (Figure 16.4).

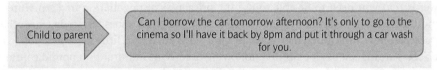

Figure 16.4 A more complex deal between parent and child

The child attempts to predict factors that might deter the parent from accepting the bargain and negate them in order to gain agreement (a venue not associated with alcohol consumption and an early return time). This is supported with an incentive (washing the car) that involves little effort or loss to the child but which is consistent with the notion of taking care of another's property.

We also learn the value of allowing room for manoeuvre and of asking questions to elicit information about the concerns of the other party.

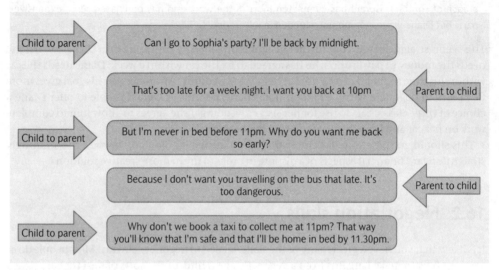

Figure 16.5 Room to manoeuvre

The child starts with a later return time so that she can be seen to make concessions but still stay until the desired time of 11 p.m. This gives room for movement and prevents an appearance of stubbornness. By asking questions about the parent's concerns, the child is able to make a suggestion that overcomes these fears and contributes to achieving her own objective.

From these simple examples of negotiation that have resonance with the everyday experience of many people, we can identify some key negotiation strategies:

- The deal needs to be attractive to the other party so you need to offer them something of value
- Find out (by asking questions) or predict (on the basis of your knowledge of the other party) what will hold value for them
- Enhance your offer by 'throwing in' things of little value to you (this illustrates the variable nature of 'value': what holds value for one person may be of little significance to another)
- Keep the tone of negotiation amicable by making reasonable offers that leave you room to manoeuvre

You may wonder why you need this chapter if negotiation skills are learned in childhood. The answer is that you need to be able to use the principles of negotiation in a structured and methodical way in relation to multifaceted and complex issues. Everyday negotiations between parents and children may give you some skills but it does little to prepare you to negotiate access arrangements for children following divorce or multimillion pound commercial negotiations.

Overall, although it is fair to say that most individuals have some experience of the basic tools of negotiation, they are not sufficiently developed or sophisticated to deal with the complexities of conducting legal negotiations on behalf of a client. They do, however, provide a basis upon which we can build.

16.3 Preparing to negotiate

Simulated negotiations involve two teams (usually with two students in each team) who each represent one party to a legal dispute. It is usual for each team to be given a set of written facts that outline the facts of the dispute from the perspective of their client, although some negotiations may also involve a set of common facts which are distributed to both teams. In more sophisticated negotiations, the parties may have the opportunity to ask questions of their client, usually by email to a member of staff responsible for the negotiation who formulates an appropriate response. There is an excellent example of an interactive negotiation to be found on the University of Strathclyde website.[3] It is more usual for the facts to be limited to a written outline.

It is sometimes the case that students negotiate, having done nothing more than read though their instructions. This tends to lead to a weak performance as the team is not sufficiently familiar with the facts and has not undertaken the necessary research and preparation to reach a favourable settlement.

Rather than thinking of 'the negotiation' as solely concerned with the face-to-face discussion between the teams, it is preferable to think of it as a two-stage process.

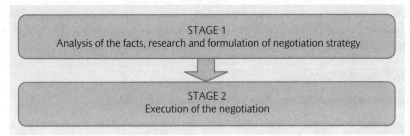

Figure 16.6 Negotiation as a two-stage process

Although settlement is reached at the second stage, the preparatory process should be viewed as the essential foundation to conducting a negotiation and should be undertaken with diligence. The second stage simply cannot be completed with success if the first has not been undertaken thoroughly.

16.3.1 Analysis of the scenario

As the scenario is the only information that the team has as the basis of the negotiation (plus common facts if they are available), it is essential that it is subjected to careful analysis to identify the client's interests and priorities, whether explicit or implicit, and to determine what, if any, instructions limit the scope of the settlement.

Working as a team has advantages in terms of the execution of the negotiation but it is useful during the preparation too as two pairs of eyes minimize the risk that a key fact will be overlooked. It may also draw attention to ambiguities in the scenario if the team members have drawn different inferences from the same facts or reached divergent conclusions about the client's priorities.

When analysing the scenario, make a note of the key points:

- What does the claim concern? In other words, identify the relevant area of law, e.g. contract, family law, negligence, personal injury

---

3.   www.strath.gla.ac.uk/synergy/law.html.

- What does the client want? Make a list of things that you need to achieve for your client during the negotiation, taking note of implied as well as express aims such as a quick resolution, a desire for an amicable resolution, or reluctance to litigate

- What are the client's interests? Again, these might be stated explicitly in the scenario or you may need to read between the lines. Exercise caution in doing this; remember the pitfalls of making false assumptions about the client's interest noted earlier. Identify the client's interests by working down the list of 'wants' and asking the question 'why'. For example, the client may want to avoid court action but do you know why? It may be because it is expensive or in order to avoid any negative publicity and maintain an undamaged reputation. The underlying issue is likely to have an impact on the way in which the negotiation is handled

- What, if any, limitations are there? For example, are you instructed to prioritize a particular aspect of the negotiation? Are you told that a particular outcome is unacceptable?

- What, if anything, does the scenario suggest about the issues that are important to the other party? Are there any clues that provide insight into their priorities?

- What are your strengths and weaknesses and how do you plan to deal with them in the negotiation?

 This is an example of a scenario that might be given to one team. This negotiation will be used as the basis for many of the practical exercises in the remainder of this chapter. The facts that would be given to the opposing team can be found on the Online Resource Centre.

Donkey Negotiation Scenario A:

Instructions for Representatives of the Henley Animal Centre (HAC)

HAC is an animal rescue centre in the New Forest run by Kate and Dave. It was established in 1990 as a ferret rescue centre but has expanded to take in a range of animals, including two horses and two donkeys. One donkey is a pure-bred Andalucían stallion named Loppy (HAC have registration papers that establish Loppy is pure-bred). HAC is struggling to make an income as visitor numbers are significantly down on the previous year and the rent for the land has just been increased. Unless things improve dramatically, HAC will close within two years.

Kate and Dave want to use Loppy for breeding. Andalucían donkeys are an endangered breed and activities that contribute towards their preservation attract significant financial support. Preliminary research indicates that they will receive £150,000 if they initiate a breeding programme that results in the birth of one pure-bred foal. Kate and Dave believe that a rare donkey foal would attract publicity from the local media and increase visitor numbers. Their attempts to find a breeding partner in Spain have failed and they have not been able to locate an Andalucían donkey mare in this country.

Dave read an article in the *Donkey Herald* about Island Farm Donkey Sanctuary (IFDS) in Oxfordshire that had been swindled out of large sums of money by its fund-raising manager. The article was accompanied by a photograph of two Andalucían donkey mares, Mabel and Mrs P, owned by IFDS. He approached the owners with a view to establishing a breeding programme. IFDS is agreeable provided satisfactory arrangements can be made.

Dave wants Loppy to breed with both IFDS mares to increase the chances of a successful outcome. He is aware he could charge stud fees for the use of Loppy but prefers an agreement with long-term benefits by having both foals at HAC to attract more visitors. If IFDS objects to this, he would be prepared to let them keep one foal but only if this was the only way that IFDS would agree to a breeding programme. He would like the foals to be born at HAC as this will attract more publicity but he does not want the mares for any longer than necessary owing to the costs of accommodating

(*Cont.*)

them. Ideally, he would like the mares to arrive one week prior to the birth of the foals. He appreci-ates that the mares will need to stay until the foals are weaned but would like IFDS to pay 'board and lodging' for the mares during that time and be accompanied by at least one handler, as he lacks expertise in donkey breeding and would not want to be responsible for the foals when they were newly born. He is also concerned about the cost of any veterinary care that might be necessary and wants IFDS to agree to contribute as much as possible towards any such costs. He is prepared to transport Loppy to IFDS as many times as is necessary to ensure that both mares are impregnated.

Dave has instructed you to reach an agreement within the spirit of these instructions that involves as little financial outlay as possible. He would share income from the breeding grants with IFDS if this will help to reach agreement but, given the precarious finances of HAC, wants to share as little as possible.

 Self-test questions

Analyse the donkey-breeding scenario, remembering to take into account the six points noted above:

1. What is the legal framework for the negotiation?
2. What does your client want?
3. What are your client's interests?
4. What boundaries are placed upon the negotiation?
5. What are the other side likely to want?
6. What are your strengths and weaknesses?

You will find answers to these questions and guidance on how they were reached on the Online Resource Centre. There is also an analysis of the other side of the negotiation but it might be useful if you do not look at it yet as it will be harder for your work on this side if you have already seen what the other party wants and how it plans to tackle the negotiation.

16.3.2 Research

Once you have a good grasp of the facts of the scenario and have identified the general area of law raised, you will be ready to engage in research.

16.3.2.1 Researching the law

Researching the legal issue should be straightforward as it should be apparent what area of law is raised by the scenario. The emphasis in negotiation is on use of the facts, so it should not be necessary to do any more than read the relevant sections in one or two textbooks to gain an appropriate grasp of the law.

It may be that your scenario raises issues that you have not covered in mainstream textbooks; for instance, there may be legal limitations on road transport of pregnant livestock. If you can identify any uncommon legal issues, you will need to use some of the methods outlined in chapters 2 and 5 for finding the relevant legal provision.

You must be focused in your legal research. Try and isolate particular questions that need to be answered. One of your key tasks should be to work out how the case would be decided if it went to court. This gives rise to two questions, the answers to which should help you to formulate a negotiation strategy:

1. **If this case was heard in court, would I win?** Unless the answer is an unequivocal 'yes', you have every incentive to work towards a negotiated settlement, even if this means achieving an outcome that is less than your client hoped; remember, part of something is better than all of nothing. Even if you are confident that your case would succeed in court, there are still incentives to negotiate. Litigation is costly and time-consuming and it may be that your client is unwilling to go to court. Moreover, there is more flexibility in negotiation for your client to determine the shape of the settlement that is reached to suit his or her requirements.

2. **If this case succeeded in court, what would I receive?** This should be your bottom line as there are few advantages to reaching a negotiated settlement that leaves your client with a worse outcome than that which would have been imposed by the court. You will need to take into account factors such as the cost of litigation and the likely time frame of events, so be sure to work this into your calculation. Remember to take advantage of tables for calculating damages,[4] for example, in working out the likely position of your client following court action or looking for decided cases with analogous facts as a basis for comparison. You can refer to these in your negotiation, to give support to your arguments.

> **BATNA** (best alternative to a negotiated agreement) is an acronym used to describe the best possible outcome that will result for your client if you do not negotiate or if the negotiation fails. This will be explored in more detail in relation to negotiation strategy but needs to be taken into account at this stage because you need to know whether your case would win or lose at court and what the outcome would be if you won in order to work out your BATNA.

These two questions may not be relevant if the scenario involves preliminary steps to enter into legal relations as illustrated by the donkey negotiation used in this chapter where the parties are hoping to enter into a contract. If this is the case, you should research the relevant law on contract formation to ensure that you cover all the necessary requirements to enter into a contract during your negotiation.

Remember that negotiation is an agreed settlement and is not binding. This is important, whether the negotiation is aimed at resolving a dispute or if it is a facilitative negotiation, i.e. agreeing the terms of a contract. The lack of enforceability should give you cause to consider one further question that is pertinent to your legal research:

3. **What will happen if the agreement is breached?** If the negotiation is aimed at dispute resolution, the answer is usually that the injured party will either give up or the case will end up in court. Therefore, there is a real need to ensure that the settlement is genuinely acceptable to both parties as this minimizes the chances of breach. If the negotiation is aimed at agreeing terms of a contract, do not forget to consider the consequences of breach. Think about all the possible things that could go wrong and try to ensure that you find a way to write ways of dealing with these problems into the contract.

16.3.2.2 Researching the facts

Conducting research into other issues is less straightforward as the scenario will often involve factual issues about which you have no prior knowledge. This is a fair approximation of what will happen in legal practice. However, in simulated negotiations, unlike practice, you cannot

---

4. *Kemp and Kemp on Damages.*

simply ask the client for that information. In any case, you should never place too great a reliance on the facts presented by a client if they can be objectively ascertained. A client may be misguided or simply have chosen the facts that most suits their expected outcome. For example, imagine conducting a negotiation for the sale of a property based exclusively on the client's estimation of the value of the property! You would not place reliance on this and you should always ensure that facts which are objectively determinable are objectively determined. In other words, if it is possible for you to find something out for yourself, you should do so as only then will be you be confident that you are basing your negotiations on accurate and unbiased information.

It is impossible to cover all the sorts of questions that you would want to research given the infinite range of scenarios that you might encounter, so this aspect of research will be demonstrated in relation the donkey breeding negotiation.

Practical exercise

Think about the facts you would need to know in preparation for the donkey-breeding negotiation. You will find some suggestions on the Online Resource Centre along with explanations of the reasoning behind them.

It is important to research the facts as well as the law as this may disclose all manner of negotiation points that you would not have considered otherwise, particularly if you keep your client's interests in mind.

Take the facts at face value and research accordingly. For example, you know that the stallion is in Southampton and the mares are in Oxfordshire, so you could make an estimation of transport methods and costs. Equally, you know that your client wants more visitors, so could a dual publicity-raising scheme be entered into between the parties? Try to be flexible and creative—what alternative ways could you suggest to achieve the client's goals without departing from the instructions given?

It is worth emphasizing that your research into factual issues must be conducted in an honest manner. Please do not mislead the Donkey Breed Society into thinking that you have an Andalucían stallion that you want to breed in order to obtain the information that you want; it is simply unethical. The Internet is a wonderful repository of all sorts of information that is readily available to researchers prepared to exercise a little effort and ingenuity.

16.3.3 Strategy

Formulating a research strategy is not a straightforward matter as there are a multitude of factors to take into account. Foremost amongst these is the need to evaluate the strength of your case and the various potential outcomes of the negotiation.

16.3.3.1 Identifying potential outcomes

In light of your analysis of the scenario and your research, you should be able to establish four things (Figure 16.7 overleaf).

It is essential that you establish each of these as this will enable you to calculate a strategy designed to achieve the most favourable outcome for your client.

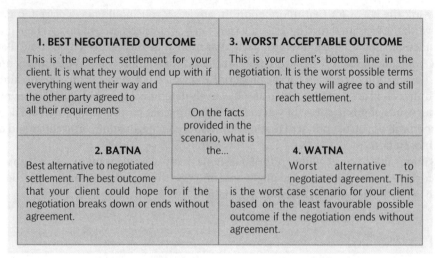

1. BEST NEGOTIATED OUTCOME	3. WORST ACCEPTABLE OUTCOME
This is the perfect settlement for your client. It is what they would end up with if everything went their way and the other party agreed to all their requirements	This is your client's bottom line in the negotiation. It is the worst possible terms that they will agree to and still reach settlement.
2. BATNA	**4. WATNA**
Best alternative to negotiated settlement. The best outcome that your client could hope for if the negotiation breaks down or ends without agreement.	Worst alternative to negotiated agreement. This is the worst case scenario for your client based on the least favourable possible outcome if the negotiation ends without agreement.

On the facts provided in the scenario, what is the...

Figure 16.7 Identifying potential outcomes

Self-test questions

In relation to the donkey negotiation, calculate:

1. Best negotiated outcome.

2. BATNA.

3. Worst acceptable outcome.

4. WATNA.

Having done this, consider the strength of the client's position to negotiate? What do you consider to be the characteristics of a strong bargaining position?

 Answers to the self-test questions can be found on the Online Resource Centre.

16.3.3.2 Formulating the issues

Once you have identified the most beneficial negotiated outcome for your client, you can break this down into a series of issues that can be dealt with individually within the negotiation.

For example, in relation to the donkey negotiation, you may have decided that the best negotiated outcome for the client is for their stallion to cover both mares at Island Farm, which results in two foals, both of which are owned by the client who incurs no costs at any point in the process.

This can be broken down into three separate issues:

1. Location: where will the stallion cover the mares and where will the births take place?

2. Costs: what costs will be incurred and which party shall bear these?

3. Ownership: who will own the foals?

Once you have identified the issues, you might want to decide in what order you would like to take them. There is no right or wrong answer to this but be prepared to justify your decision. For example, given that the ownership of the foals is at the heart of the negotiation, it could be beneficial to deal with it first as there is no point in agreeing the other issues if this point cannot be settled. Alternatively, given that the client needs to reach an agreement (because the BATNA is not particularly advantageous), it might be preferable to start with an issue such as the location of insemination because the client is prepared to transport the stallion, so the negotiation starts with the client offering something advantageous to the other party.

Practical exercise

1. Do you agree with the division of the negotiation into these three issues? Are there other issues that could be included? Could any of these issues be (a) combined or (b) divided and what are the advantages of taking this action?

2. What order would you take the points in and why? What other order did you consider and why did you reject it?

It is important that you reflect upon the reasons for your decisions. In a negotiation competition, the judge(s) will ask you why you chose a particular course of action and expect you to have a reasoned explanation for this, so it is useful to form the habit of scrutinizing your own decision-making process.

 Answers to these questions can be found on the Online Resource Centre.

16.3.3.3 Balancing the issues

Negotiations involving multiple issues can be difficult because you cannot expect to achieve your desired outcome on every issue. You need to be able to see the relationship between the issues so that you can exercise flexibility on one issue in order to gain ground on another.

There are two aspects to this process:

1. Establishing a top and bottom line of each of the issues

2. Ranking them in order of importance to the client.

When you can see the boundaries of each issue and their relative importance to the client, you can start to think about trading them off against each other. You may have to make concessions on one issue in order to gain ground on another issue. This is an effective negotiation strategy, provided you always keep the 'big picture' of the client's goals in mind and you do not act contrary to any explicit instructions.

For example, the most pressing need for the client in the donkey negotiation is to generate income, otherwise the rescue centre will have to close. Therefore, although they might like to do this by having two rare donkey foals to gain publicity and attract visitors, provided a solution can be found that generates income so that they do not have to close, the client is likely to be satisfied. As such, you may be able to make concessions on the ownership of the foals if the breeding agreement is a profitable enterprise for the client overall. This would not be a possibility if, for example, the instructions said that it was essential for the client to have ownership of at least one foal.

Self-test questions

1. Rank the issues in the donkey negotiation in order of importance to the client. Note that this may well differ from the order in which you decided to negotiate the issues.

2. Calculate the boundaries of each of the issues, i.e. work out the best and worst outcome on each issue to determine how much bargaining scope there is on each point.

3. Consider ways in which you could offer concessions on one issue in order to gain something beneficial for the client on one of the other issues.

 Answers to the self-test questions can be found on the Online Resource Centre.

16.3.3.4 Generating more options

The negotiation scenario does not provide detailed instructions of all the potential outcomes that are agreeable to your client. You are provided with some indication of their aims and also of their broader interests and you should have tried to anticipate what the other party will want from your client. Working within this framework, try to generate some creative ways in which the aims of both parties could be satisfied.

For example, if the issue of ownership of the foals become contentious, i.e. both parties are insistent that they want both foals, it could be a useful way of breaking a potential deadlock to offer a two-year breeding programme in which the other party has both foals born this year, in return for some significant financial concessions for your client, whilst ownership of the next batch of foals goes to your client.

This are just one example of a creative use of the facts that could help you to reach an agreement. Remember that you are not permitted to make up facts that are not included in your scenario (and in competition will be heavily penalized for doing so) but you can make reasonable inferences from the facts provided that you are acting within the spirit of your instructions.

 Self-test questions

Go back to the donkey negotiation scenario and review your analysis of it. Can you think of any other creative ways in which the needs of the parties can be fulfilled that are not immediately obvious. Try to focus in particular on what your client has identified as a potential difficulty: that both parties want ownership of the foals. Your client is prepared to accept one foal but will that be acceptable to the other party (remember that cutting the orange in half did not work in the example given above). Assuming that both parties would ideally like two foals, are there any other ways that this could be achieved? Think about the interests of your client and think of potential interests that could be motivating the other party; does this help to formulate creative solutions to this Solomon-esque dilemma.

Answers to the self-test questions can be found on the Online Resource Centre.

16.3.3.5 Negotiation plan

Once all the analysis and planning is complete, you might find it useful to prepare yourself a schedule of negotiation that notes the issues that you need to discuss, the order in which you would like to address them and your best and worst outcome on each issue so that you can see quite clearly how much scope for negotiation there is on each point. This can serve as a particularly useful reminder not to move outside of your instructions. This need be no more than one side of A4 and should be used as a reminder of your key issues rather than a strict schedule (you will be expected to demonstrate flexibility, so must be prepared to depart from your plan) or a crib sheet (good negotiations involve personal contact, not paper shuffling).

16.4 Conducting the negotiation

Negotiation is an inherently reflexive activity. The ability to listen and ask appropriate questions are essential skills that contribute to a successful negotiation as they will help you to piece together a complete picture of events. A good negotiator will be able to elicit information from the other parties and incorporate this into their understanding of the situation in order to make appropriate proposals for resolution based upon the information received. It is essential that you do take the other party's interests into account as a negotiated settlement is one that suits both sides rather than one in which the stronger party forces an outcome on the weaker party.

This final section of the chapter covers some of the key components of an effective negotiation.

16.4.1 Preliminary matters

It will be tempting, particularly in a competition that involves completing the negotiation within a tight time frame, to jump straight into a discussion of the first issue but there are certain preliminary matters that will need to be completed before the negotiation proper commences. Not the least of these is reaching an agreement with the other parties as to what is the first issue for consideration.

16.4.1.1 Introductions

It is a matter of good practice to introduce yourself and identify the party that you are representing. This need not be a lengthy business and involves little more than a handshake and a brief sentence. More important than the words themselves can be the manner in which the introductions are undertaken. First impressions are important, so think carefully about what image you want to present, both individually and as a team.

16.4.1.2 Establishing the framework for negotiation

It is useful to outline, in a couple of sentences, the factual basis of the negotiation. This should be a very basic statement of the facts that are likely to be agreed between both sides. For example:

> We have been instructed by Henley Animal Centre to seek to reach an agreement regarding a breeding programme involving their Andalucían stallion, Loppy, with Island Farm Donkey Sanctuary's Andalucían mares, Mabel and Mrs P.

16.4.1.3 Setting an agenda

As part of your preparation, you will have decided the order in which you want to negotiate the various issues. As outlined earlier in this chapter, there are various factors that might influence how you prioritize the order of your issues and decide what issue to deal with first:

- The issue that is of primary importance to the client as settlement may not be possible unless a core objective of the client is achieved
- The most complicated issue to get it out of the way, or
- The most straightforward issue so that the negotiation starts with an issue on which agreement is reached easily, as this sets a positive tone for the remainder of the negotiation.

It is possible that the other side will disagree either about the issues for negotiation or about the order in which they should be addressed. This can lead to a 'negotiation within a negotiation' as the agenda itself becomes a contentious issue. This process might set the tone for the negotiation, so treat it with importance but do not fall into the trap of spending too much valuable time determining the agenda. Ultimately, provided all your issues are on the agenda, the order in which they are discussed should not make too much difference to the overall outcome. This stage can be important, however, in setting the tone of the negotiation, so it is important that you do not become too insistent about following your own agenda or allow the other party wholly to override your wishes.

The overall objective at this stage is to establish an agreed agenda.

16.4.2 Fact-finding

Eliciting information from the other team is an important aspect of negotiation. It should not be confined to the start of the negotiation but should take place throughout the discussions.

It can be a useful starting point if one of the parties commences by providing a brief summary of their client's position. Some students are reluctant to do this as they feel that it 'gives away' important information to the opposing team; try to remember that a negotiated outcome is one that suits both sides, so there is little to be gained by being reticent with information. However, that does not mean that you have to be wholly forthcoming at this stage, particularly with information that weakens your client's position.

If you decide to offer an outline, select your facts carefully. Do not overwhelm the opposing side with detail. Try to contain your outline to the material facts that provide the framework for the negotiation. If the opposing team offers an outline of their facts, try not to interrupt even if you disagree with them; after all, they are giving you information that you need to know in order to understand their position, so it is important to listen carefully and make notes of any key points.

Good negotiation involves interactive, not unidirectional, communication. This means that it is important that each side has the chance to ask questions, to seek clarification, and to add information. Ending the summary of the facts with an invitation to comment will facilitate interactive communication:

- Is there anything that you would like to add?
- Do you have any questions?

16.4.2.1 Ask questions

The most effective means of eliciting information is to ask questions. If you are unclear about something or are struggling to grasp the other party's position, you should ask questions to help you gain a better understanding. These fall into two general categories (Figure 16.8).

Remember the importance of 'why' questions that provide insight into the motivation of the client and shed light on the 'big' aims that the client wishes to achieve. If you can elicit

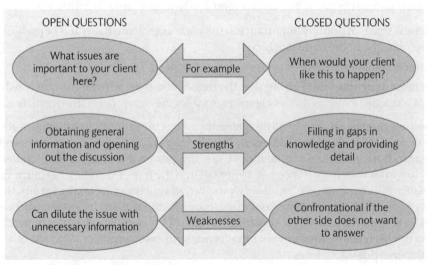

Figure16.8 Open and closed questioning

information about the overall objective of the other client, you will be better placed to make creative solutions that might achieve that objective.

It can be helpful if you prepare a list of information that you feel you need to know prior to the start of the negotiation and then think of the most effective types of question to ask to elicit this information. If you prepare this as a grid, you can tick off the questions that have been answered (to avoid repetition) and make a quick note of the answer:

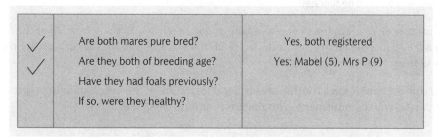

✓	Are both mares pure bred?	Yes, both registered
✓	Are they both of breeding age?	Yes: Mabel (5), Mrs P (9)
	Have they had foals previously?	
	If so, were they healthy?	

Figure 16.9 Question checklist

16.4.2.2 Give reasons

If you tell the other team that you do not understand or provide some other explanation of why you want to know a particular piece of information, it makes it harder for the other team to refuse to provide it.

- I don't understand why your client wants to achieve this in such a tight time frame. Are there other factors that are important here that I need to take into account?

- You don't seem receptive to my suggestion of a shared advertising campaign. I thought this would be a mutually beneficially enterprise so is there some reason that you feel this would not be attractive to your client?

16.4.3 Breaking deadlock

Deadlock occurs when the parties cannot reach agreement on a particular issue and are no longer prepared to make any movement towards each other. This can occur all too easily. Imagine the following situation:

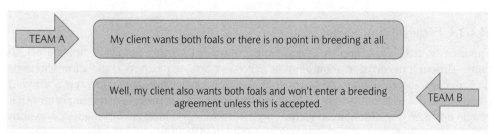

TEAM A — My client wants both foals or there is no point in breeding at all.

Well, my client also wants both foals and won't enter a breeding agreement unless this is accepted. — TEAM B

Figure 16.10 Deadlock

16.4.3.1 Avoiding deadlock

The most effective strategy is to avoid deadlock occurring in the first place. Try to avoid making 'make or break' demands in absolute terms. If you allow yourself no room for movement, there is nowhere for you to go if the other side refuses to agree with your requirements. Moreover, backing the other side into a corner in which they either have to stand against you or give in entirely is confrontational and aggressive, so is viewed as bad negotiation practice. You are supposed to be reaching mutual agreement, not imposing your will on others.

16.4.3.2 Keep the negotiation moving

If you cannot settle a particular issue, it can be a good idea to move away from it and find an issue where agreement can be reached:

> It seems that we're struggling to find common ground in relation to the ownership of the foals. Would it help to move on to consider the financial arrangements between the parties to see if this helps us to resolve the ownership issue?

Even if this does not resolve the disputed issue, at least it keeps the negotiation in progress and demonstrates your commitment to finding a way around deadlock.

16.4.3.3 Ask questions and offer solutions

As mentioned previously, if you can gain insight into why the other team is adopting a particular position, you may be able to find an alternative way to help them to achieve their objectives:

- Why is ownership of both foals so important to your client?

If the other team is not forthcoming with explanations, it might help to posit potential explanations:

- Is your client unwilling to entrust the foals to us because we are a general rescue centre rather than a specialist donkey centre? If so, perhaps we could agree a programme of care for the foals based upon your client's expertise and arrange for periodic visits by your client.

The other team will either have to agree and confirm that your speculation was correct, in which case you can work towards resolving the problems or they will deny that this is the reason, in which case you can at least rule it out as a possibility. Whichever of these applies, you will have demonstrated your willingness to explore all the options and an inclination to reach agreement, both of which are key negotiation skills.

Be creative in the solutions that you offer but do ensure that they are within the overall spirit of your instructions. There is no point in finding a solution to the problem that your client finds unacceptable.

16.4.3.4 Highlight concessions

This is an assertive way of applying reasonable pressure to the other team to demonstrate flexibility. Although negotiation should not be aggressive, undue passivity could allow you to be pressured into accepting an agreement that is not on particularly favourable terms for your client, so do not be afraid to apply a little pressure if it seems appropriate. It is important that you do not seem unreasonable, so identifying areas where you have already made concessions can underline the facts that you have been reasonable and flexible whilst the opposing team has been inflexible:

- I understand that the issue of ownership of the foals is important to your client but it would help us to reach agreement if you could be a little flexible here. After all, the issue of finance was important to our client and yet we moved towards you considerably on this point by accepting responsibility for all veterinary costs.

It is for this reason that it can be useful to move away from a contentious issue into more straightforward areas as settlement reached elsewhere can be a useful lever to prompt settlement once the difficult issue is revisited.

16.4.3.5 Take a break

There is provision within most negotiation competition rules for both teams to take a short break during the negotiation. This can be used effectively in a number of ways but can be a particularly useful strategy for breaking deadlock, especially if relations between the teams have become strained. It will give you the opportunity to have a private discussion with your team mate in which you can discuss how to deal with the situation. Remember to cast off any negative emotions during this period and come back into the negotiation room in an objective and professional frame of mind.

16.4.3.6 Walk away

There is no point in reaching an agreement that is unacceptable to your client, so if none of the other strategies succeed in breaking the deadlock and the other team's requirements are outside your instructions, there is no option other than to end the negotiation without reaching agreement. If you contemplate doing this, you should cast your mind back to your BATNA and WATNA as these were the possible outcomes if no agreement could be reached. However, if you make it clear that you are contemplating ending the negotiation without agreement, the other team will also reflect about their BATNA and WATNA which might make them realize that there is room for movement after all.

16.4.4 Teamwork

One of the criteria upon which your negotiation will be judged is your ability to work effectively with the other member of your team. It would be useful to give this some thought during the planning period and consider how you are going to relate to each other in the most effective way. Factors that you might like to take into account are as follows:

- Your relative skills as communicators (assertive, conciliatory, patient, forceful, etc.) and how these can be used to best effect in the negotiation
- Distribution of workload such as allocation of issues, responsibility for note-taking, strategies for intervention if the other person is struggling, and dealing with opening and closing the negotiation
- Dealing with conflict within the negotiation. It can be useful to decide how you will respond if the other team introduces an option that you had not considered if you disagree about its value to your client. Never argue with each other

16.4.5 Ethical considerations

It is important that your negotiation is conducted within the parameters of professional practice, which means that you must act in an ethical manner. It is of the utmost importance that you do not misrepresent your position or otherwise mislead the other team. Not only must you not do this deliberately, you must be cautious in your choice of language to avoid any possibility that you will mislead the other team inadvertently.

It can be particularly tempting to misrepresent the upper and lower limits in relation to a financial issue, for example, in order to obtain a more favourable deal for your client. You must not do this.

Imagine that you are trying to negotiate a settlement for personal injury following an accident that the other team concedes was the fault of their client. Your client has instructed you to get 'as much as possible and certainly not less then £5,000'. If the other team suggests £6,500, you are not compelled to accept it but you cannot say 'my client would not agree to that, he would rather go to court' as this is simply not true. You need to find alternative ways of seeking to persuade the other team to increase their offer without making false representations of your instructions:

- That is towards the lower end of the usual award of damages for this type of injury. Let's not forget that your client was wholly responsible for the accident and my client has suffered a great deal of pain since this happened.

16.4.6 Closing the negotiation

It is important to close the negotiation in an effective way so that everybody is clear about the terms of the agreement that has been reached. It can be useful to refer back to the agreed agenda and make a note of the outcome of each point that was listed, drawing particular reference to any issues that might require further consultation. Remember that the agreement that you have reached is subject to your client's agreement, so be sure to reflect this in your closing comments.

16.5 Post-negotiation reflection

Most negotiation competitions allocate a period of time at the end of the negotiation in which each team deliberates on their performance in the presence of the judges. This is not done in the presence of the opposing team. This stage of the negotiation gives the judges insight into the success of the negotiation from the perspective of the teams. This should include:

- Did the negotiation go according to plan? If not, what aspect of it was unexpected and could a different approach to planning and preparation prevent such an occurrence in subsequent negotiations?

- How well did the team work with each other and how well did they relate to the other team? If there were problems, what was the cause of these and were they resolved in an effective and professional manner?

- Was the outcome of the negotiation acceptable? Did the team gain a better deal for their client than they had anticipated or is the agreement that is reached disappointing? What factors might account for this?

- What were the strengths and weaknesses of the negotiation? Do not be afraid to identify weaknesses as this demonstrates to the judges that you are aware of the shortcomings of your own performance. If you are able to suggest ways that you would improve upon these areas in the future, this will satisfy the judge that you have gained something of value from participation in the negotiation

- If you conducted the negotiation again, what would you do differently and why?

It can be difficult to reach an understanding of such a practical activity from reading a chapter such as this, so you might find it useful to look at some of the examples of negotiation on the Online Resource Centre and think about the commentary that accompanies the clips.

» CHAPTER SUMMARY

Planning and preparation

- Analyse the negotiation scenario to ensure that you have a clear grasp of the issues that need to be resolved

- Use the strategies outlined in this chapter to assess the strength of your position. Work out the scope of movement in relation to each issue and consider how the issues can be used in conjunction to strengthen your bargaining power

- Research the relevant law and the facts to ensure that you have a thorough grasp of the key information

- Take a holistic view of your client's aims and think of creative ways to achieve these objectives within the spirit of your instructions

Conducting the negotiation

- Make a firm professional start with clear introductions, a summary of the factual situation, and a suggested agenda. Be prepared to amend your proposed agenda to reflect the requirements of the other team

- Remember that you only know half the story, so take time to find out about the issues that concern the other team and fill in the gaps of your factual knowledge

- Elicit information by asking questions. Remember that 'why' questions give insight into the aims of the other team's client and this may enable you to propose creative solutions that facilitate agreement

- A skilled negotiator will try and work around obstacles rather than stopping when confronted with them to try to use a range of different strategies to avoid or break deadlock

- It is important to evolve a strategy that enables you to work as a team and to form an effective working relationship with the other team, irrespective of their approach to negotiation

- Ensure that you are always ethical in your dealings with the other team, taking care not to mislead them or misrepresent your position

- Conclude by outlining the proposed agreement to ensure that everyone is clear on its terms

- Critical reflection will help you to improve your negotiation skills and enable you to improve upon your performance